A SUMMARY

of

CHRISTIAN DOCTRINE

A Popular Presentation of the
Teachings of the Bible

By

EDWARD W. A. KOEHLER, D.D.

(1875-1951)

Member of Faculty of Concordia Teachers College
River Forest, Illinois
(1909-1951)

Second Revised Edition
prepared for publication by

ALFRED W. KOEHLER

Reprint 1971
by
Concordia Publishing House
St. Louis, Missouri 63118

ISBN 0-570-03216-4

Printed in U.S.A.

FOREWORD TO FIRST EDITION

If the truth of God's Word is to accomplish its divinely intended purpose, it must be taught and accepted as it is revealed in Holy Scriptures. Any change or corruption of these teachings will necessarily affect the influence they have on the hearts and the lives of men. Guided by wrong information, man will go wrong. Only the right doctrine can create the right faith in our hearts and lead us in the right way through life.

Conscious of this, the author in writing this *Summary of Christian Doctrine* was guided by no other consideration than this, What does God say in His Word? and has, therefore, documented his statements with pertinent Bible references. With the exception of a few instances, he has not attempted to disprove erroneous teachings, but has rather in a positive way set forth what the Scriptures teach. Those who seek information on the doctrinal position of the churches of Christendom and of other religious bodies are referred to that excellent book, *Popular Symbolics,* published by Concordia Publishing House, St. Louis, Mo.

The reason for writing this *Summary* was to provide students with a suitable manual to be used in connection with the Bible as the basis for class discussion of Christian doctrines. Between the Catechism, used in elementary instruction, and the larger works on Dogmatics, used in theological seminaries, we have at present no book which in a concise form and yet in a fairly comprehensive manner systematically treats the doctrines of the Scriptures. While not supplanting the more scholarly works used in theological seminaries, the *Summary* may supply a real need in Christian colleges.

However, the *Summary* may also serve pastors in office as a convenient review in Christian doctrine, recalling to their minds what they have learned, crystallizing their doctrinal concepts, and inciting them to dig deeper into the divine truths. The material has been so arranged that it can easily be expanded into doctrinal papers and lectures at conferences and in congregations. But especially to teachers in parish and Sunday schools the *Summary* might prove helpful in clarifying and widening their knowledge of those truths which they would teach their pupils. No teacher should think that, while he must continue his studies in other fields of learning, he knows enough to teach children the simple truths of the Catechism, and has, therefore, no need of further study. Confused teaching is often due to confused knowledge. One must know well to teach well, and one must know more than just the lesson he wishes to impart. Hence, Paul says: "Give attendance to reading," 1 Tim. 4: 13. A study of the *Summary* will help us better to understand the Catechism, giving us a deeper insight into its teachings. For this reason the *Summary* may profitably be used for private study and also as a basic text in Sunday school teachers' classes and institutes.

The *Summary* is a plain and simple statement of the doctrines of the Bible. Avoiding technical terms and discussions, it should appeal also to the average layman. Ignorance begets indifference, and indifference leads to the loss of the truth. In our day and age religious knowledge is in many quarters very vague and superficial. In the press and over the radio "religious" ideas and opinions are ventilated that becloud, obscure, and distort fundamental truths of the Bible. It is important, therefore, that also the laymen of the Church are well indoctrinated, that they grow in knowledge of God's Word beyond the elementary instruction they received in their youth. It is not enough that we have the truth in our books and Bibles; we must know the truth. The knowledge of the truth fortifies us against error.

The works of many recognized writers in the field of Christian doctrine were consulted in the writing of this *Summary*, and they were directly quoted when, in the opinion of the author, they adequately expressed the point under discussion. Numerous Bible references will be found, and these should be carefully studied, so that the reader may see for himself whether the doctrines set forth agree with the Word of God (Acts 17: 11). Our faith must not be built on what men say, but on what God says in His Book; only in this way can our hearts be established (Hebr. 13: 9). The frequent references to, and quotations from, the Confessions of our Church serve the definite purpose of showing that the teachings of the Lutheran Church are in full agreement with the Bible. It is, therefore, hoped that a study of the *Summary* will encourage many to study also the Confessions of the Lutheran Church to the end that a true unity of faith may ultimately be achieved by all who profess adherence thereto.

The author would express his indebtedness to all those who encouraged and helped him to get out this book; especially to Dr. C. F. Brommer of Seward, Nebr., and to Dr. Th. Engelder of St. Louis, Mo., who have read the manuscript and offered many helpful suggestions.

May the Lord bless the study of this *Summary* so that we may better understand and more firmly believe the truth that makes us free. "Unto Him be glory in the Church by Christ Jesus."

River Forest, Ill., January 29, 1939.
　　River Forest, Ill., January 29, 1939.
　　Centennial of the Saxon Immigration.
　　　　　　　　　　　　EDWARD W. A. KOEHLER.

FOREWORD TO SECOND EDITION

The great popularity and evident usefulness of the first edition of *A Summary of Christian Doctrine,* as well as the express desire of Dr. Koehler to issue a second revised edition, has led his children to have this book published. To the undersigned was given the joyful task to examine and to arrange the manuscript and notes, which Dr. Koehler had almost completed for publication prior to his death. While the second edition generally follows the copy of the first, certain portions have been clarified and elaborated upon. We issue this book in the hope that many will be led to God's truth through it, and many more confirmed therein.

Oakland, California, November 19, 1951.
　　　　　　　　　　　　ALFRED W. KOEHLER.

TABLE OF CONTENTS

PART I. The Holy Scriptures

PART II. Of God

PART III. Creation and Providence

PART IV. Of the Angels and of Man

PART V. Of the Law and of Sin

PART VI. Salvation by the Grace of God through the Redemption in Christ Jesus

so intimately joined as to make but one person. This personal union is a mystery. When and how this union was effected. 4. The communication of attributes: the idiomatic, the majestic, the apotelesmatic genus. 5. Why did our Savior have to be God and man?

1. The humiliation. What it is not. Definition. Bible proof. Purpose and necessity. 2. Stages of humiliation: conception and birth, Christ's life, His suffering, death, and burial. 3. The exaltation. Definition and proof. 4. Stages of exaltation: descent into hell, the fact and the meaning of the resurrection, the forty days, the ascension, session at the right hand of God, return to judgment.

The work of Christ is a unit, yet we distinguish three offices. 1. The prophetic office. What is a prophet? Christ the Prophet, who revealed the will of God to man through the holy men of God, personally, and still does so through the ministry. Content of this revelation. 2. The priestly office. What is a priest? Christ our High Priest and Sacrifice. Meaning of Old Testament sacrifices. 3. The work of our High Priest. The ransom. Satisfaction by His active and passive obedience. Universal redemption. The fruit of redemption: Christ redeemed us from sin, from death, and from the power of the devil. Priestly office in the state of exaltation. 4. The kingly office. Christ a King, not a worldly king. Kingdom of power, of grace, of glory. Relation of these kingdoms to each other. 5. The purpose of Christ's work.

PART VII. Salvation by the Grace of God through the Sanctification of the Holy Ghost

Relation between the work of redemption and the work of sanctification. 1. Conversion not the work of man. Synergistic views. Man is capable of conversion. Man cannot believe in Christ by his own reason, strength, and will; but he is not converted against his will. 2. Conversion the work of the Holy Ghost. A work of divine grace. The Holy Ghost operates through the means of grace. The method of grace.

PART X. Civil Estates

PART I. THE HOLY SCRIPTURES

I. THE BIBLE, THE SOURCE AND NORM OF CHRISTIAN DOCTRINE

1. Before it is possible to determine what is to be regarded as *Christian doctrine*, it is necessary to agree on the *source* from which such doctrine is to be drawn, and on the *norm* by which it must be judged; otherwise it is impossible to reach an agreement.

2. No one can tell us what God wants us to believe and to do but God Himself. " . . . the things of God knoweth no man, but the Spirit of God" (1 Cor. 2: 9-11). Therefore our knowledge of God and of His will toward us can be derived from no other source than from God's own Word. "Should not a people seek unto their God? . . . To the law and to the testimony: if they speak not according to this word, it is because there is no light in them" (Is. 8: 19. 20). This Word of God must also be the norm and criterion according to which teachings and teachers are to be judged. "If ye continue in My Word, then are ye My disciples indeed; and ye shall know the truth" (John 8: 31. 32). "If any man speak, let him speak as the oracles of God" (1 Pet. 4: 11).

The Lutheran Confessions, therefore, state: "We believe, teach, and confess that the sole rule and standard according to which all dogmas together with all teachers should be estimated and judged are the prophetic and apostolic Scriptures of the Old and of the New Testament alone" (*Triglot,* p. 777).

3. If we wish to convey our thoughts to a person, we must do so in a language he understands. Because the Word of God was intended for human beings to learn and to know, it was necessary that it be revealed in words of human language, intelligible to human minds. The Word of God does not work like a magic formula which need not be understood, but we must learn and know what it means. In searching the Scriptures we must, therefore, use our knowledge of language and grammar, use the faculties of our mind to discover the sense and meaning of what we read, and we may then formulate

1

our findings into doctrinal statements, or creeds, as we do in the Confessions of our Church. Such *instrumental* use of our mental faculties is proper and necessary if we would know the Scriptures.

4. It is not our business to sit in judgment on what we have learned to be the plain sense of the Bible text, accepting what agrees, and rejecting what does not agree with our personal views and rationalizations. This *judicial* or *critical* use of human reason is absolutely out of place with respect to divine truths. Where God has spoken, the right of private judgment ceases. "Casting down imaginations, and every high thing that exalteth itself against the knowledge of God, and bringing into captivity every thought to the obedience of Christ" (2 Cor. 10: 5). We must take the words of the Scriptures in the sense and meaning they convey; we may not add thereto nor take away anything from it (Deut. 4: 2), nor corrupt the Word of God by putting our own meaning into the text (2 Cor. 2: 17). We must, therefore, not "correct" the Scriptures according to our ideas and logical deductions, but we must correct our thoughts and ideas according to the Scriptures.

5. To interpret the Scriptures means that in our own words we explain and restate what the texts of the Bible actually mean and teach. "Sensus literalis unus est." A Scripture text can have but one divinely intended sense and meaning; two contradictory interpretations of the same text cannot both be correct. A true interpretation of the Bible, therefore, consists in finding, setting forth, and reaffirming the divinely intended meaning of the statements of the Scriptures, taking the words as they read, in their proper and plain sense, as determined by the context, and ruling out whatever conflicts with the "analogy of faith," that is, with other clear passages of the Bible, which teach that particular doctrine. There are doctrines in the Bible which do not agree with our way of thinking; there are others which we cannot harmonize with each other; but there are none that contradict each other. "Thy Word is truth" (John 17: 17). It is, therefore, not our purpose to prove the teachings of the Bible true to the satisfaction of human reason, but merely to show that we teach in agreement with the Bible.

6. To be true, a doctrine need not agree with the resolu-

tions of church councils, the confessional writings of a church, the deductions of human reason, the "findings" of science, etc., but it must in all parts and points agree with the clear statements of the Scriptures. As sources and norms of Christian doctrine we, therefore, reject every type and form of human authority, such as: church fathers, church councils, church confessions; human reason, philosophy, science, private opinions; the "inner light" of enthusiasts, new revelations, the "shrine of the Pope's heart."

7. To accept man-made doctrines as the doctrines of God

(a) is foolish. "In vain they do worship Me, teaching for doctrines the commandments of men" (Matt. 15: 9);

(b) will not "establish," give firm assurance to, the heart. "Be not carried about with divers and strange doctrines. For it is a good thing that the heart be established with grace" (Hebr. 13: 9);

(c) is dangerous, because it destroys the right faith. "Beware of false prophets which come to you in sheep's clothing, but inwardly they are ravening wolves" (Matt. 7: 15);

(d) is sinful, because God forbids it. "Behold, I am against the prophets, saith the Lord, that use their tongues, and say, He saith" (Jer. 23: 31).

8. Our Lutheran Confessions are very explicit on this point. "We receive and embrace with our whole heart the Prophetic and Apostolic Scriptures of the Old and New Testament as the pure, clear fountain of Israel, which is the only true standard by which teachers and doctrines are to be judged" (F. C., Th. D., Sum., 3, *Triglot*, p. 851).

"For it will not do to frame articles of faith from the works and words of the fathers. . . . The rule is: The Word of God shall establish articles of faith and no one else, not even an angel" (S. A., Part II, Art. II, 15, *Triglot*, p. 467).

"We concede neither to the Pope nor to the Church the power to make decrees against the consensus of the prophets" (Apol., Art. XII, 66, *Triglot*, p. 271).

"We are certainly in duty bound not to interpret and explain these words of the eternal, true, and almighty Son of God . . . according as it seems agreeable to our reason, but with simple faith and due obedience to receive the words as they read, in their proper and plain sense, and allow ourselves

to be diverted therefrom by no objections or human contra-
dictions spun from reason, however charming they may appear to reason" (F. C., Th. D., Art. VII, 45, *Triglot*, p. 987).

II. ORIGIN AND INSPIRATION OF THE BIBLE

1. **Different human writers, but one divine Author.**—
The Bible is a collection of books, written at different times
and by different men. Moses and the prophets wrote the
canonical books of the Old Testament in the Hebrew and
Aramaic languages; the evangelists and the apostles wrote
the canonical books of the New Testament in the Greek language. Still, there is but ONE Author of the entire Bible,
and this Author is God. The Bible is God's own Book, which
not merely contains the Word of God intermingled with many
human additions and interpolations, but which in all its parts
IS the Word of God.

Of the Old Testament writers we read: "All Scripture is
given by inspiration of God" (2 Tim. 3: 16). Also: "God, who
at sundry times and in divers manners spake in time past unto the fathers by the prophets, hath in these last days spoken
unto us by His Son" (Hebr. 1: 1. 2). And of the New Testament writers Paul says: "When ye received the Word of God
which ye heard of us, ye received it not as the word of men,
but as it is in truth, the Word of God" (1 Thess. 2: 13).

Not all God ever said and did is recorded in the Bible (John
21: 25); nor have we in the Bible a complete revelation of
God in the sense that all we should like to know of His essence, judgments, and purposes is made known to us (Rom.
11: 33-36); but all that is necessary and profitable for us to
know, God has made known; hence "we know in part" (1 Cor.
13: 9).

2. The divine inspiration of the Bible may be considered
under the following three headings: (a) *When* the holy men
were to write; (b) *What* they were to write; (c) *How* they
were to write.

(a) **The divine impulse.**—The men whom God employed
as His penmen, no doubt, spoke and wrote also other things
during their lifetime; but only then did they speak and write
the Word of God, when there was a divine impulse and command, when they were moved by the Holy Ghost. "The

prophecy came not in old time by the will of man: but holy men of God spake as they were moved by the Holy Ghost" (2 Pet. 1: 21). Inspiration, therefore, includes the antecedent divine instigation or peculiar impulse of the will to engage in writing.

(b) **The divine thought content.**—The Holy Ghost not only moved these men when to write, but He also suggested, inspired, and controlled what they wrote. The thought content of the Bible, the facts recorded, the truth revealed, the doctrines taught, are in all parts and particulars what God wanted them to write, and in no instance did they write anything God did not want them to write. This is true not only of the things which pertain to our salvation, but also of historical events, of happenings in nature, of personal experiences, and the like.

Peter writes (1 Pet. 1: 10-12): "Of which salvation the prophets have enquired and searched diligently, who prophesied of the grace that should come unto you: searching what, or what manner of time the Spirit of Christ which was in them did signify, when it testified beforehand the sufferings of Christ, and the glory that should follow. Unto whom it was revealed, that not unto themselves, but unto us they did minister the things, which are now reported unto you by them that have preached the Gospel unto you with the Holy Ghost sent down from heaven." Very definitely Peter here speaks of the *content* of the prophecy, and tells us that the Spirit of Christ was in the prophets and testified beforehand of His redemptive work, and that its fulfillment was now preached through the Holy Ghost in the Gospel.

Paul writes (2 Tim. 3: 16): "All Scripture is given by inspiration of God." From this text it is evident that the men of God were not merely moved by the Holy Ghost to speak, but that also what they spoke and wrote, "all Scripture," was God-inspired, God-inbreathed. Inspiration, therefore, had for its object not the writers themselves, who were only the instruments of the Holy Ghost and were soon to pass away, but the writings, the books, the Holy Scriptures, which were to continue in the Church unto the end of time. What Paul says of the Old Testament is true also of the New Testament. Jesus had promised His disciples the Holy Ghost, of whom

He said: "He shall teach you all things, and bring all things to your remembrance, whatsoever I have said unto you" (John 14: 26); and again: "He will guide you into all truth" (John 16: 13). This was fulfilled, for Paul writes (1 Cor. 2: 13): "Which things also we speak, not in the words which man's wisdom teacheth, but which the Holy Ghost teacheth; comparing spiritual things with spiritual," i.e., matching spiritual things with spiritual words, expressing the truths of the Spirit in the words of the Spirit.

The inspiration of the thought content of the Bible is by no means identical with revelation. "To reveal" means "to make unknown things known." All that is written in the Bible is inspired, but not everything therein was divinely revealed. Some of the things recorded in the Bible no man could know of himself; these are the mysteries of God, and they were divinely revealed unto the writers (1 Cor. 2: 7-13; Eph. 3: 2-6). However, other things the writers knew from personal observation and experience (1 John 1: 1-3). Others they learned by inquiry and investigation (Luke 1: 1-3). Still others are the expression of their personal sentiments and feelings, as we find them in many of the Psalms. *Inspiration refers to the speaking* (2 Pet. 1: 21) *and to the writing* (2 Tim. 3: 16) *of these things.* When speaking or writing of these matters, which they had learned from various sources, these men were so controlled by the Holy Ghost, that whatever they spoke or wrote was what God wanted them to speak or to write.

(c) **The divine words, or verbal inspiration.**—Inspiration covers not only the subject matter of the Bible, but it extends to the words, yea, to the very forms of words that were used to express the divine thoughts. The Holy Ghost moved these men *how* they were to write. To Jeremiah God said: "Write thee all the words that I have spoken unto thee in a book" (Jer. 30: 2). David says: "The Spirit of the Lord spake by me, and His word was in my tongue" (2 Sam. 23: 2). Peter tells us that the holy men of God spake, uttered words, as they were moved by the Holy Ghost (2 Pet. 1: 21). Paul informs us that the things he taught were expressed in "words . . . which the Holy Ghost teacheth" (1 Cor. 2: 13). Christ points to a single word, "gods," and adds that the Scripture cannot be broken (John 10: 34. 35; Ps. 82: 6). Paul builds up an entire argument on the singular form of the word "seed" (Gal. 3: 16). It did not merely so happen that Moses (Gen. 22: 18) used the singular form, "in thy Seed," but it was the will of God that this form was used.

As an illustration of what inspiration was like, we may point to the Pentecostal miracle, when the disciples were moved by the Holy Ghost, and spoke of the wonderful works of God as the Spirit gave them utterance (Acts 2: 4. 11).

We must insist on the verbal inspiration of the Bible, because the Bible teaches it, and because we otherwise could never be sure whether the words used by the holy men of God express exactly the thoughts and truths of God. The words a man speaks do not always clearly express his own thoughts; much more difficult it is for one to express the thoughts of another. If, then, the Holy Ghost had not controlled the very words the holy writers used, we might well ask: "Did God really mean what the words of these men say?"

If, because of the variant readings found in manuscripts, one would reject the *verbal* inspiration of the Bible, one should, consistently, have to reject the *entire doctrine of inspiration.* For how could we know that *any copy* still contains the inspired text? Then the Bible is just an ordinary human book, and not God's Word. "Variant readings" are the result of making new copies of the Scriptures by hand with pen and ink. Despite all the care exercised to keep them out, flaws were inadvertently introduced as the copies were made. The variant readings number perhaps 150,000. An analysis of these readings quickly dispels any alarm, which may have arisen. For the most part they are of *no authority;* no one can suppose them to be genuine. Of the remainder, most are of *no importance* as affecting the sense. When we compare the Revised Version of the New Testament (with the marginal notes) with the text of the Common or Authorized Version, we shall see of how much, or rather, of how little importance, for the most part, the remainder are. None of the variant readings changes or destroys one single doctrine of the Bible.

3. **This all-inclusive control exercised by the Holy Spirit in inspiration did not reduce the human writers to mere automata.** They were not like mechanical instruments in the

hand of God, not knowing what they were doing; but the act of writing was on their part a conscious, volitional, and intelligent act; they knew what they were doing and writing. David knew that the Spirit of God spake by him (2 Sam. 23: 2), and Paul was fully conscious when he wrote his letters to the churches (2 Thess. 3: 17).

Nor must we conceive of inspiration as a mechanical dictation, as when a man dictates a letter to his stenographer. Each writer used his mental powers, arranged his thoughts and arguments, chose his words, constructed his sentences, and retained his own style and diction. Nevertheless, in all this the men were under the constant control of the Holy Ghost, who set in motion, "moved," their mental apparatus, and made use of their education and learning, so that their searching and thinking, their choice of words and arrangement of arguments was taken into service by the Holy Ghost, and made the medium of His activity and speaking. The Holy Ghost employed different types of men as His scribes: kings and peasants, fishermen and scholars, making use of their several abilities, learning, and styles of writing.

This inspiration is a profound mystery. It has never been duplicated. It cannot be demonstrated by any psychological experiment, nor can its inner and deeper working be explained, even as we cannot explain the active immanence of God in His creatures (Acts 17: 28). The Bible teaches the *fact* of its inspiration, but not the *"how,"* and there is nothing in the realm of human experience that could explain to us the "theopneustos" of the Scripture.

4. **The inspiration of the Bible is an article of faith** to be believed on the Bible's own testimony concerning itself. The objection that the Bible cannot testify in its own behalf is not valid. Even in human affairs we do not determine the essence of a thing by external testimony, but by evidence furnished by the thing itself. When the Levites wanted to know who John the Baptist was, they went to him directly and asked: "What sayest thou of thyself?" (John 1: 19-28). If, therefore, we wish to know what the Bible is, the only rational thing to do is to find out what the Bible says about itself. And it does say that it is the Word of God, given by inspiration of the Holy Ghost. And this testimony of the Scrip-

tures concerning itself carries conviction, divine conviction. The Bible is self-authenticating. Whoever denies in part or in whole the inspiration of the Bible cannot do so on the basis of Scriptural evidence, but does so for other, rational or moral, reasons.

5. **All Scripture inspired.**—What has been said about inspiration applies equally to all canonical books of both Testaments. Hence the writings of the "apostles and prophets" (Eph. 2: 20) are in an equal sense the foundation of the Church. As there are no degrees of inspiration, there is no difference in authority.

Unless we accept "all Scripture" as given by inspiration, we have no foundation whatever for our faith. If men are to determine what in the Bible is inspired and what is not, we shall in the end have nothing left; for there is not a single part or doctrine in the Bible which someone will not discard as not inspired. If because of human objection we give up one part, we must for the same reason give up every other part; tear up one plank, and the whole platform becomes insecure. Even though all would agree on certain matters, our faith would in that case still rest on the judgment of fallible men. It is either all or nothing. If the record of the creation is a myth, then there is no reason why the Gospel of our salvation is not likewise a myth. They who assail the plenary inspiration of the Bible are tearing up the very foundation, and leave nothing behind but rubbish and ruin, nothing on which to build our faith.

"If only the mysteries of the faith, which are contained in the Sacred Scriptures, depend upon inspiration, and that all the rest, which may be known by the light of nature, depends merely upon divine direction, then the whole of Scripture is not inspired. But Paul declares that the whole of Scripture is divinely inspired. Therefore not only the mysteries of faith, but also the remaining truths that may be known by the light of nature, which are contained in Scripture, are divinely suggested and inspired." (Hollaz)

6. **The apocryphal books,** which were never included in the term "Holy Scriptures," were not written under inspiration. They are profitable to read, but are human documents which cannot be used to establish divine truths.

7. Copies and translations of the Scripture are not inspired. Strictly speaking, only the original manuscripts were written under the inspiration of the Holy Ghost. The original documents are no longer in existence. We possess copies only, in fact only copies of a long series of prior copies. Nevertheless, a correct copy or version of the original text is as truly the Word of God as the original itself. A sermon or treatise explaining a Bible truth is not inspired; but inasmuch as it really presents the Bible truth, it is truly the Word of God. An error by the copyist, the translator, or the commentator is not invested with divine authority.

III. ATTRIBUTES OF THE BIBLE

1. The authority of the Bible.—It is not the authority of man, of Moses, of Paul, or of Peter, but the authority of the sovereign God Himself that stands behind every statement, doctrine, promise, and command of the Bible. "God . . . spake . . . by the prophets" (Hebr. 1: 1). "The things that I write unto you are the commandments of the Lord" (1 Cor. 14: 37). This authority cannot be superseded by any other. "If any man teach otherwise, and consent not to the wholesome words, even the words of our Lord Jesus Christ, and to the doctrine which is according to godliness; he is proud, knowing nothing, but doting about questions and strifes of words" (1 Tim. 6: 3. 4); (Gal. 1: 8. 9). To this authority all men, the wise and the simple, must submit without quibble and reservation (2 Cor. 10: 5). It calls for instant and unqualified acceptance of every statement of the Bible on the part of man. "My heart standeth in awe of Thy Word" (Ps. 119: 161); (Is. 66: 2). To ignore, disregard, or reject any doctrine of the Bible is rebellion against God's authority, and will not go unpunished. "He that rejecteth Me, and receiveth not My Words, hath one that judgeth him" (John 12: 48).

2. The inerrancy and the truth of the Bible.—Human writers make mistakes in their books; but when the holy men of God spake as they were moved by the Holy Ghost, every possibility of error, not only in the presentation of the fundamental doctrines, but also in such references as pertain to nature and history, was eliminated from the outset. Referring to one word, "gods" (Ps. 82: 6), Christ says: "The Scripture cannot be broken" (John 10: 35). The Bible does not contain, besides some divine truths, also myths, fables, errors, or antiquated ideas, which must be deleted from its sacred pages. As all Scripture is given by inspiration of God, we grant to no man the right to decide what in the Bible is true and what is not true.

The statements and doctrines of the Bible are not merely subjectively true, i.e., only true to him who believes them to be so, but they are objectively true, i.e., they are true in themselves, because they are the Word of God. "Thy Word is truth" (John 17: 17). This objective truth of God's Word is not in the least affected by what men think about it (Rom. 3: 3. 4). He who continues in the words of Christ knows the truth (John 8: 31. 32). He who builds his faith on them has built on a sure foundation (Matt. 7: 24), and shall not be confounded (1 Pet. 2: 6). The promises of God are absolutely reliable. "The promises of God in Him are yea, and in Him Amen" (2 Cor. 1: 20). For this reason the Word of God is more sure than the testimony of our own senses (2 Pet. 1: 16-19). Any doctrine that does not fully agree with the teachings of God's Word is of necessity false, no matter how sincerely believed. Sincerity of faith does not prove the correctness of a doctrine or the truth of a man's religion.

What Satan (Gen. 3: 4), Gehazi (2 Kings 5: 22), and Peter (Mark 14: 71) said was not true to the facts, but the record of what they said is true. Whatever the Bible records as sins, lies, errors, superstition, etc., is exactly what the Bible says of it.

3. **The efficacy of the Bible.**—"The efficacy of the Bible is that property by which the Bible has indissolubly united with the true and genuine sense, as expressed in its words, the power of the Holy Ghost, who has made it for all times the ordinary means by which He operates on and in the minds and hearts of those who properly hear and read it" (A. L. Graebner, *Doctrinal Theology*, p. 12).

The Word of God is efficacious; it has the power to produce an effect, to make an impression on the heart. The effect is not produced by the mere external contact with the Word, but the Word must be learned and its true sense and meaning must be apperceived by the mind.

The Bible is efficacious not only because to the consciousness of the hearer the authority of God stands behind its every
statement, but chiefly because the Holy Ghost operates
through and by the Word. "The words that I speak to you,
they are spirit, and they are life" (John 6: 63). The Word
of God, therefore, is not a dead letter, but it is powerful. "The
Word of God is quick, and powerful, and sharper than any
two-edged sword, piercing even to the dividing asunder of
soul and spirit, and of the joints and marrow, and is a dis-
cerner of the thoughts and intents of the heart" (Hebr. 4: 12);
(Jer. 23: 29; 1 Thess. 1: 5; 1 Cor. 2: 4).

Even the words spoken by men have the power to impress
others for evil or for good (Acts 19: 28; 5: 34-40). Thoughts
conveyed to others have the inherent power to affect the heart,
and will so affect it unless hindered by dominating inhibitory
influences. In a much greater degree does the Word of God
possess this power, because it is God Himself who operates
through His Word.

The effect of a message is determined by the content of the
message. Not every teaching of the Word of God will produce the same effect. Because of its peculiar content, the Law
produces knowledge of sin and contrition of heart (Rom. 3:
20); the Gospel, being the glad tidings of the grace of God,
produces faith and hope (Rom. 10: 17). Thus the Scriptures
are really able to make men wise unto salvation through faith
in Christ (2 Tim. 3: 15).

"With this Word of God the Holy Ghost is present, and
opens hearts, so that they, as Lydia in Acts 16: 14, are attentive to it and are thus converted" (F. C., Epit., Art. II, 5,
Triglot, p. 787).

4. **The sufficiency of the Bible.**—"The sufficiency of the
Bible is that perfection according to which the Bible contains
all that is necessary for the achievement of the end and aim
of the Holy Scriptures" (A. L. Graebner, *Doctrinal Theology,*
p. 13).

As the Bible contains "all the counsel of God" (Acts 20: 27),
it is sufficient to "make us wise unto salvation" (2 Tim. 3: 15),
and to educate or train us in righteousness of life (2 Tim. 3:
16. 17). For this reason the rich man was told that his brothers
had "Moses and the prophets" (Luke 16: 29), and that if they

believed their words, they would escape the torments of hell; they needed nothing more. Hence, there are no deficiencies in the Bible to be supplied by oral tradition, pronouncements of Popes, new revelations, modern development of doctrine, etc. Today the Bible is as sufficient to accomplish its purpose as it ever was.

The Confessions of the Church must in no wise be regarded as additions to the Bible, supplementing it with additional or more complete truths; they are merely restatements of the doctrines of Scripture over against errors that have developed in the course of time.

5. **The perspicuity or clearness of the Bible.**—"The perspicuity of the Bible is that clearness of Holy Writ which renders all the doctrines and precepts laid down in the inspired Word freely accessible to every reader and hearer of average human intelligence and sufficient knowledge of the language employed, and of a mind not in a manner so preoccupied by error as to preclude the apprehension of the truths themselves, however clearly set forth in words of human speech" (A. L. Graebner, *Doctrinal Theology*, p. 11).

As the Bible was given to man in words of human language, it must be granted from the outset that man must also be able to understand its teachings. The principal doctrines are expressed in language sufficiently clear to be understood by all men of normal intelligence. For this reason the Bible is called "a light" (Ps. 119: 105; 2 Pet. 1: 19). It can make wise the simple (Ps. 19: 7). Even children can know the Scriptures (2 Tim. 3: 15).

We admit that the teachings of Holy Writ do not always agree with the deductions of human reason (2 Cor. 10: 5); that there are "some things hard to be understood" (2 Pet. 3: 16); (Rom. 11: 33); that there are texts difficult to interpret because of our lack of knowledge either of the language or of the conditions to which the texts refer; that, as in Revelation, we cannot always with absolute certainty determine the meaning and import of the highly figurative language employed. Still, the doctrines which we must know to be saved and to lead a holy life on earth are clearly stated for all to understand.

"Over against the view that the Scripture is obscure, waiting for priest and Pope, the theologian and council, to demonstrate its real meaning, the Lutheran Church upholds the perspicuity of Scripture, 'the clear word and teaching of the apostles' (Ap. VII and VIII, 25), 'the pure, clear fountain of Israel' (F. C., Th. D., Comp. Sum., 3)," (*Popular Symbolics*, 23, p. 28).

IV. DIVISIONS OF THE BIBLE

1. The Bible is divided into two major parts, the Old Testament and the New Testament. The former consists of 39 books, which were written at different times during the period approximately from 1500 to 400 B. C. Its principal theme is: Salvation promised in the Messiah. The latter consists of 27 books, written during the second half of the first century after Christ. Its principal theme is: Salvation accomplished by Christ.

2. Another convenient division respects the general character of the various books. Thus the Old Testament is divided into a) the Pentateuch or the Five Books of Moses, b) the historical books from Joshua to Esther, c) the devotional or poetic books from Job to the Song of Solomon, d) the prophetic books from Isaiah to Malachi. In the New Testament we have a) historical books: the four Gospels and the Acts, b) didactical books: the Epistles of the Apostles, c) prophetic book: the Revelation of John.

3. A third division, which runs practically through all the books of the Bible, pertains to its two fundamental doctrines, the Law and the Gospel. While both are the Word of God, they are radically different as to content, purpose, and effect, and must be carefully distinguished from each other (2 Tim. 2: 15).

V. THE PURPOSE OF THE BIBLE

1. **Threefold purpose.**—God gave His Word to man for a very definite purpose, namely: a) to save man from sin and damnation through faith in Christ, b) to educate and train His children in holiness of life, c) to magnify His glory.

(a) Man had been created for a life of joy and bliss in the communion with his God. By sin he lost all this, and became subject to eternal death. Moved by His infinite compassion,

God determined to save guilty man from the dire consequences of his transgression, and to restore him to blissful
communion with Himself. To accomplish this, He not only
redeemed us through the death of His Son (Rom. 5: 8. 9), but
also gave us the Scripture, which "is able to make us wise
unto salvation through faith, which is in Christ Jesus" (2 Tim.
3: 15). For this reason Christ says: "Search the Scriptures:
for in them ye think ye have eternal life: and they are they
which testify of Me" (John 5: 39). Again we read: "These
are written, that ye might believe that Jesus is the Christ, the
Son of God, and that believing ye might have life through
His name" (John 20: 31).

(b) The second purpose of the Bible is to teach and train
all believers in Christ to serve God in righteousness and true
holiness. Jesus prayed for His disciples that God would
"sanctify them through Thy truth" (John 17: 17). To this
end the Word of God is "a lamp unto our feet, and a light
unto our path" (Ps. 119: 105). Paul informs us that "all
Scripture is profitable . . . for instruction in righteousness:
that the man of God may be perfect, throughly furnished unto all good works" (2 Tim. 3: 16. 17).

(c) Both of these objectives culminate in the ultimate purpose, the glory of God. "If any man speak, let him speak as
the oracles of God; if any man minister, let him do it as of
the ability which God giveth: that God in all things may be
glorified through Jesus Christ, to whom be praise and dominion for ever and ever. Amen" (1 Pet. 4: 11).

2. **No other book can accomplish this purpose,** because no
other book in the world can give us reliable information concerning these matters. Only God can tell us how we can be
reconciled to Him, and how we are to worship and serve Him.
It is utterly futile and presumptuous for any man to devise a
plan according to which God is to give eternal life to sinners,
and to determine what manner of conduct and works will
please God (Matt. 15: 9).

The plan of salvation, as revealed in the Bible, sets this
Book apart from all other so-called sacred books in the world.
These other books all teach that man must, in some way or
other, save himself. The Bible teaches that God saves man by
grace for Christ's sake through faith. Such a plan human in-

genuity could never have devised; it marks the Bible as the revelation of God (1 Cor. 2: 7-10).

3. **The entire Bible serves this purpose.**—The Bible treats of various matters, some of which, individually considered, do not seem to have any bearing on the purpose mentioned above. Still, whatever the apostles and prophets wrote and taught was for our learning (Rom. 15: 4), and constitutes the foundation of the Church, in which the doctrine of Christ and of His redemption is the chief cornerstone (Eph. 2: 20). The Bible is a unit in which all parts, statements, doctrines, commandments, and promises, either directly or indirectly, serve the purpose of teaching men how to be saved through faith in the Saviour, and how to live as the children of God in this world to the glory of their Lord. It is for this purpose that the Word of God should be used (John 5: 39); using it for other purposes means taking the name of God in vain (Exodus 20: 7).

VI. THE USE OF THE BIBLE

1. **All men should use the Bible.**—In order that the purpose for which God gave His Word might be accomplished, the Bible must be used. If unknown or unused, it does not help any man. But should this Sacred Volume be placed into the hands of all men? Is it safe to let the laity read and study this Book? The oracles of God were, indeed, committed unto the Jews (Rom. 3: 2), but they were not intended for them exclusively. "The earth shall be full of the knowledge of the Lord" (Is. 11: 9), and the Gospel is to be preached to all men (Mark 16: 15). The use of the Bible is not restricted to the clergy, but all men may and should read and study the Word of God. When Christ says: "Search the Scriptures," He places the Bible into the hands of every man, woman, and child. The Epistles were addressed to, and read by, the entire congregation (Rom. 1: 7; Col. 4: 16; 1 Thess. 5: 27), including children (1 John 2: 13. 14; 2 Tim. 3: 15).

2. **How to use the Bible.**—We should *hear* the Word of God. "Blessed are they that hear the Word of God and keep it" (Luke 11: 28). "Hear ye Him," says God of His Son (Matt. 17: 5). "He that heareth you, heareth Me," says Christ to His disciples (Luke 10: 16).

We should *read and study* the Word of God. "Search the Scriptures" (John 5: 39). This is not to be a heedless but an attentive reading, which endeavors to grasp and to retain in the mind what we read. "Whoso readeth, let him understand" (Matt. 24: 15).

We are to *meditate* on what we have learned. "This book of the law shall not depart out of thy mouth; but thou shalt meditate therein day and night" (Joshua 1: 8). "These words which I command thee this day, shall be in thine heart" (Deut. 6: 6). "Mary kept all these things, and pondered them in her heart" (Luke 2: 19). It is by means of such meditation on our part that the meaning of Scripture texts and truths unfolds itself more fully to our minds and sinks deeper into our hearts.

We are to *accept as true and to believe* the Word of God. Isaiah complains that Israel had not believed his report (Is. 53: 1). Christ says: "Believe the Gospel" (Mark 1: 15). The nobleman believed the words Jesus had spoken (John 4: 50). Do not criticize, but accept and believe the Word of your God.

We are to *observe* the Word of God in our lives. "That thou mayest observe to do according to all that is written therein" (Joshua 1: 8). "Teaching them to observe all things whatsoever I have commanded you" (Matt. 28: 20). We are to learn the Scriptures not merely to know them intellectually, but to make practical use of their teachings both in our hearts and in our lives.

We are to *teach* the Word of God to others. "Thou shalt teach them diligently unto thy children" (Deut. 6: 7); (Ps. 78: 5). "Preach the Gospel to every creature" (Mark 16: 15); (Col. 4: 16). Those that have and know the truth of God should teach those that have it not and know it not.

3. **Various uses of the Bible.**—The Bible is to be used for doctrine, for reproof, for correction, for instruction in righteousness (2 Tim. 3: 16), for comfort (Rom. 15: 4).

For doctrine.—The Bible is the source-book of all Christian doctrine. It is in this Book that God tells us what He would have us know, believe, and do, and we must study this Book to learn what it teaches. Every doctrine taught in God's Church must be taken from God's Book, and must in all parts agree with it. Whenever this is the case, then we know and have the truth (John 8: 31. 32). Such use of the Bible is fundamental. Only when we know the truth can we be helped; only when we know God's promises can we believe them; only when we know His precepts can we observe them; only when we know His assurances of grace and help can we be comforted; only when we know the Bible truth can we recognize error.

However, we are not using the Bible aright if we acquire only an intellectual knowledge of its teachings. These truths must mean something to us personally. In studying the Commandments, we must apply them to ourselves, learn to know our sins (Rom. 3: 20), and our lost condition (Rom. 7: 14. 23. 24). In studying the Gospel, we must take its promises to heart, and thus be made wise unto salvation through faith in Christ (2 Tim. 3: 15). In every case we must study the Scriptures in such a manner as to be spiritually benefited thereby.

For reproof.—Men have ever tried to palm off their own dreams and inventions as the doctrines of God (Jer. 23: 31; Matt. 15: 9), or to gainsay the teachings of the Bible. To recognize error, it must be tested by the Word of God (1 John 4: 1). "If they speak not according to this word, it is because there is no light in them" (Is. 8: 20). False doctrines cannot be proved to be scripturally wrong with arguments drawn from human reason and science. By sound doctrine we must exhort and convince the gainsayer (Tit. 1: 9).

For correction.—Though we are God's children by faith in Christ, we still have the old Adam with his deceitful lusts (Eph. 4: 22). We should use the Bible that from it we may learn where our lives are in need of correction and improvement. It teaches us what is displeasing to God, and urges us by the mercies of God that we be not conformed to the ways of the world (Rom. 12: 1. 2), that we deny ungodliness (Tit. 2: 12), and put off and suppress the old Adam.

For instruction, training, in righteousness.—A Christian loves God, and is willing to serve Him. "Thy people shall be willing in the day of Thy power, in the beauties of holiness" (Ps. 110: 3). While the Gospel inspires us with willingness and strength to lead a godly life, the Law is the rule and guide which shows us the way we should go, and the works we should do (Ps. 119: 9; Micah 6: 8). Thus we should use the

Word of God that thereby we might be sanctified in our lives. No book on ethics written by men can be compared with the Bible, which not only teaches the highest type of morality, but also supplies willingness and strength to follow its precepts.

For comfort.—In the world we have tribulations; but in His Word God cheers us with the assurance of His protection and the promise of His grace (John 16: 33). Therefore in the midst of adversity and affliction His Word is to us the joy and rejoicing of our heart (Jer. 15: 16). The burden of all Gospel preaching is: "Comfort ye, comfort ye my people, saith your God" (Is. 40: 1). "For whatsoever things were written aforetime were written for our learning, that we through patience and comfort of the Scriptures might have hope" (Rom. 15: 4).

In the Preface to his Large Catechism Luther says: "If I were to recount all the profit and fruit which the Word of God produces, whence would I get enough paper and time?"

Wrong use of the Bible.—It is a wrong and sinful use of the Bible when we quote Scripture to defend false doctrine and a wicked life. The devil misquoted Scripture (Matt. 4: 6). To use the Bible for some superstitious purpose, to quote texts and stories of the Bible "just to be funny" and to entertain others, is a gross misuse of the Word of God. "Thou shalt not take the name of the Lord, thy God, in vain" (Exodus 20: 7).

PART II. OF GOD

VII. NATURAL AND REVEALED KNOWLEDGE
OF GOD

1. Nature proves the existence of God.—"No man hath seen God at any time" (John 1: 18). To our physical senses God is invisible and intangible. Nevertheless, he is a fool who denies the existence of God (Ps. 14: 1); "because that which may be known of God is manifest to them; for God hath shewed it unto them. For the invisible things of Him from the creation of the world are clearly seen, being understood by the things that are made, even His eternal power and God-head; so that they are without excuse" (Rom. 1: 19. 20). "Every house is builded by some man; but He that built all things is God" (Hebr. 3: 4). Neither the origin nor the continued existence of this world can be satisfactorily explained, unless there be a Prime Cause that brought it into being, and an omnipotent Power that sustains and governs it. Though we do not see God, still we know of Him from His works.

It is preposterous folly to assume that the things we see about us in nature came of themselves, and that this well-ordered universe with its myriads of diverse animate and in-animate beings is the product of blind chance and evolution. As rational man contemplates the wonderful works of nature, he must ask himself whence these things came and by what they exist. His ordinary common sense will tell him that there must have been Some One who made them, and that there still is Some One by whose power they continue to ex-ist. And this Some One is God.

While God indeed manifests Himself in nature, neither nature itself nor the forces in nature may be identified with God. Pantheism is the belief that God and the universe are identical. As we distinguish the building from the builder, so must we distinguish creation from the Creator. "He is before all things, and by Him all things consist" (Col. 1: 17).

2. The conscience of man proves the existence of God.—Of the Gentiles Paul says that they "show the work of the

Law written in their hearts, their conscience also bearing witness, and their thoughts the meanwhile" (between themselves) "accusing or else excusing one another" (Rom. 2: 15), and "who knowing the judgment of God, that they which commit such things are worthy of death" (Rom. 1: 32). Conscience, therefore, holding man accountable for his deeds to a Power higher than himself, testifies to the existence of God.

3. Belief in the existence of God is universal.—The testimony of nature and of conscience for the existence of God is a fact which no sane person will deny. Hence it has ever been the concern of rational man to establish some sort of relation between himself and God. "No people has ever been so reprobate as not to institute and observe some divine worship" (Large Cat., I Com., 17, *Triglot*, p. 585). It would simply be impossible to account for the religious worship we find among pagan people, if there were not some basic knowledge of the existence of a Higher Being.

However, following their vain imaginations, men have built upon the foundation of the natural knowledge of God systems of religion, which are superstitious, idolatrous, and abominable (Rom. 1: 21-25; Acts 17: 22-25). "The heathen had to a certain extent a knowledge of God from the natural Law, although they neither knew Him aright nor glorified Him aright" (F. C., Th. D., Art. V, 22, *Triglot*, p. 959).

4. The extent and the limit of this knowledge.—Nature, history, and conscience teach not only the existence of God, but also that He is a living God (Acts 17: 27); that He is almighty (Rom. 1: 20); that He is wise (Prov. 3: 19); that He is good to His creatures (Acts 14: 17); that He is holy and just, commanding and rewarding what is good, and forbidding and punishing what is evil (Rom. 1: 32; 2: 15).

The true God reveals Himself to us in nature, but nature does not reveal to us who this true God is. No heathen people ever learned from the book of nature that God is the Triune God: Father, Son, and Holy Ghost. When, on the basis of what men know of God from nature, they try to determine who He is, they invariably make an idol of Him. "For all the gods of the nations are idols" (Ps. 96: 5); (Rom. 1: 21-23). "The heathen really make their self-invented notions and dreams of God an idol, and put their trust in what is altogether nothing" (Large Cat., I Com., 20, *Triglot,* p. 585).

Nor is this natural knowledge of God sufficient unto salvation; because the grace of God in Christ is revealed to man only in the Gospel, of which men know nothing by nature (1 Cor. 2: 9-11). Hence, the Gentiles "have no hope, and are without God in the world" (Eph. 2: 12).

5. **The purpose of this knowledge,** especially as it acts through the conscience, is to maintain outward discipline among men, who know the judgment of God upon them that do evil (Rom. 1: 32). The knowledge of the existence of God should, furthermore, incite men to seek Him that they may learn who He is, and what His will is towards men (Acts 17: 27). If they neglect to do this, they will be "without excuse" in the Day of Judgment (Rom. 1: 20).

6. **The revealed knowledge of God.**—In order that man might know who the true God is, and how to worship Him aright, God has revealed Himself more fully in the Bible. The Bible not only corroborates the knowledge of God which men have from and by nature, but it amplifies the same and adds such things as could never be learned otherwise (1 Cor. 2: 7-11). While nature tells us *that* there is a God, the Bible tells us *who* this God is. While nature and conscience reveal to us many of the attributes of God, the Bible not only re-emphasizes them, but also tells us of His love and grace in Christ, and of the salvation He has prepared for us. We are, therefore, not permitted to have our own ideas about God, as the heathen have; but our thoughts and concepts of God must, as far as this is possible for our finite minds, conform to what the Scriptures say of Him. Nor may we worship Him in any manner we please, but we must worship and serve Him according to His Word (Matt. 15: 9).

VIII. THE ESSENCE AND THE ATTRIBUTES OF GOD

A. The Divine Essence

1. God is not a mere idea, existing in the imagination of man, and lacking objective reality; but GOD IS. "I AM THAT I AM" (Ex. 3: 14). This "I AM" is a reality; He is the Absolute and Supreme BEING. By comparison, the idols of the Gentiles are "nothing"; they do not exist as real gods, but they

exist only in the minds of their worshipers (Is. 41: 24; 1 Cor. 8: 4).

2. God is not of a material nature, visible and tangible to our physical senses, but "GOD IS A SPIRIT" (John 4: 24). No man knows of what this spiritual essence of God consists.

But God is not an invisible, lifeless "something," not the "omnia agens," the driving actuating force in nature, not merely the living principle in man, beast, and plant. GOD IS A PERSONAL BEING. "I AM," says He. It was a Personal Being that spoke to Moses, a being that is distinct from all created things and forces. "By Him were all things created, that are in heaven, and that are in earth, visible and invisible" (Col. 1: 16).

God did not evolve out of something that was before Him, nor is His existence dependent on something beside Him; but GOD IS AND SUBSISTS OF AND BY HIMSELF. "I am the first, and I am the last; and beside Me there is no God" (Is. 44: 6). All other beings have their existence from and in God (Acts 17: 28); but God's existence centers in Himself. He "hath life in Himself" (John 5: 26).

Sometimes the Bible speaks of God as though He were a human being, having arm, hand, finger, face (Ex. 6: 6; Eph. 1: 20; Luke 11: 20; Num. 6: 24-26). Such figurative language with respect to God is called anthropomorphism; it is an adaptation to our finite mind, which cannot conceive and realize the spiritual essence of an infinite God. In heaven we shall see God, as He is, in all the inexpressible beauty of His holiness and love (1 John 3: 2).

B. The Divine Attributes

1. **God is one.**—"I am the Lord, and there is none else, there is no God beside Me" (Is. 45: 5). "There is none other God but one" (1 Cor. 8: 4). Hence, "thou shalt have no other gods before Me" (Ex. 20: 3). "Thou shalt worship the Lord thy God, and Him only shalt thou serve" (Matt. 4: 10).

2. **God is a simple, indivisible essence.**—When God says: "I am that I am," He would also have us understand that He is not a compound of parts and elements, but that He is absolutely simple in His essence. Being one, He cannot consist of two or more constituent parts. "There is one divine Essence

which is called, and which is God: eternal, without body, without parts" (A. C., Art. I, 2, *Triglot*, p. 43). "God is a spiritual, undivided essence" (F. C., Th. D., Art. VIII, 68, *Triglot*, p. 1039).

3. **God is immutable** in His essence, in His attributes, and in His will. "I am the Lord, I change not" (Mal. 3: 6). "With whom is no variableness, neither shadow of turning" (James 1: 17). There can be no development or evolution, neither improvement nor deterioration, neither growth nor decline, no change whatever in God. He is what He is, what He always was, and what He ever will be: "semper idem." "Thou are the same, and Thy years shall have no end" (Ps. 102: 27). God is not fickle like man. His judgments and His promises stand. This should be to us a warning and a comfort.

4. **God is infinite,** not limited by, and confined to, space; hence, He is omnipresent. Dimensions of space belong to this created world; there is no infinite space; God alone is infinite. "The heaven and heaven of heavens cannot contain Thee" (1 Kings 8: 27). "Can any hide himself in secret places that I shall not see him? saith the Lord. Do not I fill heaven and earth? saith the Lord" (Jer. 23: 24); (Ps. 139: 7-12). God is, therefore, not confined to a certain locality, but is present in all places, at the same time, not in part, but wholly. We cannot hide nor escape from His presence; He is about us whereever we may be. "He is not far from every one of us: for in Him we live, and move, and have our being" (Acts 17: 27. 28). This is a warning to us (Gen. 17: 1), and a comfort (Is. 41: 10; Ps. 23: 4).

5. **God is eternal,** not limited by time. "Even from everlasting to everlasting, Thou art God" (Ps. 90: 2). God is timeless. With Him there is neither past nor future, but one everlasting presence; "This day" (eternity) "have I begotten Thee" (Ps. 2: 7). "One day is with the Lord as a thousand years, and a thousand years as one day" (2 Pet. 3: 8). The eternity of God is incomprehensible to us; even the span of time from the beginning of the world to the end thereof is not a fraction of eternity as this term applies to God.

When applied to creatures, the term "eternal" is used in a restricted sense, as having a beginning, but no end; men and angels have their beginning, but both shall continue to exist

forever (Matt. 25: 41. 46). The word "everlasting" is sometimes used in the sense of a long period of time (Gen. 17: 8).

6. **God is a living, rational, active being,** not a dead, lifeless something. "But the Lord is the true God, He is the living God" (Jer. 10: 10). "The Father hath life in Himself"
(John 5: 26). God is a rational being. He has wisdom and
knowledge (Rom. 11: 33). He purposes and plans His acts,
and is intent upon their execution (Is. 46: 10. 11). God is
constantly active in preserving and governing the world. "My
Father worketh hitherto, and I work," says Christ (John 5:
17). He is therefore the source of all life and activity in the
world, "for in Him we live, and move, and have our being"
(Acts 17: 28). This is a warning to all unbelievers (Hebr. 10:
31); but it is a comfort to us Christians, for "we trust in the
living God" (1 Tim. 4: 10).

7. **God is omniscient,** has a perfect knowledge of all things.
"The Lord is a God of knowledge" (1 Sam. 2: 3). "God is
greater than our heart, and knoweth all things" (1 John 3:
20). "The eyes of the Lord are in every place, beholding the
evil and the good" (Prov. 15: 3); (Ps. 139: 1-4). It is a warning to realize that we cannot hide anything from Him (Prov.
28: 13); it is a comfort to realize that He knows our sorrows
and troubles, and is ready to help us (Is. 66: 2).

8. **God is wise.** "With Him is wisdom and strength, He
hath counsel and understanding" (Job 12: 13). God knows
in every case what to do and how to do it, how to dispose
and ordain all causes and effects for the attainment of His
purposes. The wisdom of God is manifest in the works of
nature (Ps. 104: 24), and in the work of our redemption and
salvation (1 Cor. 2: 6. 7). The wisdom of God far surpasses
the understanding of man (Rom. 11: 33), who, therefore,
should beware of criticizing the ways and the Word of his God.

9. **God has a will,** inasmuch, as He consciously prompts
His own acts and is intent upon the execution of His pur-
poses. "My counsel shall stand, and I will do all My pleasure.
I have purposed it, I will also do it" (Is. 46: 10. 11).

We distinguish between the revealed will of God, as we
have it in the Bible, and the hidden or secret will of God
(Deut. 29: 29). There are many things in the mind of God
which He has not made known to us (Rom. 11: 33. 34).

The antecedent will of God is that He will have all men to be saved (Ezek. 33: 11); the consequent will of God is that He will surely damn those who reject His saving grace (Mark 16: 16).

Men can resist the will of God when He calls them through the Gospel to come to Him and be saved (Matt. 23: 37); but when on the Last Day He calls the dead from their graves, His will is irresistible (John 5: 28. 29; 2 Cor. 5: 10).

The holy will of God is revealed in the Law; His good and gracious will is made known to us in the Gospel.

10. **The holiness of God** denotes His majesty and glory as exalted above all created things. "Holy, holy, holy is the Lord of hosts: the whole earth is full of His glory" (Is. 6: 3). "Who is like unto Thee, O Lord, among the gods?" (mighty ones) "who is like Thee, glorious in holiness, fearful in praises, doing wonders?" (Ex. 15: 11).

The holiness of God denotes also His opposition to, and abhorrence of, every type of iniquity and sin. "Ye shall be holy; for I the Lord your God am holy" (Lev. 19: 2). "Thou art not a God that hath pleasure in wickedness; neither shall evil dwell with Thee" (Ps. 5: 4).

11. **God is just and righteous.** The *personal* righteousness of God does not consist in this that He conforms to the Law He has given to man, or to another and higher law; for God is "exlex," outside of, above the law; He is His own perfect ethical norm, and whatever He pleases to do or not to do is of itself right and just. "A God of truth and without iniquity, just and right is He" (Deut. 32: 4). "The Lord is upright . . . there is no unrighteousness in Him" (Ps. 92: 15). We must not judge God in His dealings with men by human standards. Whatever God does is right, and it is a heinous blasphemy to accuse Him of injustice.

The righteousness of God *in the Law* is that righteousness which He demands of men; namely, perfect conformity with all His commandments (Matt. 5: 48). His justice under the Law is that He will punish those who fail in the least point (Gal. 3: 10), and to reward those who keep His commandments.

The righteousness of God *in the Gospel* is that righteousness which He graciously imputes unto sinners for Christ's sake, forgiving their sins and declaring them righteous. "The righteousness of God without the Law is manifested . . . even the righteousness of God which is by faith of Jesus Christ" (Rom. 3: 21. 22). The justice of God in the Gospel is that, because Christ has atoned for our sins, God will not hold them against us, but will impart forgiveness to all who penitently confess their sins and believe in Jesus Christ. "He is faithful and just to forgive us our sins, and to cleanse us from all unrighteousness" (1 John 1: 9).

12. **God is truth,** inasmuch as His words and promises truly express His intention and will. "The Word of the Lord is right; and all His works are done in truth" (Ps. 33: 4). "Which keepeth truth forever" (Ps. 146: 6). "God, that cannot lie" (Tit. 1: 2). The absolute truthfulness of God pertains to all that is written in His Word. "Thy Word is truth" (John 17: 17). God's promises do not fail (2 Cor. 1: 20).

13. **God is omnipotent,** inasmuch as He can do and does do whatever He purposes to do. "He hath done whatsoever He hath pleased" (Ps. 115: 3). The power and might of God is as infinite as He Himself is; it never exhausts itself. He "is able to do exceeding abundantly above all that we ask or think" (Eph. 3: 20). "With God nothing shall be impossible" (Luke 1: 37). This, however, does not mean that God could do anything that would involve a contradiction of and disagreement with Himself, as, for instance: God cannot cease to exist; He cannot lie; He cannot do evil; He cannot contradict Himself.

The almighty power of God worked *immediately, directly,* in the creation of the world. "He spake, and it was done; He commanded, and it stood fast" (Ps. 33: 9). "Deus producit volendo," meaning: God produces a thing by willing it. This same power works *mediately,* through natural means, such as food; "Thou givest them their meat in due season . . . and satisfiest the desire of every living thing" (Ps. 145: 15. 16). This power works mediately through the means of grace in creating and preserving faith; the Gospel is "the power of God unto salvation" (Rom. 1: 16). When the power of God acts directly, in uncovered majesty, there is nothing that can resist, as was evidenced in the creation of the world and will be in the resurrection of the dead (John 5: 28. 29). But when the power of God operates through means, as in the Gospel, then man can resist; "ye do always resist the Holy Ghost" (Acts 7: 51).

14. **The goodness of God** includes a number of important and to us very comforting attributes.

God Himself is absolutely good; there is no fault or defect in Him; He is perfect in every respect. "There is none good but one, that is, God" (Matt. 19: 17).

God is good and kind to His creatures, benevolent, and desirous to bless them. "The Lord is good to all; and His tender mercies are over all His works" (Ps. 145: 9).

God is love, desirous of bringing the lost children of men back into union and communion with Himself. "God is love" (1 John 4: 8); (John 3: 16). "Yea, I have loved thee with an everlasting love: therefore with loving-kindness have I drawn thee" (Jer. 31: 3).

God is merciful, having compassion with the afflicted and bestowing His blessings upon them. "The Lord, the Lord God, merciful and gracious, longsuffering, and abundant in goodness and truth" (Ex. 34: 6).

God is gracious, inasmuch as He offers and confers His blessings regardless of the merits or demerits of the objects of His benevolence. "If by grace, then it is no more of works: otherwise grace is no more grace. But if it be of works," (merit of our works) "then it is no more grace: otherwise work is no more work" (Rom. 11: 6). This grace is not a gift or virtue which God imparts to man, no infused grace, but it is an attribute and an attitude of God. It is the "favor Dei," the favor, the good will of God toward those who are utterly unworthy of His blessings. It is the unmerited love of God toward man.

God is longsuffering, slow to anger. "But Thou art a God ready to pardon, gracious and merciful, slow to anger, and of great kindness" (Neh. 9: 17). "The Lord is not slack concerning His promise, as some men count slackness; but is longsuffering to us-ward, not willing that any should perish, but that all should come to repentance" (2 Pet. 3: 9).

IX. THE TRIUNE GOD

A. The Unity of God

1. **"There is ONE Divine Essence** which is called, and which is God" (A. C., Art. I, 2, *Triglot*, p. 43). "The Lord our God is one Lord . . . There is one God; and there is none other but He" (Mark 12: 29. 32); (Is. 44: 6).

2. **The Bible teaches a strict monotheism,** and definitely excludes every form of dualism and polytheism. Dualism teaches the existence of two mutually hostile superior beings, one representing everything morally good and beneficial to man, while the other is the source of all sin and evil. Polytheism is the belief in more gods than one, as we find in the religion of the ancient Greeks and Romans. Both, dualism and polytheism, virtually destroy the concept of God as the Highest Essence. If there are more gods than one, each must necessarily be limited in his sphere by the other, and it is possible to think of a god who is higher than the others. Indeed, there are many that are called gods by men (1 Cor. 8: 5); however, these are not gods in essence, but are merely regarded and worshiped as gods; they are not gods, but men make them gods. "We know that an idol is nothing in the world, and that there is none other God but one" (1 Cor. 8: 4).

3. **Practical importance.**—Worshiping this one God, we do not get into conflict with any other. If He blesses us, no other god can curse us. "If God be for us, who can be against us?" (Rom. 8: 31). But if He is turned against us, "there is none that can deliver out of Thine hand" (Job 10: 7). There is no appeal from Him to a higher and mightier one, for there is no God beside Him. Hence, it is He, and He only, whom we must worship, and to whom we must turn for help and salvation. "This is life eternal, that they might know Thee the only true God, and Jesus Christ, whom Thou hast sent" (John 17: 3).

B. The Trinity of God

1. **Three distinct Persons.**—In the undivided and indivisible Essence of God there are *three distinct Persons.* "And the term 'person' they use as the Fathers have used it, to signify, not a part or a quality in another, but that which subsists of itself" (A. C., Art. I, 4, *Triglot*, p. 43).

Bible proof.—The doctrine of the Trinity is not a New Testament development, as some hold, but is clearly taught also in the Old Testament. "Come ye near unto Me, hear ye this; I have not spoken in secret from the beginning; from the time that it was, there am I: and now the Lord God, and His Spirit hath sent Me" (Is. 48: 16). Here three Persons are clearly distinguished. "Thy throne, O God, is forever and ever: the sceptre of Thy kingdom is a right sceptre. Thou lovest righteousness, and hatest wickedness: therefore God, Thy God, hath anointed Thee with the oil of gladness above Thy fellows" (Ps. 45: 6. 7). Here God is anointed by God with the oil of gladness, which is the Holy Ghost (Acts 10: 38). In the very first verses of the Bible we learn of God and of the Spirit of God and of the Word of God, by whom all things were made (Gen. 1: 1-3); (John 1: 1-3). Because there are more Persons than one, God said: "Let *us* make man in *our* image, after *our* likeness" (Gen. 1: 26). From the New Testament we learn that three distinct Persons were revealed at the baptism of Christ (Matt. 3: 16. 17), and that all nations should be baptized "in the name of the Father, and of the Son, and of the Holy Ghost" (Matt. 28: 19); (2 Cor. 13: 14).

2. **The Father is true God.**—Of the Father Jesus says that He is "the only true God" (John 17: 3). Paul writes: "But to us there is but one God, the Father, of whom are all things, and we in Him" (1 Cor. 8: 6).

He is a Person distinct from the Son. God "gave His only begotten Son" (John 3: 16); in the fulness of time "God sent forth His Son" (Gal. 4: 4). He is distinct also from the Holy Ghost, since He anointed "Jesus of Nazareth with the Holy Ghost and with power" (Acts 10: 38). In Gal. 4: 6 He is distinguished from the Son and the Spirit: "God hath sent forth the Spirit of His Son into your hearts."

The Father, Himself unbegotten, begat the Son from eternity. "The Lord hath said unto Me, Thou art My Son; this day have I begotten Thee" (Ps. 2: 7). Together with the Son He spirates the Holy Ghost from eternity. "When the Comforter is come, whom I will send unto you from the Father, even the Spirit of truth, which proceedeth from the Father, He shall testify of Me" (John 15: 26).

3. **The Son is true God.**—"This" (Jesus Christ) "is the true

God, and eternal life" (1 John 5: 20). Paul says of Him that He "is over all, God blessed forever" (Rom. 9: 5). He is not merely similar (homoi-ousios) to the Father, as Arius taught, but He is coequal with, and of the same essence as, the Father (homo-ousios). Hence, "all men should honor the Son, even as they honor the Father" (John 5: 23).

He is distinct from the Father (John 3: 16; Gal. 4: 4), and from the Holy Ghost, whom He calls "another Comforter" than Himself (John 14: 16. 17).

He is begotten from the Father from eternity (Ps. 2: 7; John 3: 16), and together with the Father He sends forth the Spirit of truth (John 15: 26).

4. **The Holy Ghost is true God.**—Peter tells Ananias that, when he lied unto the Holy Ghost, he had lied unto God (Acts 5: 3. 4). Christians are called the temple of God, because the Holy Ghost dwells in them (1 Cor. 3: 16).

He is distinct from the Father and the Son, for in John 14: 16 Christ clearly differentiates between Himself, the Father, and the Comforter.

The Holy Ghost did not beget, nor was He begotten, but He proceeds from the Father and the Son from eternity. He is the Spirit both of the Father (Matt. 10: 20) and of the Son (Gal. 4: 6). He proceeds from the Father, and is at the same time sent by the Son (John 15: 26). "Jesus breathed on them, and saith unto them, Receive ye the Holy Ghost" (John 20: 22).

The eternal generation of the Son by the Father and the eternal spiration of the Holy Ghost by the Father and the Son are facts plainly taught in the Bible; but they are not explained, hence are profound mysteries to us. We learn and believe what the Bible says about this and other mysteries, but we cannot comprehend how these things can be.

5. **Trinity in unity.**—The Father is God; the Son is God; the Holy Ghost is God. Yet there are not three Gods, but only ONE God. "As we are compelled by Christian verity to acknowledge every Person by Himself to be God and Lord, so we are forbidden by the catholic religion to say, There are three Gods, or three Lords" (The Athanasian Creed). Neither is the Deity split into three parts, each Person being one-third of the Godhead; but each Person is the fullness of the God-

head (Col. 2: 9). Neither is each only a different manifestation, or phase, of the one divine Essence, as ice and steam are but different forms of water, but each is a distinct Person, and each is the full and complete God. Thus the Father is the one and only God (John 17: 3); the Son is the one and only God (1 John 5: 20); the Holy Ghost is the one and only God (Acts 5: 3. 4). There is no subordination of one Person to the other, but the three Persons are of equal rank and majesty, none to be preferred before the other (John 5: 23). While definitely distinct in person, they are one in essence. Christ says: "He that hath seen Me, hath seen the Father" (John 14: 9), and "I and My Father are one" (John 10: 30). In this text the Greek has for "one" the neuter "hen," and not the masculine "heis," which shows that they are one in essence, but not one in person. When Christ says: "My Father is greater than I" (John 14: 28), this must not be understood of the Deity, but of the humanity of Christ in His humiliation. "Equal to the Father as touching His Godhead, and inferior to the Father as touching His manhood." . . . "We worship one God in Trinity, and Trinity in Unity; neither confounding the Persons, nor dividing the Substance" (Athanasian Creed).

6. **Ours is an incomprehensible God.**—He is incomprehensible in His essence; we do not know what His essence is, and of what it consists. He is incomprehensible also in His attributes. According to the Scriptures we, indeed, distinguish between essence and attributes. Still, God's attributes are not qualities inherent in a divine substance, but as God is an absolutely simple and indivisible Being, His essence and His attributes are one. "God *is* love" (1 John 4: 8). God is incomprehensible in His Trinity in Unity. There is no analogy, no simile, no illustration in the wide realm of human thought which could clarify for us this profound mystery.

It is futile and foolish for man to try to penetrate deeper into the mystery of God than it is revealed to us in the Bible. The finite mind of man simply cannot comprehend the infinite God. He transcends conceptual thought and eludes intellectual grasp. For the present let us be content with what we read in the Bible: "Beloved, now are we the sons of God, and it doth not yet appear what we shall be; but we know that, when He shall appear, we shall be like Him; for we shall see Him as He is" (1 John 3: 2).

7. **The doctrine of the Holy Trinity is a fundamental article of our Christian faith.**—"He, therefore, that will be saved must thus think of the Trinity" (Athanasian Creed). Faith in the Triune God means more than accepting the bare teaching of Three Persons in One Essence; it includes reliance and confidence in the saving work of the Trinity. A reading of the Athanasian Creed will bring out this fact very clearly.

PART III. OF CREATION AND OF PROVIDENCE

X. THE CREATION OF THE WORLD

1. Source.—In Genesis, chapters 1 and 2, we have the only authentic and reliable record of the creation of the world. No man was present at the time to report this great event, neither can geology and astronomy tell us how in the beginning all things came into being. Whether Moses received his information by direct revelation from God, or by tradition from Adam, is of no consequence, since also this part of the Bible was written under inspiration of God, and is, therefore, God's own record of His own work.

2. The Creator.—"In the beginning God created the heaven and the earth" (Gen. 1: 1). While the work of creation is primarily, not exclusively, ascribed to the Father, the other Persons of the Trinity concurred in this creative act. The three Persons are referred to in the very first verses of the Bible. God created heaven and earth; the Spirit of God moved upon the face of the waters; and when God *said*, "Let there be light," it was the Word, by whom all things were made (John 1: 1-3; Col. 1: 16; Hebr. 1: 2; Ps. 33: 6).

The creation was not a necessary, but a free and voluntary act of God; "He hath done whatsoever He hath pleased" (Ps. 115: 3). Whether God created or is still creating other worlds, is an idle question. The Bible speaks of the creation of the world in which we now live.

3. The creation.—Before the "beginning" there was neither time nor space nor any pre-existing material, from which this world was fashioned; but there was only God, who "is before all things" (Col. 1: 17); (Ps. 90: 2; John 1: 1). But God did not create the world from His own essence, so that every creature was and still is a part of the Deity (pantheism); He created the world out of nothing. There was no substance of any kind which God used in forming the universe, but all things that now exist were by Him called into being. "Through faith we understand that the worlds were framed by the Word

34

of God, so that things which are seen were not made of things which do appear" (Hebr. 11: 3). By His omnipotent "fiat" God called all things into existence. "By the Word of the Lord were the heavens made; and all the host of them by the Breath of His mouth. . . . He spake, and it was done; He commanded, and it stood fast" (Ps. 33: 6. 9). Thus the very existence of the entire universe depends solely on the will of God. "By Him all things consist" (Col. 1: 17).

4. **Time.**—God might have created the entire universe, as it now is, in the twinkling of an eye. He might have allowed it to develop over long periods of time. But He definitely tells us that He began and completed the work in six consecutive days. The expression "evening and morning" marks the days of creation as ordinary days of twenty-four hours each. Beginning with the fourth day (Gen. 1: 14-19), the present solar system was put into operation, the sun to rule the day and the moon the night. These days, therefore, controlled by the same lights as ours are, were not longer than our days are at present. The same holds good of the first three days, which, like the last three, are described as "evening and morning." This is further substantiated by the reference of Exodus 20: 9-11 to the days of creation. Texts like Ps. 90: 4 and 2 Pet. 3: 8 do not show that those days may have been indeterminably long periods, but merely prove that God is timeless. The creation days, however, are very definitely measures of time. Whoever believes these days to have been long periods, does so not on the basis of Scriptural evidence. The omnipotent God did not need any period of time, long or short, to finish His creative work.

5. **Orderly progression.**—God began the work by first creating the crude material: heaven and earth, water, and elementary light (Gen. 1: 1-5).—The second day He made the firmament to divide the waters below from the waters above the firmament (Gen. 1: 6-8).—On the third day He separated the land from the sea, and caused the land to bring forth grass, the herb yielding seed, and the tree yielding fruit, whose seed was in itself. Thus the naked earth was clothed with a variegated flora, each species so constituted as to propagate by producing its own seed (Gen. 1: 9-13).—The next day God made the sun, the moon, and the numerous stars,

placing them in the canopy of heaven. The elementary light was now concentrated into these heavenly luminaries. Their purpose is to give light on earth, and to divide time into days, months, seasons, and years; and they have continued to do this ever since. How deep this firmament is, in which these lights move, we do not know; but since God set these lights in the firmament of the heaven (Gen. 1: 17), this firmament must be as deep as the distance between the light nearest to us and the star farthest from us (Gen. 1: 14-19).—The earth had now become a fit habitation for living beings. Hence, God proceeded to call forth numerous and various species of fish and of fowl, and, blessing them, enabled them to multiply on earth (Gen. 1: 20-23).—On the sixth day God commanded the earth to bring forth all manner of living creatures, cattle and beasts and creeping things, each after his kind, bestowing on them the same blessing. Finally, God formed the most noble creature, for whose benefit, use, and enjoyment He had produced all the rest; God made man (Gen. 1: 24-28).

6. **The ultimate end of creation is the glory of God.**— "Thou art worthy, O Lord, to receive glory and honor and power; for Thou hast created all things, and for Thy pleasure they are and were created" (Rev. 4: 11).

Inasmuch as God created all things from nothing by His word and will, the entire creation is a manifestation of His omnipotent power. "Ah Lord God! behold, Thou hast made the heaven and the earth by Thy power and stretched-out arm, and there is nothing too hard for Thee" (Jer. 32: 17).

In the multitude, variety, order, and harmony of all created things shines forth the wisdom of God. "O Lord, how manifold are Thy works! in wisdom hast Thou made them all: the earth is full of Thy riches" (Ps. 104: 24).

Inasmuch as all things God made are in themselves "very good" (Gen. 1: 31), and are intended for the use and the benefit of man (Gen. 1: 28), the entire creation proclaims the goodness of the Lord.

7. **The Bible record of the creation is reasonable.**—Compared with the creation myths of the heathen and with the theories of modern evolutionists, the Bible record of the creation commends itself to every thinking man as the most sane and reasonable. It is irrational to assume that the basic mat-

ter constituting this universe should have sprung into existence without some primary or first Cause, without the creative
act of some Supreme Being. It is equally irrational to believe
that this material should of itself, without any intelligent direction and purposeful influence by that same Being, have developed in a series of haphazard evolutions into those many
and manifold forms we now find in nature. Even from the
viewpoint of reason the account of the Bible regarding the
creation of the world is far more believable than all the theories of scientists. If we must admit that it requires a Supreme
Power to create the material of which this world is composed,
we must also admit that He is well able to put this material
in shape and order within six days, and that evolutionary
periods of unknown length are not at all necessary to produce
our present world. Since no human being was present when
the world was made, no man can from his own observation
give us reliable information as to how this world came into
existence. The only one who can speak with authority on
this subject is the Creator Himself, and His account we find
in Genesis, chapter 1. What the various schools of evolution
have taught, or still teach, are mere theories. They do not
teach facts, verified by observation and experience, but mere
human opinions and speculations, acclaimed today and rejected tomorrow. Whether a man accepts the theories of evolution, or the record of the Bible, in both cases he believes.
The question is whether we shall believe men when they
theorize on matters of which they know nothing, or whether
we shall believe our God.

XI. DIVINE PROVIDENCE
or
The Preservation and the Government of the World

1. **God rested.**—"On the seventh day God ended His work
which He had made; and He rested on the seventh day from
all His work which He had made" (Gen. 2: 2). This "rest"
of God, which has continued ever since, does not mean that
God ceased working; for Christ tells us: "My Father worketh
hitherto, and I work" (John 5: 17). It simply means that
God ceased creating new and additional things; but He did

not withdraw from His finished work, letting it shift for itself according to previously established laws.

2. Immediate preservation.—Neither the world at large nor the individual creatures in the world have the inherent power to subsist in themselves; but their continued existence rests and depends solely upon the will and power of God, without which they would immediately vanish into nothing. "All things were created by Him . . . and by Him all things consist" (Col. 1: 16. 17). As by His almighty Word God called all things into being, so does He now by the same power keep them in existence, "upholding all things by the Word of His power" (Hebr. 1: 3). God, therefore, is not resting in the distant heavens, unconcerned about His creation, but He is constantly and actively present with all things He has made, keeping and sustaining, directing and governing them. "He is not far from every one of us: for in Him we live, and move, and have our being" (Acts 17: 27. 28). Preservation, then, is that act of the Triune God by which He continuously sustains all things He has made, so that they continue in being, each with the properties and powers implanted in its nature at creation. "O Lord, Thou preservest man and beast" (Ps. 36: 6).

3. Mediate preservation.—While God keeps all things in existence directly and immediately by the sheer power of His will, He at the same time employs His creatures as means to give support and sustenance to each other. When God had created man, He gave to him the herb of the field and the fruit of the tree "for meat" (Gen. 1: 29). After the fall of man this was expanded so as to include the flesh of animals. To Noah God said: "Every moving thing that liveth shall be meat for you; even as the green herb have I given you all things" (Gen. 9: 3); (Ps. 104; 14. 15). While directly, therefore, our existence and life is dependent on the will of God (Acts 17: 28), it is indirectly dependent upon the means of livelihood, which He gives us. Hence, "the eyes of all wait upon Thee; and Thou givest them their meat in due season. Thou openest Thine hand, and satisfiest the desire of every living thing" (Ps. 145: 15. 16).

God gives us our daily bread, but we must work for it. Not even in the garden of Eden was man to spend his days in idleness, but he was to dress it and keep it (Gen. 2: 15). After

the fall into sin, work became toilsome labor (Gen. 3: 19);
and to this day it is the will of God "that if any would not
work, neither should he eat" (2 Thess. 3: 10). In order that
our work be not in vain, other agencies are called into service: the soil, the sun, the weather, the seasons, the air, etc.
Thus the entire creation is a wonderful workshop of God, in
which all things are integrated for mutual service, one sup-
plying the other with what it needs for its subsistence.

"I believe that God has made me and all creatures; that
He has given me my body and soul, eyes, ears, and all my
members, my reason and all my senses, and still preserves
them; also clothing and shoes, meat and drink, house and
home, wife and children, fields, cattle, and all my goods; that
He daily and richly provides me with all that I need to support this body and life." Thus we confess with Luther in the
explanation of the First Article of the Apostles' Creed.

4. **The concurrence of God.**—The means which God employs for our preservation are endowed with definite properties and powers. However, these means do not function independently of God, but it is He Himself who operates through
them according to the measure of their peculiar properties
and powers and for those ends which He has fixed. "God
worketh all in all" (1 Cor. 12: 6). This text indeed speaks of
spiritual gifts and operations; but since God bestowed upon
each of His creatures natural gifts and fitted them for special
functions, we may apply these words also to all natural operations of His creatures. Such concurrence, or cooperation, of
God, as the prime cause, with His creatures, as the secondary
cause, may be exemplified thus:

We say it is natural for the sun to rise, and the rain to fall
from the clouds; yet very definitely the Bible tells us that it
is God, who maketh the sun to rise, and it is He that sendeth
the rain (Matt. 5: 45). So neither the sun nor the rain act
independently, but God, who sustains them, also works and
operates in them.—We say it is natural for seed to germinate,
for grass to grow and to yield seed after its kind. Yet, the
almighty power of God is at all times operating in, with, and
through the germinating seed, the growing grass, etc. "He
causeth the grass to grow for the cattle, and herb for the
service of man" (Ps. 104: 14).—We say it is natural for chem-

icals, medicines, or food to produce certain effects, each after
its kind. Still, without the concurrent power and operation
of God they would be absolutely ineffective. "Man doth not
live by bread only, but by every word that proceedeth out of
the mouth of the Lord doth man live" (Deut. 8: 3); (Matt.
4: 4). Here we not only learn that God can sustain man without the use of natural means such as bread, but also are reminded that bread originally received its nutritive power from
God through His Word.—Living creatures have the ability to
move about at will. Yet, without God's will and concurrence
the sparrow could not flap its wings, nor man move a finger
(Matt. 10: 29; Acts 17: 28). No creature, animate or inani-
mate, acts independently of God, even as it does not exist independently of God. God concurs in whatever a creature does
according to the properties and abilities of its nature. "Der
durch seine grosze Kraft alles wirket, tut und schafft"
(Luther).

We identify God neither with nature nor with the forces
and laws of nature. Still, the latter do not function independently of God, but rather it is the will and power of God that
operates in and through the creatures within the limits of
those properties and powers He has given them, and for those
ends He has determined. Thus: fire is hot, ice is cold, poison
kills, food nourishes; each creature acts according to its peculiar nature. But in and through each one of them operates the
power of Him in whom all things live and move and have
their being. Since God is the author of the laws of nature,
He controls them, and they do not control Him. In the case
of a miracle He simply suspends the natural limitations and
function of a creature, and makes it serve His own purpose.

This doctrine of the concurrence of God is by no means an
idle speculation, but has practical significance. We pray to
this God, and He has promised to hear us (Ps. 50: 15). The
fact that He concurs in all the functions of His creatures
strengthens in us the assurance that He can easily make them
serve our needs.

5. **The concurrence of God in the evil and the good works
of man.**—Man is not only a physical creature; he is also a
moral being. Hence, we must differentiate between the physical acts (materiale) and its moral quality (formale). Physi-

cally two men may perform the same act, yet morally it need not be the same. One man picks up a dollar and keeps it, and he is an honest man, because the money is his. The other does the same thing, and he is a thief, because he knows that the money belongs to somebody else. In both cases God concurs in the physical performance of the act; also the thief could not move his hand without God's cooperation. But God has absolutely no part in the sinfulness of the act, for He is not a God that hath pleasure in wickedness (Ps. 5: 4). God concurs in the physical part of an evil act, but not in the moral depravity of this act. Why does God not refrain to cooperate in the physical performance of such acts as are morally contrary to His will? We do not know. However, it is blasphemous if on that account we hold Him responsible for our evil deeds. "Let no man say when he is tempted, I am tempted of God: for God cannot be tempted with evil, neither tempteth He any man; but every man is tempted, when he is drawn away of his own lust and enticed" (James 1: 13. 14).

As to the moral quality of the good works men do, we know that in the case of the Gentiles God urges them through their conscience to do the works of the Law (Rom. 2: 14. 15); and in the case of the believers He actuates them by His Holy Spirit to will and to do of His good pleasure (Phil. 2: 13). Thus God concurs not only in the physical performance of, but also supplies the motive for and gives direction to, the good works of His Christians.

The fact that "in God we live and move and have our being" does not reduce man to an automaton, deprived of freedom of will and action. For man often thinks, wills, and does what God would not have him think, will, and do, which plainly shows that man has a will of his own. Hence, according to the witness of his own conscience (Rom. 2: 14. 15), and of the Scriptures (Matt. 12: 36), man, and not God, is responsible for his thoughts, words, and deeds. The idea of fatalism is contrary to the teachings of the Bible. Therefore our Confessions deny "that everything that man does, even in outward things, he does by compulsion, and that he is coerced to evil works and deeds" (F. C., Epit., Art. II, 8, *Triglot*, p. 789), and they state that "the human will has liberty in the choice

of works and things which reason comprehends by itself"
(A. C., Art. XVIII, 70, *Triglot*, p. 335).

6. **The government of God.**—God actively participates in
all that happens for the express purpose of governing the
world. He most excellently orders, regulates, and directs the
affairs and actions of all creatures according to His wisdom,
justice, and goodness for the glory of His name and the welfare of men.

As the Sovereign Ruler of the universe (a) God controls
the laws of nature. We have seedtime and harvest, cold and
heat, summer and winter, day and night, because God so wills
it (Gen. 8: 22). He makes the sun to rise on the evil and the
just (Matt. 5: 45), and gives rain from heaven and fruitful
seasons (Acts 14: 17). (b) He governs also the destiny of
nations, as we see from the history of Israel, of the Assyrians,
and of others recorded in the Bible. (c) Yea, He orders also
the lives of individual men, as we see from the lives of Abraham, of Moses, and others. "A man's heart deviseth his way;
but the Lord directeth his steps" (Prov. 16: 9); (Ps. 33: 13-
15). As we, therefore, plan our work and our future, we
should do so subject to the will and good pleasure of God
(James 4: 13-15). (d) God also controls the evil in the world.
At times God suffers evil to happen, and permits men to walk
in their perverse ways (Ps. 81: 12; Acts 14: 16; Rom. 1: 24).
Then again, He breaks up the evil counsel and will of men,
as in the case of Saul (Acts 9; Ps. 33: 10), or he hinders and
frustrates their wicked purpose. It is as Joseph said to his
brethren: "Ye thought evil against me; but God meant it unto good" (Gen. 50: 20). He defends us against danger, as He
defended Lot in Sodom and Israel at the Red Sea. Without
His will no sparrow shall fall to the ground, and not a hair
from our head (Matt. 10: 29. 30). He guards and protects us
from all evil (Ps. 91: 10-12). Even the evil men do is subject
to His control, and must serve His purposes: the betrayal of
Judas and the judicial murder of Christ He used to carry out
His plan of redemption. (See also Gen. 50: 20). He determines the length to which wicked men may go, and so regulates and limits the results of their actions that all things
must in the end work out for the good of His children (Rom.
8: 28). The "foreknowledge of God observes its order also in

wicked acts and works, inasmuch as a limit and measure is fixed by God to the evil, which God does not will, how far it should go, and how long it should last, when and how He will hinder and punish it; for all of this God the Lord so overrules that it must redound to the glory of the divine name and to the salvation of His elect, and the godless, on this account, must be put to confusion" (F. C., Th. D., Art. XI, 6, *Triglot*, p. 1065).

This government of God is so comprehensive that it concerns itself not only with the great events in history, but also with the smallest details of our personal lives. A study of this doctrine should make us feel very humble, as we must realize our utter dependence on God for our life and being. On the other hand, it should fill our hearts with joy and comfort, because we know ourselves to be at all times in the hands of our heavenly Father. "He defends me against all danger, and guards and protects me from all evil; and all this purely out of fatherly, divine goodness and mercy, without any merit or worthiness in me; for all which it is my duty to thank and praise, to serve and obey Him. This is most certainly true." Thus we confess with Luther in the explanation of the First Article of the Apostles' Creed.

PART IV.   OF THE ANGELS AND OF MAN

XII.   OF THE ANGELS

1. **Existence of angels.**—"The Sadducees say that there is no resurrection, neither angel, nor spirit" (Acts 23: 8). Also in our day there are those who doubt and even deny the existence of angels, especially, of the devil. Indeed, we find no evidence of their existence in nature, but numerous texts of the Bible definitely prove that angels do exist (Ps. 103: 20. 21).

2. **Time of their creation.**—Before the beginning nothing existed but God (John 1: 1-3). After the sixth day no new creatures were made (Gen. 2: 1. 2). Hence, the angels must have been created sometime within the six days of creation.

God made one man and one woman, who were to replenish the earth; but the angels are sexless; they do not propagate (Matt. 22: 30). Hence, all the angels, and there are hosts of them (Rev. 5: 11; Luke 2: 13), were created at the beginning. Their number is neither increased nor diminished.

3. **The nature of angels.**—Angels are not mere physical or moral forces, but distinct spiritual beings, which God created. "Who maketh His angels spirits" (Ps. 104: 4); (Hebr. 1: 14). Though at times they assumed human forms (Gen. 18: 2), they possess no material bodies, "for a spirit hath not flesh and bones" (Luke 24: 39). We do not know of what substance these angelic spirits consist.

Unlike the human soul, which is also a spirit, but ordinarily lives in a physical body, the angel spirits have no bodies in which they live, but are complete in their spiritual nature. Angels are not omnipresent, but are present only in one particular place at a time. However, they are illocally present; they do not occupy and fill a definite circumscribed space, where their presence could be felt.

Angels are personal beings. "I am Gabriel, that stand in the presence of God" (Luke 1: 19). The text plainly shows that this angel was conscious of his existence and of his personality. Angels are rational beings, who experience joy over a sinner's repentance (Luke 15: 10), and desire to look into

44

the things that pertain to the kingdom of Christ (1 Pet. 1: 12). They possess knowledge and wisdom; "My lord is wise, according to the wisdom of an angel of God" (2 Sam. 14: 20). They excel in strength (Ps. 103: 20). However, they are neither almighty nor omniscient (Mark 13: 32).

There are various ranks and orders among angels: Cherubim (Gen. 3: 24); Seraphim (Is. 6: 2); Thrones, Dominions, Principalities, Powers (Col. 1: 16); Archangels (1 Thess. 4: 16). The Scriptures also mention the names of a few angels: Gabriel (Luke 1: 19); Michael (Dan. 10: 13).

Angels do not marry and propagate their kind, as men do (Matt. 22: 30). "The sons of God," who took to wives the daughters of men (Gen. 6: 2), were not the angels of God, but children of godly parents, who were still numbered with God's people and who married the daughters of the world. Angels are immortal; "neither can they die any more, for they are equal unto the angels" (Luke 20: 36).

4. **The good angels.**—All angels were created equally good and holy, for "God saw everything that He had made, and behold, it was very good" (Gen. 1: 31). All angels were at first in a state of trial and probation, in which they were able to sin and able not to sin. Some of them did sin; "God spared not the angels that sinned" (2 Pet. 2: 4). Others did not sin, but kept the first estate in which they were created. These are now confirmed in their holiness, are unable to sin, are "holy angels" (Matt. 25: 31), and "always beholding the face" of God in heaven, they enjoy everlasting bliss and communion with God (Matt. 18: 10), which they owe exclusively to His goodness.

The bliss of these angels does not consist in idleness, but in willing and joyful service. They praise and worship God (Luke 2: 13. 14; Is. 6: 2. 3). They "do His commandments, hearkening unto the voice of His word" (Ps. 103: 20. 21); (2 Kings 19: 35; Luke 1: 19. 26; Matt. 1: 20; 4: 11; 25: 31; 1 Thess. 4: 16). Especially are they employed to promote the work of the Church, and to protect its servants (Dan. 6: 22; Acts 5: 18-20; 12: 7-9), and to minister to all that fear God and walk in His ways (Ps. 34: 7; 91: 11), that they may attain to eternal life (Hebr. 1: 14; Luke 16: 22).

If God would open our eyes, as He opened the eyes of the

youth (2 Kings 6: 16. 17), we also would see the guardian angels that encamp round about us. There is no Word of God which tells us that we should invoke these angels for help, neither are we to adore them (Rev. 22: 8. 9).

5. **The evil angels.**—Evil angels are not a personification of the wickedness in the world or in man, but they are personal spiritual beings, as may be seen from the temptation of Jesus in the wilderness (Matt. 4: 3); (Mark 5: 9).

These angels, originally good and holy, sinned (2 Pet. 2: 4), not through any defect in their nature, nor because of some outward instigation, as in the case of man, but in full possession of their intellect, with deliberate design, and voluntary abuse of their will. They "abode not in the truth" (John 8: 44), "kept not their first estate, but left their own habitation" (Jude 6); they made a beginning of sin (1 John 3: 8). It does not appear what their first offense was; nor do we know the date of their fall, but their rebellion against God must have happened after the sixth day of the creation and before the devil tempted our first parents.

These evil angels are now forever rejected, "reserved in everlasting chains under darkness unto judgment" (Jude 6). There is no redemption for them; no promise of grace applies to them; no Gospel is preached to them. They will never return into the communion with God, for "everlasting fire" was prepared for the devil and his angels (Matt. 25: 41).

There are many devil spirits; "my name is legion: for we are many" (Mark 5: 9). They are powerful (Eph. 6: 12); they know God and their judgment (James 2: 19; Matt. 8: 29); they are cunning and deceitful even when they quote Scriptures (Gen. 3: 1; Matt. 4: 6; 2 Cor. 11: 14); they are liars and murderers (John 8: 44); utterly depraved and perverted, unclean and wicked (Mark 1: 23; Eph. 6: 12).

Until the Day of Judgment God permits these evil spirits to roam on earth (Job 1: 7; 1 Pet. 5: 8; Matt. 8: 29. 31). Being the adversaries of God and man, they are ever bent upon destroying the works of God to counteract His gracious purposes with man, as we may see from the temptation in Paradise and from the temptation of Christ. They are the secret sinister power that holds the heathen in abject idolatry and superstition (1 Cor. 10: 20; Acts 26: 18); they are the driving force behind the wickedness of the world (Eph. 6: 12). They are assiduously plotting to disturb and to destroy the Church (Matt. 16: 18), by scattering heresies (1 Tim. 4: 1), by hindering the work of pious ministers (1 Thess. 2: 18), by turning the minds of the hearers from the meditation on God's Word, from prayer, and the practice of the divine truths (Luke 8: 12), and by inciting persecutions (Luke 22: 31). They tempt men to sin (John 13: 2), keep them in ignorance and unbelief of the Word (2 Cor. 4: 4), and molest them in their bodies (2 Cor. 12: 7; Luke 13: 16).

Nevertheless, these wicked spirits are subject to God's supreme dominion and control, and they cannot go beyond what He permits them to do (Job 1: 12; 2: 6). Neither shall they prevail against the Church (Matt. 16: 18; Rom. 16: 20), but they must serve the purposes of God in chastising the pious, as God permitted them to do to Job, and in punishing the wicked (Ps. 78: 49).

XIII. OF MAN

1. **The creation of man.**—On the sixth day the Triune God made man (Gen. 1: 26. 27. 31). The details of this creation, as recorded in the Scriptures, mark man as the chief and foremost of all visible creatures. Not only did God, as it were, take counsel with Himself, but He fashioned the body of a mature man, Adam, from the dust of the ground, and breathed into his nostrils the breath of life (Gen. 2: 7), gave him a rational soul and a conscience, and created him in His own image. On the same day God made one mature woman, Eve, of a rib, which He had taken from Adam (Gen. 2: 21. 22).

This record of man's creation seems puerile and silly to many, fit for the kindergarten, but not to be accepted as an actual fact by men and women of modern learning and attainments. But, in all fairness, compare this record with the theory of the descent of man that is advanced by evolutionists, and then judge for yourself which is more rational and more worthy of the position man holds in the world. This is a simple story, but not at all unbelievable, since there is an Almighty God, who stands behind it. The theories of evolutionists are not based on facts, but on the opinions of men, and they require a goodly portion of credulity on the part of those who accept them. Christians believe that God has made man; let others believe that they are the descendants of anthropoid apes.

2. **The nature of man.**—Man consists of body and soul in one complete person (Gen. 2: 7; Eccl. 12: 7). The *body of man* is of the dust of the ground (Gen. 3: 19). Its anatomy shows it to be a most wonderful piece of workmanship; eyes that see, ears that hear, a heart that beats and sends the bloodstream through the lungs to be purified and through the entire body to build up its tissues, a delicate nervous system that carries messages to and from the brain, and all members so constructed as to serve their purpose most admirably. "I will praise Thee; for I am fearfully and wonderfully made: marvelous are Thy works; and that my soul knoweth right well" (Ps. 139: 14). It is difficult to understand how any one who studies the human body, its various members and organs, and their specific functions, can still be an atheist, believing that this body is the product of blind chance and evolution.

The *soul of man* is not a material, but an immortal, living, spiritual essence, the composition and structure of which we do not understand. It dwells in the body (Acts 20: 10), but takes up no room or space. It gives life to the body, and makes use of its several members according to the purpose for which they are designed. The interrelation and interaction of soul and body is a profound mystery.

The fact that God breathed into man the breath of life shows that the soul of man is different from the life principle in animals. However, it is not a part of the divine Essence, for the souls of the unbelievers God shall "destroy" in hell (Matt. 10: 28), and it is preposterous to think that God would "destroy" a part of His own Essence. Like the angel spirits, the soul of man is a creature of God.

Man is a *rational* soul. He can learn, think, and reason. The ideas of his mind stir up in his heart emotions and feelings, which, in turn, press upon his will and produce voluntary action. And of all this man is conscious. Thus Adam was able to distinguish and to name the creatures, which God brought to him (Gen. 2: 19. 20). The forbidden fruit was pleasant to the eyes of Eve, and to be desired (Gen. 3: 6); both, Adam and Eve, voluntarily ate thereof. The fact that

God put man on probation, forbidding him to eat of the tree of knowledge of good and evil (Gen. 2: 16. 17), shows that man is a *moral* creature, who has some knowledge of God and His law, and a conscience, which urges him to comply with this law, and holds him guilty if he fails to do so. None of these things can be said of the irrational brute, their instincts or unreasoning promptings to action notwithstanding.

The soul is carrier of man's personality, of his conscious self, his "ego"; for the dead body knows nothing, feels nothing, wills nothing (Eccl. 9: 5).

Dichotomy and trichotomy.—The Bible teaches dichotomy, that is, man consists of two chief parts, body and soul (Matt. 10: 28), or body and spirit (Eccl. 12: 7). Trichotomy holds that man consists of three parts: body, soul, and spirit. In Luke 1: 46. 47 the words "soul" and "spirit" are parallel terms. Both indicate the same immaterial element as contrasted to the body, however with this difference: the soul indicates the living, rational, active function in its relation to earthly experiences, while the spirit refers more to its relation with God and spiritual things. Thus the soul is fully active in believers and unbelievers, while the spirit is alive to God in believers, but dead to God in unbelievers. This distinction, however, is not always strictly observed.

We do not speak of the soul of God, but we do speak of the soul of Christ in His humanity (Matt. 26: 38).

3. **Propagation.**—In the beginning God made one man and one woman, and joined them in wedlock to be one flesh (Gen. 2: 18. 21-24), that they should be fruitful and multiply and replenish the earth (Gen. 1: 27. 28). Since then men and women are no longer created in the same manner as Adam and Eve were created, but they are begotten and born of their parents, through whom God gives them body and soul, eyes, ears, and all their members, their reason and all their senses. Adam begat a son (Gen. 5: 3) and Eve bare Cain (Gen. 4: 1); (Job 14: 1). Parents beget not only the body, but living children; therefore also the rational soul is passed on by parents to their children; this doctrine is called traducianism. Nevertheless, it is God who forms the child in the mother's womb (Jer. 1: 5), and gives it life and breath (Acts 17: 25; Zech. 12: 1). Thus God "hath made of one blood all

nations of men for to dwell on all the face of the earth" (Acts 17: 26).

4. **The primeval state of man.**—In his original state man was "very good" in every respect. (a) The physical condition of his body was perfect; there was no weak and defective organ, no germ of disease or of death; he was potentially immortal (Gen. 2: 17; Rom. 5: 12). The rational powers of his soul were likewise perfect. Christ excepted, Adam and Eve before the fall into sin were the only human beings that ever were perfectly healthy in their bodies and perfectly sane in their minds.

(b) The spiritual relation of man to his God was perfect. Both, man and woman, were created in the image of God (Gen. 1: 27), which, being a spiritual likeness, had its seat in the soul, and was reflected in their lives. It consisted in blissful knowledge of God (Col. 3: 10), and in perfect righteousness and true holiness of life (Eph. 4: 24; Eccl. 7: 29). There was no evil, no sin in man; he was innocent, hence, not ashamed of his nakedness (Gen. 2: 25). Man knew the will of his God, and was fully able to conform to it in thought, word, and deed. However, in the state of probation he possessed also the freedom to use his powers against God and to transgress His commandment. It was possible for him to sin, and also possible not to sin (posse peccare et posse non peccare).

(c) The mutual relation between the man and the woman was ideal, each of them fully understanding and observing the duties and restrictions of his position, and regarding each other as a precious gift of their Creator. "It is not good that the man should be alone; I will make him an help meet for him" (Gen. 2: 18). "This is now bone of my bones, and flesh of my flesh: she shall be called Woman, because she was taken out of Man" (Gen. 2: 23). And Paul writes: "Man is the image and glory of God; but the woman is the glory of the man. For man is not of the woman; but woman is of the man. Neither was the man created for the woman; but the woman for the man" (1 Cor. 11: 7-9). From this it appears that also in the state of integrity the man was the head of the wife, and she was an helpmeet for him. The full measure of happiness, which the estate of matrimony was intended to bring both, was realized while Adam and Eve remained sinless.

(d) The relation of man to the other creatures was one of dominion and rule. God gave man dominion over every living thing that moved on the earth (Gen. 1: 28); all herbs and fruit He gave him for meat (Gen. 1: 29); the lights of the firmament and whatever else God had made were for the benefit, service, and enjoyment of man. However, also in the garden of Eden God wanted man to work (Gen. 2: 15); but work was pastime and joy, not a toilsome burden.

5. **The fall of man.**—The original state of innocence came to an abrupt end when man fell into sin. We do not know how long after the creation this happened, but our first parents sinned before the conception of their first offspring (Gen. 4: 1).

Eve, tempted by Satan (Rev. 12: 9), ate of the tree of which God, to test man's obedience, had told him not to eat; she then gave unto her husband, and he also did eat (Gen. 3: 1-6). This disobedience was in no wise due to any defect in man, for God had made him "very good" (Gen. 1: 31); nor was it purposed and decreed by God, for He had definitely forbidden man to eat of this tree (Gen. 2: 17); but it was entirely a voluntary act on the part of man. Knowing the express will of God, Eve gave way to doubt, selfish pride, and an inordinate desire for the forbidden fruit, which led to the sinful act (James 1: 13-15). Adam and Eve were fully able to resist the temptation of Satan, but they yielded knowingly and willingly, hence, theirs was the responsibility.

By transgressing this one positive and express commandment, which God had given to our first parents to test and to try their obedience, Adam and Eve virtually transgressed the whole Law (James 2: 10), because thereby they broke through the restraint of the entire moral Law, within which God wanted them to live. By this disobedience man consciously set himself in opposition to God, and thus severed that spiritual union and communion with his Maker, in which he had lived.

The immediate result of man's fall into sin was the loss of the image of God. Having sinned, man was no longer holy; being guilty, he was no longer innocent; he had exchanged the fellowship with God for the fellowship with the devil, for "he that committeth sin is of the devil" (1 John 3: 8). Because of all this he was under the just wrath and curse of God (Gen. 2: 17); the happiness and bliss of Paradise was lost, and depravity, misery, and death was his lot.

(a) Thus man's holy relation to God had ceased; his heart had departed from the Lord. There was no longer a reverential fear, a filial love, an implicit trust in God; man was "afraid" of God, hiding himself among the trees from the presence of the Lord (Gen. 3: 8). He mistrusted God, lied to Him, and would fain blame Him for his sin (Gen. 3: 10-12). Man is now spiritually dead (Eph. 2: 1), an enemy of God (Rom. 8: 7). He still knows that there is a God, to whom he is responsible; yet this is not a blissful knowledge, but one of dread and fear.

(b) Man's moral relation to his neighbor is changed. To clear himself, he blames the woman; he is selfish, pitiless, cruel. Love for the neighbor is lost and selfishness fills the heart. There were other dire consequences.

(c) The dominion of man over nature is curtailed; the ground is cursed (Gen. 3: 17). Life becomes a fierce battle, "ein Kampf ums Dasein." All created things were made subject to vanity and corruption (Rom. 8: 20-22).

(d) The mental faculties of man had lost their pristine perfection, and physically he was weakened. His body needs more protection (Gen. 3: 21), and is subject to pain and sorrow and death (Gen. 3: 16-19; Rom. 5: 12; 6: 23), and eternal damnation (Rom. 5: 18), for he may not eat of the tree of life (Gen. 3: 22).

Thus this first transgression of Adam and Eve was of disastrous consequences; it brought misery and woe on them personally and upon all their children (Rom. 5: 12).

Man was in past ages not a brute, which by a process of evolution gradually became a moral being, and is still advancing toward higher levels of knowledge, perfection, and righteousness, but there was a decided deterioration, and never will he in this life again attain that state of perfection which Adam and Eve possessed before they fell into sin.

PART V. OF THE LAW AND OF SIN

XIV. OF THE LAW

1. **The natural knowledge of the Law.**—God gave to man not only the one command recorded in Gen. 2: 17: "Of the tree of knowledge of good and evil, thou shalt not eat of it," but, creating man in His image, He inscribed the knowledge of His will, the moral Law, in man's heart (Col. 3: 10). "Even our first parents before the fall did not live without Law, who had the Law of God written also into their hearts, because they were created in the image of God (Gen. 1: 26 f; 2: 16 ff; 3: 3)" (F. C., Epit., Art. VI, 2, *Triglot*, p. 805).

By the fall this knowledge was indeed obscured, but not totally effaced, because to this day all men have by nature some knowledge of God's Law, according to which their conscience judges their deeds and words. "For the Gentiles, which have not the Law, do by nature the things contained in the Law, these, having not the Law, are a law unto themselves: which shew the work of the Law written in their hearts, their conscience also bearing witness, and their thoughts the mean while" (between themselves) "accusing or else excusing one another" (Rom. 2: 14. 15).

This innate knowledge of the Law is by no means perfect, and it is furthermore darkened and suppressed in various degrees under the influence of sinful habits and customs (Rom. 1: 21; Eph. 4: 17-19). Still, whatever remained of this knowledge is sufficient to convict man of his sinfulness and of his guilt before God (Rom. 1: 32; 3: 19. 20). In no other way can we explain the efforts of the Gentiles to atone for their sins by all manner of sacrifices. The conscience of man, though also impaired and more or less perverted and benumbed, is still active and bears witness to the Law and its stringency, and to man's responsibility for his acts, and to the sinner's just condemnation according to the judgment of an omniscient and almighty God.

2. **Conscience.**—Conscience is not a faculty that can be acquired; but every human being has it by nature. It is a pre-

cious gift of God, which distinguishes man from the beast of
the field, and is a powerful force and monitor in his life; for
it is conscience that urges him to do, or not to do, what he
himself believes to be right or wrong. Conscience must, therefore, not be identified with man's moral convictions, nor with
the natural knowledge of the Law, to which it "bears witness"; but as we distinguish between a judge in court and the
law according to which he judges, so must we also distinguish
between conscience and our knowledge of right and wrong.

Conscience never acts independently of our moral convictions; where these are lacking, it cannot act. It does not examine the correctness of our convictions; whatever our convictions may be, conscience simply urges us to comply with
them in our lives, and judges our actions according to them.
We may, therefore, define conscience as a feeling of compulsion; we feel that we ought to do what we believe to be right,
and that we ought to avoid what we believe to be wrong.
Conscience centers not in the mind or in the will, but rather
in the emotions; it is a feeling which urges and moves us to
will and to do what the mind regards as right and true, and
it deters us from willing and doing what we believe to be
wrong. Our conscience acts in response to *our own* convictions, and never in response to the convictions of another. In
order, then, that our conscience may guide us aright, it is
absolutely necessary that we first have the right moral convictions, and these we must receive from the Word of God;
for in moral matters the conscience of man should be subject
to no other rule than the Law of God.

Conscience is not always active, but only when in a given
case our moral convictions are put to a test. It is then that it
obligates us to comply with them. It warns us not to do what
we believe to be wrong, and urges us to do what we believe
to be right. Whenever we obey its voice, it approves ("ex-
cuses") what we have done, but it "accuses" and holds us
guilty whenever we fail to do so.

"Conscience is that God-given feeling or emotion which,
before the act, prompts us to do what we believe to be right,
and deters us from doing that which we believe to be wrong.
And after the act, it commends us for having done what we

believed to be right, or condemns us for having done what we believed to be wrong." (Scaer, *Conscience,* p. 13).

To disregard the voice of conscience is always a sin. "Whatsoever is not of faith is sin" (Rom. 14: 23). The word "faith" is in this text contrasted to doubt, and does not mean the saving faith in Christ, but it means conviction, the personal assurance that what we do is right and in agreement with a recognized norm or law. Whatever the convictions of a person may be in moral matters, it is a sin to act contrary to them. It is wrong to do what you believe to be wrong.

While the witness of conscience must not be ignored, it is, in itself, not an infallible guide of conduct. For, controlled by a wrong rule or law, conscience will urge us to comply with said rule or law. Thus Paul thought that he ought to do many things contrary to the name of Christ (Acts 26: 9). And Christ tells us that people will think they are doing God a service when persecuting the disciples (John 16: 2). Others, because of false convictions, regard as wrong what God has allowed (Rom. 14: 14. 22), such as eating meat that had been sacrificed to an idol, or eating meat on Friday. With these people the eating of meat is a matter of conscience, and it is a real sin if they do eat meat.

A conscience controlled by a wrong norm is often called an "erring conscience." But conscience never errs in its peculiar functions; the error lies in the norm or conviction, to which conscience bears witness. The remedy is not to act against your conviction, but to correct it according to the Word of God.

Again, we speak of a "doubting conscience." Yet conscience never doubts; the doubt is lodged in the mind; we do not know whether a thing is right or wrong. In such cases we must suspend action (Rom. 14: 23), until from the Word of God we become "fully persuaded in our own mind" (Rom. 14: 5).

All this emphasizes the importance of right instruction from the Word of God, by which right convictions are created in the heart, on the basis of which conscience will urge us to will and to do the right thing.—The cure for a guilty conscience is faith in the forgiving grace of God (Hebr. 10: 22).

3. **The revealed Law.**—Whether the natural Law written

in man's heart was amplified by any revealed Law between the time of Adam and Moses, we know not. However, on Mount Sinai this Law was amplified and codified in the Ten Commandments by God Himself, and published through Moses (Deut. 4: 13). The two tables of stone, on which these "Ten Words" were originally written, are lost, but God had the Commandments recorded also in the Bible (Exodus 20; Deut. 5: 6-22).

The Old Testament wording of the Decalogue contains statements that pertained to the Jews only (Exodus 20: 2. 9-11. 12). An authoritative exposition of these brief Ten Words we find in the New Testament, particularly in Christ's Sermon on the Mount (Matt. 5; 6; 7). For the New Testament interpretation of the Third Commandment see Mark 2: 27. 28 and Col. 2: 16; and for the New Testament version of the Fourth Commandment we have Eph. 6: 2. 3. (See Luther's classical explanations of the Commandments).

The Law we have in the Decalogue is called the Moral Law. Its meaning and implications are expounded and illustrated in many texts and stories of the Bible. It is a fuller exposition of the natural Law written in the heart of man, and is binding on all men (Gal. 3: 10; Deut. 27: 26).

Those rules and regulations governing the ritual of the Old Testament worship service and its sacrifices are called the Ceremonial Law. Being a shadow of Christ (Col. 2: 16. 17), their authority and force ceased when Christ had come.

God gave unto Israel also divers Political Laws and ordinances, which regulated the civil affairs of the people, so that external discipline might be preserved in civil society; for example see Matt. 19: 7. 8, and Deut. 24: 1-5. These laws continued in force only as long as the Jews were a nation.

4. **Definition and authority of the Law.**—"We unanimously believe, teach, and confess that the Law is properly a divine doctrine, in which the righteous, immutable will of God is revealed, what is to be the quality of man in his nature, thoughts, words, and works, in order that he may be pleasing to God; and that it threatens its transgressors with God's wrath and temporal and eternal punishment" (F. C., Th. D., Art. V, 17, *Triglot,* p. 957).

Not the authority of Moses, but the authority of the Holy

and Almighty God stands behind each Commandment. "I am the Lord thy God" (Exodus 20: 2) is the introduction to the Decalogue. Therefore no man, prince or priest, congregation or synod, or the whole Christian Church on earth can invalidate the least of these Commandments either for themselves or for others (Matt. 5: 19).—The law concerning the seventh day of the week as the Sabbath of the Lord, on which the Jews were to rest from all labor, was not changed by any human authority, but was abrogated by the Lord Himself (Matt. 12: 8; Col. 2: 16; Rom. 14: 5. 6). Neither God nor the apostles appointed Sunday or any other day as the day of rest and worship, but of their own free choice the early Christians met on the first day of the week for worship (Acts 20: 7; 1 Cor. 16: 2).

Obedience to the Moral Law is not optional, subject to the willingness or the ability of man, but it is mandatory, and must be perfect (Matt. 5: 48). We must confirm, fulfill, all the words of the Law (Deut. 27: 26), and do it from unselfish love (Matt. 22: 36-40). Not only in our external actions (Eph. 5: 5), but also in our words (Matt. 12: 36), in our thoughts and feelings (Matt. 5: 22. 28), yea, in our entire being (Lev. 19: 2), we must conform to the requirements of God's holy Law.

5. **The fulfillment of the Law.**—*Before the fall* man not only knew the will of God, but also was able to keep it perfectly; for the image of God implied, on the part of man, perfect conformity to the will of his Maker.

Since the fall unregenerate man cannot keep the Law of God at all. Speaking of the children of men, David says: "They are all gone aside, they are all together become filthy: there is none that doeth good, no, not one" (Ps. 14: 3). Solomon says: "There is not a just man upon earth, that doeth good, and sinneth not" (Eccl. 7: 20). Though externally one may comply with certain demands of the Law, and thus effect a civil righteousness, man cannot keep the Law in the right spirit, which is love to God. The attitude of natural man being inimical to God (Rom. 8: 7), there is in his heart no true fear and love of God; hence he does not keep the Commandments for God's sake, but for his own sake, from fear of punishment or from selfishness and self-righteousness. Lacking the proper motive, it is simply impossible for natural man to keep the Law as God wants it to be kept. What men, therefore, regard as "righteousness," is before God "as filthy rags" (Is. 64: 6).

Even Christians cannot keep the Law perfectly, as some imagine they can. Indeed, because their faith worketh by love (Gal. 5: 6), they want to keep God's Commandments, and, in a measure, they do; but because of their flesh, which clings to them through life and which is sinful, they never become perfect. Paul was a Christian; yet he admits that he is not perfect in his life, but that he is unceasingly striving after a more perfect fulfillment of the Law (Phil. 3: 12; Rom. 7: 14-23). David, a servant of God, knows that neither he nor any other man is just before God (Ps. 143: 2). The best of Christians will have to admit many transgressions (1 John 1: 8. 9), and each transgression renders him guilty of the whole Law (James 2: 10).

6. **The curse of the Law.**—The Law carries with it the threat of punishment. "In the day that thou eatest thereof thou shalt surely die" (Gen. 2: 17); (Exod. 20: 5). "Cursed be he that confirmeth not all the words of this Law to do them. And all the people shall say, Amen" (Deut. 27: 26). Not only does God pronounce His curse upon the transgressor, but all the people shall agree that such a one is accursed. This curse implies the wrath and displeasure of God, temporal punishment, and eternal damnation. "The soul that sinneth, it shall die" (Ezek. 18: 20); (Rom. 6: 23). These threats of punishment are not empty words, for God is a lawgiver, "who is able to save and to destroy" (James 4: 12); (Matt. 10: 28). This He demonstrated in punishing Adam and Eve (Gen. 3: 16-19), in sending the Deluge (Gen. 7), in the destruction of Sodom (Gen. 19), in the destruction of Jerusalem (Luke 19: 43. 44), and He will prove it in the Final Judgment (Matt. 25: 41).

Not only in general does God threaten to punish transgressions of the Law, but He threatens also with regard to the transgression of each Commandment: First Commandment (Jer. 17: 5); Second (Exod. 20: 7; Lev. 24: 15. 16); Third (Hosea 4: 6); Fourth (Prov. 30: 17; Rom. 13: 2); Fifth (Gen. 9: 6; Matt. 5: 21. 22); Sixth (Eph. 5: 5); Seventh (1 Thess. 4:

6); Eighth (Prov. 19: 5; Ps. 50: 19-22); Ninth and Tenth (Matt. 23: 14). Every single transgression of any one Commandment brings down on man the wrath and displeasure of God, temporal punishment, and the threat of eternal damnation. "Whosoever shall keep the whole Law, and yet offend in one point, he is guilty of all" (James 2: 10). "For Thou art not a God that hath pleasure in wickedness: neither shall evil dwell with Thee" (Ps. 5: 4); therefore, "the wrath of God is revealed from heaven against all ungodliness and unrighteousness of men" (Rom. 1: 18; 2: 5-9).

Men do not like such a strict interpretation of the Law, and would fain tone down its requirements and threats. But it does not at all depend upon what we think, and how we feel, about this matter, but on what God says. And He says thus: "I the Lord thy God am a jealous God, visiting the iniquity of the fathers upon the children unto the third and fourth generation of them that hate Me" (Exod. 20: 5). "The soul that sinneth, it shall die" (Ezek. 18: 20).

7. **The purpose of the Law:**

(a) *It is not the purpose of the Law to save man.* "The Law is holy, and the commandment holy and just and good" (Rom. 7: 12); "the man which doeth those things shall live by them" (Rom. 10: 5); (Luke 10: 28). Thus the Law indeed reveals a perfect way to heaven. But since the fall of man this Law, which was ordained unto life (Rom. 7: 10), "was weak through the flesh" (Rom. 8: 3), inasmuch as no man is able to measure up to the holiness and perfection demanded in it (Eccl. 7: 20; Rom. 3: 23). Whoever, therefore, seeks salvation under the Law not only exposes himself to its curse, but, failing to keep it, he actually merits this curse (Gal. 3: 10). Hence, "by the deeds of the Law there shall no flesh be justified in His sight" (Rom. 3: 20). The Law, then, while revealing a perfect way to heaven, cannot achieve this objective in man because of man's impossibility to conform to its requirements. If men try to achieve salvation by the deeds of the Law, they sin. This does not detract from the goodness of the Law, nor from its life-giving end, if perfectly kept; it merely shows that man's own wickedness makes the Law an impossible way of salvation for man, and that the Law, therefore, cannot have the purpose of salvation with regard to man.

"Because, therefore, men by their own strength cannot fulfill the Law of God, and are all under sin, and subject to eternal wrath and death, on this account we cannot be freed by the Law from sin and be justified" (Apol., Art. IV, 40, *Triglot,* p. 131).

God's purpose in giving the Law on Mount Sinai was not at all that man should and could earn salvation for himself by keeping its Commandments; for not only did God know that this was impossible for man, but He had four hundred and thirty years before given the inheritance to Abraham by promise. Paul speaks of the matter (Gal. 3: 14-18), where we read in part: "The covenant, that was confirmed before of God in Christ, the Law, which was four hundred and thirty years after, cannot disannul, that it should make the promise of none effect. For if the inheritance be of the Law, it is no more of promise: but God gave it to Abraham by promise."

(b) *The Law is a mirror to show us our sins.* "Wherefore then serveth the Law? It was added because of transgressions" (Gal. 3: 19). "I had not known sin, but by the Law: for I had not known lust" (namely, that lust is really sin), "except the Law had said, Thou shalt not covet" (Rom. 7: 7). "For by the Law is the knowledge of sin" (Rom. 3: 20). Since the fall of man, the chief purpose of the Law is to convict man of his innate sinfulness and of his manifold offenses against the holy will of God, of the guilt incurred by sin, and of the righteous wrath of God (Rom. 3: 19; Dan. 9: 10. 11). Thus the Law performs a very distinct and important office: it is to break down in man that self-sufficiency, that self-righteousness, that pride before God which boasts and trusts in one's own merits, and spurns all offers of grace; it is to humble man before God and fill his heart with terror and dismay: "for mine iniquities are gone over mine head: as an heavy burden they are too heavy for me" (Ps. 38: 4). Thus the Law makes us realize our lost condition and the need of a saviour (Rom. 7: 24. 25). The chief purpose of the Law, therefore, is to work knowledge of, and sorrow over, sin.

(c) *The Law serves as a guide in our lives.* Christians, inasmuch as they are regenerated through faith in Christ, are indeed free from the bondage of the Law (Rom. 6: 14). Without being coerced and driven by its stern commands, "Thou shalt" and "Thou shalt not," they are willing from love of God to do whatever is pleasing to Him. They need only be shown what God would have them do, and forthwith they will gladly do it. This is the new obedience which springs from faith, the free obedience of a loving child, not the forced obedience of a slave. To God's children the Law is merely a guide and a rule, which no longer commands and compels their obedience, but which directs and guides them by pointing out what is truly good and pleasing in the sight of God (Rom. 12: 1. 2; Micah 6: 8; Ps. 119: 9). "Thus the Law is and remains both to the penitent and impenitent, both to regenerate and unregenerate men, one and the same Law, the immutable will of God; and the difference, so far as concerns obedience, is alone in man, inasmuch as one who is not yet regenerate does for the Law out of constraint and unwillingly what it requires of him; but the believer, so far as he is regenerate, does without constraint and with a willing spirit that which no threatening of the Law could ever extort from him" (F. C., Epit., Art. VI, 7, *Triglot*, p. 807).

(d) *The Law serves as a curb.* The Law is useful also to the end that thereby external discipline and decency are maintained against wild and disobedient men, and gross outbursts of sin are, in a measure, repressed. "The Law is not made for a righteous man, but for the lawless and disobedient, for the ungodly and for sinners . . . " (1 Tim. 1: 9. 10). This means that for the ungodly the Law with its threat of punishment is to act as a curb, which restrains, holds back, and checks, in a measure, coarse outbursts of sin. For though men have little respect for the Law itself, they are afraid of the punishment it threatens. In this way the natural Law functions in the conscience of men, who often refrain from doing wrong from fear of punishment. The revealed Law also serves this purpose. "God threatens to punish all that transgress these Commandments. Therefore we should fear His wrath, and not act contrary to them. But He promises grace and every blessing to all that keep these Commandments. Therefore we should also love Him, trust in Him, and willingly do according to His Commandments" (Luther's explanation in *Small Catechism*). The external civil righteousness of men, while not proceeding from the right motive, is a product of this use of the Law, without which men would live like the beasts of the field.

8. **The Christian and the Law.**— To the Christians Paul writes: "Ye are not under the Law, but under grace" (Rom. 6: 14). This does not mean that they may disregard and ignore the Law. It means that they neither seek salvation by the Law, nor are they actuated in their lives by its commandments; but by grace they are saved, and in this grace they live and do God's will out of love. Because of the old Adam in them, Christians do continue to use the Law as a mirror. But chiefly they use it as a rule and guide for the new man to do what is pleasing unto God.

XV. OF SIN

1. **Definition.**— The Bible defines sin as "the transgression of the Law," as "anomia," lawlessness (1 John 3: 4). No deed, word, thought, or desire are in themselves sin, but become sin by being at variance with the Law of God. To eat the fruit of a tree seems to us a rather innocent matter, but since God had forbidden it, it was a sin to Adam and Eve (Gen. 2: 17). When Saul spared Agag, the king of Amalek, and the best of the sheep and oxen for sacrifice, it looked like a humane and pious thing; yet God had commanded him to destroy Amalek utterly, and so it was a sin to spare them (1 Sam. 15). When at the exodus from Egypt the children of Israel borrowed jewels of silver and of gold from the Egyptians (Exod. 12: 35. 36), without returning them, it was not a sin, because God expressly commanded them to do this (Exod. 3: 22). Whether or not anything is a sin is not determined by what we think, or how we feel, about it, but solely by this: does it or does it not agree with the Word of God? Sin is not a physical, but a moral condition, and it consists in this that a given act, behavior, or condition of man is not what God wants it to be; it is nonconformity with the will of God. Thus, to sin means to do what God forbids (Gen. 2: 17), or not to do what He enjoins (James 4: 17), or not to be as He wants us to be (Lev. 19: 2). Hence, with respect to the Law, sin is a departure from its rule; with respect to God, sin is disobedience to His will.

Every departure from the Law is sin, whether this be great or small, known or unknown, intended or accidental, or even when it is against our will (Rom. 7: 19). The question whether anything is or is not sin, is not determined by our personal opinion, our knowledge, our intention, or our will, but solely by this one fact, whether or not it is in agreement with the will of God. Our personal attitude may aggravate or mitigate our guilt, but it does not change the nature of the act or the conduct as a transgression of the Law. Even the good intention and purpose one may have, will not change an unlawful act into a lawful one (1 Sam. 15: 1-26). We cannot sin to the glory of God (Rom. 6: 1).

On the other hand, *only* what is at variance with the Word of God is sin. Transgressing man-made rules and laws may not be regarded a sin, unless in so doing we also transgress a Commandment of God. Thus, in transgressing the laws of the government, we sin against God, who has commanded us to submit to every ordinance of man (1 Pet. 2: 13). To disobey parents is to sin also against God who says: "Children, obey your parents in all things" (Col. 3: 20). Likewise we sin when we act against our own conscience (Rom. 14: 23), and when by an inconsiderate use of our liberty we give offense to a weak brother (1 Cor. 8: 9-13). However, when men ask of us anything that is contrary to the Word of God, then it is not a sin, if we disobey them, but is loyalty to God, for "we ought to obey God rather than men" (Acts 5: 29).

Things, which God neither forbids nor commands, are in themselves indifferent (Mitteldinge, Adiaphora), and it is no sin either to do or not to do them. However, also in such matters we must remember: "Whether, therefore, ye eat, or drink, or whatsoever ye do, do all to the glory of God" (1 Cor. 10: 31); (Rom. 14: 6). If done from a selfish motive, without regard for the glory of God and the welfare of our neighbor, even such indifferent things are displeasing to God. (Read: F. C., Th. D., Art. X, *Triglot*, p. 1053 ff.)

Modernists very much agree with the view of Christian Science, which teaches that sin does not really exist, but is merely the delusion of the mortal mind; that there is no sin, except men believe it to be so. To them sin is nothing more than a subjective view men have of things, acquired by a faulty education. However, sin is a fact, as the conscience of every man and the Scriptures testify.

To clear themselves of guilt, men often deny the sinfulness of a given act, or excuse themselves saying, that they did not know it was wrong, that they did not mean to do it. But our personal attitude does not determine the sinfulness of an act; the fact that it does not conform to the Law makes it a sin, for "sin is the transgression of the Law."

2. **The cause of sin.**—*In no sense is God the cause and author of sin.* He did not create man to sin (Gen. 1: 31); neither did He decree that man should become a sinner; nor did He approve of sin when it was introduced into the world; nor does He in any way incite man to sin. "God cannot be tempted with evil, neither tempteth He any man" (James 1: 13). "Thou art not a God that hath pleasure in wickedness: neither shall evil dwell with Thee" (Ps. 5: 4); (Zech. 8: 17). The fact that God concurs in the physical performance of a sinful act does not make Him the author or the abettor of the sinful quality of the act. It is a presumptuous question for man to ask: "Why did and does God permit sin if He hates it?" We are not to sit in judgment and to criticize the ways of God. "God is not a creator, author, or cause of sin, but by the instigation of the devil through one man sin has entered the world" (F. C., Th. D., Art. I, 7, *Triglot*, p. 861).

The devil is the *external* cause of sin. Created good and holy, the devil was not tempted and seduced by any one else, but the first thought of sin and rebellion against God originated with him. "The devil sinneth from the beginning" (1 John 3: 8). How it was possible for a perfectly good and holy angel to conceive the thought of sin, we do not know, and it is futile to try to trace the origin and cause of sin beyond the devil. Inasmuch as he tempted and seduced Eve (Gen. 3: 1-6), he became the external cause of sin in the human race (Rev. 12: 9). He is to this day the driving force in the children of unbelief (John 8: 44; 1 John 3: 8), and is tempting the Christians to evil (2 Cor. 11: 3; 1 Pet. 5: 8. 9). He is not resting on his first success in the garden of Eden, but has since been the prime mover of all evil.

The heart of man is the *internal* cause of sin. Sin is not like the dust of the road, which settles on the body, a mere external pollution; but each sin we commit has its start in our own hearts. The temptations, which approach us from without, touch and stir our hearts, and it is there where our sins begin. The temptation which beset Eve from the devil was not the sin which Eve committed; her sin began as soon as she lost faith in God's Word and, believing the word of the devil, desired to eat of the forbidden fruit (Gen. 3: 6). Even without such external temptation the heart of natural man is inclined to all evil, "for the imagination of man's heart is evil from his youth" (Gen. 8: 21). To this day man sins when he is "drawn away of his own lust, and enticed" (James 1: 14); to this day evil thoughts and sinful works proceed out of his own heart (Matt. 15: 19; Rom. 7: 18). Let us not blame the devil for the evil we do; God did not accept that excuse in Paradise (Gen. 3: 13. 16), neither will He now. The responsibility and guilt are ours.

As the image of God inhered in the soul, so sin likewise has its seat and origin there, and not in the material body. The physical body is, indeed, called "the body of sin" (Rom. 6: 6), because it is the organ through which the soul works. We have not a pure soul imprisoned in a sinful body, but the body is controlled and dominated by a sinful soul (Rom. 6: 12. 13).

3. **The consequences of sin.**—Every transgression of the Law is inseparably connected with *guilt;* "he hath sinned, and is guilty" (Lev. 6: 4). The act of sin is not identical with the guilt of sin. The guilt continues to weigh on our conscience long after the sinful act is finished.

While we speak of a man being guilty of this or that sin, he is, in fact, guilty of the whole Law. All the Commandments are the expression of the holy will of God, and are, therefore, a unit. By transgressing a single one of these Commandments man breaks through the restraint of the whole Law. (Illustration: breaking through a fence, or breaking a chain.) "Whosoever shall keep the whole Law, and yet offend in one point, he is guilty of all" (James 2: 10). As all men have sinned (Rom. 3: 23), all the world is guilty before God (Rom. 3: 19).

We often speak of small sins and great sins; yet every sin, however small it may appear to us, is an offense against the

Majesty of God, and its guilt must be measured by the exalted position of Him, against whom it is committed. The eating of the forbidden fruit by Adam and Eve does not seem to us to have been such a great crime; yet it was the disobedience against God, manifested in this apparently innocent act, that made it a damnable sin. The greatness of our guilt can be measured by one yardstick only, namely the infinite Majesty of God, against whom we sinned. We have become callous in this respect, and have lost the sense of the enormity of our guilt. If we fully realized that by our sins we offend the holy Majesty of the omnipotent God, we should hardly live through our first sin, but would, like Judas, be driven to utter despair. But let us remember that Christ redeemed us from the guilt of sin (2 Cor. 5: 12), and in Him our hearts are sprinkled from an evil conscience (Hebr. 10: 22).

Guilt entails *punishment;* in this case, it is death. "The wages of sin is death" (Rom. 6: 23); (Gen. 2: 17; Rom. 5: 12). We distinguish a threefold death: spiritual death, temporal death, eternal death. Essentially, death is separation.

Spiritual death is the separation of the soul from God. The moment man sinned, his heart departed from the Lord; he lost all true fear and love of God and trust in Him; he was afraid of God, and fled from Him; he was spiritually dead.— This is the condition of all men by nature; they are dead in trespasses and sins (Eph. 2: 1); they are dead to God, dead in spirit while they live in the body (1 Tim. 5: 6). There is no yearning, no longing for God, but all the inclinations and appetites of man are toward the earth, toward sin (Gen. 8: 21). This estrangement from God accounts for all the griefs and sorrows, worries and heartaches, the restlessness and un- happiness, the despondency and despair of the human heart. —Through faith in Christ we are quickened unto a new spir- itual life (Eph. 2: 5), are begotten again unto a lively hope (1 Pet. 1: 3), and have again become His children and heirs of salvation (Gal. 3: 26; Rom. 8: 16. 17).

Temporal death is the separation of the body and the soul, the violent tearing asunder of those two parts which God had joined together to make a human person. To this death Adam was subject from the moment he sinned; to this death all men are subject from the moment of their birth. Man, who was created to live, is now born to die. His way through life is a way to the grave. "It is appointed unto men once to die" (Hebr. 9: 27). All bodily ills and evils, pains and diseases, toilsome labor and misfortunes, are but precursors of his final death. For us Christians all these have lost their sting (1 Cor. 15: 55), and work together for our good (Rom. 8: 28).

Eternal death is the eternal separation of man from the blissful presence of God. "Depart from Me, ye cursed, into everlasting fire, prepared for the devil and his angels" (Matt. 25: 41), where "there shall be weeping and gnashing of teeth" (Matt. 25: 30). This death is not annihilation, but everlasting punishment (Matt. 25: 46).—But Christ has delivered us from the fear of death (Hebr. 2: 15), and in Him we shall have everlasting life (John 3: 16; Matt. 25: 34. 46).

XVI. ORIGINAL SIN

1. The sin of our first parents was of disastrous consequence not only to them personally, but also to all their offspring, inasmuch as the guilt of their first transgression is imputed, and the corruption of their nature is transmitted, to all their children. The first is called hereditary guilt, the other, hereditary depravity.

2. **Hereditary guilt.**—The sin which Adam committed was, indeed, first charged to Adam himself, and he died of that sin. But it was imputed also to all his children, and to this day men die of the sin of Adam. Paul tells us that by the obedience of One, that is Christ, many were made righteous —constituted righteous, because the obedience of Christ is imputed or credited to them—and "by one man's disobedience many were made sinners"—were constituted sinners, because the disobedience of Adam was imputed or charged to them (Rom. 5: 19). "By the offense of one, judgment came upon all men to condemnation" (Rom. 5: 18). This he proves by the fact that from Adam to Moses men died, even though they had not sinned "after the similitude of Adam," transgressing as Adam had done an express command of God, to which the penalty of death was affixed (Gen. 2: 17). But they died "through the offense of one" (Rom. 5: 14. 15); (1 Cor. 15: 22). Hence, the offense of Adam must have been charged to them,

and because of this offense they died. 'Tis true, also the sins men commit personally are worthy of death (Rom. 6: 23). Paul emphasizes how sin and its guilt came into the world, into the human race. Adam's sin killed our entire race, made death reign supreme. By their very entrance into this world, sin and death reached all men. "As by one man sin entered into the world, and death by sin; and so death passed upon all men, for that all have sinned" (Rom. 5: 12). That the guilt of Adam's sin is charged to us appears also from the fact that the punishment meted out to him and Eve for their specific transgression (Gen. 3: 16-19), is suffered by all men and women to this day. Illustration: A man, who gambled away his freedom and became a slave, by this act brought slavery also upon his children, who had not gambled as their father did. In a similar manner the guilt of Adam, and whatever goes with it, is visited upon all his children.

In this connection we must, however, remember that the same God who imputes to us the sin of Adam and condemns us on its account, has likewise imputed to us the righteousness of Christ and declared us just for His sake (Rom. 5: 18. 19).

3. **Hereditary depravity.**—In another direction did the fall of Adam bring woe upon him and his kin. By their sin our first parents lost the image of God and became altogether sinful and corrupt in their nature. As children inherit from their parents certain features and traits, sometimes even bodily weaknesses and diseases, so have all men inherited that deep-seated spiritual corruption, which we call original depravity. This is not a sin which men do or commit in their lives, but a sinful condition of their nature, which they have by birth. Having himself lost the image of God, Adam begat a son "in his own likeness" (Gen. 5: 3). Like himself, his children were destitute of righteousness, holiness, and innocence; they were selfish, seeking only their own advantage and pleasure and honor; they were inclined to, and capable of, any sin and crime. Cain was a murderer. Men do evil, because by nature they are evil (Gen. 4: 8; 6: 3. 5; 8: 21).

"Since the fall of Adam, all men begotten in a natural way are born with sin, that is, without fear of God, without trust in God, with concupiscence; and this disease, or vice of origin, is truly sin, even now condemning and bringing eternal wrath upon those not born again through Baptism and the Holy Ghost" (A. C., Art. II, *Triglot*, p. 43).

Bible proof.—Man is "flesh born of flesh" (John 3: 6), that is, he is the sinful child of sinful parents. "Behold, I was shapen in iniquity, and in sin did my mother conceive me" (Ps. 51: 5). In his flesh dwelleth no good thing (Rom. 7: 18). By nature there is in him no true fear of God, no love of God, no trust in God, no willingness to serve God and to do good to his neighbor. On the contrary, his old Adam "is corrupt according to the deceitful lusts" (Eph. 4: 22). All manner of lusts arise in him, but they are deceitful, do not lead him in the right way, because his heart, alienated from God, is inclined toward evil (Gen. 8: 21). Man covets, because by nature he is covetous; he sins, because by nature he is sinful, and given to "inordinate affection, evil concupiscence, and covetousness" (Col. 3: 5). Thus, by nature man loves himself more than he loves God or his neighbor; he envies others, is selfish and self-centered. Whatever he plans, purposes, and does, must in some way serve his own personal interests, or flatter his vanity. He has become his own god. In spiritual things his understanding is darkened (Eph. 4: 18); he cannot discern or appreciate them, for they are foolishness to him (1 Cor. 2: 14). Being carnally minded, his will is not free or neutral, but set on the things of the flesh (Rom. 8: 5), and against the things of the Spirit (Gal. 5: 17); hence he is by nature an enemy of God (Rom. 8: 7; Col. 1: 21). Being dead in sin (Eph. 2: 1), man has no strength to work out his spiritual restoration.

This description of the spiritual condition of natural man is by no means flattering to his vanity, but such it is according to the Word of Him who "knew what was in man" (John 2: 25). This inherited corruption, which vitiated and depraved primarily the faculties of the soul, enslaves in the service of sin also the members of the body (Rom. 6: 12. 13a; 7: 23. 24).

Original sin does not constitute an essential part of the soul, which God created, nor is it a self-existing essence; but it is the corrupt quality and condition of the soul, brought on by the fall of man, and passed on by birth to his children.

It is not the sinful act which Adam committed, but the depravity and corruption of the entire nature contracted by, and resulting from, that act. It is the sinfulness of our whole nature, which is ours by birth, and because of which we are constantly at variance with the demand of God: "Ye shall be holy" (Lev. 19: 2). Because we are not as God made us at the beginning, and as He wants us to be, we are by nature under His wrath (Eph. 2: 3).

"Original sin is not properly the nature, substance, or essence of man, that is, man's body and soul, which even now, since the Fall, are and remain the creation and creatures of God in us, but it is something *in* the nature, body, and soul of man, and in all his powers, namely, a horrible, deep, inexpressible corruption of the same, so that man is destitute of the righteousness wherein he was originally created, and in spiritual things is dead to good and perverted to all evil. . . . Now, since the Fall, man inherits an inborn, wicked disposition and inward impurity of heart, evil lust and propensity" (F. C., Th. D., I, 2. 11, *Triglot,* p. 859. 863).

Other names for this original depravity are "old Adam," because we inherited it from Adam. It is also called "flesh" (Rom. 8: 13); "old man" (Eph. 4: 22); "sin that dwelleth in us" (Rom. 7: 17).

"**Original sin is universal,** inherited by 'all men begotten in the natural way' (A. C., Art. II). The universal scope of Job 14: 4; John 3: 6; Rom. 5: 12 leaves no room for excepting the Virgin Mary. She did not except herself, but placed her sole hope of salvation in her 'Saviour' (Luke 1: 47). The only human being, untainted by original sin is the Virgin's Son, Jesus Christ, who was immaculately conceived through the power of the Holy Ghost (Luke 1: 35; Hebr. 7: 26; 2 Cor. 5: 21)." (*Popular Symbolics,* §48).

Original sin clings to us through life.—It is not eradicated in Baptism, as the Roman Catholic Church teaches. (*Popular Symbolics,* §227). By faith in Christ we are freed from its guilt and punishment; but the corruption itself, concupiscence, remains, as Paul experienced (Rom. 7: 14-25), and as every Christian still experiences. (Apol., Art. II, 35-37, *Triglot,* p. 113). By faith Christians will with the aid of the Holy Ghost constantly strive to suppress this old Adam (Eph.

4: 22; Gal. 5: 24); in this life they will never succeed in totally destroying him. (Cf., F. C., Th. D., Art. I).

XVII. ACTUAL SIN

1. **Definition.**—As distinguished from original sin, actual
sin involves some activity, either external or internal, on the
part of man. Speaking of actual sins, Christ says: "Out of
the heart proceed evil thoughts, murders, adulteries, fornications, thefts, false witness, blasphemies" (Matt. 15: 19). And
Paul writes: "The works of the flesh are manifest, which are
these: adultery, fornication, uncleanness, lasciviousness, idolatry, witchcraft, hatred, variance, emulations, wrath, strife,
seditions, heresies, envyings, murders, drunkenness, revellings,
and such like" (Gal. 5: 19-21). Thus, whatever one may do,
speak, think, feel, or will contrary to the Law of God is actual
sin. However, man becomes guilty of actual sin also by not
doing what the Law requires. "To him that knoweth to do
good and doeth it not, to him it is sin" (James 4: 17). The
slothful servant, who had not done what was expected of him,
was justly punished (Matt. 25: 24-30).

A knowledge of sinning and an intent to sin are not necessary to make an act against God's will a sin. An act contrary
to the Law of God is sin, even though it be committed un-
knowingly or without intent. Paul states that the natural
evil condition, which the Christian does not want in his life,
still bears the character of sin. "The evil which I would not,
that I do" (Rom. 7: 19). Together with the Apology (Art. II,
43, *Triglot,* p. 117) we reject the sentences: "Nothing is sin,
unless it be voluntary," and: "Thoughts are exempt from
custom and punishment."

2. **Classification of sins.**—

(a) All sins are committed against God (Ps. 51: 4), since
they are transgressions of His Law. But some sins are directed against God personally and directly, since they are
transgressions of those Commandments involving our relationship to Him (the First Table of the Law). Others are
directed against our neighbor, since they are transgressions
of those Commandments involving our relationship to our
neighbor (the Second Table of the Law). Others are directed

against one's self (1 Cor. 6: 18; Eph. 5: 18); the suicide of Judas.

(b) External sins are those of word and deed; internal sins are those of thought and heart.

(c) It is a sin of commission when we do what is forbidden; it is a sin of omission when we fail to do what is commanded.

(d) Known sins are those which we know to be against the Law; unknown sins are those of which we are not conscious, or of which we do not know that they are sins (Lev. 4: 2; Rom. 7: 7).

(e) Voluntary sins are sins we commit by deliberate volition, contrary to our conscience; involuntary sins are those which a man commits when he is carried away by the lust of his flesh to do what otherwise he would not do (Rom. 7: 15).

(f) Venial sins are sins of weakness; they are limited to believers, and do not kill faith, because they are not done intentionally. In themselves they are real sins and are worthy of death, but through faith Christians have forgiveness for them. Mortal sins are such as kill faith, and drive the Holy Spirit from the heart, because no man can sin wilfully and intentionally and at the same time believe in Christ for the forgiveness of his sins.

(g) Sins which we commit ourselves, and sins of others of which we become partakers (Eph. 5: 7; 1 Tim. 5: 22). We must not in our hearts approve a sin which another has committed, but must regard and reprove it as sin (Deut. 27: 26).

(h) Occasional and habitual sins. It is dangerous to dally with sin; at first it is like a spider's web, but finally it becomes like a steel cable, which we cannot break.

Pardonable and unpardonable sins.—"All manner of sin and blasphemy shall be forgiven unto men: but the blasphemy against the Holy Ghost shall not be forgiven unto men. . . . " (Matt. 12: 31. 32). The sin against the Holy Ghost is directed against the work which the Holy Ghost is doing in the heart of the person committing the sin. It consists in this that such a person from sheer spite and malice rejects and blasphemes those truths of which the Holy Ghost is convincing, or has convinced him. If a man blasphemes divine truths of which he is not convinced in his heart, he has not committed this sin. If he is convinced, and he rejects and blasphemes them from fear of men, as did Peter (Mark 14: 66-72), from love of the world, from pride, selfishness, self-righteousness, the unpardonable sin has not yet been committed; for it is possible that all these are eventually overcome by the influence of the Holy Ghost. When all other motives for resisting the work of the Holy Ghost are no longer operating and determining the action of said person, but when pure contrariness, spite, and malice against Him, whose influence he feels in his heart, dictates his action, then it is simply impossible for the Holy Ghost to win that person; for every attempt to draw him to Christ is resisted with more vehement malice and blasphemy. In that case the very fact that the person feels the "pull" of the Holy Ghost in his heart incites him to resist and to blaspheme Him, and to harden his heart against His influence.

When Christ had cast out a devil (Matt. 12: 22), the Pharisees were, no doubt, impressed and convinced that this was a work of God. The Holy Ghost had worked that in their hearts. But they would not yield, and said: "This fellow doth not cast out devils, but by Beelzebub the prince of devils" (Matt. 12: 24), thereby wishing to counteract the impression which this miracle had made on themselves and on others. To call a manifest work of God the work of the devil, indeed, is blasphemy. It is in this connection that Jesus, who "knew their thoughts," speaks of the sin against the Holy Ghost. He does not say that these men had actually committed this sin, but there was danger that they might. Hence, Christ warns them, lest their hatred of Him, perhaps still motivated by pride and self-righteousness, turn into spite and malice to resist wilfully every influence of the Holy Ghost to draw them to Christ.

We should not charge anyone with this sin, since we do not know whether or not a person is really convinced of the truth he blasphemes, nor can we tell whether he is doing it from spite and malice; we cannot look into his heart. Those who are disturbed in their minds that they might have committed this sin, have definitely not committed it, because their very fear proves that there is no spite and malice in their hearts. Those who have committed this sin are not in the least disturbed about it. "To all godly Christians who feel and experience in their hearts a small spark or longing for divine grace and eternal salvation, this precious passage (Phil. 2: 13) is very comforting; for they know that God has kindled in their hearts this beginning of true godliness, and that He will further strengthen and help them in their weakness to persevere in the true faith unto the end" (F. C., Th. D., Art. II, 14, *Triglot*, p. 885).

The reason why this sin cannot be forgiven is not that it is too great—though great it is—but that it makes repentance impossible, since it is directed against every effort of the Holy Ghost to convert man. We should be warned not to resist the Holy Ghost when He touches our hearts.

The hardening of the heart differs from the sin against the Holy Ghost in this, that it is not necessarily spite and malice connected with blasphemy that brings it about. If a person for any reason whatsoever continues to harden his heart against the influence of the Holy Ghost, as Pharaoh hardened his heart, God may, as an act of judgment, at any time harden the heart of that person (John 12: 40), and thus cut short his time of grace, while he still continues to live in this world. While with those who die in impenitence the time of grace is ordinarily cut off in death, it is cut off during the lifetime of those whom God has hardened. (Cf., F. C., Th. D., Art. XI, 85. 86, *Triglot*, p. 1091).

Sins against conscience.—A right conscience is controlled by convictions and knowledge gained from the Word of God. To act against such a conscience is a grievous sin, inasmuch as such a person so doing sins against the Word of God not from ignorance, but with full knowledge and in spite of the warning of his conscience; it destroys faith (1 Tim. 1: 19). If persisted in, it MAY lead finally to the hardening of the heart, or to the sin against the Holy Ghost.—A person has a "doubting conscience" when he is not sure whether the thing he proposes to do is morally right or wrong; he has misgivings about it. In such a case one should not act (Rom. 14: 23). "Let every man be fully persuaded in his own mind" (Rom. 14: 5).—An "erring conscience" is one that is controlled by a conviction which regards as forbidden what is allowed or what is commanded, or as commanded what is free or definitely forbidden. A person whose conscience is bound in things that are free must obey his conscience until he is convinced that the things he believed to be wrong are allowed. —Cure of a guilty conscience is faith in the pardoning grace of God (1 John 3: 20; Hebr. 9: 14).

3. **Origin and cause of actual sin.**—The evil heart is the internal cause of actual sin. "Out of the heart proceed evil thoughts, murders, adulteries, fornications, thefts, false witness, blasphemies" (Matt. 15: 19). Thus, the evil heart, the original depravity, is the source and fountain of all our actual transgressions of the Law (Rom. 7: 17).

There are also external causes that incite man to sin. The devil put it into the heart of Judas to betray the Lord (John 13: 2). It is he that works in the ungodly (Eph. 2: 2), and stirs up the old Adam in the Christians (Luke 22: 31). The world is another powerful factor to excite evil lusts in our hearts. Sinful men entice us (Prov. 1: 10; Gen. 39: 7-9); the things that are in the world: prevailing ideas, practices, conditions, environment, suggest and incite sin (1 John 2: 15-17; Matt. 18: 7). But whatever the external stimuli and excitations, in each case man is drawn away by his own lust and enticed (James 1: 14. 15).

4. **Temptation.**—There are two kinds of temptation: temptations for good and temptations for evil.

God, indeed, tempts and tries His children (Gen. 22: 1-9; Mark 7: 25-30), permitting such conditions and circumstances to develop in their lives where they are put to the test to decide for or against Him, for good or for evil (Job 1; Deut. 13: 1-3). In so doing it is God's purpose to purify and to strengthen their faith, and to draw them closer to Himself, as we see from the story of the woman of Canaan (Matt. 15: 21-28); (James 1: 3. 12). It is never the intention of God that in such temptation we should decide against Him for evil (James 1: 13), and, therefore, He will not suffer us to be tempted above what we are able (1 Cor. 10: 13).

But the very temptation which God permits for a good purpose, the devil uses for an evil purpose to draw us away from God, to destroy our faith, and to seduce us into sin, as we learn from the temptation of Adam and Eve in Paradise. The same is true of those temptations which originate in the world and in our own flesh. God permits these temptations to come that by resisting them our faith may be purified and strengthened; but the devil, the world, and our flesh, plying us with them, want us to yield and submit. Hence, the same temptation which God permits to strengthen our faith, the devil uses to destroy our faith (1 Pet. 5: 8. 9; Luke 22: 31. 32).

"Watch and pray that ye enter not into temptation" (Matt. 26: 41). We must not wilfully expose ourselves to temptation, nor to be over-confident, as Peter was (Matt. 26: 33-35). "Let him that thinketh he standeth take heed lest he fall" (1 Cor. 10: 12).

5. **Offenses.**—"Woe unto the world because of offenses! for it must needs be that offenses come; but woe to that man by whom the offense cometh" (Matt. 18: 7). The word "offend" is here not used in the popular meaning of causing dislike, anger, displeasure, of hurting one's feelings, but in the sense of causing one to stumble in his faith, to fall into sin. An offense, therefore, is anything that is likely to lead a person into unbelief, misbelief, or sin, or anything whereby he is encouraged to continue therein. Such offense is given by false teaching (Rom. 16: 17), by setting a bad example (Rom. 2: 23. 24), by an inconsiderate use of our Christian liberty without due regard for the weak in faith (Rom. 14: 13).— The sins we commit are harmful not only to ourselves, but also to those who are thereby tempted to follow our example. We are, therefore, responsible for the influence we exert on others by our conduct. The influence of our lives should be a wholesome salt, and not a vicious poison.

We must not *give offense* to any man (1 Cor. 10: 32); especially not to children, who are easily influenced by what they see or hear others do and say (Matt. 18: 6), nor to those who are weak in faith (Rom. 14: 13), nor to the world (Rom. 2: 23. 24). In its effect offense is soul murder. Therefore, "Woe to the man by whom the offense cometh!"—On the other hand, we must not *take offense*. The world being what it is, it must needs be that offenses come. But this is no excuse for us to stumble in our faith and to fall into sin. To be tempted to sin is not an excuse for yielding to such temptation. Offenses and temptations are there for us to overcome (Deut.

13: 1-3). "Resist the devil, and he will flee from you" (James 4: 7); (Prov. 1: 10).

6. **Adiaphora.**—In speaking of sins, it is necessary to speak also of things which God has neither commanded nor forbidden, which are in themselves indifferent, and are called adiaphora, or "Mitteldinge." There are many of these in our daily lives, but there are others concerning which there have been controversies in the Church. Such things are the eating of certain meats (Acts 10: 11-14; Rom. 14: 14), the observance of certain days, particularly, of the Sabbath (Rom. 14: 5. 6; Col. 2: 16. 17), the mode of baptizing, whether by sprinkling or immersion (Mark 7: 4), and many others. While under the Law we are at liberty to do as we please in these matters, we sin if by an inconsiderate use of our liberty we lead a weak brother to act against his erring conscience (Rom. 14: 15. 20; 1 Cor. 8: 8. 9).

If, however, a person insists that we abstain from things which God has allowed, and observe as obligatory what He has not commanded, if he demands that by our compliance we recognize and support his erroneous views as though they were divine requirements, then we may not yield to him. Paul did not circumcise Titus when some false brethren insisted that it must be done (Gal. 2: 3-5), while, under other circumstances, he did circumcise Timothy (Acts 16: 3). For the sake of charity to a weak brother we should be ready to refrain from the use of our liberty (Rom. 14: 15; 1 Cor. 8: 9); but if a confession of the truth is involved, then we must stand in the liberty wherewith Christ has made us free, and not be again entangled with the yoke of bondage (Gal. 5: 1). nor let our liberty be judged by another man's conscience (1 Cor. 10: 29). (Cf., F. C., Th. D., Art. X, 10-14, *Triglot*, p. 1055).

PART VI. SALVATION BY THE GRACE OF GOD THROUGH THE REDEMPTION IN CHRIST JESUS

XVIII. THE SAVING GRACE OF GOD

1. **The necessity of grace.**— All men have sinned (Rom. 3: 23), and are, therefore, guilty before God (Rom. 3: 19), under the curse of the Law (Gal. 3: 10), and deserving of death (Rom. 6: 23). Left to himself, it is absolutely impossible for man to achieve his own salvation, for "by the deeds of the Law shall no flesh be justified" (Rom. 3: 20). Salvation by the merit of our works is impossible; hence, divine grace is necessary for us to be saved.

2. **The certainty of divine grace.**—The grace of God is not an imagination or a possibility, but a divinely revealed fact. Moved by His love and compassion for man, God resolved to save him by the death of His Son (John 3: 16; Rom. 5: 8. 10). The grace of God, then, is the *moving* cause, and the redemption through Christ is the *meritorious* cause of our salvation. Man, lost by his own works, is saved by the grace of God in Christ. "For the grace of God that bringeth salvation hath appeared to all men" (Titus 2: 11). "By grace are ye saved through faith . . . not of works, lest any man should boast" (Eph. 2: 8. 9). Salvation by works is impossible, by grace it is sure. "Therefore it is of faith, that it might be by grace; to the end the promise might be sure to all the seed" (Rom. 4: 16).

This doctrine of salvation by grace distinguishes the Christian religion from all other religions in the world. All others teach that, because man sinned, man must make amends and appease the wrath of God. While they differ as to method and means by which this may be done, they are agreed in principle that man must achieve his salvation by his own efforts and works.—The Bible teaches that man's salvation is achieved exclusively by the grace of God. Human ingenuity never could have devised the plan of salvation as it is revealed in the Bible (1 Cor. 2: 6-10); it runs utterly contrary to our

78

way of thinking; it is "foolishness" to us (1 Cor. 2: 14). This doctrine, being the chief doctrine of our faith, marks the Christian religion to be of divine origin, while all others are human inventions.

3. **Definition of grace.**—In our definition of "grace" we do not include that goodness which God shows to all His creatures (Ps. 145: 9), but confine ourselves to the grace by which God saves sinners.

The word "grace" is sometimes used of a gift, quality, virtue, or power which God imparts to man gratuitously (Rom. 15: 15; 1 Pet. 4: 10). But when we speak of "saving grace," we do not mean any of these things, nor do we mean an "infused" or a "prevenient" grace, by the proper use of which man is supposed to be able to effect his conversion. The grace by which God saves us is a personal attribute or quality in God, which manifests itself in His attitude toward man and in His promises and gifts, but which is not imparted to man. (Example: We can show our love to our neighbor in various ways, but we cannot impart our love to him.) According to Romish teaching "grace" is not a quality in God, but an infused "quality inhering in the soul" of man, by the aid of which he is to do good and to obtain forgiveness. When the Romish Church says that we are saved "by grace," it means something entirely different from what we mean when we say that we are saved by grace. The grace of God by which we are saved is the "favor Dei," which is that merciful, affectionate disposition, that good will of God toward men, according to which He forgives sins to those who are worthy of eternal death. It is the unmerited love of God toward men (John 3: 16; Titus 3: 4. 5).—From this concept of grace must be excluded every regard for the merit of man. God's grace is not in the least affected, motivated, or influenced by any worthiness in us; in fact, the slightest injection of man's merit and worthiness utterly destroys the concept of grace. "If by grace, then it is no more of works; otherwise grace is no more grace. But if it be of works, then it is no more grace; otherwise work is no more work" (Rom. 11: 6). The grace of God and the merit of man are exclusive terms. Man cannot be saved partly by the grace of God and partly by his own merit; it might, conceivably, be the one or the other, but never both.

As man cannot be saved by the merit of his works, it follows that his salvation is possible only by the grace of God.

It is a grace *in Christ Jesus.* While the merits of man are indeed excluded from the concept of grace, the merits of Christ must necessarily be included. "Being justified freely by His grace through the redemption that is in Christ Jesus" (Rom. 3: 24). There could be no grace for sinners with God, unless the demands of His holiness and justice had been fully satisfied by the active and passive obedience of our Redeemer. Hence, we may not think of the grace of God apart from the redemption by Christ. God is gracious to sinners only in Christ and for Christ's sake. They who trust in the grace of God, but reject the vicarious atonement of Christ, trust in something that does not exist, and will some day find God to be a consuming fire (Hebr. 12: 29). The grace of God is given us by Jesus Christ (1 Cor. 1: 4).

4. **Attributes of saving grace.**—

(a) The grace of God is *universal.* It is not limited to certain individuals, the elect, as Reformed theology teaches, but it extends to all men. "The grace of God that bringeth salvation hath appeared to all men" (Tit. 2: 11). "God so loved the world that He gave His only begotten Son" (John 3: 16). "God will have all men to be saved, and to come unto the knowledge of the truth" (1 Tim. 2: 4); (Ezek. 33: 11). As Christ is the propitiation for the sins of the whole world (1 John 2: 1. 2), so also the grace of God in Christ goes out to all men. But the Bible does not reveal that there is grace and redemption also for the fallen angels.

The fact that only few are saved (Matt. 7: 13. 14), and that these are saved solely by the grace of God, does not invalidate the truth that God is gracious to all men. Both propositions, that grace is universal, and that grace alone saves, must be maintained on the basis of the Scriptures. If the grace of God did not include all men, no man could be sure of it, because every one must then be in doubt whether God's grace is really intended for him. Neither can any one be sure of God's grace if in any way it depended on his merit, because he could never be certain that he is personally worthy of it.

(b) The grace of God is *active.* God's grace is not an idle sentiment, but it manifests itself in what He did and what He still does for the salvation of men. Because God loved the world, He sent His Son to save the world (John 3: 16). "God commendeth His love toward us, in that, while we were yet sinners, Christ died for us" (Rom. 5: 8). By the preaching of the "Gospel of grace" (Acts 20: 24), God continues to offer to all men the saving benefits of Christ's redemption. All the acts of God, whereby men are brought to faith, justified, sanctified, preserved, and finally saved through faith, are motivated by this grace. "By grace are ye saved through faith" (Eph. 2: 8).

(c) God's grace is *serious and sincere*. This appears not only from what His grace prompted, and still prompts, Him to do, but also from definite statements to that effect. God swears, saying: "As I live, saith the Lord God, I have no pleasure in the death of the wicked, but that the wicked turn from his way and live" (Ezek. 33: 11). Christ weeps over impenitent Jerusalem (Luke 19: 41) and says: "How often would I have gathered thy children together, even as a hen gathereth her chickens under her wings, and ye would not" (Matt. 23: 37). There should be no doubt in the mind of any one that the grace of God is unfeigned, honest, and sincere.

(d) The grace of God is *efficacious*. The declaration and offer of God's grace in the Gospel possesses inherent power to impress and move the heart and to work acceptance of the offer. The Word of God, which offers this grace, works effectually in them that believe (1 Thess. 2: 13). As the offer of grace by the governor of the state has power to work in the heart of the convict the acceptance thereof, so the offer of God's grace has power to work in the heart of the sinner that faith, by which he accepts it. The reason that it does not always do this, lies not in a lack, deficiency, or weakness of the offered grace, but in the perverse will of man. "Ye would not" (Matt. 23: 37). "Ye do always resist the Holy Ghost" (Acts 7: 51).

XIX. THE PERSON OF CHRIST

While it was grace that moved God to *provide* salvation for lost mankind, it was the redemption by Jesus Christ that *procured and earned* this salvation. For this reason it is important that we should now study the Person of our Redeemer.

In so doing we shall discuss His Names, His Natures, the Personal Union, the Communication of Attributes, and finally, Why Our Saviour had to be both man and God.

1. The Names of the Redeemer

The names of the Saviour are Jesus Christ, which names do not, like the names of other persons, merely distinguish Him from others, but which definitely describe Him as what He is.

(a) **Jesus is the personal name,** by which the Redeemer was known and called in His day. This name was selected by God Himself. "She shall bring forth a Son, and thou shalt call His name Jesus, for He shall save His people from their sins" (Matt. 1: 21). The meaning of Jesus is "helper, savior"; in this particular case, a helper and savior from sin. He is the Savior not only of the Jews, who were His people by race, but of all men. "He is the propitiation for our sins, and not for ours only, but also for the sins of the whole world" (1 John 2: 2). And He is the *only* Savior; there is none beside Him. "Neither is there salvation in any other; for there is none other name under heaven given among men, whereby we must be saved" (Acts 4: 12). "I am the way, the truth, and the life: no man cometh unto the Father, but by Me" (John 14: 6).

(b) **Christ is the official name** of the Savior. Christ, which is the Greek word for the Hebrew word Messiah, means "the Anointed." To be anointed with oil signified that one received an office, and for this office the gift of the Holy Ghost; thus David was anointed to be king of Israel (1 Sam. 16: 13). —That Jesus is the Anointed of God appears from Hebr. 1: 8. 9: "But unto the Son He saith, Thy throne, O God, is for ever and ever: a scepter of righteousness is the scepter of Thy kingdom. Thou hast loved righteousness, and hated iniquity; therefore God, even Thy God, hath anointed Thee with the oil of gladness above Thy fellows." The oil of gladness, with which the human nature of Jesus was anointed (Acts 10: 38), is the Holy Ghost. Jesus did not become the Christ of God at His baptism, but He was the Anointed of God from and by the incarnation, when by the operation of the Holy Ghost the Virgin Mary conceived the child, in whom dwelt the fulness of the Godhead bodily (Luke 1: 35).—"Fellows" are such as had likewise been anointed for an office, as were priests (Exod. 29: 4-7), prophets and kings (1 Kings 19: 16), in the Old Testament. "Above Thy fellows" indicates that Christ's office was higher than theirs, since He was anointed with the Holy Ghost without measure, "for God giveth not the Spirit by measure unto Him" (John 3: 34). His office was not limited as was the office of the prophets, priests, and kings of old, who were but shadows and types of the future Messiah; Christ was anointed to be our *real* Prophet, Priest, and King. Calling Jesus "the Christ" (Matt. 16: 16) means just this, that He is recognized and accepted as the promised Messiah.

2. The Natures of Christ

In Luther's explanation of the Second Article of the Apostles' Creed we confess that "Jesus Christ is true God, begotten of the Father from eternity, and also true man, born of the Virgin Mary." This is a wonderful statement to make about Jesus; yet this is exactly what the Scriptures teach concerning Him.

(a) **Christ is true God.**—The Jews regarded the statement of Jesus that He was the Son of God as blasphemy (Matt. 26: 63-65). In the fourth century Arius, a presbyter in Alexandria, taught that Jesus was only similar (homoi-ousios) to, but not coequal (homo-ousios) with, the Father. The Church rejected Arianism in the Nicene and the Athanasian Creeds. In our day the Deity of Christ is denied by many without and within the visible Church; to them Jesus is a model man, a great teacher and reformer, but not the very God. But if Christ is not the true God, then He is neither a model of virtue and truthfulness, nor a great teacher, but, as the Jews said of Him, a deceiver (Matt. 27: 63), and His religion is a fraud; nor can He then be the Savior from sin.

The Deity of Christ is a fundamental doctrine, a denial of which is a serious matter. "Who is a liar but he that denieth that Jesus is the Christ? He is antichrist, that denieth the Father and the Son. Whosoever denieth the Son, the same hath not the Father" (1 John 2: 22. 23); (1 John 4: 3; 5: 12. 13). Such denial makes saving faith impossible. In this, as in all matters of doctrine, we must not follow human reason, but believe what the Scriptures teach, and these are very definite on this point.

Jesus was not made a god at His baptism or at His resurrection, nor was He subsequently deified by His followers, who believed Him to be God, while He Himself never made such a claim; but from His conception Jesus was, and still is, and ever will be, the true God.

Testimony of prophecy.—Speaking of the future Messiah, Isaiah tells us: "Unto us a Child is born, unto us a Son is given . . . and His name shall be called . . . the mighty God, the everlasting Father" (Is. 9: 6). Unto the Virgin Mary the angel said: "That Holy Thing which shall be born of thee shall be called the Son of God" (Luke 1: 35). At His birth the angels proclaimed the Babe of Bethlehem to be "Christ the Lord" (Luke 2: 11).

Christ's own testimony.—Usually Jesus referred to Himself as "the Son of Man" (Matt. 18: 11). However, He not only accepted the answer of Peter: "Thou art the Christ, the Son of the living God," but added that this knowledge had been given to Peter "by My Father which is in heaven" (Matt. 16: 13-17). Still more directly does He emphasize His Deity in John 10: 28-30. While He differentiates between Himself and the Father, who gave Him the sheep (a difference in person), He identifies Himself with the Father in saying that the sheep are both in His hand and in the hand of the Father, adding: "I and the Father are one" (unity of essence). This unity of essence is demonstrated in the unity of action, as we see from John 5: 17-19: "My Father worketh hitherto, and I work . . . The Son can do nothing of Himself, but what He seeth the Father do; for what things soever He doeth, these also doeth the Son likewise." In John 10: 37. 38 Christ refers to His works as evidence of His Deity: "If I do not the works of My Father, believe Me not. But if I do, though ye believe not Me, believe the works: that ye may know, and believe, that the Father is in Me, and I in Him." When asked by the priests and scribes to tell them whether He was the Son of God, He said unto them: "Ye say that I am" (Luke 22: 70).

Testimony of the Scripture.—Scripture definitely calls Jesus the true God. "This is the true God and eternal life" (1 John

5: 20). "Christ, who is over all, God blessed forever" (Rom.
9: 5). These *divine names* are not empty honorary titles, but
"the Word was made flesh, and dwelt among us, and we beheld His glory, the glory as of the only begotten of the Father,
full of grace and truth" (John 1: 14). His resurrection also
is proof of His Deity (Rom. 1: 4). Scripture ascribes to Him
divine attributes. He is omniscient; "Lord, Thou knowest all
things" (John 21: 17); (John 1: 47-49). He is omnipotent
(John 10: 28-30; Matt. 28: 18). He does *divine works*. By
Him were all things created (John 1: 3; Col. 1: 16. 17). He
preserves all things (Hebr. 1: 3). He raises the dead, and
judges the world (John 5: 21. 27). *Divine honor* is His. He
is to be worshiped as God by men and angels (John 5: 23;
Phil. 2: 9. 11).

Whoever denies the Deity of Christ certainly cannot do so
on the basis of Scriptural evidence, but does it for other reasons. The Confessions of the Church are in full agreement
with the Bible. "I believe . . . in one Lord Jesus Christ, the
only-begotten Son of God, begotten of His Father before all
worlds, God of God, Light of Light, Very God of Very God,
begotten, not made, being of one substance with the Father"
(Excerpt from the *Nicene Creed*).

(b) **Christ is true man.**—While the Jews never doubted
that Jesus, who lived and moved among them, was a real
human being, there arose later a heresy, called Docetism,
which held that Christ was only seemingly a human being,
and not so in reality. Some denied that He had a human
body; others, that He had a human soul; or a human will, etc.
In our day Christian Science, which teaches that matter is
non-existent, must consistently teach that Jesus had no material body. This error may not be regarded a trivial matter,
for what Christ has not assumed, He has not redeemed. If He
did not take on the full human nature, then the full human
nature is not saved. It is futile to speculate on the possibility
whether the eternal Son of God could have become a real
man; the fact that He did is clearly established in the Scriptures.

Jesus has human ancestors (Rom. 9: 5). He is called "the
son of David" (Matt. 21: 9); (Jer. 23: 5). He was born of
a human mother, from whom He received a human nature

(Luke 1: 35); hence, He is a real human being. He has a body, consisting of flesh and blood and bones (Luke 24: 39; Hebr. 2: 14). He has a human soul (Matt. 26: 38), which functioned as a human soul in this that He acquired wisdom (Luke 2: 52), had emotions (John 11: 33; Hebr. 4: 15), and a will (Luke 22: 42). Jesus calls Himself "the Son of Man" (Matt. 9; 6), is called "man" (1 Tim. 2: 5). He acted like a man: He was born, increased in knowledge (Luke 2: 7. 52), was hungry (Matt. 4: 2), thirsty (John 19: 28), ate and drank (Matt. 11: 19), slept (Mark 4: 38), suffered and died (Matt. 20: 18. 19; John 19: 30).

Having called attention to the fact that Christ did not take on the nature of angels but of the seed of Abraham, Scripture points out the peculiar comfort which lies therein. Christ not only has a knowledge of our weaknesses, but is also touched with a sympathetic "feeling of our infirmities" (Hebr. 2: 17); (Hebr. 4: 15).

(c) **Peculiarities of the human nature of Christ.**—While on the basis of Scripture we insist that Jesus has a real and true human nature, we must call attention to certain peculiarities of this nature.

Virgin-birth.—Since Adam and Eve, all men are begotten of a human father and born of a human mother. It was not so with Jesus. He was born of a human mother, the Virgin Mary, but He was not begotten of a human father. He is the "Seed of the woman" (Gen. 3: 15), the Son of a Virgin (Is. 7: 14; Matt. 1: 23), who by the miraculous operation of the Holy Ghost conceived the Child (Matt. 1: 18; Luke 1: 35). Whoever believes that God is almighty (Luke 1: 37), will not stumble in his faith at the virgin-birth of the Savior.

Sinlessness.—"All men begotten in a natural way are born with sin" (A. C., Art. II, 1, *Triglot*, p. 43). As Jesus was not begotten in a natural way, this does not apply to Him; hence, we learn that it was a "Holy Thing" that was born of the Virgin (Luke 1: 35). Neither was hereditary guilt and original depravity transmitted to Him through birth; nor did He ever commit any actual sin in His life. "Which of you convinceth Me of sin?" (John 8: 46). "Who knew no sin" (2 Cor. 5: 21). "Who did no sin, neither was guile found in His mouth" (1 Pet. 2: 22). Since sin is not an essential part of the human nature, it was indeed possible for Christ to be a true man, and to be without sin both by birth and in His life. —This personal sinlessness of Christ is not disproved by Rom. 8: 3, where we read: "God sending His own Son in the likeness of sinful flesh." He who knew no sin was made to be sin for us, and, therefore, exhibited in His human nature the weaknesses and infirmities of the "sinful flesh." Because of our sins Christ's human nature did not appear in the likeness of Adam's nature before the Fall, but in the likeness of human nature after the Fall.—Since in this particular human nature dwelt the fulness of the Godhead bodily (Col. 2: 9), it was not possible for the human nature of Christ to sin, unless we are ready to admit that God can sin when He takes on a human nature.

Immortality.—Because of sinlessness, this human nature is immortal. We die as a consequence of our sins. Christ has no sins of His own; hence, He did not have to die. He could not have died of any bodily illness or of old age. When He died, His death was a voluntary act. "No man taketh it" (My life) "from Me, but I lay it down of Myself. I have power to lay it down, and I have power to take it again" (John 10: 18); (John 19: 30). Personally sinless and immortal, Jesus died for our sins, because He wanted to die; and He died at the very moment He wanted to die.

Impersonality.—Ordinarily a human nature exists as a human person, having its own and individual existence. The human nature of Jesus was from the moment of the incarnation assumed by the Son of God. "The Word was made flesh" (John 1: 14). "God sent forth His Son, made of a woman" (Gal. 4: 4). At no time did the human nature of Christ exist for and by itself, constituting in itself a person; but from its beginning it had its existence in the Person of the Son of God. Nor were the two natures merged into one new person, but the eternal Person of the Godhead, the Son, assumed the human nature; hence, the impersonality of His human nature. The Son of God supplied the personality of the God-man Jesus Christ.

3. The Personal Union of the Natures in Christ

(a) **Christ is one person, but has a complete divine and a complete human nature.**—According to Rom. 9: 5 Jesus has human fathers, and is, therefore, Himself a true human being; but at the same time He is "God blessed forever." Thus it appears that the two natures are united so as to constitute one person, an individuality. Hence, there is one Christ, who is both true God and true man. (Cf., Athanasian Creed, 28-35, *Triglot,* p. 35).

"We believe, teach, and confess that the Son of God, although from eternity He has been a particular, distinct, entire divine person, and thus, with the Father and the Holy Ghost, true, essential, perfect God, nevertheless, in the fulness of time assumed also human nature into the unity of His Person, not in such a way that there are now two persons or two Christs, but that Jesus Christ is now in one person at the same time true, eternal God, born of the Father from eternity, and true man, born of the most blessed Virgin Mary" (F. C., Th. D., Art. VIII, 6, *Triglot,* p. 1017).

(b) **This personal union of the two natures in Christ is a profound mystery,** (1 Tim. 3: 16). However, to give us some faint idea, Scripture compares it to the union existing between body and soul. "In Him dwelleth all the fulness of the Godhead bodily" (Col. 2: 9). The two natures are not so mixed and mingled as to make a new composition; neither has one changed into the other, losing its own identity; but, like body and soul, they remain distinct. Nor do they exist beside each other, like two boards glued together, without having any communion with, and interrelation to, each other; but again, like body and soul, the divine nature so permeates and penetrates the human nature, and the human nature is so permeated and penetrated by the divine nature, that both natures make one person. "As the reasonable soul and flesh is one man, so God and man is one in Christ" (Athanasian Creed). "The union of the two natures is so close and inseparable that the one can no longer be conceived of as without or away from the other, but both are to be regarded in all respects united, yet in such a way that each of the two natures retains its own essential character and peculiarities as before, and remains unmingled with the other" (Schmid, *Doctrinal Theology*, p. 317). This particular human nature belongs to, and is possessed of, the Son of God. Where, therefore, the Son of God, the divine nature, is, there is likewise the Son of Man, the human nature. Ever since the Word was made flesh (John 1: 14), the flesh is not without the Word, and the Word is not without the flesh. The two natures are inseparable, though distinct.

(c) **How and when was this personal union effected?**— The flesh was not made God. Jesus was not a mere man for a number of years, and was then elevated to the Deity; but "the Word was made flesh" (John 1: 14); "God sent forth His Son, made of a woman" (Gal. 4: 4). The personal union was, then, brought about in this way, that the eternal Son of God received and incorporated into His divine Person another, a human, nature. This happened at the conception of Jesus (Luke 1: 35); the unborn Child of Mary is called "Lord" (Luke 1: 43). At no time, not even in the death of Jesus, did the human nature exist outside of, and apart from, the Word, but from its very beginning it had its existence, and will to all eternity have its existence, in the Person of the Son of God.

(d) Because of the personal union of the divine and the human nature in Christ it is perfectly proper to say not only, "Christ is God" (cf., 1 John 5: 20), and "Christ is man" (cf., 1 Tim. 2: 5), but also to say of Him, "This man is God," or "The Son of Man is the Son of God" (cf., Matt. 16: 13-17), and "God is man" (cf., John 1: 14). "Hence, we believe, teach, and confess that God is man and man is God, which could not be if the divine and human natures had in deed and truth absolutely no communion with one another" (F. C., Epit., Art. VIII, 10, *Triglot*, p. 819). These personal propositions, therefore, express the intimate union and communion existing between the two natures in Christ.

4. The Communication of Attributes

Because of the Personal Union of the two natures in Christ, we may speak also of the Communication of Attributes, of which there are three kinds or genera: the idiomatic, the majestic, the apotelesmatic.

The Idiomatic Genus

(a) Illustration: A person consists of body and soul; each of these has its own peculiar attributes and properties. But as both, body and soul, belong to the same person, the attributes of either body or soul are ascribed to the entire person. Example: "N. N. weighs 150 pounds," which can properly be said only of his physical body. "N. N. is happy and joyful," which can properly be predicated only of his soul.

(b) Thus Christ has two distinct natures, a human and a divine, each of which has its own essential attributes, functions, and activities. But as both natures belong to the same Person, the attributes and properties of either may be ascribed to the Person. Christ was begotten of the Father from eternity according to His divine nature (Ps. 2: 7); Christ was born of the Virgin Mary in the fulness of time according to His human nature (Gal. 4: 4). Jesus was thirty years old according to His human nature (Luke 3: 23); according to His divine nature He could say: "Before Abraham was, I am" (John 8: 58). Christ is "equal to the Father as touching His Godhead, and inferior to the Father as touching His manhood." (Cf., Athanasian Creed).

(c) The Bible even names the Person of Christ according to one nature, and predicates of Him attributes of the other nature. The Son of God was made of the seed of David according to the flesh (Rom. 1: 3). The Jews killed the Prince of Life (Acts 3: 15), and crucified the Lord of glory (1 Cor. 2: 8). Thus we confess in the Second Article of the Apostles' Creed concerning Jesus Christ, the Son of God, that He was conceived and born, was crucified, dead, and buried. As little as we may separate the human nature from the Son of God, so little may we separate from Him what this human nature did and suffered. In other texts the Savior is designated according to His human nature, but things are predicated of Him which properly apply to His divine nature. "What and if ye shall see the Son of man ascend up where He was before?" (John 6: 62).

Thus the idiomatic genus is this, that such things as are peculiar to the divine or to the human nature are truly and really ascribed to the entire Person of Christ, designated by either nature or by both. It does not follow, however, that what is ascribed to the person is at the same time a property of both natures, or an inherent attribute of both natures, but it is distinctively explained what nature it is according to which anything is ascribed to the person. Hence, things divine are ascribed to the entire Person of Christ *according to* the divine nature, and things human are ascribed to the entire Person of Christ *according to* the human nature. (Cf., Rom. 1: 3; 1 Pet. 3: 18; 4: 1). (Cf., F. C., Th. D., Art. VIII, 36. 37, *Triglot*, p. 1027).

The Majestic Genus

(a) Illustration: The human body in itself is dead; but when joined to the living soul, this soul imparts and communicates life to the body. Thereby the life of the soul is not diminished or divided, but it remains fully intact. However, at times this life manifests itself in the body less than at other times, less, for example, when a person sleeps than when he is awake; but the body does not impart anything to the soul.

(b) When the Son of God assumed the human nature, He imparted and communicated to it divine majesty, glory, and attributes. Thereby the majesty of the divine nature was in no wise lessened or divided, but remained fully intact in both natures. However, in the state of humiliation Christ did not always and fully manifest this divine majesty in His human nature (Phil. 2: 6-8). That the fulness of the majesty of God was communicated to the human nature is clearly seen from this Scripture: "In Him dwelleth all the fulness of the Godhead bodily" (Col. 2: 9). And this fact was also evident to men, for "God was manifest in the flesh" (1 Tim. 3: 16), and the disciples "beheld His glory, the glory as of the Only-begotten of the Father" (John 1: 14); (2 Pet. 1: 17. 18; Matt. 17: 1. 2). In His divine nature the Son of God always did have divine glory and majesty (John 17: 15); but to His human nature all this was given (Dan. 7: 13. 14; Hebr. 2: 7. 8). Jesus expresses the same truth, saying: "All power is given unto Me in heaven and in earth" (Matt. 28: 18). And He, to whom all power is given, promises to be with His disciples unto the end of the world (Matt. 28: 20). Thus by virtue of the personal union of the two natures in Christ the human nature became omnipotent and omnipresent. That also the human nature of Christ is omnipresent we learn from Eph. 4: 10, where we are told that Christ ascended "far above all heavens that He might fill all things." That Christ is omniscient we see from John 21: 17 and John 2: 24. 25.

(c) While, therefore, the divine attributes belong essentially to the divine nature, they belong by communication also to the human nature. Like as heat is communicated to iron, and life to the body, so is divine majesty communicated to the human nature. But the human nature does not communicate anything to the divine nature, because the divine nature is perfect, and nothing can be added thereto. (Cf., F. C., Th. D., Art. VIII, 48-87, *Triglot,* p. 1031-1045).

The Apotelesmatic Genus

(a) Illustration: Whenever a person performs a voluntary act, not only his body, nor only his soul acts, but both act conjointly, each contributing its part. Without the soul the body does not move nor do anything, and we know of no soul action which does not somehow employ the organs of the body. —"Apotelesmatic" means "pertaining to the final result to be accomplished." Applied to the Person of Christ, it refers to the result to be accomplished by the God-man, namely, His work as Prophet, Priest, and King to redeem the human race.

(b) The Word was made flesh for the express purpose of saving sinful mankind. Whatever the Savior did and still does to accomplish this blessed purpose may not be ascribed to either of His. natures exclusively, but must be ascribed to both natures conjointly. Christ is our Savior not according to one of His natures only, but according to both natures, the divine nature using the human nature as its organ, and participating in everything this nature did and suffered.

"For this purpose the Son of God was manifested" (in the flesh) "that He might destroy the works of the devil" (1 John 3: 8). "To destroy the works of the devil" summarizes the entire work of redemption, and this was the work of the Son of God. However, this work was not performed outside and independently of the human nature, but through this nature; the Son of God was manifested in the flesh that in and through the flesh He might perform this work. This is very plain also from this passage: "Forasmuch then as the children are partakers of flesh and blood, He also Himself likewise took part of the same; that through death" (suffered in His human nature) "He" (the Son of God) "might destroy him that had the power of death, that is, the devil" (Hebr. 2: 14). Again we read: "When the fulness of the time was come, God sent forth His Son, made of a woman, made under the Law, to redeem them that were under the Law, that we might receive the adoption of sons" (Gal. 4: 4. 5). If only the human nature had been under the Law, the obedience of Christ would have no greater value than that of a saint. But the text tells us that the Son of God was made man, and that in and with His human nature the Son of God fulfilled the Law for us. In Acts 20: 28 we read that God purchased the Church with His own blood. Plainly, the divine and the human nature cooperated in this work of redemption. From 2 Cor. 5: 19 we learn that "God was in Christ," evidently in His human nature, "reconciling the world unto Himself." Reconciliation is a work which God did, but He did it in and through the human nature. Thus in all works pertaining to the office of Christ as Prophet, Priest, and King both natures act in conjunction with each other, each nature doing what is peculiar to the same. (Cf., F. C., Th. D., Art. VIII, 46, *Triglot,* p. 1031).

5. Why Did Our Savior Have to Be God and Man?

Jesus Christ was indeed a unique person, true God and true man in one undivided and indivisible Person. Why did our Savior have to be God and man?

(a) **Why true man?**—As Christ was to save mankind (Matt. 18: 11), He had to take the place of man, become the substitute for man. " . . . He took not on Him the nature of angels, but He took on Him the seed of Abraham. Wherefore in all things it behooved Him to be made like unto His brethren" (Hebr. 2: 14-17). To redeem man it was necessary for Him to do two things, both of which required that He be true man.

To satisfy the demands of God's holiness it was necessary that the Law be fulfilled (Lev. 19: 2). Man did not and could not do this; hence, Christ takes this duty and burden on

Himself. But as the keeping of the Law was really man's work, and not God's, the Son of God was made man, and was made under the Law, that in man's place and stead He might fulfill all righteousness (Gal. 4: 4; Matt. 3: 15; Rom. 10: 4).

To satisfy the demands of God's justice it was necessary that full atonement be made for the transgressions of man by suffering the penalty. "The wages of sin is death" (Rom. 6: 23). "Without shedding of blood is no remission" (Hebr. 9: 22). To be a propitiation for our sins the Savior must needs shed His blood and die (Hebr. 9: 12). Therefore He had to be true man, that He might be capable of suffering and dying for us. This is clearly stated in Hebr. 2: 14, where we are told that He took on flesh and blood for this very purpose, that He might be able to die and through His death destroy the devil.

(b) **Why true God?**—A mere man, be he sinner or saint, could never have redeemed us. A sinner cannot save himself, much less can he save another; a perfect saint, if there were such, would indeed be saved, but he would have no superfluous merit, which he could pass on to some one else. "None of them can by any means redeem his brother, nor give to God a ransom for him: (for the redemption of their soul is precious, and it ceaseth forever)" (Ps. 49: 7. 8). The redemption of a soul costs so much, that man must forever cease in his attempts to redeem his brother. Since man was to be reconciled to God, none other than God Himself could furnish a ransom that would fully meet the demands of divine holiness and justice. Only God could render full satisfaction to God. For this reason any reconciliation attempted by one who is less than God must necessarily fail. But the work of Christ was sufficiently precious to redeem all men, because "God was in Christ reconciling the world unto Himself" (2 Cor. 5: 19), because it was God's blood that was shed for us (1 John 1: 7; Acts 20: 28b). The fact that it was God in Christ who fulfilled the Law, and suffered for our sins, gives infinite value and saving power to the work of our Redeemer. Since it was God Himself who reconciled the world to Himself, we know for a certainty that all was done that was necessary for such reconciliation.

XX. THE LIFE OF THE REDEEMER IN THE STATES OF HUMILIATION AND EXALTATION

Scripture presents Christ to us both in the state of humiliation and in the state of exaltation (Phil. 2: 6-11). The humiliation comprises the "days of His flesh" (Hebr. 5: 7), from His conception to His burial. The exaltation begins with His vivification and continues forever.

Both, the humiliation and the exaltation, do not pertain to the divine nature of Christ, because in this nature He is always the same (Hebr. 13: 8), and can neither be humbled nor exalted. It was in the human nature that Christ humbled Himself and was exalted.

1. The Humiliation

(a) **What it is not.**—The humiliation did not consist in this that the Son of God was made man; incarnation is not identical with humiliation. Otherwise the opposite of humiliation, namely, exaltation, would be that He ceased to be man, which He never did. Nor did the humiliation consist in this that in the days of His flesh the human nature of Christ did not possess divine majesty and glory, and that divine attributes were first bestowed on Him in His exaltation. For not only are we told that in Him dwelt all the fulness of the Godhead bodily (Col. 2: 9), but in His miracles, which He performed in His own name and power, He manifested His glory as the Only-begotten of the Father (John 1: 14; 2: 11).

(b) **Definition.**—What the humiliation was like, we may make clear to ourselves by an illustration. A giant has great strength of body, but if he does not make use of it, weak children can bind him and put him to death. Thus it was with Christ. In His divine nature Christ always and fully did use His majesty and power (John 5: 17; Hebr. 1: 3); but in His human nature, to which all this majesty and power had been communicated, He did not make constant and full use of the same. The humiliation of Christ, therefore, consists in the non-use of the divine power and majesty which He possessed also in His human nature.

(c) **Bible proof.**—"Let this mind be in you which was also in Christ Jesus; who being in the form of God, thought it not

robbery to be equal with God, but made Himself of no reputation, and took upon Him the form of a servant, and was
made in the likeness of man; being found in fashion as a man,
He humbled Himself, and became obedient unto death, even
the death of the cross" (Phil. 2: 5-8). Jesus really was in the
"form of God." This does not mean an external form; but it
means that in Him dwelled the fulness of the Godhead bodily
(Col. 2: 9) and that divine attributes had been communicated
to His human nature, and that, therefore, He was truly "equal
with God." The expression "to think a thing robbery" is not
very familiar to us in our day. When in those days a victorious general returned from war, he would publicly show and
display the spoils of battle. Thus did the Roman emperor
Titus, who, after the destruction of Jerusalem and its temple,
returned home, and, entering the city of Rome in a triumphant
procession, publicly displayed the spoils of conquest. (See also Col. 2: 15). To think or treat a thing as robbery means to
make a public show of it. The meaning of our text, therefore,
is: Although Christ was in "the form of God," He did not
constantly show that He was "equal with God"; in other
words, although He possessed divine power and majesty, He
did not always make use thereof in His human nature. Thus
it was that people did not at once recognize Him as "the Lord
of glory." Ordinarily, as He moved among men, He did not
show "the form of God," but rather "took upon Him the form
of a servant," showing Himself in the fashion of a common,
lowly, and weak man. Occasionally, as when He performed
miracles (John 2: 11), and on the Mount of Transfiguration
(Matt. 17: 2), He, indeed, manifested "the form of God," flash-
ing forth rays of hidden glory; but ordinarily He looked and
acted like a common man, refraining to use the divine attributes He possessed. He was like a king, who hides his royal
garments beneath a beggar's cloak. He was like a strong giant,
who does not use the strength he has, but allows little children to capture and to crucify him. In John 18: 6. 12 we
have an example of Christ's use and non-use of the divine
power in His human nature.

"This majesty Christ always had according to the personal
union, and yet He abstained from it in the state of humiliation, and on this account truly increased in all wisdom and

favor with God and men; therefore He exercised this majesty, not always, but as often as it pleased Him" (F. C., Epit. Art. II, 16, *Triglot,* p. 8,21).

(d) **The purpose and the necessity of the humiliation** are indicated in the words: "And became obedient unto death, even the death of the cross." Had Christ during His life on earth made full and constant use of His divine majesty in His human nature also, the world would have been amazed, but not saved; for then He could not have been put under the Law, could not have been bound and killed (John 18: 6). But He was like the strong giant who refrained from using his strength so that weak dwarfs might be able to put him to death. All this He did in obedience to God, that He might be able to suffer and die for our sins.

The humiliation of Christ is also to teach us an important lesson. Men like to "show off" and let people know what they are. But our text says: "Let this mind be in you which was also in Christ Jesus." We should be humble, meek, and lowly of heart (Matt. 11: 29), not think of ourselves more highly than we ought to think (Rom. 12: 3).

2. Stages of Humiliation

(a) **Not steps, but stages.**—As the humiliation is the non-use of divine majesty and power communicated to the human nature, we cannot speak of degrees of humiliation. In the non-use of a thing there can be no degrees. Properly speaking, there is no deep and deeper and deepest humiliation, though sometimes we use such expressions with reference to our Lord's Passion. With the exception of those instances when in His miracles He flashed forth rays of hidden glory, the humiliation was on the same level throughout His life. Therefore, we prefer to speak of stages of humiliation.

(b) **Conception and birth.**—On the basis of Luke 1: 35 we believe that Christ was, by the miraculous working of the Holy Ghost, conceived a true human being by the Virgin Mary. His, and His alone, was an "immaculate conception." From Luke 2: 1-14 we learn that He was born of His Virgin mother a true human child. Not the fact that the Word was made flesh, but the manner in which it was done shows the humiliation. He was "made of a woman" (Gal. 4: 4); He is the fruit of Mary's womb (Luke 1: 42); He is made under the Law (Gal. 4: 4); He was born in great lowliness and poverty (Luke 2: 7). The Child of Bethlehem was "the mighty God" (Is. 9: 6), but there was nothing in His actions and appearance that revealed this fact. Even at this stage His humiliation was linked up with His work of redemption; He was "made under the Law to redeem them that were under the Law" (Gal. 4: 4).

(c) **Christ's life.**—Physically and mentally Jesus grew up and developed as any other child. "And Jesus increased in wisdom and stature, and in favor with God and man" (Luke 2: 52). "And Jesus Himself began to be about thirty years of age, being (as was supposed) the son of Joseph" (Luke 3: 23). "In all things it behooved Him to be made like unto His brethren" (Hebr. 2: 17). Except when He performed miracles, He showed Himself "in the fashion as a man," living the life of a Jewish rabbi. Jesus was not a rich man, not even well-to-do, but very poor (Matt. 8: 20), depending for His sustenance on the ministration of His friends (Luke 8: 3). Yet behind this "form of a servant" was hid the "form of God."

Morally there was, indeed, a great difference between Him and others. He was born without sin (Luke 1: 35); His life as a child, as a boy, as a young man was absolutely sinless (John 8: 46; Hebr. 7: 26). In His relation to God, to His parents, to His fellow-men He kept the Law perfectly.—His holy life was as much a part of His redemptive work (active obedience) as was His suffering and death, and is to be an example to us for a God-pleasing life.

(d) **Suffering, death, and burial.**—The entire life of Christ was a continuous suffering; He bore the weaknesses and infirmities common to man (Hebr. 2: 17; 4: 15; Is. 53: 3). He knew Himself burdened with the sins of the world (John 1: 29), being always conscious of our guilt that was imputed to Him (2 Cor. 5: 21). His suffering was intensified in Gethsemane and on Golgotha, and reached its climax when He exclaimed: "My God, My God, why hast Thou forsaken Me?" (Mark 15: 34). This suffering of the Holy One can be understood only if we bear in mind that the Lord had laid on Him the iniquity of us all (Is. 53: 6), and that in His conscience

Jesus felt these sins as though they were His own; hence the agony of His soul (Matt. 26: 38). He experienced in His heart the fierceness of the wrath of God (Ps. 22: 14. 15). When He was forsaken of God, He suffered torments of hell. While the physical suffering of Christ was perhaps not greater than that of the malefactor, His soul suffering was incomprehensibly great. The eternity of hell torment we should have suffered was in the case of Christ counter-balanced by the fact that He is God. The damned in hell despair, but Christ in the midst of deepest agony clings to God and cries: "My God, My God." — And Christ really died; He "gave up the ghost" (Mark 15: 37); the soul departed from the body. The soldiers attest to the death of Christ (John 19: 28-37).

The personal union of the two natures in Christ was not disrupted by the death of His human nature. The soul of Christ was in Paradise (Luke 23: 43), and the lifeless body in the grave was still the body of the Son of God. The fact that this body did not see corruption (Acts 2: 31), shows that it still was in communion with the divine nature.

The death of Christ was an absolutely voluntary act on His part. "Therefore doth My Father love Me, because I lay down My life, that I might take it again. No man taketh it from Me, but I lay it down of Myself. I have power to lay it down, and I have power to take it again" (John 10: 17. 18). Men die, whether they will or not (Hebr. 9: 27); death is inevitable, brought on by various causes. However, when Christ bowed His head and gave up the ghost (John 19: 30), it was not of physical exhaustion or any other cause, but because He willed to die just then.

The suffering and the death were inflicted upon our Savior by God (Is. 53: 4), through men, the Jews, Pontius Pilate and the soldiers, because of our sins (Is. 53: 5). (Passive obedience.)

3. The Exaltation

(a) **Definition.**—Whereas the humiliation consisted in this that Christ did not constantly and fully use and display the divine majesty He possessed in His human nature, the exaltation, being the opposite, consists in this, that now also in

His human nature He fully and without restraint and inter-
ruption exercises the prerogatives of the divine nature.

(b) **Bible proof.**—Of the same Christ who had humbled
Himself we read: "Wherefore God also hath highly exalted
Him, and given Him a name which is above every name; that
at the name of Jesus every knee should bow, of things in
heaven, and things in earth, and things under the earth; and
that every tongue should confess that Jesus Christ is Lord,
to the glory of God the Father" (Phil. 2: 9-11). In the days
of His flesh Jesus hid the "form of God" under the "form of
a servant"; hence, many of the Jews failed to recognize Him
as "the Lord of glory" (1 Cor. 2: 8); but if the exalted Savior
were to appear among men now, as He will on the Day of
Judgment, then every knee would bow to Him, and every
tongue would confess that He is the Lord. The state of exaltation is not one merely of honor and glory, but one of power
and dominion, for God "set Him at His own right hand in the
heavenly places, far above all principality, and power, and
might, and dominion, and every name that is named, not only
in this world, but also in that which is to come: and hath put
all things under His feet" (Eph. 1: 20. 21); (1 Pet. 3: 22).

The exaltation, therefore, does not consist in this that the
human nature was received into union with the Son of God,
nor in this that divine attributes were communicated to the
human nature, but simply in this, that also in His human nature Christ now and forever makes full use of His divine
majesty and power, being present everywhere and upholding
and governing all things.

4. Stages of Exaltation

(a) **The descent of Christ into hell.**—The exaltation of
Christ began with His vivification, in which He exercised the
"power to take it" (His life) "again" (John 10: 18). After this
He immediately descended into hell. "Being put to death in
the flesh, but quickened by (in) the spirit; by (in) which
also He went, and preached to the spirits in prison, which
sometime were disobedient . . . " (1 Pet. 3: 18-20). "In the
flesh" does not mean the human nature of Christ, for in this
nature, the flesh, He was not only put to death, but also
quickened again; both, the death and the vivification took

place in the human nature. The term "in the flesh" refers to "the days of His flesh" (Hebr. 5: 7), to His earthly life, which began with His conception and ended with His death and burial. To be put to death, therefore, belonged to that part of life which He lived "in the flesh." "In the spirit" does not mean "by the Spirit," for we do not read that the Holy Spirit made Christ alive, but that it was Christ Himself who did this (John 10: 18). "In the spirit" is here used in contrast to "in the flesh," and it denotes that new life which began with His vivification, and which never ends. Hence, that Christ was put to death and buried, happened to Him in His earthly life; but that He was quickened and descended into hell, belongs into the new life "in the spirit."

Christ did not descend into hell only in His divine nature, or only in His soul; He descended also in His human nature, after He was quickened and the soul had returned into the body. The Savior went to that prison in which were the souls, spirits, of those who during their life on earth had been disobedient, unbelieving, when the Word of God was preached to them, as it had been to the generation in the days of Noah. Hence, Christ did not preach unto them repentance and forgiveness; but since they had despised the longsuffering of God when grace was offered to them, Christ now preached judgment to them, manifesting Himself, whom they had rejected, as the Victor over death and hell. In what manner this preaching was done, we do not know; but the mere fact that Christ showed Himself alive to those lost souls was enough to convince them of their just judgment.

Christ did not preach the Gospel of salvation to the damned souls in hell. One cannot prove this from 1 Pet. 4: 6, for this text speaks of men who now are dead, but to whom during their lives on earth the Gospel was preached for the purpose that, even though they die in the flesh, their souls should live. If, because of their disobedience, this gracious purpose of God was not achieved during their lives, they are, when dead, subject to His wrath and judgment (1 Pet. 4: 5).—Nor did Christ descend into hell to finish the work of redemption by further suffering. Christ's work was finished on the cross.—Nor did Christ descend into hell to liberate the souls of the Old Testament patriarchs from the "limbus patrum," as Romanists teach.

(b) **The resurrection of Christ a fact.**—There is no record that any man saw Jesus come out of the grave. When the angel rolled back the stone from the grave, Christ had already risen (Matt. 28: 1-7). Nevertheless, the resurrection of Christ is an established fact, which no one can disprove, although this has been tried in various ways.

The swoon theory: The theory that Christ fainted on the cross, was laid into the grave because the disciples "believed" Him to be dead, and that He, regaining consciousness, issued from the grave, and made His disciples believe that He had risen, must be dismissed in view of the certified fact that He really died on the cross (John 19: 30-36). It is exceedingly ridiculous for any one who lives nineteen hundred years after the event to entertain such a theory, since men, friends and foes of the Crucified, who were present on Calvary, testify to the death of Christ.

The theft theory: The Jews and Pontius Pilate were personally very much interested in this matter. They sealed the stone and set a watch (Matt. 27: 62-66). If the disciples had stolen the body (Matt. 28: 11-15), it would have been an easy matter for the public authorities to apprehend the thieves, and to force them to produce the body. And the Jews would have done so, if for no other reason than to ease their own conscience (Acts 5: 28). The theft theory lacks every reasonable foundation.

The hallucination theory: The disciples themselves were slow to believe that Christ had risen (Luke 24: 25; John 20: 25; Luke 24: 11). However, at different times, under different circumstances, He appeared to different groups of them. They saw Him, ate with Him, handled Him, and were thus in every conceivable way convinced of the fact that Christ had risen (Acts 1: 3; 2: 32; 1 Cor. 15: 4-8; Luke 24: 36-43). In view of these facts, the hallucination theory, according to which the disciples are said to have imagined that they had seen the Lord, is itself a hallucination.

The fraud theory: Nor was the testimony of these men a fraud and fabrication; for if it had been, the Jews could easily have proved it to be such. Besides, can any sane person assume that these disciples would have endured persecution and death (Acts 5: 41; 7: 56; 2 Cor. 11: 23-27), unless they had actually seen and heard the things they preached? (Acts 4: 20).

The resurrected body of Christ was the identical body that had died on the cross, and had been laid into the grave (John 20: 20-27). However, it had become a spiritual body, which is no longer subject to the laws and conditions to which it was subject before; it did not require food, rest, etc. The fact that the risen Savior did eat was to convince the disciples that He was not a spirit, but that He had a real body (Luke 24: 39-43). The resurrection fact is important because of its meaning.

The meaning of Christ's resurrection.—(1) Christ had repeatedly told the Jews that He is the Son of God (John 5: 17-23; 10: 30), and that His doctrine is of God (John 7: 16. 17; 8: 31. 32). While His miracles were sufficient to establish this claim (John 5: 36; 10: 25), the Jews again and again sought of Him a sign from heaven as a proof of His divine mission and authority. In answer to their request Christ points to His resurrection (Matt. 12: 38-40; John 2: 19). Since Christ did arise, He was by this resurrection declared to be the Son of God with power (Rom. 1: 4). If He is the Son of God, it follows that His doctrine is true.—Christ was either the Son of God, or a base deceiver, who pretended to be the Son of God; there is no other possibility. If He had been the latter, God certainly would not have permitted Him to arise, and thus help Him in His fraud. But "this Jesus hath God raised up, whereof we are witnesses" (Acts 2: 32). Thereby God Himself definitely showed that this Jesus is indeed His beloved Son, and that His doctrines are divine truths. The resurrection fact makes the position of modernists, who praise Christ as a model man but deny His Deity, absolutely untenable; while for Christians it strengthens their faith when doubts assail them.

(2) "Christ died for our sins" (1 Cor. 15: 3). If Christ had not risen, it would clearly show that His suffering and death had not been sufficient to atone for our sins and to reconcile us with God. Therefore Paul says: "If Christ be not raised, your faith is vain; ye are yet in your sins" (1 Cor. 15: 17). But now Christ is risen, and this is conclusive evidence that the Father accepted the sacrifice of His Son for the reconcili-

ation of the world. "Christ was delivered for our offenses, and was raised again for our justification" (Rom. 4: 25). Indeed, the resurrection of Christ does not make us just before God in the sense that it was a part of the ransom He paid for our sins, for the redemption was finished on the cross; but the resurrection *proves* to us that by His suffering and death Christ really did fully atone for our iniquities. Since it was God Himself who raised up Christ, God thereby declared that full satisfaction was rendered, that all sins are forgiven, and that we are just and righteous before Him. Since our surety is free, we, too, are free.—As Christ bore the sins of the whole world (John 1: 29), and died for all men (2 Cor. 5: 15), His resurrection proves that the sins of all men are fully expiated, that the world is reconciled to God, and that, therefore, the sins of men are no longer imputed to them, but forgiven (2 Cor. 5: 19). The resurrection of Christ is, therefore, of utmost significance to the whole world, inasmuch as it is the actual declaration on the part of God that, because of the redemption through Christ, He has in His heart absolved men of all sins, and regards men just and righteous, for we read: "By the righteousness of one the free gift came upon all men unto justification of life, for . . . by the obedience of one shall ·many be made righteous" (Rom. 5: 18. 19). This is commonly called Universal or Objective Justification. This justification, which took place in the court of heaven, would have remained unknown to man, if God had not revealed it in the Gospel. The Gospel, moreover, freely offers to all men this justification as an accomplished fact and for the purpose that men should by faith apply this fact to themselves and, in so doing, become personally justified (Rom. 3: 28). This we call Individual or Subjective Justification. This personal justification by faith is possible only because faith appropriates to itself the universal general justification. Without the preceding universal general justification there could be no Gospel to offer it, and no justification for faith to apprehend. Before a gift can be offered to man and be received and enjoyed by him, it must be ready. The resurrection of Christ proves that the gift of forgiveness before God is ready for all men.

(3) The resurrection of Christ proves that there is such a

thing as a resurrection of the dead (1 Cor. 15: 12. 16. 20), and that for the believers there is a resurrection unto life (John 14: 19; 11: 25. 26). Christ, who raised Himself from death (John 2: 19), has power to raise also us from death, and to give us eternal life (John 6: 40).

(c) **The forty days.**—During the forty days following His resurrection Christ did not live and sojourn with His disciples as He had done for about three years, "while I was yet with you" (Luke 24: 44). But He repeatedly appeared to them at different times and in different places to convince them of the fact of the resurrection, to expound to them the Scriptures (Luke 24: 25. 44. 45), and to give them further instruction concerning the kingdom of God and their mission on earth (Acts 1: 3-8).

(d) **The ascension of Christ.** — The ascension of Christ from Mount Olivet was in part witnessed by the disciples. "While they beheld, He was taken up; and a cloud received Him out of their sight" (Acts 1: 9). While He thus withdrew from them His visible presence, He promised to be with them unto the end of the world (Matt. 28: 20). His human nature, therefore, is not confined somewhere to a definite circumscribed place, for He "ascended up far above all heavens, that He might fill all things" (Eph. 4: 10). Hence, in both, His divine and His human nature, Christ is still with us, and present everywhere.—Having finished His work on earth, He triumphantly returned as the Victor over sin and hell (Eph. 4: 8) into the glory of His Father (John 17: 4. 5; Luke 24: 26). This heaven is not a limited space in, or part of, this created physical world; it is the Father's house in which there are many mansions, where Christ has gone to prepare a place for us, and where we shall be with Him (John 14: 2. 3; Phil. 1: 23); it is the right hand of the majesty of God (Hebr. 1: 3).

(e) **Session at the right hand of God.**—"He was received up into heaven, and sat on the right hand of God" (Mark 16: 19). The right hand of God is not a circumscribed locality in a spatial heaven, but the infinite power and majesty of God, filling all in all and ruling all things (Exod. 15: 6; Ps. 118: 16; 139: 7-10; Is. 48: 13; Matt. 26: 64). To sit at the right hand of God, therefore, means to occupy a position of supreme power and dominion. God "set Him at His own right hand in the heavenly places, far above all principality, and power, and might, and dominion, and every name that is named, not only in this world, but also in that which is to come; and hath put all things under His feet, and gave Him to be the Head over all things to the Church, which is His body, the fulness of Him that filleth all in all" (Eph. 1: 20-23; 1 Pet. 3: 22).

The divine nature of Christ always was at the right hand of God, i.e., it always exercised sovereign dominion over all things (John 5: 17-23). Also to the human nature this majesty was communicated; but during His humiliation Christ refrained from making full use thereof. But now also this human nature fully participates in the actual exercise of this sovereign authority and dominion. (Cf., F. C., Th. D., Art. VIII, 78, *Triglot*, p. 1043).

It is a great comfort for us Christians to know that He, who has all power in heaven and on earth, is our dear Savior. He, who is the Lord over all, is also the Head of the Church, which is His spiritual body. His Christians are closer to Him than anything else; hence, He uses His sovereign power over all things in the interest and for the benefit of His friends. As Joseph in Egypt used his royal power for the benefit of his brethren (Gen. 46 and 47), so Christ governs the universe for the particular well-being of His Christians. As the head makes everything subservient to the welfare of the body, so Christ, the Head of the Church, lovingly governs and mightily protects His Church, and manages the affairs of the world so that all things work together for the good of His Christians (Rom. 8: 28).

The exalted Savior continues to perform His threefold office as Prophet, Priest, and King. As our Prophet He gives us teachers (Eph. 4: 8-12); as our High Priest He intercedes for us (Rom. 8: 34); as our King He governs the kingdom of power in the interest of His kingdom of grace (Eph. 1: 20-23).

(f) **For the return of Christ unto judgment,** which also belongs to the state of exaltation, cf., pp. 296 ff., 304 ff.

XXI. THE WORK OR OFFICE OF THE REDEEMER

The work of Christ was repeatedly referred to in the discussion of His theanthropic person and of His life in the states of humiliation and exaltation. Briefly stated, it consists in this: "The Son of Man is come to save that which was lost" (Matt. 18: 11); "Christ came into the world to save sinners" (1 Tim. 1: 15). Whatever Christ did and still does serves this one purpose, and is motivated by the tender mercies and love of God for man (John 3: 16; 1 John 4: 9. 10; Luke 1: 78). Thus, the work of Christ is a unit, having for its single purpose the salvation of mankind.

However, Scripture distinguishes three distinct phases of this work. Christ Himself says: "The Spirit of the Lord is upon Me, because He hath anointed Me to preach the Gospel to the poor" (Luke 4: 18); "the Son of Man came . . . to give His life a ransom for many" (Matt. 20: 28); "thou sayest that I am a King" (John 18: 37). On the basis of such and similar statements, we differentiate between the Prophetic, the Priestly, and the Kingly Office of Christ.

1. The Prophetic Office

(a) **What is a prophet?**—A prophet is one who speaks for another, as Aaron was to speak to Pharaoh for Moses (Exod. 7: 1). A prophet of God is one who speaks for God, making known and interpreting the word and will of God to man. A prophet, therefore, is God's representative and ambassador to man (2 Cor. 5: 20).

Christ is a prophet.—That the Messiah was to be a prophet is revealed in the Old Testament. "The Lord, thy God, will raise up unto thee a Prophet" (Deut. 18: 15). That these words apply to Jesus we learn from Acts 3: 19-26. When God, speaking of Jesus, commands us: "Hear ye Him" (Matt. 17: 5), He thereby designates Him as His Prophet who is to speak to us for God. In Luke 13: 33 Christ refers to Himself as a prophet, and He was regarded by His followers as "a prophet mighty in deed and word before God and all the people" (Luke 24: 19); (Luke 4: 18).

Christ is The Prophet.—Christ is not a prophet of the same type and rank as other prophets mentioned in Scripture. Moses tells the Jews: "Unto Him ye shall hearken" (Deut. 18: 15), thereby placing that future prophet above himself. (Cf., Hebr. 3: 1-6). In fact, all revelation of God to man comes to us through Christ. "No man hath seen God at any time; the only begotten Son, which is in the bosom of the Father,

He hath declared Him" (John 1: 18). It is for this reason that He is called "Word" or "Logos" (John 1: 1). As words reveal our hidden thoughts, so the Son of God is called the "Word" of God, because He declared, made known, to man the thoughts, the will, of God. God dwells in a light which no man can approach unto (1 Tim. 6: 16), and no man can of himself know anything of God. But He who is in the bosom of the Father and, therefore, has intimate knowledge of the innermost thoughts of God, has declared and revealed Him to man. In this sense Christ is the one and only Prophet, and there is no revelation of the true God but by Him.

(b) **Christ performed His prophetic office through the holy men of God.**—Peter tells us that the holy men of God spake as they were moved by the Holy Ghost (2 Pet. 1: 21). The same apostle informs us that it was the Spirit of Christ which was in these holy men (1 Pet. 1: 11). And Paul tells us that it was Christ who dealt with the children of Israel in the wilderness (1 Cor. 10: 4. 9). Hence, even before His incarnation it was Christ, the Son of God, who made known to Moses and the prophets the word and will of God by sending His Spirit into their hearts.—The same is true of the New Testament writers, of whom Paul tells us that they spoke as the Holy Ghost taught them (1 Cor. 2: 13). But also here it was Christ who, according to His promise (John 15: 26), gave to the evangelists and apostles the Spirit of truth that guided them into all truth (John 16: 13. 14; Gal. 1: 12). Thus, all revelation of God as we have it in the Bible comes to us from Christ through the Holy Ghost, "who spake by the prophets."

Christ performed His prophetic office directly.—In the days of His flesh the Son of God did not speak to the people through inspired men, but He spoke to them personally and directly. "God, who at sundry times and in divers manners spake in time past unto the fathers by the prophets, hath in these last days spoken unto us by His Son" (Hebr. 1: 1. 2). However, there is this difference between Christ and the prophets: they spoke by inspiration of the Holy Ghost, but Christ spoke from personal and immediate knowledge. Jesus did not receive His knowledge of divine truths by revelation of the Holy Ghost, but His divine nature possessed it originally from the beginning, because He was in the bosom of the

Father (John 1: 18). And when the Word was made flesh, He communicated this knowledge to His human nature. Hence, He could say: "All things that I have heard of My Father I have made known unto you" (John 15: 15); "I speak to the world those things which I have heard of Him" (John 8: 26); (John 3: 11). John the Baptist says of Him: "He that cometh from heaven is above all. And what He hath seen and heard, that He testifieth" (John 3: 31. 32). As Christ performed miracles by His own power, so He spoke from His own knowledge.

Christ performs His prophetic office through the ministry of the Word.—He gave unto His disciples His Word (John 17: 14), and charged them to teach all nations the things He had commanded them (Matt. 28: 20). As they do so, Christ Himself, through their teaching and preaching, still makes known to men the Word and will of God. "He that heareth you heareth Me" (Luke 10: 16). Moreover, it is the exalted Savior who continues to give to His Church men that teach and preach His Gospel (Eph. 4: 11. 12). Whenever, therefore, these men continue faithfully in the word of Christ, as they should (John 8: 31), then it is Christ Himself who through them performs to this day His prophetic office. But if any one teaches error and false doctrine, then it is not Christ who performs His prophetic office through him (1 Tim. 4: 1).

(c) **The content of this prophecy.**—In a wider sense the prophecy of Christ comprised the revelation of all the will of God, both Law and Gospel. In the Sermon on the Mount Jesus did not become a new lawgiver, but He merely restated and expounded what He had before revealed through Moses.

However, the Law is not the chief part of God's revelation to man (Gal. 3: 17-24). The promises of the Messiah and their fulfillment in Christ, which is the Gospel, is the principal thing. Hence, Christ preached the "Gospel of the kingdom of God" (Mark 1: 14), and tells us that He was anointed to preach the Gospel to the poor (Luke 4: 18). Thus the entire prophecy of Christ centers in His person and in His work (John 3: 14-17). He revealed Himself and by the preaching of the Gospel still reveals Himself to men as the Son of God and the Redeemer of the world. In other words, in His prophetic office He makes known to the world what He procured for all men in His priestly office.

2. The Priestly Office

(a) **What is a priest?**—A priest is one who by means of intercession and sacrifice aims to reconcile man to God, i.e., to restore man to the favor of God. He deals with God for, and in behalf of, man. "Every high priest taken from among men is ordained for men in things pertaining to God, that he may offer both gifts and sacrifices for sins" (Hebr. 5: 1); (Lev. 16). While the prophet deals with men for God in God's place, the priest deals with God for man in man's place. The priest represents man before God.

Christ is our High Priest.—That the Messiah was to be a priest was foretold in the Old Testament (Ps. 110: 14; Zech. 6: 13), and foreshadowed in the Levitical priesthood of Israel. In the New Testament the Epistle to the Hebrews, chapters 5-10, shows that Christ is the one and only High Priest that actually reconciled the world unto God.

"For such an High Priest became us" (we had need of) "who is holy, harmless, undefiled, separate from sinners, and made higher than the heavens; who needeth not daily, as those high priests, to offer up sacrifice, first for His own sins, and then for the people's: for this He did once, when He offered up Himself. For the law maketh men high priests which have infirmity; but the word of the oath, which was since the law, maketh the Son, who is consecrated for evermore" (Hebr. 7: 26-28). This text clearly points out the difference between Christ and the other priests. They were men, having sin and infirmity; Christ is the Son of God, holy and perfect and higher than the heavens. They had to sacrifice first for their own sins; Christ had no sins of His own for which to sacrifice. They offered animals; Christ offered up Himself, and thus He was both the Priest and the Sacrifice. The necessary repetition of their sacrifices proved them to be ineffective (Hebr. 10: 1. 2); by one sacrifice Christ effected an eternal redemption (Hebr. 9: 12; 10: 14).

(b) **Meaning of Old Testament sacrifices.**—As "it is not possible that the blood of bulls and of goats should take away sins" (Hebr. 10: 4), so the sacrifices of the Old Testament could not atone for sin. Still, they were by no means useless and without benefit to the people. They were shadows of the good things to come, and had value and power inasmuch as they prefigured Christ's sacrifice on Calvary. As a gold certificate is secured by the gold in the government's treasury, so these sacrifices were secured by God's own sacrifice on the cross, and were means by which the merits of this sacrifice were offered to the faithful. By their own virtue these sacrifices did not expiate sin (Micah 6: 6. 7; Hebr. 10: 4), but being symbolical shadows of Christ, they offered the forgiveness achieved by His sacrifice. Thus, in appearance they were sacrifices, but in their effect they were sacraments or means of grace.

3. The Work of Our High Priest

(a) **The ransom.**—To reconcile sinful man to God, our High Priest had to give a ransom that was sufficient and acceptable to God. Such a ransom was not silver and gold (1 Pet. 1: 18). The redemption of a soul is so precious, costs so much, that all the treasures of this world are of no avail to achieve redemption. Here the rich man has no advantage over his poor neighbor; his millions will not win for him the favor of God, and buy him a place in heaven (Ps. 49: 6-8). Nor can the blood of bulls and goats cleanse us from sin (Hebr. 10: 4). Not even a human sacrifice is sufficiently precious. "Shall I give my firstborn for my transgression, the fruit of my body for the sin of my soul?" (Micah 6: 7). Deep heartfelt sorrow and penitent tears will not blot out our transgressions, and many good works will not make amends for one sin we have committed.

Only God can reconcile the world unto Himself. The sin we commit may seem small to us, but, being committed against God (Ps. 51: 4), its guilt must be measured by the greatness of Him against whom it is committed. Likewise must the value of the sacrifice for sin measure up to the greatness of Him, who is to be appeased and conciliated thereby. Not beast, not man, but God alone can expiate and extinguish our guilt of sin and reconcile us to God. If Christ had not been true God, His life and death would not have been a sufficient ransom for our souls. But "God was in Christ, reconciling the world unto Himself" (2 Cor. 5: 19). The value of Christ's ransom is, therefore, not determined by the duration and the intensity of His suffering, but by the fact that He was and is true God. Luther says: "We Christians must know that if God is not also in the balance, and gives the weight, we sink to the bottom with our scale. By this I mean: If it were not to be said, God has died for us, but only man, we should be lost" (F. C., Th. D., Art. VIII, 44, *Triglot,* p. 1029). The fact that God was in Christ gives infinite worth to all our Savior did and suffered, and is, at the same time, the absolute guaranty that His sacrifice is sufficient and acceptable to God; for God certainly would not so atone for our sins that He Himself is not satisfied therewith.

(b) **Satisfaction.**— To reconcile man unto God, our High Priest had to do two things: He had to satisfy the demands of God's holiness by His active obedience, and also the demands of God's justice by His passive obedience.

The active obedience of Christ.—God is holy. He made man holy, and demands that man be and remain holy (Lev. 19: 2; Matt. 5: 48). To meet this demand of God it was necessary for man to keep the Law perfectly, which he did not do and could not do (Eccl. 7:20). *Without a perfect fulfillment of the Law a reconciliation with God is impossible.* To satisfy these demands of God's Law, and to make good our delinquencies and shortcomings, the Son of God was made man, became our substitute, was made under the Law, that He might keep and fulfill it in our stead (Gal. 4: 4. 5; Matt. 5: 17; 3: 15). This He did, for He is "the end of the Law" (Rom. 10: 4). During His entire life Jesus kept the Law fully and perfectly, not for Himself, but for us, "who were under the Law." This holy life, in which by His active obedience He satisfied the demands of God's holiness with respect to our obligations under the Law, is one part of the ransom and sacrifice of Christ for our reconciliation with God.

The passive obedience of Christ.—God is just. He cannot condone sin (Ps. 5: 4. 5). No sin is forgiven unless it is atoned for, and full satisfaction is made by suffering the penalty. *Without a full atonement for sin a reconciliation with God is impossible.* Since man cannot do this, Christ again takes man's place. "The Lord laid on Him the iniquity of us all" (Is. 53:

6), and visited our sins upon Him (Is. 53: 5). Christ bare our sins in His own body on the tree (1 Pet. 2: 24), and thus was made a curse for us (Gal. 3: 13). In the suffering of Christ God "declared His righteousness" (Rom. 3: 25), His justice, which demands that the sins of the world must be expiated, if they are to be forgiven. Since by His holy precious blood and His innocent suffering and death (1 Pet. 1: 18. 19), Christ did fully atone for the sins of men, as proved by His resurrection from the dead, God no longer imputes them to us (2 Cor. 5: 19), but has forgiven them. Thus, by His vicarious suffering and death Christ satisfied the demands of God's justice with respect to the punishment man should have suffered for his sins. The passive obedience is the other part of the ransom Christ paid for the redemption of our souls.

(c) **Universal redemption.** — When Paul writes: "Christ loved the Church and gave Himself for it" (Eph. 5: 25), he does not mean to say that the redemption was limited to the Church, the believers, the elect. For while it is true that these are the only ones who actually receive the benefit of His redemption, the Bible is very explicit in stating that Christ redeemed all men. He is the Lamb of God that taketh away the sins of the world (John 1: 29); He is the propitiation for the sins of the whole world (1 John 2: 2; 1 Tim. 2: 6); He reconciled the world unto God (2 Cor. 5: 19); even they who are ultimately lost in hell were bought by Him (2 Pet. 2: 1). There is no human being that was overlooked, for Christ tasted death for every man (Hebr. 2: 9). While there is no redemption for the fallen angels, there is a perfect redemption for all men, even for the vilest of them. "This is a faithful saying, and worthy of all acceptation, that Christ Jesus came into the world to save sinners; of whom I am chief" (1 Tim. 1: 15). All nations and races may gather under the cross of Christ, and find redemption there.

(d) **The fruit of the redemption.**—In Luther's explanation of the Second Article of the Apostles' Creed we confess that Christ has redeemed us from sin, from death, and from the power of the devil.

Christ redeemed us from sin.—Christ did not free us from sin in the sense that He committed the act of sin for us; for **the fact that** we sinned cannot be undone. We must distinguish the act of sin from the guilt of sin. As we committed the act, the guilt really was ours (Rom. 3: 19), but our *guilt* was laid on, and charged to, Christ, who assumed all blame and responsibility for our transgressions (Is. 53: 4-6). The act was ours, the guilt became His. Thus He, who knew no sin, was made to be sin for us, and we, who are guilty, become righteous through Him (2 Cor. 5: 21).—They who trust in the merits of Christ have, therefore, a good conscience before God, a conscience free from guilt (Hebr. 9: 14; 1 Pet. 3: 21). Faith in Christ is the only and the sure remedy for a guilty conscience.

Since Christ bore our guilt, He took on Himself also our *punishment*. He was made a curse for us (Gal. 3: 13); He suffered our chastisement (Is. 53: 5), our death (Hebr. 2: 9); (cf., the story of Christ's Passion). Because the Lord had laid on Him the iniquity of us all, it pleased God to bruise Him and put Him to grief (Is. 53: 6. 10). In our place He suffered what we had deserved, hence we are free from the curse and the punishment of sin, and may look forward to meet our God without fear and trembling. "Verily, verily, I say unto you, he that heareth My word, and believeth on Him that sent Me, hath everlasting life, and shall not come into condemnation; but is passed from death unto life" (John 5: 24). Faith in Christ banishes from the heart all fear of judgment and punishment.

The external consequences of sin, indeed, remain, such as toilsome labor, tribulation, disease, pain, temporal death, etc., (Gen. 3: 16-19; Acts 14: 22); yet these are no longer to be regarded as punishments for sin, but are fatherly chastisements intended for our good (Hebr. 12: 6. 7). The cross we bear has disciplinary, pedagogical value (1 Cor. 11: 32; Hebr. 12: 11).

By nature man is a servant and slave of sin; he can do nothing but sin (Rom. 7: 14); but Christ has redeemed us from the *dominion and bondage* of sin, from the "vain conversation," worthless manner of living, from a life controlled by sin (1 Pet. 1: 18. 19). Christ "gave Himself for us, that He might redeem us from all iniquity, and purify unto Himself a peculiar people, zealous of good works" (Titus 2: 14). Here Paul does not teach that Christ redeemed us from the guilt of our iniquity before God, but from the power and control of sin in our personal lives. They who believe in Christ are by this faith sanctified that they need not, and will not, let sin reign in their mortal bodies to obey the lusts thereof. Sin shall have no dominion over them, who by faith stand in the grace of God (Rom. 6: 12-14; 2 Cor. 5: 15). Indeed, also the believers still have their old Adam, which lusteth against the Spirit (Gal. 5: 17; Rom. 7: 14-21), but while they sin daily, faith in Christ enables them to resist sin, so that it does not gain dominion over them.

Christ redeemed us from death. — Death is separation. Spiritual death is separation of the heart, the soul from God; "whose heart departeth from the Lord" (Jer. 17: 5). Temporal death is separation of the soul from the body; "Jesus . . . yielded up the ghost" (Matt. 27: 50). Eternal death is the eternal separation of body and soul from the blissful presence of God; "depart from Me, ye cursed, into everlasting fire" (Matt. 25: 41).

Spiritual death consists in this that the heart of man is given to sin (Eph. 2: 1), and is without true fear and love of God and without trust in Him. If Christ had not redeemed us from sin, we could never trustingly believe in God for the remission of our sins, and we could not truly fear and love Him. Hence, we should have to remain in despair and spiritual death. But the redemption through Christ makes it possible for us to believe in a merciful God, who forgives sin, and thereby spiritual life is regained (Eph. 2: 5. 6). This is the "first resurrection" as distinguished from the "second" or bodily resurrection (John 5: 25. 28).

Although by faith in Christ we have regained spiritual life, we are, nevertheless, subject to temporal death (Gen. 3: 19; Hebr. 9: 27). As man was not created to die, he experiences a natural horror of death. But Christ "delivered them who through fear of death were all their lifetime subject to bondage" (Hebr. 2: 15). For Christians temporal death is no longer a punishment, but merely a change of existence, and a change for the better; it is the passageway that leads us to the beautiful mansions of God in heaven. "Blessed are the dead which die in the Lord from henceforth" (Rev. 14: 13). Knowing that heaven is beyond, they are not terrified at the thought of death, for death has lost its sting, and the grave its victory (1 Cor. 15: 55-57); they have much rather "a desire to depart, and to be with Christ, which is far better" (Phil. 1: 23). It is this hope of salvation that helps us to overcome the natural dread of death.

Eternal death has no power over Christians, because Christ has "abolished death, and hath brought life and immortality to light" (2 Tim. 1: 10). They who believe in Him shall not die eternally (John 11: 26), but have everlasting life (John 3: 16). Thus Christ redeemed us from eternal death, the fear of which hangs like a gloomy pall over the lives of men.

Christ redeemed us from the power of the devil.—It is by sin that the devil gained power over man (Gen. 3). Whoever, therefore, commits sin, is of the devil (1 John 3: 8), who seeks to fasten his control over him by tempting and leading him deeper into sin (1 Thess. 3: 5). Because of our sinfulness we are utterly helpless against these temptations. The devil also has power to accuse us before God (Rev. 12: 10), and we cannot deny his charges.

"The Son of God was manifested, that He might destroy the works of the devil" (1 John 3: 8). He did this when as our substitute He successfully resisted the temptation of the devil (Matt. 4: 3-11), and when by His vicarious death He fully paid the penalty of our guilt (Gen. 3: 15; Hebr. 2: 14).

While this deliverance from the power of the devil is procured for all men, only they enjoy it who personally believe in Jesus Christ. They are able in the strength of faith to resist and to overcome the temptations of the devil (1 Pet. 5: 8. 9; Eph. 6: 11; James 4: 7). Though by reason of the weakness of their flesh they still fall into sin, the devil cannot accuse them before God, because Christ is their Advocate (1 John 2: 1. 2), and no one may lay anything to their charge (Rom. 8: 33).

It was by sin that man brought upon himself guilt and punishment; thereby he became subject to spiritual, temporal, and eternal death; thereby he put himself under the power of the devil. By redeeming us from sin Christ delivered us from all of these.

(e) **The priestly office of Christ in the state of exaltation.** —The priestly office of Christ did not cease with His sacrificial death on the cross, but is continued in heaven (Hebr. 7: 24. 25). However, He no longer atones for our sins (Rom. 6: 9; Hebr. 9: 12. 13; 7: 27), but on the basis of His redemptive work, finished in the state of humiliation, He now intercedes, speaks, pleads for men that the merits of His work be applied to them for righteousness and salvation (Rom. 8: 34; Hebr. 7: 25). "If any man sin, we have an Advocate with the Father, Jesus Christ the righteous: and He is the propitiation for our sins: and not for our's only, but also for the sins of the whole world" (1 John 2: 1. 2). If we fall into sin, the devil, our adversary, has indeed a good case against us to accuse us before God (Rev. 12: 10). It is then that our Advocate intercedes for us, and, pointing to His propitiation for the sins of the world, He pleads for mercy and grace. But Christ does not intercede for those who, having died in unbelief, are in hell. To them He is not an Advocate, but the Judge. He intercedes only for those who still live in this world.

That Christ intercedes for the believers we see from Rom. 8: 33. 34, where we read: "Who shall lay anything to the charge of God's elect? It is God that justifieth. Who is he that condemneth? It is Christ that died, yea rather, that is risen again, who is even at the right hand of God, who also maketh intercession for us." Christ prayed for His disciples and for all those who should believe on Him through their word (John 17: 20). He makes intercession for them that come unto God by Him (Hebr. 7: 25). What a comfort for us to know that in spite of our sins and weaknesses Christ pleads for us, shielding us with the merits of His redemption, in which we trust. Christ takes a very personal interest in each of His believers.

Christ prays also for the world, but not that it might continue in its wicked ways (John 17: 9), but that the time of grace be extended (Luke 13: 6-9), and that men might hear the Gospel and be converted (Rom. 2: 4; 2 Pet. 3: 9). That the unbeliever, the fruitless tree, is not cut off in his sins, but continues to live and has opportunity to hear the Gospel, he owes to the intercession of the Savior. The intercession of Christ for the world supports our mission work.

Christ is the only Advocate (1 Tim. 2: 5). The saints and

the Virgin Mary are not qualified for this work, as they are neither personally righteous, nor have they done anything that might support their reputed plea in our behalf. But Christ is righteous, and He is the propitiation for the sins of the world. He, therefore, has a right to speak for us, and His intercession is effective (Rom. 8: 34).

4. The Kingly Office

(a) **Christ a King.**—A king is he who has power and authority to rule a country. That the Messiah was to be a King was prophesied (2 Sam. 7: 12), where God promised to establish the kingdom of David's Son. And in Zech. 9: 9 the prophet exhorts Jerusalem to rejoice at the coming of its King. Christ was of the house and lineage of David (Luke 2: 4), and when He was born, the Wise Men from the East inquired about the new-born King of the Jews (Matt. 2: 2). Jerusalem hailed Him as its King (Luke 19: 38), and before Pilate Jesus testified that He was indeed a King (John 18: 37).

Christ is not a worldly king.—Jesus was not the kind of king the Jews, or even His disciples, expected—a king who was to "restore again the kingdom of Israel" (Acts 1: 6). For unto Pilate Jesus said: "My kingdom is not of this world . . . but now is My kingdom not from hence" (John 18: 36). Christ was not an earthly king, not a rival of Herod and of Caesar; His kingdom is not like that of David and of Solomon. His kingship and His kingdom are far greater than that of any earthly potentate.

(b) It is customary to distinguish the kingdom of power, and of grace, and of glory.

The kingdom of power is not limited to any geographic region on earth, but it comprehends the entire universe, and extends to all creatures, visible and invisible. Christ says: "All power is given unto Me in heaven and in earth" (Matt. 28: 18). God "hath put all things under His feet" (Eph. 1: 22); (1 Cor. 15: 25). And there is nothing that is not under Him (Hebr. 2: 8). He upholds all things by the word of His power (Hebr. 1: 3). He controls the forces of nature and the destiny of nations; without His will not a sparrow falls to the ground, nor a hair from our head. Good and evil are subject to Him (Ps. 110: 2; Phil. 2: 9-11). He is the Lord of lords, the King of kings (Rev. 17: 14). (Cf., Divine Providence, p. 37 ff.).

The kingdom of grace does not include all creatures, not even all men, but only those who through the preaching of the Gospel of the kingdom (Mark 1: 14. 15) have been born again (John 3: 3. 5). Only true believers are citizens in this kingdom (Eph. 2: 19). This kingdom Christ Himself describes as one which is established, not by war and bloodshed, but by the witness of the truth, and which is governed not by man-made laws and ordinances, but solely by His Word (John 18: 37). This kingdom has proved itself stronger than the kingdoms of this world; the mighty Roman Empire, which Pilate represented, has passed away, but the kingdom of the Crucified One has continued and flourished in spite of bloody persecution, frivolous ridicule, disrupting heresy, and science falsely so called, and it will continue to the end of time (Ps. 2: 1-9; 46: 4. 5; Matt. 16: 18).

It is called the kingdom of grace, because it is the promise and offer of divine grace that wins men for this kingdom; it is the acceptance of this grace by faith that makes them citizens in this kingdom; it is the appreciation of this grace that makes them render willing obedience to their King. The essence of this kingdom, therefore, is not an external organization, like a congregation, a denomination, or the visible church in the world, but ". . . the kingdom of God is within you" (Luke 17: 20. 21); it is the rule of Christ in the hearts of His believers. For the individual the kingdom of God consists in his personal relation to Christ, established by faith, by which he trusts in the grace of his Savior and renders joyful service to his Lord. This kingdom, therefore, comes to us "when our heavenly Father gives us His Holy Spirit, so that by His grace we believe His holy Word, and lead a godly life" (Luther's explanation to the Second Petition of the Lord's Prayer). But as there are many others who thus believe in Christ and serve Him, the kingdom of grace includes all those whom Christ gathers by the preaching of the Gospel, who acknowledge Him their King, and are governed by His Spirit. (Cf., Of the Church, p. 236).

The kingdom of glory is not on earth, but in heaven, where Christ Himself shall have all glory (Luke 24: 26; 2 Tim. 4: 18;

John 17: 24), and where those who have been faithful unto death shall likewise be crowned with glory and honor (Phil. 3: 21; Rom. 8: 18). The souls of the believers enter this kingdom of glory in the hour of death (Luke 23: 43); after the resurrection also their bodies shall inherit the kingdom prepared for them (Matt. 25: 34). (Cf., Eternal Salvation, p. 313 ff.).

(c) **Distinct but not separate.**—While we properly distinguish a threefold kingdom, we must not separate one from the other as though they had nothing in common. As a matter of fact, there is a close relation between them. There is one and the same King, who rules these three kingdoms, and there is one dominant purpose in their government.

Christ rules the kingdom of power for the benefit of His kingdom of grace. From Eph. 1: 20-23 we learn that Christ, who has supreme rule over all things (kingdom of power), is the Head of the Church, which is His body (kingdom of grace). This means that Christ exercises His lordship and power over all things in the interest of those people who constitute His spiritual body. As Joseph used his high position in Egypt for the benefit of his brethren, giving them the best land (Gen. 47: 11), even so does Christ use His omnipotent power and dominion over all things for the particular benefit of His brethren in the flesh. Thus the world continues to exist, and is governed by Christ to this end that He might gather and build His Church, bringing men to faith and preserving them therein. Because He has all power in heaven and on earth, He sends out His Christians to preach the Gospel to all men (Matt. 28: 18. 19), and so protects His Church that the forces of evil shall not prevail against it (Matt. 16: 18). Since we know that our Friend and Savior is the Sovereign Ruler of all things, we may rest assured "that all things work together for good to them that love God" (Rom. 8: 28). The salvation of sinners is by no means an incidental side issue in the government of the world, but it is the chief issue. The world continues for no other purpose than this, that sinners might come to repentance (2 Pet. 3: 9).

The kingdom of grace serves the kingdom of glory. Christ's purpose in building His Church in this world is not merely to establish an ecclesiastical organization which is to serve temporal interests. It is true that Christians are the salt of the earth (Matt. 5: 13), who by their good influence counteract the moral corruption among men. However, the chief purpose of the kingdom of grace is to win and to prepare men for the kingdom of heaven. We hope in Christ not only in this life (1 Cor. 15: 19), but are begotten again unto a lively hope, to an inheritance incorruptible and undefiled, that fadeth not away, and is reserved in heaven for us who are kept by the power of God unto salvation (1 Pet. 1: 3-5).

Neither the world nor the Church exist for purposes of their own, but for this one thing, that sinners may be converted and be won for the kingdom of glory. In order that this may be accomplished, the government of the world and of the Church is placed in the hands of Him who came to save sinners.

5. The Purpose of the Work of Christ

The purpose of the work of Christ in His threefold office is the salvation of sinners. In His priestly office He procured for all men forgiveness of sins, life, and salvation. In His prophetic office He makes this fact known to men, and freely offers to all the blessings of His redemption, and thus would draw them to Himself. In His regal office He so rules all things that through the ministry of the Church men attain to the glory prepared for them.

For the individual the purpose of Christ's work is adequately expressed in the words of Luther's explanation of the Second Article of the Apostles' Creed, where he says: ". . . that I may be His own, and live under Him in His kingdom, and serve Him in everlasting righteousness, innocence, and blessedness, even as He is risen from the dead, lives and reigns to all eternity." We are not our own (1 Cor. 6: 19) to live as we please, and to do what our natural heart desires, and to walk in our own selfish ways. But since God has purchased us with His blood (Acts 20: 28; 1 Cor. 6: 20), we now belong to Him, and are His purchased possession (Eph. 1: 14). In grateful appreciation of our deliverance from sin, death, and the power of the devil we should glorify God in body and soul (1 Cor. 6: 20), by living under Him in His kingdom of grace, and gladly serving Him in righteousness and holiness all the days of our lives (Luke 1: 74. 75). "He died for all that they which live should not henceforth live unto themselves, but unto Him which died for them and rose again" (2 Cor. 5: 15).

As Christ is risen, lives and reigns to all eternity, so we likewise shall arise from death, and live and reign with our Lord in the kingdom of glory to all eternity. "It is a faithful saying: For if we be dead with Him, we shall also live with Him: if we suffer, we shall also reign with Him" (2 Tim. 2: 11. 12). "My sheep hear My voice, and I know them, and they follow Me: and I give unto them eternal life; and they shall never perish, neither shall any man pluck them out of My hand" (John 10: 27. 28).

PART VII. SALVATION BY THE GRACE OF GOD THROUGH THE SANCTIFICATION OF THE HOLY SPIRIT

XXII. CONVERSION NOT THE WORK OF MAN, BUT OF GOD

Relation between the work of redemption and the work of sanctification.—By the work of redemption Christ procured for all men forgiveness of sins, life, and eternal salvation. But all this would not benefit any man if it were not for the work of sanctification. For if men are to be saved by the redemption in Christ, its merits must be offered, imparted to, and received by them. This work is especially ascribed to the Holy Ghost, and is called the work of sanctification. This term, when taken in its wider sense, comprehends all those phases of the Holy Spirit's work, by which He leads sinners from the state of wrath into the state of grace, and preserves them therein until they enter into the state of glory in heaven.

A. Conversion Not the Work of Man

Pelagianism and the various forms of Synergism hold that natural man can by his own powers turn from sin to the Savior, believe in Him, and thus be saved; or that he can, in a measure at least, cooperate with the Holy Ghost in bringing about his own conversion. They admit that the redemption was effected without man's cooperation; but they insist that man can and must contribute something positive, be it ever so little, towards his conversion, and unless he does so, he cannot be converted. Synergism is a false teaching, resulting from attempts to explain why some are converted, while others remain unconverted. But we shall see that, while man can be converted, he can do nothing towards his conversion.

Man is capable of conversion.—As man is not an insensible block nor an irrational brute, but is endowed with a rational soul, which possesses mental, emotional, and volitional powers, his conversion is, indeed, possible, as is evidenced by the fact that men are actually converted. However, the fact that man is capable of being converted does not prove that he is also able to convert himself or to contribute anything towards his conversion. Iron can be melted, but it cannot melt itself; the dead shall be raised, but they cannot raise themselves; men are converted, but no one has ever converted himself or helped in bringing about his conversion. Conversion is a passive experience. "It is true that man before his conversion is still a rational creature, having an understanding and a will, however, not an understanding with respect to divine things, or a will to will something good and salutary" (F. C., Th. D., Art. II, 59, *Triglot,* p. 905).

Natural man can by diligent study acquire an intellectual knowledge (Kopferkenntnis) of the truths of the Gospel; he can meditate upon them and discourse concerning them. (F. C., Th. D., Art. II, 24, *Triglot,* p. 891). Such knowledge is indeed necessary for faith (Rom. 10: 14); but, in itself, it is not faith, and a person having only this knowledge is not converted. There are those who know the truths of the Gospel, and they know them well; still, they do not believe them, do not put their trust in them, but are perhaps vehemently opposed to them.—The powers of the mind are instruments by which we acquire knowledge and understanding, but in no case do they, of themselves, affect and touch the heart to accept and to believe what we have learned. The power to do this lies not in the means by which we learn, but in the *things* which we have learned. Thus a message may, according to its peculiar content, either gladden or sadden our hearts. Yet it is not our psychic faculties that produce this effect; they only make us capable of experiencing it. The effect is produced by the message itself. Thus it is with the Law and the Gospel; they are the *external* means, by which God teaches us His truths. Our mental powers are the *internal* means, by which we learn and apperceive them. But it is the truths that make an impression on us, creating in us an emotional response. The Law works in us sorrow, contrition, and despair; the Gospel works faith and love and hope. It is, therefore, not anything in us that produces these effects, but it is the Word of God that enlightens our mind, touches our heart, and turns our will (Rom. 10: 17; Hebr. 4: 12).

Man cannot by his own reason believe in Christ.—Reason

is a precious gift of God, by which we acquire knowledge; but it cannot work faith in our hearts. Unconverted man may have a thorough intellectual knowledge of the things, the teachings, of the Spirit of God. But for some reason or other he regards them as foolishness. The crucified Christ is to the Jews a stumbling block, and to the Greeks foolishness (1 Cor. 1: 23). As long as this condition obtains, it is simply impossible for natural man to receive the truths of the Gospel with a believing heart and to put his trust in them. "The natural man receiveth not the things of the Spirit of God: for they are foolishness unto him: neither can he know them, because they are spiritually discerned" (1 Cor. 2: 14). Even historical, rational, and philosophical considerations cannot create in his heart that faith which trusts in the merits of Christ. "Neither can he know them, because they are spiritually discerned." As it requires a musical sense properly to judge and to appreciate a musical composition, so it requires a spiritual sense to discern, judge, and appreciate the things of the Spirit. But by nature man is carnally minded (Rom. 8: 5); he utterly lacks this spiritual sense. While, therefore, he may know the truths of the Gospel intellectually, he cannot know them spiritually and cannot receive them with a believing heart. The power to work this spiritual understanding lies not in the reason of man, but in the truth of the Gospel and with the Holy Ghost working through this Gospel.

Man cannot by his own strength believe in Christ.— Faith is essentially trust and confidence of the heart. Also a heathen may have a real, though a false, faith in his idol. However, even he cannot produce such faith and trust by his own effort, for it is created in him by what he knows and thinks of his idol. Also we Christians cannot believe in Christ or come to Him by our own strength; our faith is in no wise the product of our own effort. Faith is the echo of our hearts to the voice of God in the Gospel. The utter inability of man to turn to Christ and convert himself appears from this passage from Scripture: "Even when we were dead in sins" (God) "hath quickened us together with Christ" (Eph. 2: 5). Physically, these people had been alive and very active in committing all manner of sins. However, these very sins showed that they had no true fear and love of God, and did not trust in Him. Their hearts, alive with evil lusts, were dead to God. The heart of natural man, therefore, is not like a charged battery, which needs only to be touched to produce the spark of faith; it is spiritually dead. There is no dormant strength and energy that might be roused, but a new life must be created. This happens in conversion (Eph. 2: 10). As little as a dead body can quicken itself, so little can the spiritually dead raise themselves to spiritual life. — There is no medial state, in which man is neither spiritually dead nor spiritually alive, no longer unconverted nor yet fully converted; he is either one or the other.

The words of Christ: "Repent ye, and believe the Gospel" (Mark 1: 15), do not prove that man is able to do this by his own powers. Christ also commanded Lazarus to come out of the grave (John 11: 43. 44); still, of himself, Lazarus could not have done so. Even so natural man, dead in sins, does not raise himself spiritually, but he is raised and converted by the power of God through the Word (Ps. 19: 7). "No man can come to Me, except the Father, which hath sent Me, draw him" (John 6: 44). "Inasmuch as man before his conversion is dead in sins (Eph. 2: 5), there can be in him no power to work anything good in divine things" (F. C., Th. D., Art. II, 61, *Triglot*, p. 905).

Man cannot by his own will believe in Christ.—God endowed man with a will. Natural man, therefore, can will something. But this will never acts on its own initiative, for every intelligent voluntary act is stimulated by some consideration or motive, by some idea and its resultant emotion. However, there is absolutely nothing in the mind and heart of natural man that could possibly incline his will toward God. On the contrary, the imagination of his heart is evil from his youth (Gen. 8: 21); his mind is set on carnal things (Rom. 8: 5; Gal. 5: 19-21); his desires and lusts are towards evil (Eph. 2: 2. 3; 4: 22). The natural depravity of man determines the direction of his will towards those things which God hates and forbids. Therefore Paul says: "The carnal mind is enmity against God" (Rom. 8: 7). Natural man, as much as in him lies, does not want to come to God; he is afraid of Him; he flees from Him and hates Him. He is not merely a spiritual cripple who, though lacking strength, has some yearning and will to believe in Christ, but is by nature an enemy of God, whose mind and will are set against God. Some influence from without must produce in him a change of mind and heart, a "metanoia" (Matt. 3: 2; 4: 17), before he can be willing to come to Christ (Phil. 2: 13).

This, however, does not mean that conversion is forced on man against his will. (F. C., Th. D., Art. II, 60. 73, *Triglot*, p. 905. 909). Conversion is effected in this wise, that God through His Word brings such influence to bear upon man, that a change takes place in intellect, heart, and will, so that he, who is by nature stubborn and unwilling, becomes willing. Even as we sometimes bring about a change of mind in men by argument and persuasion, so God by the power of His Word persuades unwilling men so that willingly and joyfully they trust in His grace.

We confess with Luther in the explanation of the Third Article of the Apostles' Creed: "I believe that I cannot by my own reason or strength believe in Jesus Christ, my Lord, or come to Him." We affirm with the Lutheran Confessions: "Holy Scriptures ascribe conversion . . . not to the human powers of the natural free will, neither entirely, nor half, nor in any, even the least or most inconsiderable part, but in solidum, that is, entirely, solely, to the divine working and the Holy Ghost" (F. C., Th. D., Art. II, 25, *Triglot*, p. 891). Again: "The Scriptures deny to the intellect, heart, and will of the natural man all aptness, skill, capacity, and ability to think, to understand, to be able to do, to begin, to will, to undertake, to act, to work or to concur in working anything good and right in spiritual things as of himself" (F. C., Th. D., Art. II, 12, *Triglot*, p. 885). (Read Art. II of the Formula of Concord, Thorough Declaration, which treats the subject: Of Free Will, or Human Powers.)

B. Conversion the Work of the Holy Ghost

Conversion the work of God.—Conversion, by which men are brought to faith in Christ, is ascribed to God, in particular, to the Holy Ghost. It is the Father that draws men to Christ (John 6: 44); it is God who must turn us if we are to be turned (Jer. 31: 18); they who believe are born, not of the will of man, but of God (John 1: 12. 13), and their faith

is of the operation of God (Col. 2: 12). Only by the Holy
Ghost can men believingly call Jesus their Lord (1 Cor. 12:
3). Therefore Paul writes: "But ye are washed, but ye are
sanctified, but ye are justified in the name of the Lord Jesus,
and by the Spirit of our God" (1 Cor. 6: 11).

Conversion a work of divine grace. — It was grace that
moved God to redeem man by the death of His Son, and it
is grace, and in no sense the merit of man, that moves God
to convert man, and to impart to him the blessings of Christ's
redemption. "God hath saved us and called us with an holy
calling, not according to our works, but according to His own
purpose and grace, which was given us in Christ Jesus before
the world began" (2 Tim. 1: 9). "Not by works of righteousness which we have done, but according to His mercy He
saved us, by the washing of regeneration, and renewing of
the Holy Ghost" (Tit. 3: 5). If any man, then, is converted,
it is not because he is more worthy than others, or because
he has contributed something toward his conversion, which
others have not done, but it is entirely and solely a work of
divine grace.

The Holy Ghost operates through the means of grace.—
Contrary to the opinion of some, who state that the Holy
Ghost works directly and immediately on the hearts of men
to sanctify them by turning them to, and keeping them with,
Christ, the Bible teaches that the Holy Ghost employs certain
means, by and through which He works and preserves faith
in the hearts of men. Christ prays: "Sanctify them through
Thy truth; Thy Word is truth" (John 17: 17), and He adds
that men believe on Him through the word of the apostles
(v. 20). Paul tells us: "So then faith cometh by hearing, and
hearing by the Word of God" (Rom. 10: 17). Men are converted, or born again, by the Word of God (1 Pet. 1: 23; James
1: 18), and by Baptism (Tit. 3: 5; John 3: 5; Acts 2: 38).

"Through the Word and Sacraments, as through instruments, the Holy Ghost is given, who works faith, where and
when it pleases God, in them that hear the Gospel" (A. C.,
Art. V, *Triglot,* p. 45). (Cf., F. C., Epit., Art. II, 4, *Triglot,* p.
787; S. A., Part III, Art. VIII, 3, *Triglot,* p. 495).

We do not deny that the Holy Ghost could without the use
of means work directly on the heart of a person (Luke 1: 15.

44); but we have no word and promise whatever that He will do so. We, therefore, are bound to the means of grace. "They have Moses and the prophets; let them hear them" (Luke 16: 29). Therefore our Confessions state: "God does not wish to deal with us otherwise than through His spoken Word and the Sacraments" (S. A., Art. VIII, 10, *Triglot,* p. 497). We may not look for any other revelation, or for a direct operation of the Holy Ghost, or for other means of grace. He who refuses to use the means which God Himself has ordained, may not expect that the Holy Ghost will work on his heart to turn it to Christ. As the Gospel is to be preached to all men (Mark 16: 15), so all men must hear it if they would receive the Spirit of God (Gal. 3: 2), and come to faith in Christ (John 17: 20).

The method of grace.—God's mode of operation is adapted to the rational nature of man. It is a psychic process, which the Holy Ghost employs; in the work of conversion He uses man's intellectual, emotional, and volitional abilities, through which man is taught, moved, and converted. God makes use of this psychic equipment of man. He teaches man to know the Gospel; He impresses and moves his heart, and thus turns his will. The psychic process in conversion is the same as when in other matters a person is taught, moved, and turned. The difference, however, is this, that in order to effect the conversion of a sinner man is taught not secular, but spiritual things, which are the Word of God (1 Cor. 2: 6. 7). Furthermore, it is God who gives man knowledge and understanding (2 Cor. 4: 6); it is God who through such knowledge moves and opens the heart (Acts 16: 14); it is He who turns the will (Jer. 31: 18; Phil. 2: 13). While God makes use of the psychic functions, with which He Himself endowed the soul of man, it is He, and He alone, that turns the soul and draws it to Christ, creating a new life and bestowing spiritual powers.

"When we treat of the matter how God works in man, God has nevertheless a way of working in man, as in a rational creature, and another way of working in some other, irrational creature, or in a stone and block" (F. C., Th. D., Art. II, 62, *Triglot,* p. 905).

There is a logical sequence in conversion. In this work of **grace, by which sinners** are saved, the Holy Ghost observes a

very definite method, in which we distinguish the following
steps:

(1) By the Law He works in man knowledge of sin and
contrition of heart;

(2) By the Gospel He calls penitent sinners to Christ;

(3) He converts them by working faith in their hearts;

(4) He justifies them through this faith;

(5) He sanctifies them in this faith;

(6) He preserves them in this faith unto salvation.

While the external circumstances and conditions attending
this work vary, the means employed and the method observed
are always the same. There are not several different ways by
which the Holy Ghost leads men to heaven, but only one
(Eph. 4: 4. 5; John 14: 6). In the following chapters the
steps in the method of grace are discussed in detail.

XXIII. CONVERSION

**Conversion is wrought by the Holy Ghost in the heart
of man.**—While conversion will inevitably manifest itself in
the outward life of a person, it actually takes place in the
heart, and consists in this that the heart, broken and contrite
because of sin, trusts in Christ for grace and forgiveness. It is,
therefore, essentially the bestowal of faith. In order to effect
this change of heart, the Holy Ghost works repentance, offers
grace, and works faith.

(1) By the Law God Works Knowledge of Sin and Contrition of Heart. (Step I)

By the preaching of the Law God prepares the way for the
preaching of the Gospel. Before any man will turn to Christ
for grace and forgiveness, he must know his sins and repent
of them. "They that be whole need not a physician, but they
that are sick" (Matt. 9: 12). To convince man that he is sick
unto death because of his sins, the Holy Ghost uses the Law,
which shows man his sins (Rom. 3: 20), and the wrath and
the curse of God, which man deserved (Gal. 3: 10). Wherever
the preaching of the Law is effective, men are in their conscience convicted of their sins, realize their lost condition, are
moved to sorrow and contrition, and are driven to despair.
"The sorrow of the world worketh death" (2 Cor. 7: 10).

Such knowledge of sin, such sense of God's wrath, and such despairing of all self-help are indispensable prerequisites for conversion. No man will want forgiveness of sins if he does not know that he is a sinner, or does not feel sorry for the wrong he has done, or if he still believes that he can help himself. Faith cannot find room in a secure and self-satisfied heart, nor in a heart that loves sin. Before a man will turn to the Savior, he must realize his need of a Savior (Rom. 7: 24. 25). In this wise the Law, preceding the preaching of the Gospel, is necessary to bring man to the conviction of sin. However, the Law does not reveal the Savior; it offers no positive help; it works no faith; it cannot save. As far as the Law is concerned, it leaves man in sorrow and despair. "But whenever the Law alone, without the Gospel being added, exercises this its office, there is nothing else than death and hell, and man must despair, like Saul and Judas, as St. Paul, Rom. 7: 10, says: Through sin the Law killeth" (S. A., Part III, Art. III, 7, *Triglot*, p. 481).

(2) The Holy Ghost Calls Men by the Gospel. (Step II)

Gospel invitation and offer of grace.—When the Law has accomplished its purpose in working contrition of heart, the Holy Ghost has the Gospel, the glad tidings of the grace of God in Christ, preached unto man. "Preach the Gospel to every creature" (Mark 16: 15). By such preaching He calls and invites men to come to Christ, and offers to them the blessings of His salvation. "Come, for all things are now ready" (Luke 14: 17). "Incline your ear, and come unto Me; hear, and your soul shall live; and I will make an everlasting covenant with you, even the sure mercies of David" (Is. 55: 3). "I have blotted out, as a thick cloud, thy transgressions, and, as a cloud, thy sins: return unto Me; for I have redeemed thee" (Is. 44: 22). "Come unto Me, all ye that labor and are heavy laden, and I will give you rest" (Matt. 11: 28).

This invitation is *absolutely free;* it does not impose new conditions and obligations, which must be fulfilled before it may be accepted, but it offers to every sin-sick soul grace and forgiveness "without money and without price" (Is. 55: 1).

This invitation is *universal,* inasmuch as it is addressed to all men without exception and distinction (Mark 16: 15; Luke

24: 47; Rev. 14: 6). For this reason the Gospel must be preached among all nations until the end of time (Mark 13: 10).

This invitation is *sincere* in every case, no matter who reads or hears it. Even those who refuse to accept it are sincerely called. "All day long I have stretched forth My hands unto a disobedient and gainsaying people" (Rom. 10: 21). "How often would I have gathered thy children together, even as a hen gathereth her chickens under her wings, and ye would not" (Matt. 23: 37).

This invitation is *always efficacious,* that is, because of the blessings it freely offers and because of the power of God operating through it, it is always able to work acceptance in the hearts of men (Hebr. 4: 12; Rom. 1: 16; 2 Tim. 3: 15).

The fact that the Gospel invitation is *not always effective,* or does not always produce in the hearts of all that hear it the desired effect, is not in the least due to a lack of sincerity on the part of God, who calls, nor to a lack of power in the Gospel, whereby men are called, but solely to the perverse will of man. "Ye would not" (Matt. 23: 37); "Ye do always resist the Holy Ghost" (Acts 7: 51). Thus the conversion of man, which God would effect through the Gospel, can be, and often is, frustrated by man, because inhibitory influences, such as self-righteousness, love of sin, pride, despair, etc., dominate his heart, and will not allow the Word to take root.

(3) The Holy Ghost Enlightens Man with His Gifts by Working Faith in His Heart. (Step III)

(a) **The effective Gospel call.**—Whenever the Gospel call is effective, it works in the heart of man the acceptance of its invitation; it works faith. Thus the Word of God "effectually worketh also in you that believe" (1 Thess. 2: 13). By the holy calling we were actually "saved," i.e., converted (2 Tim. 1: 9). Thereby we were called "out of darkness into His marvelous light" (1 Pet. 2: 9), i.e., out of spiritual ignorance and despair into spiritual knowledge and faith in the grace of God. This is what Paul means, when he says: "God, who commanded the light to shine out of darkness, hath shined in our hearts to give the light of the knowledge of the glory of God in the face of Jesus Christ" (2 Cor. 4: 6). As in the beginning

God by His creative Word called the physical light into existence, so has He by His Word of grace enlightened our dark and despairing hearts by giving us knowledge of His glorious grace as it is revealed in Christ Jesus. As little as the moon contributes anything towards the light which the sun sheds upon it, so little does the heart of man contribute anything towards the light of knowledge with which God enlightens it. The knowledge of faith is a gift of God (Phil. 1: 29), wrought in us by means of the Gospel (Rom. 10: 17).

(b) **Intellectual and spiritual knowledge.**—We must distinguish between an intellectual knowledge of spiritual things and the spiritual knowledge of these things. A bare intellectual knowledge, which also an unbeliever may have, is dead; it makes no impression and creates no emotion in the heart; it "leaves a person cold." But it becomes alive the moment it affects one personally, creates in the heart a feeling, an echo, an affirmative response. The knowledge of the Law is dead, as long as one is not moved thereby; but it becomes alive the moment it creates fear and sorrow in the heart. Thus also the knowledge of the Gospel and its precious promises is dead, as long as it does not stir and move the heart; but it becomes alive the moment it creates in the heart a longing for the promised gifts, a trust and confidence in the promises of God. Spiritual knowledge, therefore, is not a bare knowledge of the mind, but it definitely includes the effect this knowledge has on the heart. Intellectual knowledge of the Gospel is, indeed, a prerequisite for faith, for "how shall they believe in Him of whom they have not heard" (Rom. 10: 14). Such knowledge is only a means through which the Holy Ghost works on the heart, wishing to touch and move it, to incline it unto the testimonies of the Lord (Ps. 119: 37). And it is only then when the knowledge of the mind registers in the heart, creating therein an affirmative response, a longing for and a trust and confidence in the promised grace, that conversion is effected.

(c) **Spiritual knowledge of the Gospel is faith.**—This spiritual knowledge, no matter how weak and small it may be at first, is true saving faith, by which the heart, though yet timidly, turns to and reaches out for the grace of God offered in the Gospel. Each increase and strengthening of this knowledge is an additional gift, whereby the first faint longing of the heart grows into joyful assurance. Thus the Holy Ghost enlightens us with His gifts. (Cf., F. C., Th. D., Art. II, 14, *Triglot,* p. 885). The very moment that this "small spark or longing for divine grace and eternal salvation" moves the heart, the attitude of natural man toward God is radically changed; man is converted. The promises of the Gospel are no longer "foolishness" unto him, but precious "wisdom" (1 Cor. 1: 23. 24). The heart is no longer apathetic, dead, but it is touched, moved, and quickened (Eph. 2: 5. 6). Man is no longer an enemy of God, but has now returned to the Shepherd of his soul (1 Pet. 2: 25).—We have, therefore, no right to demand a certain degree of contrition and of faith before a person may regard himself converted and a child of God. But it is necessary that his repentance and faith are sincere. "Him that cometh to Me I will in no wise cast out" (John 6: 37).

(d) **Conversion is not an extended process, but an instantaneous change.**—For days and weeks a person may experience in his heart deep contrition and sorrow over sin; but this does not mean that he is, at least partly, converted. (Example: Judas.) Conversion takes place the very moment that the first faint longing for grace moves the heart; at the first glimmer of the spark of hope in the Savior conversion is effected. There is no middle ground between being converted and not being converted, between spiritual life and spiritual death. A man is either one or the other; he either trusts in Christ, or he does not. "He that is not with Me is against Me" (Luke 11: 23). The change from death to life, from despair to hope, is always instantaneous.

(e) **Reiterated conversion.**—As conversion is essentially the bestowal of faith, it is quite obvious that a person is and remains converted as long as he has faith. "Whoever believeth that Jesus is the Christ *is* born of God" (1 John 5: 1). It is possible to lose this faith (Luke 8: 13), and the moment faith is lost, man returns to his former state of sin and wrath; he is no longer converted. If such a person is to be saved, he must again be converted (Luke 22: 32). Such reiterated conversions—and a person may experience many of them—are effected in the same way as the first conversion. (See "The fluctuations and the loss of faith" pp. 142. 143.)

"Once in grace, always in grace; once converted, always converted," is not true. No one should rely on the fact that years ago he was converted. In the Bible we are told: "Examine yourselves, whether ye be in the faith; prove your own selves" (2 Cor. 13: 5). It is only when and while we are in the faith that we are the children of God. "Without faith it is impossible to please Him" (God) (Hebr. 11: 6). A person who has lost his faith is neither converted, nor is he in the state of grace. (Cf., S. A., Part III, 42-44, *Triglot*, p. 491).

(f) **Knowledge of our conversion.**—As little as we understand how thoughts create emotions, so little do we understand how intellectual knowledge of the Gospel works spiritual knowledge, or faith, in our hearts. Sometimes it does not work faith, because other, inhibitory influences dominate us, such as love of sin, self-righteousness, indifference, despair, etc. Whenever such intellectual knowledge of the Gospel works spiritual knowledge, it is like a seed that germinates and grows, and we know not how (Mark 4: 27).—Nor do we always remember when we were converted, as Paul remembered it (Acts 22: 6-11), and it is not at all essential that we do. It is more important for us to know that we are converted, and this, indeed, we can know (2 Cor. 13: 5; 1 John 3: 14).

(g) **Terminology.**—To describe this change of heart, which takes place when a man comes to faith, Scripture employs various terms. It is called "turning" (Jer. 31: 18; 1 Pet. 2: 25), or "conversion" (Is. 60: 5; James 5: 20; Ps. 51: 13), because the heart of man turns from sin to grace. It is called "enlightenment" (2 Cor. 4: 6), because the heart which was dark with despair is made bright and cheerful by faith and hope. The terms "regeneration" or "new birth" (1 Pet. 1: 23; John 3: 5; Tit. 3: 5) indicate that a new spiritual life began the moment faith was worked in the heart. The terms "quickening" or "resurrection" (Eph. 2: 5. 6; Rev. 20: 5) tell us that by faith we have been raised from spiritual death to spiritual life. All these terms are figurative, and they describe exactly the same thing, namely, that by the operation of the Holy Ghost faith is worked in the heart.

Repentance.—Repentance is more than a ritual observance or an outward confession; it is something that takes place in the heart. The term, which is the translation of a Greek word meaning "change of mind," is used in a narrower and in a wider sense. Whenever it is used together with "faith" (Acts 20: 21) and "believe" (Mark 1: 15), it denotes sorrow and contrition over sin. When it is used alone (Luke 15: 7. 10; Mark 2: 17), it usually includes both, sorrow over sin and faith in the forgiveness of sins.—Sorrow over sin is the response and reaction of the heart to the voice of the Law; faith is the response and reaction of the heart to the voice of the Gospel. The Augsburg Confession (Article XII) describes repentance thus: "Now, repentance consists properly of these two parts: One is contrition, that is, terrors smiting the conscience through the knowledge of sin; the other is faith, which is born of the Gospel, or of absolution, and believes that, for Christ's sake, sins are forgiven, comforts the conscience, and delivers from its terrors. The good works are bound to follow, which are the fruit of repentance." Strictly speaking, conversion takes place the moment a person trusts in Christ for the remission of his sins. Sorrow over sin is a prerequisite of this faith, and good works are the fruit of this faith.

Contrition is a deep, heartfelt sorrow over sin. (Cf., *Popular Symbolics,* §81). The Bible distinguishes between a "godly sorrow" and "the sorrow of the world." "Godly sorrow worketh repentance to salvation not to be repented of: but the sorrow of the world worketh death" (2 Cor. 7: 10). The latter is wrought by the Law, and springs from fear of the wrath and the punishment of God. Such contrition we find in man before his conversion, and unless he learns of the love and grace of God, it will end in despair and death. The "godly sorrow" we find in Christians only, and is a part of their daily sanctification. It is not motivated by fear of punishment, but rather by their love of God; they are sorry for having grieved God with their sins. The Christians are sorry because their sins are offensive to God; the unconverted are sorry only because their sins are detrimental to themselves. "Godly sorrow" is pleasing to God, draws us closer to Him, and is a powerful means in suppressing the old Adam.

XXIV. FAITH

1. **Faith the work of God, an act of man.**—(a) Conversion consists in the bestowal of faith. Hence, faith is not a

work of man in the sense that by his own powers he produces faith in his heart. Faith is "of the operation of God" (Col. 2: 12); it is given unto us to believe in Christ (Phil. 1: 29). Faith is, therefore, the work of God in this sense that it is He, and He alone, who creates and sustains it in our hearts. (b) However, it is not God who believes in us and for us; it is man who does the believing. "If thou canst believe, all things are possible to him that believeth. And straightway the father of the child cried out and said with tears, Lord, I believe; help Thou mine unbelief" (Mark 9: 23. 24). "What shall we do that we might work the works of God?" (works which God requires of us). "Jesus answered and said unto them, This is the work of God, that ye believe on Him whom He hath sent" (John 6: 28. 29). These texts plainly show that faith is indeed an act or a work of man, which he performs in his heart. To be sure, it is not a physical act, but, like fearing, loving, and hoping, believing is something we do in our hearts and souls. To illustrate: I live, but it is God who gives and sustains this physical life of mine; so also, I believe in Jesus as my Savior, but it is God who creates and preserves this spiritual life in my heart. Faith, therefore, is an act or work of man inasmuch as man actually does the believing.

2. **The essence of faith.**— (a) No man can believe what he does not know. "How shall they believe in Him of whom they have not heard?" (Rom. 10: 14). The promise of God's grace benefits no man who is ignorant thereof. Hence, it is necessary to learn and to know what we are to believe. "So, then, faith cometh by hearing, and hearing by the Word of God" (Rom. 10: 17). A faith without knowledge is an impossibility.—But a bare intellectual knowledge of the Gospel is not faith; it is a prerequisite, but it is not a part of faith. The fact that a person is well versed in the doctrines of the Bible does not prove that he also believes them. Nevertheless, such knowledge is necessary, inasmuch as it is the means through which the Holy Ghost works on the heart to produce faith. For no truth can touch and affect the heart unless it first be in the mind. "All who wish to be saved ought to hear this preaching of God's Word. For the preaching and hearing of God's Word are the instruments of the Holy Ghost, by, with,

and through which He desires to work efficaciously, and to convert men to God, and to work in them both to will and to do" (F. C., Th. D., Art. II, 52, *Triglot*, p. 901).

(b) No man will or can put his trust in anything he does not regard as true and reliable. As long as the things of the Spirit are foolishness to man, or as long as he doubts them, he cannot have faith in them (1 Cor. 2: 14). But while such intellectual assent is a necessary prerequisite to faith, it is not the essence of faith. If on the basis of human authority, or because of rational and philosophic considerations, one would regard and accept as true the teachings of the Gospel, this by itself would not mean that he also puts his trust and confidence in them; it would be a faith of the head, and not of the heart. We believe many facts of history, but we do not believe in them; such belief does not in the least include trust and confidence. The devils know and believe the Scriptures, but they have no faith; they tremble (James 2: 19). The word "belief" sometimes suggests little more than an intellectual assent, while the word "faith" always implies trust and confidence of the heart.

(c) Merely to accept facts and statements as true is not faith. But if these facts and statements mean something to us personally, if we feel sure that they will help and benefit us, and if we trust in them for such help, then we believe *in* them; then we have faith. While this faith is based on knowledge and conviction, it is essentially "fiducia cordis," confidence of the heart. Faith, therefore, is never a bare intellectual knowledge and assent, but it is an emotional attitude of the heart plus an act of the will. "With the heart man believeth unto salvation" (Rom. 10: 10).—Sometimes faith is called knowledge. "And this is life eternal, that they might know Thee, the only true God, and Jesus Christ, whom Thou hast sent" (John 17: 3). However, the word "knowledge" is here used in a fuller sense. It means not a purely intellectual knowledge, such as unbelievers may have, but it is a live knowledge, a "nosse cum affectu," a knowledge which has affected the heart and the will, working conviction and confidence.

There are many things we know, but we do not accept them as true. Other things we know, which we do accept as true;

but we do not put our confidence in them. Faith is the trust and confidence of the heart in things we know to be true.

The Bible defines faith thus: "Faith is the substance of things hoped for, the evidence of things not seen" (Hebr. 11: 1). Things we hope for are such as we desire for ourselves, but we do not yet have them, as for instance, the future reward of eternal salvation. Now faith is "the substance" of these things; that means we are as sure of them as though even now we actually and substantially had them. Faith is sure and firm confidence in things hoped for, the confidence underlying these things as certainly being expected and awaited by us. The "things not seen" are the things God in His Word and in the means of grace reveals, but which cannot be seen, such as: His grace, the forgiveness of sins, and all the reality, greatness, and blessedness of God's promises to Christians for time and for eternity. While we do not see them, we do not in the least doubt them, but are as certain of them as though we saw them. Luther's translation renders the sense of this text more intelligible: "Es ist aber der Glaube eine gewisse Zuversicht des, das man hoffet, und nicht zweifeln an dem, das man nicht siehet." Faith is the assurance and confidence of the heart in those invisible and spiritual things promised to us by God in His Word and Gospel. The believer not only knows the promises of his God, but there is in his heart an emotional response; they affect him; he wants them, lays hold of them, and applies them to his personal need. Thus the three phases of soul life are engaged in the act of believing; these are cognition, emotion, and volition.

Such faith we find in the centurion of Capernaum (Luke 7: 1-10), in the nobleman (John 4: 47-53), in the woman of Canaan (Matt. 15: 21-28). These not only heard and accepted as true what Christ said, but they trusted in it. Such confidence Paul expresses: "I know whom I have believed, and am persuaded that He is able to keep that which I have committed unto Him against that day" (2 Tim. 1: 12).

We read in our Lutheran Confessions: "The term 'faith' does not signify merely the knowledge of the history . . . but signifies a faith which believes . . . also the effect of the history —namely, this article: the forgiveness of sins, to wit, that we have grace, righteousness, and forgiveness of sins through

Christ" (A. C., Art. XX, 23, *Triglot,* p. 55). Again: "Faith is not only knowledge in the intellect, but also confidence in the will, i.e., it is to wish and to receive that which is offered in the promise—namely, reconciliation and remission of sins" (Apol., Art. III, 183, *Triglot,* p. 205). Again: "To believe means to rely on the mercy of God, that He desires to be gracious for Christ's sake, without our merits. That is what it means to believe the article of the forgiveness of sin. To believe this does not mean to know the history only, which the devils also know" (*Triglot,* p. 207).

Whenever the terms "knowledge" and "belief" are taken in the fuller sense so as to include "confidence of the heart," as in John 17: 3 and 1 John 5: 1, then these terms describe the entire faith.

This definition of faith as "confidence of the heart" shows that it is something very *personal.* In the first place, the faith of a man can cling to such promises only as have been made to him personally. I may regard a promise of help made to some one else as very reliable and trustworthy, but I cannot trust in it, because it does not pertain to me. The devil knows the promises of the Gospel to be true, but he personally cannot rely upon them, because they are not intended for him. However, the promises of grace are made to all men, and are intended for each one personally. "Thy sins be forgiven thee" (Matt. 9: 2). Hence, each human being should apply these promises to himself personally, and put his trust in them. In the second place, by faith, which clings to the promise, the believer takes and appropriates to himself what the promise offers to him. He does not take it for somebody else, but for himself, even as each one eats for himself. Faith apprehends and appropriates to itself whatever God offers in the promise. "Faith is that my whole heart takes to itself this treasure" (Apol., Art. IV, 48, *Triglot,* p. 135). It is impossible that one should trust in something for another. For this reason my faith does not help any one but me. Each person must believe for himself. "The just shall live by his faith" (Hab. 2: 4); (Luke 7: 50).

The experiences of peace, joy, and happiness are, in themselves, not faith, but rather are the result and fruit of faith; they are at times overshadowed by other feelings.

3. The object of faith.—Faith always requires an object, to which it clings and in which it trusts, whether this be an idol, or money, or the merits of one's good works, or the grace of God in Christ Jesus. Thus the heathen, who trust for help in an idol, have real faith and confidence. But, because it is misplaced, it is a false faith. "Their error is this that their trust is false and wrong, for it is not placed in the only God, besides whom there is no God in heaven or upon earth" (Luther's Large Cat., I Com., 18, *Triglot*, p. 585). To say that any kind of faith will help and save is as foolish as to say that anything a person eats will nourish him. It depends upon what you eat; so it depends upon what you believe, and in what you put your trust and confidence. Our faith must have the right object.

The Law can never be the object of faith. "The Law is not of faith; but the man that doeth them shall live in them" (Gal. 3: 12). We cannot believe in the Commandments; we must do them. While a self-righteous person trusts for acceptance with God in the illusion that he has kept the Law, he cannot rely upon the Law itself. Faith in Christ, indeed, prompts us to observe the Commandments, but it does not trust in them.

The promise of God and the faith of man are correlatives. Faith on the part of man presupposes a promise on the part of God. Where there is no promise, there can be no faith, but only imagination and superstition. Conversely, a promise on the part of God requires faith on the part of man, for every promise is made that it should be believed. "Wherever there is a promise, faith is required, and, conversely, wherever faith is required, there must be a promise" (Apol., Art. IV, 50, *Triglot*, p. 135). "For just as we have above said that the promise and faith stand in a reciprocal relation, and that the promise is not apprehended unless by faith, so we here say that the promised mercy correlatively requires faith, and cannot be apprehended without faith" (Apol., Art. III, 203, *Triglot*, p. 209. 210). As it is the nature of a promise to create the faith it requires, so it is the nature of faith to cling to the promise which created it. It is even so with God's promise in the Gospel. It requires faith for its acceptance; it works this faith; and it is the object of the faith it works. Therefore, Christ says: "Believe the Gospel" (Mark 1: 15).

But no promise is believed just because it is a promise, but because of what it offers. Besides the reliability of Him who makes the promise, it is the content of the promise that appeals to us. Now, all the promises of God are absolutely trustworthy (2 Cor. 1: 20). Many of them pertain to our temporal life and well-being. But the best things God offers to us in the Gospel, where He promises to lost sinners grace and forgiveness, life and salvation, for Christ's sake. Hence, we say that Christ and the merits of His redemption are the content of the Gospel and, therefore, also the object of our faith. For this reason the prison keeper was told: "Believe on the Lord Jesus Christ, and thou shalt be saved" (Acts 16: 31).

Thus, the Gospel is the object of faith, and Christ is the object of faith. Yet this does not mean that one may be the object of faith to the exclusion of the other. The saving merits of Christ are offered to us in the Gospel; hence, we cannot believe in the one without believing in the other. (Illustration: A present offered to us in a package.) While all the promises of God, also those pertaining to our bodily needs, are the object of faith, the object of *saving* faith is the promise of God's grace and forgiveness in Christ Jesus.

A faith based on anything else than on the promise of God's grace in Christ does not save, no matter how sincere this faith may be. "He that believeth on the Son hath everlasting life; and he that believeth not the Son shall not see life, but the wrath of God abideth on him" (John 3: 36).

4. **The fluctuations and the loss of faith.**—Faith in the grace of God is not of equal strength in all believers, nor does it constantly maintain a uniform strength in the same individual; but it varies and fluctuates between a feeble longing for forgiveness and the firm assurance of possessing forgiveness. While a person's faith may be strong with respect to one promise, it may be weak with respect to another. "O thou of little faith," Christ said to Peter (Matt. 14: 31). "O woman, great is thy faith," Christ said to the woman of Canaan (Matt. 15: 28). These fluctuations of faith do not affect its saving power, because both, the weak and the strong faith, trust in the same promise and receive the same grace and forgiveness. The difference lies in the hold each has on the promise; the

strong in faith have a firmer hold than the weak in faith, and are not so likely to lose it. However, these fluctuations are reflected in the sanctifying power of faith, which consists in this that faith enables us to lead a holy life. The strong in faith are more able to resist temptations, are more fruitful of every good work, enjoy a greater measure of peace of conscience and joy in the Spirit than those who are weak in faith. But he that is strong today may be weak tomorrow. "Let him that thinketh he standeth take heed lest he fall" (1 Cor. 10: 12). All of us have reason to pray: "Lord, increase our faith" (Luke 17: 5).

5. **Faith can be lost.**—In the Parable of the Sower we read of some hearers: "Which for a while believe, and in time of temptation fall away" (Luke 8: 13); (1 Cor. 10: 12). Scripture warns against defection as an ever-present danger, and cites examples of those who, at one time converted, lost their faith and again became the children of wrath. Examples: Saul, Judas. "When a righteous man turneth away from his righteousness, and committeth iniquity, and dieth in them; for his iniquity that he hath done shall he die" (Ezek. 18: 26). It is possible, then, to fall away from grace (Gal. 5: 4), and to become a castaway (1 Cor. 9: 27).—Some of the causes why men lose their faith are: spiritual starvation, which is caused by neglecting to use those means by which faith is preserved; self-righteousness, which shifts one's trust from the grace of God and the Savior to the merit of one's own works; philosophic and rationalistic pride, which will not submit to the authority of God's Word (2 Cor. 10: 5; 1 Tim. 6: 20. 21); love of the world (1 John 2: 15; 2 Pet. 2: 20. 21; John 5: 44; Luke 8: 13. 14); wilful sins against the conscience (1 Tim. 1: 19). "One is not to imagine a faith of such a kind as can exist and abide with and alongside of a wicked intention to sin and to act against conscience" (F. C., Epit., Art. III, 11, *Triglot*, p. 795).—Wilful impenitence in one sin kills faith in the forgiveness of all sins, for faith cannot live in an impenitent heart. (Cf., Apol., Art. III, 21. 22, *Triglot*, p. 161). Sins of weakness do not kill faith, for with these sins there is not present in the heart the wilful intention to sin, and they are repented of as soon as they are recognized. But faith and mortal sin cannot coexist.

A lost faith can be restored in a re-conversion, which is essentially the same as the first conversion. "Return, thou backsliding Israel" (Jer. 3: 12). David and Peter were re-converted (2 Sam. 12: 13; Luke 22: 32. 61. 62). The repent-ance of the lapsed consists in a reappropriation by faith of the grace of God and of the forgiveness of sins offered through the means of grace. On the part of God, His covenant and promise always stand (Is. 54: 10; Rom. 3: 3), and the peni-tent sinner may at all times return to them (John 6: 37; Matt. 11: 28).

6. **The functions of faith.**—Fire does two things: it con-sumes fuel, and it produces heat and light. So faith has a double function. In the first place, it clings to the promise of God, and apprehends and appropriates to itself what this promise offers—namely, the grace of God and the merits of Christ. Thus it justifies a believer before God. This is the *justifying and saving power of faith.* "Therefore we conclude that a man is justified by faith without the deeds of the Law" (Rom. 3: 28). "Faith alone is the means and instrument whereby we lay hold of Christ, and thus in Christ of that righteousness which avails before God, for whose sake this faith is imputed to us for righteousness, Rom. 4: 5" (F. C., Epit., Art. III, 5, *Triglot,* p. 793).—In the second place, faith produces something; it renews the sinner. "The life which I now live in the flesh, I live by the faith of the Son of God, who loved me and gave Himself for me" (Gal. 2: 20). "Faith worketh by love" (Gal. 5: 6). This is the *sanctifying power of faith.* The functional difference between these two powers is that faith on the one hand apprehends the merits of Christ and thus justifies, and that it on the other hand produces a holy life and good works and thus sanctifies. "Since this faith is a new life, it necessarily produces new movements and works" (Apol., Art. III, 129, *Triglot,* p. 191). "Good works certainly and without doubt follow true faith, if it is not a dead, but a living faith, as fruits of a good tree" (F. C., Epit., Art. IV, 6, *Triglot,* p. 797).

Neither of these functions can be separated from faith. True faith always trusts in the merits of Christ, and, there-fore, always justifies. But this same faith also sanctifies the sinner in his life; it always brings forth the fruit of good works. If it fails to do so, it is dead and is not a faith of the heart, but mere intellectual knowledge and assent (James 2: 17. 18). Being dead, it does not trust in the saving merits of Christ, and does not justify and save a person.

However, faith does not justify us before God because it sanctifies us in our lives before men; it does not save us because it produces good works. Faith does not trust in its own fruits, but in the saving merits of Christ. "By grace are ye saved through faith; and that not of yourselves: it is the gift of God: not of works, lest any man should boast" (Eph. 2: 8. 9). It is rather the other way around: faith sanctifies us in our lives because it first justifies us before God. The appreciation of the blessings received by and through faith prompts us to consecrate our lives to God, our Savior; because of the mercies received, we present our bodies a living sacrifice to God (Rom. 12: 2). (Cf., F. C., Th. D., Art. III, 40. 41, *Triglot*, p. 929).

XXV. JUSTIFICATION BY FAITH. (STEP IV)

1. Faith necessarily demands an object to which it clings, a foundation on which it rests. The very moment faith springs up in the heart, it clings to the very promise that created it, and apprehends what this promise offers. As the Gospel offers grace and forgiveness, the believer by and through faith immediately appropriates these blessings and makes them his own. What God has offered in His promise He confirms in the believer. Because by faith the believer has and holds the righteousness Christ earned for him, God declares him just. It is thus that faith justifies the sinner before God. "Therefore we conclude that a man is justified by faith, without the deeds of the Law" (Rom. 3: 28). By the labor of his hands a poor helpless cripple will never become rich; but if a kind friend were to give him thousands of dollars, he would become rich through this gift. Likewise we, who cannot keep the Law as God demands, cannot be justified under the Law; but as God freely gives us the righteousness of Christ through faith, we are accounted just and righteous before Him because of this gift of God.

2. **Justification in detail.**—(a) **All men are sinners.**— "There is no difference: for all have sinned, and come short

of the glory of God" (Rom. 3: 23). For this reason they all
are guilty before God and worthy of death (Rom. 3: 19).

(b) **Christ fully atoned for all sins.**—Moved by His love
and compassion, God sent His Son to be the Savior of the
world (John 3: 16), who by His vicarious life and death rendered full satisfaction for all men (1 John 2: 2). The purpose
of His work of redemption was to reconcile the world unto
God (2 Cor. 5: 19), and by His resurrection He proved that
He had accomplished it. "Who was delivered for our offenses,
and raised again for our justification" (Rom. 4: 25).

(c) **God has forgiven all sins.**—Because of the redemption
through Christ God no longer imputes sins to men (2 Cor. 5:
19); He does not charge their transgressions against them,
but credits them with the merits of Christ. "For He hath
made Him to be sin for us who knew no sin; that we might
be made the righteousness of God in Him" (2 Cor. 5: 21).
For the sake of Christ's complete satisfaction God "justifies
the ungodly" (Rom. 4: 5), i.e., they who by nature and by
their own works were altogether ungodly, were because of
the work of Christ declared and pronounced just and righteous. Therefore, "by the righteousness of one the free gift
came upon all men unto justification of life" (Rom. 5: 18).
"Justification properly consists in the non-imputation of sins,
or their forgiveness, to the sinner, which is the negative side;
and the imputation of Christ's perfect righteousness, as though
it were his own, which is the positive side" (Dr. C. H. Little
in *Lutheran Confessional Theology,* p. 149).

The fruit of Christ's redemption is not that He merely
opened for man the way to reconciliation with God, and that
God is now ready and willing to forgive sins, pending certain
conditions man must first fulfill. The fruit of Christ's redemption is that Christ actually did effect a reconciliation, that
God does no longer impute sins, but has in His heart forgiven
all sins to all men. On the part of God reconciliation and the
forgiveness of sins is not a mere possibility, but an accomplished fact, an objective reality, which is not affected by the
personal attitude of man (Rom. 3: 3; 2 Tim. 2: 13). By His
vicarious active and passive obedience Christ paid for the sins
of all men, and God, accepting this payment, has in His heart
forgiven all sins of all men. There is not a soul in all the

world which God has not already absolved from all sin. This is called objective or universal justification. "Objective justification may be defined as God's declaration of amnesty to the world of sinners on the basis of the vicarious obedience of Christ, by which He secured a perfect righteousness for all mankind, which God accepted as a reconciliation of the world to Himself, imputing to mankind the merits of the Redeemer" (Dr. C. H. Little in *Disputed Doctrines*, p. 60).

(d) **The Gospel reveals and offers to men the forgiveness of sins.**—This fact that in Christ the world is reconciled to God, and that the sins of all men are atoned for and forgiven is not known to man by nature, nor can he discover it by his own cogitation. This is a matter we can learn only by divine revelation (1 Cor. 2: 7-11). And God did make this fact known to us in the Gospel, "for therein is the righteousness of God revealed from faith to faith" (Rom. 1: 17). This is not the personal righteousness of God, nor the righteousness He demands of us in the Law, but the righteousness Christ earned for us, which is to be accepted by faith (Rom. 3: 21. 22). The Gospel, therefore, does not reveal to us a possible reconciliation, a conditional forgiveness of sins; in the Gospel the reconciliation and the forgiveness of sins are proclaimed as accomplished facts. For this reason Christ says that "remission of sins should be preached in His name among all nations" (Luke 24: 47), and the apostle Paul writes "that through this man" (Christ) "is preached unto you the forgiveness of sins" (Acts 13: 38). Real and genuine Gospel preaching, therefore, does not consist in merely giving all manner of interesting information about the forgiveness of sins, but in proclaiming to sinners the fact of the forgiveness, the fact that the world is reconciled unto God (2 Cor. 5: 19. 20). And because the Gospel is God's own proclamation of grace to a sin-cursed world, it actually promises, offers, and brings grace and forgiveness to all that hear it.

(e) **The promise of forgiveness must be accepted by faith.** —This declaration on the part of God calls for acceptance on the part of man. But it is impossible to accept it by means of works; it can be accepted only by faith, for this righteousness is revealed "from faith to faith" (Rom. 1: 17). Whoever does not accept it in this manner will not be benefited by it, for we read: "The Word preached did not profit them, not being mixed with faith in them that heard it" (Hebr. 4: 2). But faith, which is so necessary for the acceptance of this Gospel promise, is wrought in the heart of man by this very promise, for "faith cometh by hearing, and hearing by the Word of God" (Rom. 10: 17).

(f) **Faith justifies the sinner.**—Faith clings to the promise, and thereby man appropriates to himself personally what the promise offers to all men in general. Illustration: On January 1st, 1863, Lincoln declared a general emancipation of all the slaves; the individual slave heard and believed this proclamation and applied it to himself, and thus he became personally free. Thus the reconciliation of the whole world by Christ and the forgiveness of all sins of all men is an accomplished fact, which, in itself, is not affected by the attitude of men (Rom. 3: 3). This fact is proclaimed in the Gospel to every slave of sin; and the very moment that he applies this fact to himself, believing that for Christ's sake also his sins are forgiven, he *has* the forgiveness of all his sins, is free from the guilt and punishment of sin, and is personally justified before God. That is what Paul teaches (Rom. 4: 5): "To him that worketh not," does not seek to become righteous before God by his own works, "but believeth on Him that justifieth the ungodly," trusts in God, who for Christ's sake declares all the ungodly just, "his faith is counted for righteousness," he by such faith becomes personally righteous, because the righteousness of Christ, which his faith apprehends, is by God imputed to him personally. Thus by faith one puts himself into personal possession of that justification, which the Gospel offers to all men in general. This is called personal or subjective justification.

If we tell a heathen man that for Christ's sake God has forgiven all his sins, we are simply stating a fact, which the unbelief of man cannot make ineffectual, "without effect" (Rom. 3: 3). This fact must be accepted in true faith, which presupposes a penitent heart, and consists in confidence and trust in this forgiveness. The function of faith in this matter is merely instrumental; it does not achieve forgiveness of sins; it does not earn it; it does not make us worthy of it; nor does it move God to forgive us our sins. It is not a condition we must fulfil before forgiveness is available for us. On the part of God the forgiving takes place before we ever came to faith, yea, before we were born, because with God the forgiveness rests on the atonement of our sins through Christ. The forgiveness of sins and the righteousness of Christ are ready for all men, and are being freely offered to them in the Gospel. All things in the kingdom of heaven are now ready (Matt. 22: 2-4). But if they are to benefit us, we must accept them; a promised gift can be accepted in no other way than by faith. The moment, therefore, our faith trusts in the promise of God, we apply and appropriate to ourselves what the promise offers, and God confirms the gift upon us personally. Thus it is that man is justified by faith (Rom. 3: 28). The moment I accept the riches offered to me I become rich. The believer does not have to wait for the forgiveness of his sins; it is ready for him, and he *has* it the moment he takes it, and he keeps it as long as he holds it. He loses it as soon as the faith, by which he held it, ceases. Thus the function of faith in justification is that it takes and holds with a trusting heart what God offers in the Gospel.

Justification is that forensic act of God, by which He, on the basis of the perfect vicarious atonement wrought by Christ, declared the whole world to be justified in His sight (objective justification), and transmits and imputes the effect of this declaration to all whom He brings to faith by the work of the Holy Ghost through the means of grace (subjective justification).

Thus it appears that universal justification does not benefit anyone unless it is followed by personal justification, and that personal justification is possible only because of the preceding universal justification. In other words, the fact that God has forgiven all sins to all men does not help anyone unless he accepts it by faith; on the other hand, he cannot appropriate forgiveness to himself if the sins are not yet forgiven. Illustration: Bread will not nourish us, unless we eat it; but we cannot eat it unless it is there.

(g) **Justification a judicial act of God.**—Justification is not a moral transformation, effected within the sinner by virtue of some infused grace; but it is a judicial act of God, taking place outside of the sinner, by which God in mercy for Christ's sake absolves him from all sins, pronounces and declares him righteous, who has no righteousness of his own, but who trusts in the righteousness of his Savior (Rom. 4: 5-8). God justifies the sinner by imputing to him the righteousness of Christ. "The word 'justify' means in this article, to absolve, that is, to declare free from sin" (F. C., Epit., Art. III, 7, *Triglot*, p. 793). "To justify signifies, according to forensic usage, to acquit a guilty one and declare him righteous, but on account of the righteousness of another, namely, of Christ, which righteousness is communicated to us by faith" (Apol., Art. III, 184, *Triglot*, p. 205). That the word "justify" means to declare just, we see from Matt. 12: 37 and from Prov. 17: 15.

(h) **Justification is perfect.** — Justification is not partial nor progressive, but complete and perfect. The moment there is faith in the heart, by which we lay hold of God's promise of grace, at that moment there is full forgiveness of all our sins. Forgiveness of sins and the grace of God are not a quantity, of which parts and portions are meted out to us as we have need of them day by day, as it is the case with our daily bread; but grace and forgiveness are facts, proclaimed in the Gospel. Whoever trusts in this fact has the forgiveness for all his sins. God, therefore, does not justify man partially, forgiving him some of his sins while retaining others, but He forgives all sins and justifies man completely. "Who forgiveth all thine iniquities" (Ps. 103: 3); "Thou hast cast all my sins behind Thy back" (Is. 38: 17); "Having forgiven you all trespasses" (Col. 2: 13).

As Christ has atoned for all sins (1 John 2: 2), and as God has in His heart forgiven all sins to all men, and offers this forgiveness in the Gospel to all men (2 Cor. 5: 19. 20), it follows that everyone who by faith accepts this forgiveness has the forgiveness for all sins and is completely justified before God. For this reason faith does not look forward to forgiveness of sins, as a thing to be hoped for, a thing that we might obtain in the future when we meet our God; it does not say: "I am sure that God will forgive me my sins," but it says: "From the promise of God in the Gospel I know that He has forgiven all my sins." Forgiveness of sins and justification are not future blessings we are still waiting for, but they are a present possession, which we have and hold in their completeness as long as we continue in the faith.—There are degrees of faith, weak and strong, but there are no degrees of justification; for the weak in faith cling to the same promise, and obtain the same forgiveness as the strong in faith. The difference is not in what they hold, but in the weakness or the firmness of the hold they have on it.

3. **Why does faith save us?**— (a) There can be no faith in the forgiveness of sins if there is not first sorrow and contrition over sins in the heart. Whoever does not repent of his sins will not care to have forgiveness of sins. But sorrow over sin, however deep and sincere, does not give to faith its saving power. God does not forgive sin because a person is sorry for what he has done; (example: Judas).

(b) Good works and a holy life necessarily proceed from faith, for faith without works is dead (James 2: 17). "Faith worketh by love" (Gal. 5: 6). However, faith does not save us because it produces good works; the fruits of faith do not give to faith its justifying power. Man is justified without the works of the Law (Rom. 3: 28). "Contrition that precedes, and good works that follow, do not belong to the article of justification" (F. C., Epit., Art. III, 8, *Triglot*, p. 795). (Read also F. C., Th. D., Art. III, 24-29, *Triglot*, p. 923-925.)

(c) Faith itself may be regarded as a work of man, inasmuch as he does the believing. And it is also a good work, well pleasing to God (John 6: 28. 29). But it is not a meritorious work. Faith does not justify and save us because of its intrinsic worth and ethical value. Regarded as an act of man, faith is also a work of the Law. Faith is absolutely necessary as a means of salvation, but faith is not the Savior. "Faith justifies, not for this cause and reason that it is so good a work and so fair a virtue, but because it lays hold of and accepts the merits of Christ in the promise of the holy Gospel" (F. C., Th. D., Art. III, 13, *Triglot*, p. 919).

(d) Not the act of eating, but the food we eat nourishes us. Thus, not the act of believing, but what we believe saves us. However, as one must eat food that really nourishes, so one must believe what really saves. A false doctrine, no matter how sincerely believed, cannot save. The doctrines of the First Article of the Apostles' Creed are divine truths, but they are not saving truths; one may believe them with all sincerity of heart and still be lost. The saving truth, and, therefore, the chief doctrine of the Bible, is briefly expressed in the words of Paul: "God was in Christ, reconciling the world unto Himself, not imputing their trespasses unto them" (2 Cor. 5: 19); and "in Christ we have the redemption through His blood, the forgiveness of sins, according to the riches of His grace" (Eph. 1: 7); and in the words of Christ: "God so loved the world, that He gave His only begotten Son, that whosoever believeth in Him should not perish, but have everlasting life" (John 3: 16); in other words, God by grace for Christ's sake forgave us our sins. He who truly believes these words has forgiveness, is justified before God, and will be saved. As it is the gold which I hold in my hand that makes me rich, so it is the merits of Christ which I hold by faith that saves my soul. *The saving power, therefore, lies not in the hand of faith, but in the merits of Christ, which I hold by faith.* Faith is only the means, the instrument, by which I apprehend the saving merits of my Savior. At the same time, faith is the only means by which I can come into possession of these merits, because they are offered to me in an unconditional promise, which can be apprehended in no other way than by faith.

"In order, therefore, that troubled hearts may have a firm, sure consolation, also, that due honor be given to the merits of Christ and the grace of God, the Scriptures teach that the righteousness of faith before God consists alone in the gracious reconciliation or forgiveness of sins, which is presented to us out of pure grace, for the sake of the only merit of the Mediator, Christ, and is received through faith alone in the promise of the Gospel. In like manner, too, in justification before God faith relies neither upon contrition nor upon love or other virtues, but upon Christ alone, and in Him upon His complete obedience by which He fulfilled the Law for us, which obedience is imputed to believers for righteousness. Moreover, neither contrition nor love or any other virtue, but faith alone is the sole means and instrument by which and through which we can receive and accept the grace of God, the merits of Christ, and the forgiveness of sins, which are offered us in the promise of the Gospel" (F. C., Th. D., Art. III, 30. 31, *Triglot*, p. 925).

4. The results of justification.—(a) **The state of grace.**
—The moment a person is justified by faith, he is delivered
from the state of wrath, and enters the state of grace. In this
blessed state he has peace with God (Rom. 5: 1); he has a
good conscience toward God (Hebr. 9: 14; 10: 22); he has the
assurance of God's protection and guidance (Hebr. 13: 5; Rom.
8: 28); he is delivered from all fear (Ps. 34: 4; Hebr. 2: 15);
he glories in tribulation (Rom. 5: 3); he triumphs in death
(1 Pet. 1: 3; 1 Cor. 15: 55-57); he has become a child of God
(Gal. 3: 26) and an heir of heaven (Gal. 4: 7).—In this state
of grace we continue as long as we remain in the faith; however, the moment faith is lost, justification and forgiveness and
all the blessings resulting therefrom are likewise lost.

(b) **Membership in the invisible Church,** the kingdom of
grace, and title to the kingdom of glory.—Having by faith obtained the forgiveness of sins, we are translated into the kingdom of the Son of God, and are made partakers of the inheritance of the saints in light (Col. 1: 12-14). Because we are
born again of God, we are children of His household and family (Eph. 2: 19; 3: 15). Justified by faith, we join the communion of saints, the royal priesthood, etc. (1 Pet. 2: 9), and
have claim and title to the kingdom of glory. While in this
world, Christians may seem to be of low degree, they should
always be fully conscious of the high position to which they
are exalted through faith in Christ.

(c) **The indwelling of the Holy Ghost and of the entire
Trinity.**—In conversion we received the gift of the Holy Ghost
(Acts 2: 38; 10: 44; Tit. 3: 5. 6). Hence, Paul writes: "Know
ye not that ye are the temple of God, and that the Spirit of
God dwelleth in you? If any man defile the temple of God,
him shall God destroy; for the temple of God is holy, which
temple ye are" (1 Cor. 3: 16. 17); (2 Cor. 6: 16). Speaking
of the Father and of Himself, Jesus said: "And We will come
unto him" (the believer) "and make Our abode with him"
(John 14: 23). This mystical and inexplicable union and indwelling of God pertains not only to the soul, and does not consist merely in the agreement of the will of man with the will of
God, nor in the mere union of both in mutual love, nor in a
mere influence of the Holy Ghost on man, but it pertains also
to the body. "Know ye not that your body is the temple of

the Holy Ghost which is in you, which ye have of God, and ye are not your own?" (1 Cor. 6: 19).—This union must be distinguished from the indwelling mentioned in Acts 17: 28, which is common to all created things, while this indwelling is peculiar to the believers only. This indwelling of God in His believers is mystical and inexplicable, yet it is real and actual.

What does this indwelling of the Holy Ghost mean to us? Christ purchased and won all men, even those who are finally lost (1 Cor. 6: 20; 2 Pet. 2: 1); therefore all are, in a sense, His purchased possession. But personally we become His own the moment we believe in Him, for then the Holy Ghost enters our hearts and takes actual possession of us. Illustration: The home a person buys is his own, but he takes actual possession of it when he moves in. So all men are Christ's own by the redemption, but in conversion the Holy Ghost takes actual possession of the believer by dwelling in his heart. By faith we lay hold of Christ; by sealing us with the Holy Ghost God lays hold of us. "In whom also after that ye believed, ye were sealed with that Holy Spirit of promise, which is the earnest of our inheritance until the redemption of the purchased possession, unto the praise of His glory" (Eph. 1: 13. 14). From this text we learn that the Holy Ghost is the earnest of our inheritance, a pledge on the part of God to us, that He will fulfil His promise and redeem us from this vale of tears and take us to Himself in heaven. In the meantime, the Holy Spirit bears witness with our spirit, assuring us that we are the children of God and the heirs of God (Rom. 8: 16). He also supports our prayers and makes intercession for us (Rom. 8: 26. 27). He furthermore leads and rules us, that in our lives we bring forth the fruits of the Spirit (Rom. 8: 14; Gal. 5: 16-23). So the indwelling of the Holy Ghost in our hearts means much to us, and therefore we should heed the warning: "Grieve not the Holy Spirit of God, whereby ye are sealed unto the day of redemption" (Eph. 4: 30).

(d) **Initial restoration of the image of God.**—The image of God, consisting in a blissful knowledge of God and in righteousness and true holiness of life, was lost when man fell into sin. But a beginning of its restoration is made, when man is justified by faith in Christ. For the new knowledge, which the believer gained from the Gospel, fills his heart with joy and happiness, and this, in turn, moves him to forsake the ways of sin and to walk in the paths of righteousness. Because of the old Adam, this restoration of the image of God will never be perfect in this life. For this reason Paul admonishes us: "Put on the new man, which is renewed in knowledge after the image of Him that created him" (Col. 3: 10), and: "Put on the new man, which after God is created in righteousness and true holiness" (Eph. 4: 24).

XXVI. SANCTIFICATION THROUGH FAITH. (STEP V)

1. The word "sanctification" is sometimes used in a wider sense, as in 2 Thess. 2: 13: "God hath from the beginning chosen you to salvation through sanctification of the Spirit and belief of the truth." The term here comprehends the entire work of the Holy Ghost, by which He leads the sinner unto eternal life. However, it is also used in a narrower sense, as in 1 Thess. 4: 3: "This is the will of God, even your sanctification, that ye should abstain from fornication" etc. Here the term evidently refers only to that part or phase of the Spirit's work, by which He incites and directs believers to lead a godly life.

As pointed out above, we properly distinguish between the justifying and the sanctifying power of faith. It is the latter of which we speak now.

2. **Sanctification in detail.**—(a) **Renewal of the heart.**— Sanctification of life begins in the heart. By nature man is carnally minded, and an enemy of God (Rom. 8: 7). But by faith he appreciates and accepts the blessings of God's grace. Thus there is created in his heart a gratitude and a love of God. "We love Him, because He first loved us" (1 John 4: 19). His attitude toward God is changed.

This change of heart from enmity to love brings about also a change of mind with respect to the things of life. The believer's view of life and his estimate of earthly things is changed (Phil. 3: 7. 8), and his affection is set on things above (Col. 3: 2). Because the believer loves God, his mind is no longer set on the works of the flesh, which God abhors, but on the things of the Spirit, which are pleasing to God (Rom. 8: 5). What he loved before, he now hates; what he hated

before, he now loves. Because of the mercies he received from
his God, he will not be conformed to the world, but be transformed by the renewing of his mind to prove what is the good
and acceptable will of God (Rom. 12: 2). Thus the moral
attitude of man is radically changed; morally he has become
a new creature (2 Cor. 5: 17). This inward change and renewal is the essence of sanctification.

As all sins proceed from the heart (Matt. 15: 19), so does
the reformation of life make its beginning there. Compulsory
laws and rules may somewhat change the outward conduct of
man, but it is the sanctifying power of faith in Christ that
truly reforms the evildoer, and renews the image of God in
his life (Eph. 4: 24).

(b) **Struggle against sin.**—Such change of heart will inevitably induce the believer to struggle against the wicked
promptings of his flesh, in which dwelleth no good thing (Rom.
7: 18). He will not willingly yield to, and obey, the lusts
thereof (Rom. 6: 12); but he will endeavor to subdue and
suppress them. "They that are Christ's have crucified the
flesh with the affections and lusts" (Gal. 5: 24). He will
change his former manner of life, the "vain conversation received by tradition from your fathers," by putting off the old
man, which is corrupt according to the deceitful lusts (Eph.
4: 22). By daily contrition and repentance the old Adam in
the believers is to be drowned, and evil desires are to be resisted and suppressed.

But the believer will resist also temptations that approach
him from without. His faith enables him to overcome the allurements of the world (1 John 5: 4. 5; 1 Pet. 4: 2), and to
stand against the wiles of the devil (Eph. 6: 10-13; 1 Pet. 5: 8.
9). While before there was in him no power to resist, but
rather a strong inclination to yield to every evil temptation
(Gen. 8: 21), there is in him now a new power, a new will,
that struggles against Satan, the world, and the flesh.

(c) **Good works.**—This change of heart manifests itself also in a positive way. The believer will bring forth fruit meet
for repentance (Matt. 3: 8); his faith works by love (Gal. 5:
6); he will be zealous of good works (Tit. 2: 14). He is like
"a tree planted by the rivers of water, that bringeth forth
his fruit in his season" (Ps. 1: 3). His faith is a light that

continually sends forth rays of good works (Matt. 5: 16); it is a vital energy, always active in doing what is pleasing to God.

Luther writes in the Preface to St. Paul's Epistle to the Romans: "Thus faith is a divine work in us, that changes and regenerates us of God, and puts to death the old Adam, makes us entirely different men in heart, spirit, mind, and all powers, and brings with it the Holy Ghost. Oh, it is a living, busy, active, powerful thing that we have in faith, so that it is impossible for it not to do good without ceasing. Nor does it ask whether good works are to be done; but before the question is asked, it has wrought them, and is always engaged in doing them" (F. C., Th. D., Art. IV, 10, *Triglot*, p. 941).

3. **True faith always sanctifies.**—As a light sends forth rays from the moment it begins to burn until it is extinguished, so the sanctification of life begins the very moment faith is kindled in the heart, and it continues as long as the light of faith burns. There can be no true faith in the heart without having some effect on the life of a person, for faith always works by love (Gal. 5: 6). Where there is faith in the heart, there is sanctification in the life. The lives Christians lead before men are the outward evidence of their faith in God. "Faith, if it hath not works, is dead, being alone . . . Shew me thy faith without thy works" (which is impossible), "and I will shew thee my faith by my works" (James 2: 17. 18). When faith dies, sanctification of life ceases; even though the outward form of godliness may continue, its strength and essence are gone (2 Tim. 3: 5).

4. **Sanctification varies.**—The sanctifying power of faith (not its justifying power) varies according to the strength or the weakness of faith. The weak faith succumbs to temptation more easily than the strong faith, is less productive of good works, and gives way to fear and doubt in face of danger (Matt. 14: 29-31). The fluctuations of faith are reflected in the life of a person. For this reason the holiness of life is not the same in all believers; not even in the same person does it continue on the same level. Not all Christians are equally zealous and fruitful of good works. As faith weakens, love waxes cold, and good works decrease in number and quality. To achieve a greater sanctification of life, there must be a

stronger faith and a deeper appreciation of the goodness of God. Hence, it must be our constant effort to continue and to grow in the faith, so that we may grow also in holiness of life; "to be strengthened with might by His Spirit in the inner man" (Eph. 3: 16). Growing in faith, we shall abound also in charity toward each other (2 Thess. 1: 3).

5. **Sanctification is never perfect.**—Let no one imagine that it is possible for him to become perfect in his life. Paul confesses: "Not as though I had already attained, either were already perfect, but I follow after, if that I may apprehend that for which also I am apprehended of Christ Jesus" (Phil. 3: 12). Christ apprehended Paul that he should become perfect, and Paul strives to attain this end; but he admits that he has not yet succeeded. Isaiah admits that even "our righteousnesses are as filthy rags" (Is. 64: 6). "For our best works, even after the grace of the Gospel has been received, are still weak and not at all pure" (Apol., Art. III, 42, *Triglot*, p. 169). —The reason why no believer can become perfect in his life is that besides the new man, which is faith in its sanctifying function, he still has the old Adam, the flesh, original sin, which is by no means eradicated from his nature, but clings to him unto death (Rom. 7: 14-24), which continually lusts against the Spirit (Gal. 5: 17), and contaminates even the good works that proceed from faith. But while a Christian must admit imperfection in his best endeavors, he will, nevertheless, "follow after," earnestly strive for perfection, "to cleanse ourselves from all filthiness of the flesh and spirit, perfecting holiness in the fear of God" (2 Cor. 7: 1). Hence, sanctification is progressive, but never perfect in this life.

6. **Sanctification of life not optional.** — (a) "This is the will of God, even your sanctification" (1 Thess. 4: 3). We sometimes forget this, and are concerned only about our final salvation in heaven; we are anxious to live with Christ in the kingdom of glory, but are not always so eager to live under Him in His kingdom of grace. (b) However, Christ redeemed us that also in this life we should live under Him in righteousness and true holiness (2 Cor. 5: 15; Luke 1: 74. 75). (c) Also for this purpose the Holy Ghost has converted us. "We are His workmanship, created in Christ Jesus unto good works, which God hath before ordained that we should walk

in them" (Eph. 2: 10). Therefore we should follow holiness, without which no man shall see the Lord (Hebr. 12: 14), abound in every good work (2 Cor. 9: 8), and not be weary in well doing (Gal. 6: 9).

7. **Sanctification of life has no saving power.**—While the new life we lead is, indeed, a "living sacrifice, holy and acceptable unto God" (Rom. 12: 1), it is by no means a sacrifice by which we atone for past transgressions, and on account of which God declares us just. It is rather a sacrifice of thanksgiving for the mercies received, and it is not offered in expectation of a reward. A life lived and a work done in expectation of reward cease to be fruits of faith and love. God, indeed, promises to reward faithful service (Matt. 5: 12; Luke 14: 14; Gal. 6: 9); still, such service must not be rendered because, and in expectation, of such reward, but because, and in recognition, of the numerous blessings we have gratuitously received from His hands. A holy life can never proceed from a mercenary motive, but from love. Sanctification of life, therefore, can never be the cause of our justification before God, but it is the result and consequence thereof. For this reason sanctification of life can never be properly taught independent of, and separated from, justification. Our Lutheran Confessions reject as false "that man, after he has been born again, can perfectly observe and completely fulfill God's Law, and that this fulfilling is our righteousness before God, by which we merit eternal life" (F. C., Epit., Art. II, 12, *Triglot,* p. 789).

8. **The causes of sanctification.**— (a) The principal efficient cause of our sanctification is the Triune God. "The very God of peace sanctify you wholly" (1 Thess. 5: 23). "It is God which worketh in you both to will and to do of His good pleasure" (Phil. 2: 13). More especially this work is ascribed to the Holy Ghost, who prompts and induces us to mortify the flesh (Rom. 8: 13. 14), renews us (Tit. 3: 5), and brings forth good fruits (Gal. 5: 22. 23).

To do this, the Holy Ghost employs means. Since it is faith that worketh by love, it is necessary that this faith be continually stimulated and strengthened, which is done by means of the Gospel. But while the Holy Ghost uses the Gospel to energize our faith, and to make us able and willing to serve

God in our lives, He uses the Law to direct us as to what God would have us do (Rom. 12: 1. 2; Ps. 119: 9).

"For the Law says indeed that it is God's will and command that we should walk in a new life, but it does not give us the power and ability to begin and do it; but the Holy Ghost, who is given and received, not through the Law, but through the preaching of the Gospel, Gal. 3: 14, renews the heart. Thereafter the Holy Ghost employs the Law so as to teach the regenerate from it, and to point out and show them in the Ten Commandments what is the good and acceptable will of God, Rom. 12: 2, in what works God hath before ordained that they should walk, Eph. 2: 10" (F. C., Th. D., Art. VI, 11. 12, *Triglot,* p. 965).

(b) The secondary cooperating cause is man. While in his conversion man is purely passive (he does not convert himself, but is converted), he concurs in the work of his sanctification, cooperating with the Holy Ghost by virtue of the spiritual powers bestowed upon him. In leading holy lives and in doing good works Christians are not automata, but they are consciously active. It is man that suppresses evil desires, resists temptation, wills and does what is pleasing to God; but behind all this is the energizing, prompting, directing power of the Holy Ghost (Phil. 2: 13).

"As soon as the Holy Ghost through the Word and Sacraments has begun in us His work of regeneration and renewal, it is certain that through the power of the Holy Ghost we can and should cooperate, although in great weakness. But this does not occur from our carnal natural powers, but from the new powers and gifts which the Holy Ghost has begun in us in our conversion, as Paul expressly and earnestly exhorts that we as workers together with Him receive not the grace of God in vain, 2 Cor. 6: 1. But this is to be understood in no other way than that the converted man does good to such an extent and so long as God by His Spirit rules, guides, and leads him, and as soon as God withdraws His gracious hand from him, he could not for a moment persevere in obedience to God. But if this were understood thus that the converted man cooperates with the Holy Ghost in the manner as when two horses together draw a wagon, this could in no way be conceded without prejudice to the divine truth" (F. C., Th. D., Art. II, 65. 66, *Triglot,* p. 907).

XXVII. OF GOOD WORKS

1. We must differentiate between works that are good before men and works that are good before God. God often disapproves what men regard as praiseworthy, and men often ignore and despise what is good and acceptable in the sight of God. It is not for man to determine which works are pleasing to God; this only God can do (Micah 6: 8).

2. Two things are necessary for any work to qualify as a good work before God: it must conform to God's Law, and it must proceed from the proper motive.

Good works must conform to the will of God, as it is revealed to us in His Word, specifically, in the Law. It is foolish to assume that any man, whether it be priest or laymen, congregation or synod, may determine what is to please God. "In vain they do worship Me, teaching for doctrines the commandments of men" (Matt. 15: 9). God's Word is the only standard of good works. "Ye shall observe to do therefore as the Lord your God hath commanded you; ye shall not turn aside to the right hand or to the left" (Deut. 5: 32). Works performed according to other standards, such as the commandments of the church, or man's own devotion with its self-devised holiness and self-imposed exercises, are not good works, but vain worship. Neither will the good intention one may have make a plain transgression of the Law a good work. "Behold, to obey is better than sacrifice" (1 Sam. 15: 22); (John 16: 2).

Good works must proceed from love of God.—Even the works of the Law are not truly good works if done under duress, because they are commanded, or if they are done from fear of punishment, or from desire for reward. The alms and prayers of the Pharisees did not please God, because they were prompted by vainglory and self-righteousness (Matt. 6: 1-5). Any selfish consideration destroys the quality of good works. "Faith worketh by love" (Gal. 5: 6). Faith in Christ produces love in the heart, and this love manifests itself in good works. "Love is the fulfilling of the Law" (Rom. 13: 10); (Matt. 22: 36-40; 1 John 5: 3).

3. **The unregenerate cannot do truly good works.**—They can, in a measure, comply with the letter of the Law, and thus effect a civil righteousness; they may be praised by men for their philanthropy, moral purity, and honesty, "for man looketh on outward appearance, but God looketh on the heart" (1 Sam. 16: 7). It is the attitude of the heart that determines the ethical value of a work. The only motive recognized by God is selfless love, love of God. Such love is the fruit of faith, and is, therefore, found in believers only. "He that abideth in Me, and I in him, the same bringeth forth much fruit; for without Me ye can do nothing" (John 15: 5). They that believe in Christ are careful to maintain good works (Tit. 3: 8). The regenerate are inwardly qualified to do good works, and they will do them; their light of faith will shine forth in many good works (Matt. 5: 16).

"As long as a man is not regenerate, and conducts himself according to the Law and does the works because they are commanded thus, from fear of punishment or desire for reward, he is still under the Law, and his works are called by Paul properly the works of the Law, for they are extorted by the Law, as those of a slave; and these are the saints after the order of Cain, that is hypocrites. But when a man is born anew by the Spirit of God, and liberated from the Law, that is, free from the driver, and led by the Spirit of Christ, he lives according to the immutable will of God comprised in the Law, and so far as he is born anew, does everything from a free, cheerful spirit; and these are called not properly works of the Law, but works and fruits of the Spirit" (F. C., Th. D., Art. VI, 16. 17, *Triglot,* p. 967). Thus two persons may do exactly the same work, required in the Law; but the one does it, just because it is required, and he fears the punishment; the other does it from love of God and from gratitude for His mercies. It is the latter who does a good work.

4. **Not everything a Christian does is also a good work.** —He still has the old Adam, which is not a whit better than that of the unregenerate. Whatever proceeds from the flesh of a Christian is wicked and sinful (Rom. 7: 14-23). Only as we live in the Spirit, shall we walk in the Spirit (Gal. 5: 25); only as our faith works by love, shall we bring forth good fruit.—Even the good works of believers are not perfect, but

are tainted with sin. Luther said: "A pious Christian sins in all his good works." This is true because all he does is more or less contaminated with the sinfulness of his flesh, servile fear, selfishness, etc. (Is. 64: 6). But for Christ's sake even these imperfect spiritual sacrifices of His children are acceptable to God (1 Pet. 2: 5). "But how and why the good works of believers, although in this life they are imperfect and impure because of sin in the flesh, are nevertheless acceptable and well-pleasing to God, is not taught by the Law. . . . But the Gospel teaches that our spiritual offerings are acceptable to God through faith for Christ's sake" (F. C., Th. D., Art. VI, 22, *Triglot*, p. 969).

5. **Adiaphora.**—Works which God has not specifically commanded or forbidden are in themselves indifferent. (Mitteldinge. Adiaphora). But also their quality is determined by the motive that prompts them. "Whether therefore ye eat or drink, or whatsoever ye do, do all to the glory of God" (1 Cor. 10: 31). We cannot sin to the glory of God (Rom. 2: 23. 24; 6: 1). But whatever otherwise we do in our several stations of life, if we do it from love of God and to the glory of God, is a service well-pleasing to Him. Wherever God has placed us in life, whether we be employers or employees, fathers, mothers, children, teachers, students, etc., we should do our duty faithfully "as the servants of Christ, doing the will of God from the heart; with good will doing service as to the Lord, and not to men" (Eph. 6: 6. 7). If done in the right spirit, the simplest duties of our daily lives become a God-pleasing service. To work merely for money, to study merely for honor and credit, is selfish, and not a good work. But to work and study because it is God's will that we do so, and to show our appreciation of what God has done for us, is well-pleasing in the sight of God.

6. **Good works are necessary,** because God asks them of His children (Matt. 5: 16; 2 Cor. 9: 6. 8; Tit. 2: 14). They are, furthermore, the necessary fruits of repentance (Matt. 3: 8), the inevitable product of faith (Gal. 5: 6; John 15: 5). Without them faith is dead (James 2: 17). "The regenerate do good works from a free spirit, this is not to be understood as though it is at the option of the regenerate man to do or to forbear doing good when he wishes, and that he can never-

theless retain faith if he intentionally perseveres in sins"
(F. C., Epit., Art. IV, 11, *Triglot,* p. 799).

Good works are *not* necessary for justification and salvation
(Rom. 3: 28). No man is declared just before God on the
basis of his good works. When God justifies man, He does not
in any sense take into account the good a man may have done,
but He looks solely at the merits of Christ (Rom. 3: 24). Nor
do our good works complement any lack or deficiency in the
merits of the Savior; "for by one offering He hath perfected
forever them that are sanctified" (Hebr. 10: 14). Nor are
they necessary to give to our faith strength and saving power,
for faith trusts in the merits of Christ, and not in its own
fruits. Nor are they necessary to preserve faith in our hearts,
for this is done by the Holy Ghost through the Gospel. (Cf.,
F. C., Epit., and Th. D., Art. IV, *Triglot,* p. 797 ff.)

7. **Good works are rewarded.**—The reward for good works
is not a reward which we have earned, and which we may
demand as our due. "Likewise ye, when ye shall have done
all those things which are commanded you, say, We are un-
profitable servants; we have done that which was our duty
to do" (Luke 17: 10). Besides, our best works are imperfect,
and judged on their merit would earn for us only damnation.
"It is taught on our part that it is necessary to do good works,
not that we should trust to merit grace by them, but because
it is the will of God" (A. C., Art. XX, 27, *Triglot,* p. 57). It
must never be our intention to earn anything by our good
works, for this will at once destroy their character as good
works.

Nevertheless, God has promised to reward our good works
richly. "Great is your reward in heaven" (Matt. 5: 12). "Thou
shalt be recompensed at the resurrection of the just" (Luke
14: 14). "But godliness is profitable unto all things, having
promise of the life that now is, and of that which is to come"
(1 Tim. 4: 8). This is a reward, not of merit, but of grace,
one which God does not owe us, and which we may not demand as our due, but which He promises and gives freely to
His children purely out of grace. What the exact nature of
this reward will be, God has not revealed. It may be that He
will bestow special blessings upon us in our lives (Eccl. 11: 1;
Prov. 19: 17; the Fourth Commandment), or that He will

forestall harmful consequences of our own errors. In heaven this reward consists in a greater degree of glory (Matt. 25: 14-30; Luke 19: 12-26; 2 Cor. 9: 6).

XXVIII. OF PRAYER

1. **Christians pray.**—Prayer is inseparable from the spiritual life of a believer; it is the heart-beat of his faith. A person, who has become a child of God, desires to speak to, commune with, his Father in heaven; he prays. Scriptures say: "Ye have received the Spirit of adoption, whereby we cry, Abba, Father" (Rom. 8: 15).

2. **Form of prayer.**—We pray by word of mouth, sung or spoken; but also the thoughts, meditations, desires of the heart are prayers. "Let the words of my mouth and the meditation of my heart be acceptable in Thy sight, O Lord, my Strength and my Redeemer" (Ps. 19: 14). "Lord, Thou hast heard the desire of the humble" (Ps. 10: 17). Even when not consciously engaged in prayer, Christians are always in the spirit of prayer, always grateful for mercies received, always depending on God for help; "praying always with all prayer and supplication in the Spirit" (Eph. 6: 18). Of the Spirit of God dwelling in the hearts of believers we read: "The Spirit also helpeth our infirmities; for we know not what we should pray for as we ought: but the Spirit itself maketh intercession for us with groanings which cannot be uttered. And He that searcheth the hearts knoweth what is the mind of the Spirit, because He maketh intercession for the saints according to the will of God" (Rom. 8: 26. 27).

3. **Content of prayer.**—In our prayers we thank and praise God for blessings received, and ask Him for such things as we need for body and soul. "Be careful for nothing, but in everything by prayer and supplication with thanksgiving let your requests be made known unto God" (Phil. 4: 6). Do not fret and worry about your troubles, but take them to the Lord in prayer.

4. **Basis of prayer.**—Assurance of the grace of God in Christ Jesus is the prerequisite of prayer. Without this it would be presumptuous for a sinner to present a petition before God; without this no prayer of man would ever be heard. We owe it to Christ that we may approach God in prayer,

presenting our requests before Him; and only when we trust in the merits of the Savior will our prayers touch the heart of God. "Prayer relies upon God's mercy, when we believe that we are heard for the sake of Christ, the High Priest, as He Himself says, John 16: 23: 'Whatsoever ye shall ask the Father in My name, He will give it you.' In My name, He says, because without this High Priest we cannot approach the Father" (Apol., Art. III, 212, *Triglot*, p. 211). For this reason the prayers of unbelievers, however sincere, are altogether in vain. "He that turneth away his ear from hearing the Law, even his prayer shall be abomination" (Prov. 28: 9). Before a person can truly pray to God, he must by faith have entered into the right relation with God (Rom. 10: 14). Hence, an unconverted man cannot pray before his conversion, nor can he pray to be converted.

5. **Our prayers must be addressed to the Triune God,** Father, Son, and Holy Ghost. This does not mean that all three Persons must be specifically named in each prayer. The Lord's Prayer is addressed to "Our Father in heaven"; the woman of Canaan addressed her request to Jesus (Matt. 16: 22). Whichever Person of the Holy Trinity we name in our prayer, we must be conscious of the fact that we are praying to the Triune God, who revealed Himself to us in the Bible. —Prayer is an act of worship which God demands exclusively for Himself (Matt. 4: 10), and He alone can and will hear our prayer (Ps. 65: 2; Ps. 50: 15). If, when praying, we have in mind any other god, no matter by which name we call upon him, we are sinning against the First Commandment. This is true also when we pray to angels (Rev. 19: 10), to saints, to the Virgin Mary; they can neither hear nor help us (Is. 63: 16). Many prayers are lost, because they are not addressed to the true God.

6. **We are moved to pray**—(a) **by God's gracious invitation.** "Seek ye My face" (Ps. 27: 8); "call upon Me in the day of trouble" (Ps. 50: 15). This invitation and direct command should encourage us to pray; not to do so is sin. The feeling of personal unworthiness should not keep us from praying. The publican deeply realized his unworthiness, and would not lift up so much as his eyes unto heaven; never-

theless, he prayed: "God, be merciful to me, a sinner," and his prayer was heard (Luke 18: 13. 14).

(b) **by God's promise to hear us.** Such promises, as we find in Matt. 7: 7. 8; Ps. 145: 18. 19; Ps. 50: 15, are by no means vain. "O Thou that hearest prayer, unto Thee shall all flesh come" (Ps. 65: 2). "Now we know that God heareth not sinners; but if any man be a worshiper of God, and doeth His will, him He heareth" (John 9: 31); (Prov. 15: 8).

(c) **by our own and our neighbor's trouble and need.** In trouble we seek help; hence, trouble teaches us to pray. "In trouble have they visited Thee; they poured out a prayer when Thy chastening was upon them" (Is. 26: 16); (Ps. 50: 15). Our own trouble, be it great or small, bodily, as the lepers' (Luke 17: 13), or spiritual, as the publican's (Luke 18: 13), should move us to call upon God for help. But also the trouble of our neighbor should induce us to pray for him, as Abraham did for the righteous in Sodom (Gen. 18: 23-32), and as the centurion did for his servant (Matt. 8: 5. 6).

7. **What may we ask for in prayer?**—Christ says: "What things soever ye desire, when ye pray, believe that ye receive them, and ye shall have them" (Mark 11: 24). And Paul writes: "Be careful for nothing; but in everything by prayer and supplication with thanksgiving let your requests be made known unto God" (Phil. 4: 6). No matter, what may trouble and oppress us, we should not give way to anxious worry, but take it to the Lord in prayer. In "everything," things great or small, personal or general, temporal or spiritual, make your request known to God.

But we may not pray for help in things that are contrary to the honor and will of God. It is blasphemy to ask for help and protection when we are about to commit sin, or when we wilfully expose ourselves to temptation.—Our requests must be in agreement with the promise of God, and subject to His will. "This is the confidence that we have in Him, that if we ask anything according to His will, He heareth us" (1 John 5: 14).—Because God has definitely promised and will surely give to us spiritual blessings (Luke 11: 13), we may ask for them outright. In a general way we may without condition ask also for those things which we need for our temporal life, as we do in the Fourth Petition of the Lord's Prayer.—

But when we ask for specific temporal blessings, which God has not definitely promised, we must leave it to the discretion of God whether or not He will grant our request. "Lord, if Thou wilt, Thou canst make me clean" (Matt. 8: 2). "Not My will, but Thine, be done" (Luke 22: 42). However, also in such matters we should not pray with a doubting heart, but feel sure that God will hear also these prayers in a way that is best for us.

8. **For whom should we pray?**—The malefactor, the publican, and the lepers prayed for themselves; in like manner should we pray for ourselves. But we should pray also for others. "I exhort therefore that, first of all, supplication, prayers, intercessions, and giving of thanks be made for all men" (1 Tim. 2: 1). We should pray for parents and children, for government and country, for pastors and teachers of the church, for missions, for all that are in need, also for our enemies (Matt. 5: 44); but we are not to pray for the dead, since God has neither commanded nor promised to hear such prayers. We should do good to and pray for men while they live; when they are dead, neither our works nor our prayers profit them anything. Sentimental reasons and the teachings of the Romish Church do not make such prayers effectual. We have no authority for such prayers in the Word of God; for the books of the Maccabees (Romanists refer to 2 Mac. 12: 43-46) are mere human records, and express also in this matter only a human opinion, and not a divine truth.

9. **How we should pray.** — (a) We must guard against thoughtless babble. There is no magical power in the mere utterance of prayerful words, insincere and unfelt, but we must know what we are doing, and we must mean what we say. "When ye pray, use not vain repetitions, as the heathen do; for they think that they shall be heard for their much speaking" (Matt. 6: 7). The value of our prayers does not depend upon their number or length, nor on the language and grammar we use, but on this that we pray from the heart, earnestly and sincerely (Ps. 145: 18). Our prayers may be brief, but they should be strong and fervent.

(b) We must pray with a clean heart, that is, not ask favors of God while our heart is set on doing evil, or while it holds anger and a grudge against our neighbor. "I will therefore that men pray everywhere, lifting up holy hands, without wrath and doubting" (1 Tim. 2: 8); (Mark 11: 24-26). (To lift up hands is an external gesture, indicating that we are ready to receive what God may give in answer to our prayer. By folding our hands and bowing our heads we indicate that we humbly acknowledge our unworthiness of whatever the good Lord may see fit to give us.)

(c) We must pray according to God's will. (See above, under 7.)

(d) We must pray in the name of Jesus. "Verily, verily, I say unto you, Whatsoever ye shall ask the Father in My name, He will give it you" (John 16: 23). We must not expect nor ask that our prayers be heard because of our merit or worthiness, that God should give us what we ask because we have done this or that for Him; but, knowing that we are worthy of none of the things for which we pray, we ask that because of His mercy and grace in Christ He would hear us. "We do not present our supplications before Thee for our righteousness, but for Thy great mercy" (Dan. 9: 18). Whoever comes to God with this thought in mind that God owes him some consideration because of what he did and suffered in the service of God, is insulting God with his prayer. Nothing but the grace of God in Christ moves God to grant our prayers; and it is to this grace that we must appeal when we present our requests before Him.

(e) We must pray with a believing heart, that is, we must not doubt whether or not God will hear us, but firmly believe that our petitions are acceptable to our Father in heaven and heard by Him. "But let him ask in faith, nothing wavering. For he that wavereth is like a wave of the sea driven with the wind and tossed; for let not that man think that he shall receive anything of the Lord" (James 1: 6. 7). We must pray "without doubting" (1 Tim. 2: 8). Such faith is based on the certainty of God's promise. Because God has promised to hear us, we should firmly believe that He will do so. "What things soever ye desire, when ye pray, believe that ye shall receive them, and ye shall have them" (Mark 11: 24); (Matt. 21: 22). Many prayers are killed by doubts in our hearts. Instead of being fully persuaded that God will certainly hear us, we sometimes think that we may try a prayer or two with the chance of receiving some help. If in the past our prayers were not answered in a manner we expected, we are apt to think that they will not help in the future. But we should remember that we may not expect God to hear our prayer if we ourselves are in doubt whether He will do so.

10. **When and where we should pray.**—The sanctity of a place adds no potency to our prayer. Prayers offered at the sepulchre of Christ, before a shrine, or in a church are no more effectual than prayers offered anywhere else. "I will that men pray everywhere" (1 Tim. 2: 8). "Pray without ceasing" (1 Thess. 5: 17). Wherever we may be, at home, in the field, in the shop, on the street, we should always be in the spirit of prayer, always grateful for God's blessings, always looking to Him for help and protection. While not always engaged in the act of praying, Christians are always in the attitude of prayer; there is in them always that feeling of their dependence on God and the assurance of the help of God.—We should not make a show of our prayers, as the Pharisees did, but rather pray to our Father in secret, in private, where nothing will disturb us nor distract our thoughts (Matt. 6: 5. 6).

Christians should pray together with one another, as we do in public worship (Ps. 26: 12; Acts 1: 14; 2: 42). But we may not pray together with heathen, thinking that, while they pray to their idol, we may pray to the true God. At whose altar we worship, his religion we confess. Nor may we join in prayer-fellowship with those who "cause divisions and offenses contrary to the doctrine which ye have learned" (Rom. 16: 17).

While we may pray to God at any time, we should do so especially in days of trouble (Ps. 50: 15; Is. 26: 16). It is well to cultivate the habit of praying at stated times, in the morning, in the evening, at table, etc.

11. **The efficacy of prayer.**—It has been said that the value of prayer is purely subjective, and that prayers have no effect beyond making a person feel that God will help him. It is true that prayer has this reassuring effect on our troubled hearts. But the reason for this is that God has promised to hear the prayers of His children. "I will deliver thee" (Ps. 50: 15). "He will fulfill the desire of them that fear Him; He also will hear their cry, and will save them" (Ps. 145: 19). It is for this reason that "the effectual fervent prayer of a

righteous man availeth much" (James 5: 16). Prayer does not work like an opiate, having no other effect than merely to quiet the troubled heart of him who prays. God actually answers prayer (Ps. 65: 2). When at the prayer of Elijah "it rained not on earth by the space of three years and six months. And he prayed again, and the heavens gave rain," this was not a subjective delusion, but an objective fact (James 5: 17. 18). We do not pray merely to calm ourselves, but we call upon the living God, who is able and willing to help us (Ps. 50: 15).

However, God hears our prayers at His appointed time. Often He tells us: "Mine hour is not yet come" (John 2: 4). He may withhold His help to make us realize more fully how helpless we are, or to teach us to call on Him more fervently (Mark 4: 37-41; 7: 25-30); but finally He will with everlasting kindness have mercy on us (Is. 54: 7. 8).

God answers prayers in His own way, and not always in the manner we expect. Thrice Paul besought the Lord that "the thorn in the flesh" might be removed. But God did not remove it; however, He gave to Paul the strength to bear his cross, saying: "My grace is sufficient for thee; for My strength is made perfect in" (thy) "weakness" (2 Cor. 12: 9). Hence, we must prescribe to God neither the time nor the manner, when and how He should help us.

But do our prayers actually move God, so as to bring about in Him a change of mind? Read Ex. 32: 7-14. God wanted to consume the people of Israel; but when Moses interceded, "the Lord repented of the evil which He thought to do unto the people." We must bear in mind that Christians in their prayers never set their will against the will of God, but submit their wishes and requests to God's will; they pray "according to His will" (1 John 5: 14). Also the prayer of Moses was according to the will of God (Ex. 32: 13); Moses appealed to God's promise of grace made unto the fathers. The threat to destroy the people was a reaction of God's justice to the sins of the people. Christ teaches the same thing in the Parable of the Fruitless Fig Tree (Luke 13: 6-9). Beyond the facts revealed in the Bible, that God will and does hear our prayers, we must not speculate in trying to determine how our prayers can affect the will and the providence of God.

12. **Prayer is not a means of grace.**—A means of grace is that, by and through which grace and forgiveness is *offered and conveyed* to man; in prayer, however, we *ask* for grace and blessings. The grace we ask for in prayer God offers and bestows on us through His Word and the Sacraments. In prayer we deal with God; through the means of grace God deals with us.

XXIX. THE LIFE OF A CHRISTIAN A LIFE UNDER THE CROSS, BUT A LIFE OF HOPE

A. Life Under the Cross

1. While by faith in Christ we have become the children of God (John 1: 12), our lives on earth are by no means free from trouble and tribulation; but, like the Savior Himself, each of His followers must bear his own cross. "Whosoever will come after Me, let him deny himself, and take up his cross, and follow Me" (Mark 8: 34. 35). "We must through much tribulation enter into the kingdom of God" (Acts 14: 22).

2. **What may be regarded as a cross?**—The troubles and sufferings of the ungodly are not a cross, but a punishment. "Many sorrows shall be to the wicked" (Ps. 32: 10). "Evil shall slay the wicked" (Ps. 34: 21). But even these punishments have a gracious purpose. By them God would bring the wicked to their senses, that they may realize whither their sins lead them, and that they repent and turn to the Lord (Lev. 26: 14-42; Rom. 2: 4).

Christians also suffer the external consequences of their own sins and of the sin of Adam. But as they have obtained forgiveness for all sins through faith in Christ, they are not to look upon these external consequences as punishments for their sins, in the strict sense of the term, but as corrections, chastisements. Bodily afflictions, loss of property, misfortunes, etc., are real punishments to the ungodly, but chastisements to God's children; to the Christians they are administered not in the spirit of wrath and vengeance, but in the spirit of love for the purposes of correction and trial. Thus Paul was afflicted with "a thorn in the flesh . . ." (2 Cor. 12: 7-10). (Read Hebr. 12: 5-11.)

A cross is whatever Christians endure because they are Christians (1 Pet. 4: 16), whatever they suffer because they follow the Savior and in word and deed confess His name before men. "If ye be reproached for the name of Christ, happy are ye" (1 Pet. 4: 14). "Ye shall be hated of all men for My name's sake" (Matt. 10: 22).

The cross includes self-denial; "let him deny himself" (Mark 8: 34). We must "forsake," cut loose from, forego, whatever might prevent us from following Jesus (Luke 14: 33), whether this be honor before men (Matt. 5: 11), friends and relatives (Luke 14: 26. 27), earthly possessions (Matt. 19: 21. 22), or our own life (Luke 14: 26). All these are precious gifts of God for us to use; but we must not become so attached to them that they interfere in our relation to Christ. "Yea doubtless, and I count all things but loss for the excellency of the knowledge of Christ Jesus my Lord, for whom I have suffered the loss of all things, and do count them but dung, that I may win Christ" (Phil. 3: 8). Our attitude towards all earthly things must be that we have them as though we had them not (1 Cor. 7: 30). This is not an easy matter for our flesh; yet loyalty to Christ demands that, if need be, we forsake all that we have (Luke 14: 33).

The daily struggle against sin in our members (Rom. 7: 14-25), the mortification of our flesh with its affections and lusts (Gal. 5: 24; Col. 3: 5), are not the least part of the burden we bear.

3. **Each Christian has his own cross,** fitted to his particular condition and need. Let us not complain that our crosses are more burdensome than those of others, for others may feel the same way when they compare their crosses with ours. We may rest assured that our Father in heaven will never place a heavier burden upon us than we are able to bear (1 Cor. 10: 13), and He will stand by, saying: "Fear thou not; for I am with thee: be not dismayed; for I am thy God: I will strengthen thee; yea, I will help thee; yea, I will uphold thee with the right hand of My righteousness" (Is. 41: 10).

The cross must not be regarded as a mark of God's wrath, but rather as a token of His love (Hebr. 12: 6. 8. 10; 1 Cor. 11: 32). It is a testimony of the Holy Spirit that we are not of the world, but of God (1 Pet. 4: 14). It is an earnest or pledge of our salvation (Rom. 8: 17; 2 Thess. 1: 4-7). "Through the cross to the crown."

4. **The purpose of the cross** is not to trouble and vex us, but to humble us (2 Cor. 12: 7-9). It helps us to suppress the old Adam and to deny worldly lusts (1 Pet. 4: 1. 2). It tests and tries our faith (1 Pet. 1: 6. 7). It incites us to seek help from God in prayer (Is. 26: 16), and turns our attention from things temporal and earthly to things spiritual and eternal (2 Cor. 4: 16-18).

B. A Life of Hope

1. While the life of a Christian is a life under the cross, it is at the same time a life buoyed by a glorious hope. The very moment faith springs up in the heart, there is kindled not only a fervent love, which manifests itself in a life consecrated to the service of God, but also a living hope, which supports and cheers the believer in the trials and tribulations of life. "Blessed be the God and Father of our Lord Jesus Christ, which according to His abundant mercy hath begotten us again unto a lively hope by the resurrection of Jesus Christ from the dead" (1 Pet. 1: 3). Faith, therefore, is inseparably linked with love and hope.

2. **In what do we hope?**—We hope and trust in God for guidance, protection, and help in the affairs of our earthly lives. God's children do not worry about the future, for they know that their heavenly Father will provide (Matt. 6: 25-33). "Why art thou cast down, O my soul, and why art thou disquieted within me? Hope thou in God; for I shall yet praise Him, who is the health of my countenance and my God" (Ps. 42: 11). Even in tribulation they are not dismayed, for "we know that all things work together for good to them that love God" (Rom. 8: 28).

However, the believer's hope is not limited to this life. "If in this life only we have hope in Christ, we are of all men most miserable" (1 Cor. 15: 19). Here on earth we bear the cross, but our hope reaches out beyond the grave, where the hopes of the wicked cease; it reaches out into eternity. "We are begotten again unto a lively hope . . . to an inheritance incorruptible, and undefiled, and that fadeth not away, reserved in heaven for you, who are kept by the power of God through faith unto salvation ready to be revealed in the last time" (1 Pet. 1: 3-5). Christians live in constant expectancy of the realization of a glorious hope; they "live soberly, righteously, and godly in this present world, looking for the blessed hope, and the glorious appearing of the great God and our Savior Jesus Christ" (Tit. 2: 12. 13); (1 Cor. 1: 7). Though they are still in this world, their chief interests are centered in heaven, where they hold citizenship. "Our conversation" (state of which we are citizens) "is in heaven; from whence also we look for the Savior, the Lord Jesus Christ" (Phil. 3: 20). They are pilgrims, looking for the city whose builder and maker is God (Hebr. 11: 10). Thus the life of a Christian is not world-centered, but heaven-centered; his yearnings and aspirations reach out beyond the narrow limits of this present life; they are fixed on the glorious inheritance reserved for him in heaven.

3. **The hope of heaven affects our lives on earth.**—This living hope in the life to come strongly influences and determines the manner of our present life. It fills our hearts with joy (1 Pet. 1: 6). Because we have here no continuing city, but seek one to come (Hebr. 13: 14), we should not set our affections on the things of this world, but on things above (Col. 3: 1-4). Looking forward to that incorruptible inheritance, we should not put too high a value on earthly things, which pass away (Luke 12: 15-21). Because the Lord may come at any time, we should be diligent in all good works (Matt. 24: 45-47; 25: 14-23), especially in the preaching of the Gospel (Matt. 24: 14). We should keep ourselves unspotted from the world (Tit. 2: 12-14; 1 Pet. 2: 11), guard against carnal security (Matt. 24: 36-44), use the things of this world without abusing them (1 Cor. 7: 31), be moderate, yielding to all men (Phil. 4: 5), rejoice in suffering (Rom. 8: 18; 1 Pet. 4: 12. 13), and triumph in the face of death (1 Cor. 15: 52-57). Thus the entire life of a Christian here on earth should be lived in the light of heaven; his view of life and his attitude toward life should be entirely different from that of those who have no hope. Our hope of heaven should so affect the manner of our lives on earth.

The reason that our hope of heaven does not affect our lives as it should, is due to the fact that we still have the old Adam, whose inclinations and aspirations are decidedly earthward; to him the glamor and glitter, the pleasures and the treasures of this present life, have a compelling fascination. Thus it is that the devil's promise of the kingdoms of the world and the glory of them (Matt. 4: 8) often so strongly appeals even to Christians, that they forget the greater glories reserved for them in heaven. For this reason it is necessary that again and again we be reminded to set our affection on things above (Col. 3: 2).

XXX. PRESERVATION THROUGH FAITH UNTO SALVATION. (STEP VI)

1. **God keeps us in the faith.**—As it is God who gave us, and preserves in us, our natural life, so it is He who not only wrought faith and spiritual life in us, but who also keeps and preserves it. "Who are kept by the power of God through faith unto salvation" (1 Pet. 1: 5). "He which hath begun a good work in you will perform it until the day of Jesus Christ" (Phil. 1: 6). "Who shall also confirm you unto the end, that ye may be blameless in the day of our Lord Jesus Christ" (1 Cor. 1: 8). From these texts it is evident that God does not merely start men on the way of faith to heaven, but that God also "strengthens and preserves us steadfast in His Word and faith unto the end." "The decree of the Council of Trent, and whatever elsewhere is set forth in the same sense, is justly to be rejected, namely, that our good works preserve salvation or the righteousness of faith, which has been received, or even faith itself is either entirely or in part preserved by our works" (F. C., Th. D., Art. IV, 35, *Triglot*, p. 949). We reject "the doctrine of the synergists . . . that free will . . . can cooperate, by its own powers, with the Holy Ghost in the continuation and maintenance of this work" (F. C., Th. D., Art. II, 77, *Triglot*, p. 911).

"The exhortations 'Be thou faithful unto death' (Rev. 2: 10), 'Work out your own salvation with fear and trembling' (Phil. 2: 12), do not imply that a Christian achieves this perseverance by his own powers, as little as the command to believe implies that man produces faith. The powers called for in this exhortation are supplied and set in action solely by God (Phil. 2: 13). As to the argument that, since man himself brings about his defection, he must also be able to achieve his perseverance, Scripture rejects the deduction (1 Pet. 1: 5; Hos. 13: 9). And it is not even logically valid" (*Popular Symbolics*, p. 74). The fact that man is able to do one thing does not prove that he is able also to do the opposite. Man can destroy his life, but he can neither produce nor preserve it.

2. **God preserves faith through the means of grace.**— As God preserves physical life through certains means, such as food and drink, so He preserves spiritual faith and life through means, the means of grace. The same means by which He created faith He employs to nourish and to keep it, namely, the Gospel and the Sacraments. The power of God by which we are kept in the faith (1 Pet. 1: 5), operates through the Gospel, which is "the power of God unto salvation to every one that believeth" (Rom. 1: 16). It is "the Word of God, which effectually worketh also in you that believe" (1 Thess. 2: 13). "Through the same Word and the forgiveness of sins (He) bestows, increases, and strengthens faith" (Large Cat., III, 62, *Triglot*, p. 695). "Through the same Spirit and His grace, by means of daily exercise of reading and practising God's Word, He would preserve in us faith and His heavenly gifts, strengthen us from day to day, and keep us to the end" (F. C., Th. D., Art. II, 16, *Triglot*, p. 887).

3. **Man must use the means of grace.**—As man must use the means which God provides for the support and wants of the body, so he must likewise use the means by which God would preserve his faith. "Search the Scriptures" (John 5: 39). "Blessed are they that hear the Word of God, and keep it" (Luke 11: 28). "Let the Word of Christ dwell in you richly" (Col. 3: 16). "Blessed is the man . . . his delight is in the Law of the Lord; and in His Law doth he meditate day and night" (Ps. 1: 1. 2). While God could, indeed, preserve us in faith without the use of any means whatsoever, He has not promised to do so. It has pleased Him to deal with us only through His Word. If, then, we wish that faith be preserved in us, we must learn and ponder His Word, and keep it in our hearts. Whatever occupies our attention will work on our hearts. Neglecting to use the Word of God means spiritual starvation, spiritual suicide. The light of faith continues to burn as long as the Word of God supplies oil for our lamp.

4. The end of such preservation in the faith is the salvation of the soul.—"Who are kept by the power of God through faith unto salvation . . . Receiving the end of your faith, even the salvation of your souls" (1 Pet. 1: 5. 9). "God so loved the world, that He gave His only-begotten Son, that whosoever believeth in Him should not perish, but have everlasting life" (John 3: 16). Trusting in God's promise of preserving grace, the believer is assured of his final salvation. Hence, we confess with Luther in the explanation of the Third Article of the Apostles' Creed: "I believe that . . . He will give unto me and all believers in Christ eternal life. This is most certainly true." Having thus brought the sinner back to God, the Spirit's work of sanctification comes to an end.

5. Warnings against apostasy.— "The warnings against apostasy, Rom. 11: 20; 1 Cor. 10: 12, are aimed not at the confidence of faith, but at carnal security and self-confidence; heeding them, the Christian casts himself upon the Gospel promise and thus obtains and retains the certainty of final salvation. So also the 'fear and trembling' of Phil. 2: 12, resulting from the realization of our weakness and inability, does not replace the confidence of faith, but exists side by side with it and subserves it" (*Popular Symbolics*, p. 75). As we look at our weakness and the dangers that threaten us, we, like children, are filled with fear and trembling; but as we look at the sure promises of God, we are quite confident that His hand will lead us safely through all difficulties and dangers (Rom. 8: 38; John 10: 28). "The assertion that one who knows that he may become a castaway (1 Cor. 9: 27) cannot have the assurance that he will not become a castaway may be logically correct, but is theologically false; Rom. 8: 38. The difficulty which this matter presents cannot be solved by means of logic, but only by distinguishing between the Law and the Gospel. The convictions produced by the Law must not, and do not, eliminate the convictions produced by the Gospel, the assurance of perseverance, but subserve them" (*Popular Symbolics*, p. 75).

6. Salvation is exclusively a work of divine grace.—Without their merit and cooperation did the Son of God procure for all men forgiveness of sins, life, and salvation. Without our merit and cooperation did the Holy Ghost cause us to be-

lieve in Christ, and to continue in this faith unto the end.
Thus God began the good work in us, and performs it until
we are safe in heaven. No Christian may now or hereafter
claim any merit for himself, but must give all praise and glory
to God, who "hath made us meet to be partakers of the inheritance of the saints in light" (Col. 1: 12). If at any stage our
salvation depended in any measure or degree on some contribution we must make, it would at once become uncertain to
all of us, since no one could be sure whether his personal
contribution were sufficient to insure salvation. Man cannot
contribute anything toward his conversion and final salvation,
but he is saved exclusively by the monergism of divine grace.
"By grace are ye saved through faith; and that not of yourselves: it" (salvation) "is the gift of God: not of works, lest
any man should boast" (Eph. 2: 8. 9); (Rom. 4: 16).

7. **"God will have all men to be saved"** (1 Tim. 2: 4).
Whereas God alone can save sinners, the question arises,
whether He wants to save all of them. The answer is given
in the following Scripture texts. "The Lord is not willing that
any should perish, but that all should come to repentance"
(2 Pet. 3: 9). "God will have all men to be saved, and to
come to the knowledge of the truth" (1 Tim. 2: 4). "As I live,
saith the Lord God, I have no pleasure in the death of the
wicked, but that the wicked turn from his way and live"
(Ezek. 33: 11). In this last text God confirms with an oath
His serious intention of saving all men. Even of those who
are finally lost we learn, that Christ has not only bought them
(2 Pet. 2: 1), but that He also wanted to gather them to Himself (Matt. 23: 37). There is no human being whom Christ
did not redeem, and whom the Holy Ghost does not want to
bring to faith in Christ, and through such faith to heaven. If
there were but one exception, each man might think that he
is this exception, and no one could be sure of his salvation.
However, there is positively no exception; God wants all men
to be saved, and to that end has redeemed all men through
Christ.

8. **Not all men are saved.**—"Enter ye in at the strait gate:
for wide is the gate and broad is the way, that leadeth to destruction, and many there be which go in thereat: because
strait is the gate, and narrow is the way, which leadeth unto

life, and few there be that find it" (Matt. 7: 13. 14). "And
these shall go away into everlasting punishment, but the
righteous into life eternal" (Matt. 25: 46). "Many are called,
but few are chosen" (Matt. 22: 14). Thus, more are actually
lost than saved.—The reason why many do not come to Christ,
though they are called, lies in no sense with God, but solely
with man. Unto Jerusalem Christ said: "How often would I
have gathered thy children together, even as a hen gathereth
her chickens under her wings, and ye would not!" (Matt. 23:
37). Stephen told the Jews: "Ye stiffnecked and uncircum-
cised in heart and ears, ye do always resist the Holy Ghost; as
your fathers did, so do ye" (Acts 7: 51). Whoever, therefore,
is lost, is lost by his own fault; whoever is saved, is saved by
the grace and power of God. "O Israel, thou hast destroyed
thyself; but in Me is thine help" (Hos. 13: 9). Man got himself into trouble, but only God can get him out of it.

9. A difficulty.—In this connection a certain difficulty presents itself to man's way of thinking.

There is no difference among men; they all are equally unworthy to be converted and saved (2 Tim. 1: 9), equally in-
competent to convert themselves, and by nature equally unwilling to be converted (1 Cor. 2: 14; Eph. 2: 1; Rom. 8: 7;
1 Cor. 12: 3).

There is no difference in the attitude of God towards men;
He earnestly would convert and save all men (1 Tim. 2: 4),
and He alone can convert if man is to be converted (1 Cor.
12: 3; Jer. 31: 18).

From this it would seem to follow that, since the same
powerful grace of God works on all who hear the Gospel, the
same effect would result: either that all are converted, because the powerful grace of God breaks down their resistance,
or that no one is converted, because the grace of God is not
strong enough. For if the grace of God does convert one, we
see no reason why it should not do so with another, who is in
like condemnation. If it cannot or does not convert the second
person, we see no reason why it can and does convert the
first. Where the same powers operate under the same conditions, we should expect the same results. Still we find, while
the spiritual condition of all men is the same, and the con-
verting grace is equally serious and efficacious with all, there

is a difference in the result: some are converted, others are not.

Synergism would explain this different result by a difference in men. Some people, it is held, by their natural powers contribute something towards their conversion; they cooperate with the Holy Ghost, fit themselves for His work, do not resist as much as others, and therefore with them the efforts of the Holy Ghost take effect, and conversion results.

Calvinism would explain the different result by a difference in God, namely, that God does not seriously intend to convert and save all men, that He passes certain ones by with His grace. (Cf., Historical Introduction to the Symbolical Books: XIV, The Synergistic Controversy, *Triglot*, p. 124; XX, On Predestination, p. 195).

Both, Synergism and Calvinism, make salvation uncertain to the individual. The Synergist must ask himself whether he has sufficiently cooperated with the Holy Ghost to bring about a real conversion, while the Calvinist must ever be in doubt whether he really is among those whom God wanted to convert and to save.

The Bible denies that there is a difference in the spiritual attitude of natural man toward God, or in the gracious will of God towards men, and it plainly teaches that He is willing to convert and save all men, and that only He can convert and save them. *If any man is turned to God in conversion, this is solely and exclusively the work of the Holy Ghost; but if any man remains unconverted, it is solely and exclusively his own fault. Beyond this we must not try to reason.* We have no right to construct or develop a doctrine on the basis of our own rational deductions, but must bring every thought into captivity to the obedience of Christ (2 Cor. 10: 5), and bow in humble admiration to the superior wisdom of our God, as the apostle Paul did, saying: "O the depth of the riches both of the wisdom and knowledge of God! How unsearchable are His judgments, and His ways past finding out!" (Rom. 11: 33).

XXXI. THE ELECTION OF GRACE

As the work of the Holy Ghost, by which men are brought to Christ and through faith unto salvation, is but the realization of God's eternal purpose and plan, it is proper to discuss the doctrine of election at this point. "The eternal election of God, however, or predestination, that is, God's ordination to salvation, does not extend at once over the godly and the wicked, but only over the children of God" (F. C., Th. D., XI, 5, *Triglot*, p. 1065). It has no counterpart, such as a predestination to damnation.

1. **General statement.**—Before a person begins to build a house, he has in mind the purpose to build and a plan according to which he will build. And while we may not have any advance information concerning his purpose and plan, we learn to know them as the building operations begin and proceed, for the man builds as he has purposed and planned it. We also conclude that he will continue to build until his original purpose is realized. In a similar way we may consider the work of the Holy Ghost. We observe in others, and experience it also in ourselves, that the Holy Ghost has called us by the Gospel, that He has wrought faith in our hearts, that He justifies, sanctifies, and that He keeps us in this faith, and will finally save us. These are spiritual blessings, which the Holy Ghost bestows upon us during our lifetime, of which we have knowledge. Behind the work of the Holy Ghost, as it unfolds itself in our lives, stands the eternal purpose and plan of God. The entire work of the Holy Ghost is the actual fulfilling and realization of God's purpose.

Briefly stated, then, the doctrine of predestination is this: Whatever God has done, is doing, and will still do for us during our life on earth to bring us to faith in Christ and to preserve us in this faith unto eternal salvation, is not a matter of chance; neither is it motivated by any personal merit and worthiness, or better conduct, which God foresaw in some people; but God has from eternity purposed and planned it, and by grace for Christ's sake He has chosen and predestinated us to salvation before the foundation of the world.

2. **Bible proof.**—We read in Scripture: "God hath saved us and called us with an holy calling, not according to our works, but according to His purpose and grace, which was given us in Christ Jesus before the world began" (2 Tim. 1: 9). Here the apostle Paul calls attention to certain things the Christians had experienced in their lives; they had been called and converted through the Gospel. This did not happen by

chance, nor because God discovered in them some merit or
virtue; He purposed this before the world began according to
His grace in Christ Jesus.

"Blessed be the God and Father of our Lord Jesus Christ,
who hath blessed us with all spiritual blessings in heavenly
places in Christ; according as He hath chosen us in Him before the foundation of the world, that we should be holy and
without blame before Him in love, having predestinated us
unto the adoption of children by Jesus Christ to Himself, according to the good pleasure of His will, to the praise of the
glory of His grace, wherein He hath made us accepted in the
Beloved" (Eph. 1: 3-6). The apostle Paul thanks God for the
spiritual blessings the Christians at Ephesus had received, and
of which they had knowledge. Then he adds this information, that they were blessed "according as He hath chosen us
in Him before the foundation of the world." God blessed them
during their lifetime, even as He had from eternity purposed
and planned to do. The intent of this election, therefore, was
that the Ephesian Christians should be blessed with all spiritual blessings; they were chosen that they should be holy and
blameless before God in love; they were predestinated that by
faith they should become the children of God.—Furthermore,
Paul points out the cause of their election. As during their
lives they were blessed "in Christ," so they were from eternity
chosen "in Him," and predestinated "according to the good
pleasure of His will, to the praise of the glory of His grace."
Thus we see that in blessing us with spiritual blessings during our lives on earth, God carries out what He purposed to
do for us from eternity.

Other texts which clearly set forth the doctrine of election
are: Rom. 8: 28-30; 2 Thess. 2: 13; 1 Pet. 1: 2; Acts 13: 48.

3. **Election in detail.**— (a) Election is an act of God; "He
hath chosen us." Man did not choose God to be his Father,
but God chose man to be His child. And this He did not during the lifetime of a person, but "before the foundation of the
world." The question is not determined while man lives on
earth, pending his conduct, but before he is born (Rom. 9: 11),
before the world began (2 Tim. 1: 9).

(b) God was moved to do this, not by any merit or worthiness He foresaw in man (2 Tim. 1: 9; Rom. 11: 6), but solely

and exclusively by His grace in Christ Jesus; "according to the purpose of His grace given us in Christ Jesus" (2 Tim. 1: 9); "having chosen us in Him" (Christ) and "having predestinated us . . . by Jesus Christ . . . according to the good pleasure of His will, to the praise of the glory of His grace" (Eph. 1: 4-6).

(c) This predestination does not pertain to the redemption, by which salvation was to be procured for all men, nor to the means of grace, through which these spiritual blessings were to be offered and imparted to men, but it pertains to men themselves, to individual persons; "us" (Eph. 1: 4), "you" (2 Thess. 2: 13), "as many as were ordained to eternal life believed" (Acts 13: 48). The objects of election are men, human beings, not means.

(d) God chose, elected. Election, therefore, does not extend over all men, for that would not be an election. Election extended over certain ones. "Many are called, but few are chosen" (Matt. 22: 14). Who these chosen ones are, God did not reveal beforehand; but they are recognized by the results of their election in their lives, as we shall see later. The election was at the same time also a predestination; for God elected these people for a definite purpose, and ordained that this purpose be realized and accomplished with them. He resolved and decreed from the beginning what He would do for them after they are born into this world.

(e) The elect are predestinated unto being called through the Gospel and unto conversion (2 Tim. 1: 9; Rom. 8: 28), unto the obedience of faith (1 Pet. 1: 2; Acts 13: 48), unto the adoption of children by faith (Eph. 1: 5; Rom. 8: 29), unto justification through faith (1 Pet. 1: 2; Rom. 8: 30), unto sanctification of life, to "be holy and without blame before Him in love" (Eph. 1: 4), unto good works (Eph. 2: 10), unto perseverance in the faith (John 10: 28; Matt. 24: 24), and through all these unto eternal life (Acts 13: 48; 2 Thess. 2: 13).

4. Resumé.—The decree of predestination, therefore, ordains not merely the final salvation of the elect, but it includes also the entire way that leads them to heaven. In other words, God predestinated His elect *unto* eternal life *via* conversion, faith, justification, sanctification, and preservation in the faith, as Paul says: "God hath from the beginning chosen you *to*

salvation *through* sanctification of the Spirit and belief of the truth" (2 Thess. 2: 13). None of the elect get to heaven except by this way, and it is included in the decree of their election that they should get to heaven by this way. Hence, the entire work of the Holy Ghost, by which He calls, converts, justifies, sanctifies, keeps, and finally saves sinners, is but the execution and realization of God's eternal purpose concerning these individuals. This is brought out very clearly in Rom. 8: 28-30, where we read: "We know that all things work together for good to them that love God, to them who are the called according to His purpose. For whom He did foreknow, He also did predestinate to be conformed to the image of His Son, that He might be the firstborn among many brethren. Moreover whom He did predestinate, them He also called: and whom He called, them He also justified: and whom He justified, them He also glorified." In this text the word "foreknow" cannot mean merely to know beforehand, because God knew all men before they were born, yet not all men are predestinated. Here the word "foreknow" means to know as one's own, as in Matt. 7: 23; Luke 13: 27; it means to elect, to choose, as in Rom. 11: 2; Amos 3: 2. Hence, the meaning of the text is: Whom He chose, those He predestinated; and whom He predestinated, them He called by the Gospel, them He justified by faith, and them He finally glorified in heaven.

"In this counsel, purpose, and ordination God has prepared salvation not only in general, but has in His grace considered and chosen to salvation each and every person of the elect who are to be saved through Christ, also ordained that in the way just mentioned He will, by His grace, gifts, and efficacy, bring them thereto, aid, promote, strengthen, and preserve them" (F. C., Th. D., Art. XI, 23, *Triglot,* p. 1069).

Being elected *unto* conversion and faith, and *through* these unto salvation, it is evident that a person cannot be elected in view of, or because of, his faith, since faith is not a cause, but the result of his election (Acts 13: 48).

5. **Knowledge of our election.**—No man on earth has direct information as to his personal election; he can have only an inferred knowledge. In life we often infer the cause from its effects. Illustration: Perhaps we did not see or hear it rain during the night; but if in the morning we find wet ground

and water puddles, we infer that it must have rained. In like manner, we have no direct knowledge of our election, but we have the experimental knowledge of its results in our lives, namely, those spiritual blessings in Christ, from which we should infer that we were elected thereunto. From our faith in Christ, which we now have, we infer that we shall not perish, but have everlasting life (John 3: 16); from the same faith we should infer also that we were ordained to eternal life (Acts 13: 48). Faith in Christ is a matter of personal experience and direct knowledge; "I know whom I have believed" (2 Tim. 1: 12). And by this faith which I now have, I know of my election in the past and my salvation in the future. The knowledge of my election, in turn, fortifies my assurance of final salvation (Matt. 24: 24). Thus knowledge of election—not election itself—is contingent on faith. Faith in Christ does not explain why we are elected, but it shows us that we are elected. "Der Glaube ist nicht Erklaerungsgrund, wohl aber Erkenntnisgrund der Wahl."

He who would know of his election, should not begin to speculate concerning the secret and inscrutable foreknowledge of God; but let him repent of his sins, hear the Gospel of grace, by which God calls His elect; let him examine himself whether he is in the faith (2 Cor. 13: 5); then by this faith he will know also of his election. As long as a person is in the faith, he should regard himself an elect, even as he regards himself an heir of salvation as long as he believes in Christ. In like manner must we, as Paul did (2 Thess. 2: 13), look upon all as being elected, whom we must assume to be believers.

As long as a person is without faith, he cannot *know* and regard himself as being elected. But this does by no means say that he is *not* elected; for God may still call him by the Gospel and begin in him that good work, which will end in heaven. Let him hear the Gospel, believe in Christ, his Savior, and then he will by this faith also know of his election. (Cf., F. C., Th. D., Art. XI, 25-33, *Triglot*, p. 1071).

6. **The comfort of this doctrine.**—This doctrine is by no means a useless speculation, but very comforting; it shows us that our salvation and everything pertaining thereto is not a matter of chance, nor, on our part, a matter of personal choice

(Rom. 9: 16), or of personal merit (Rom. 11: 6), but is a matter of deep concern to God, who purposed it before the world began, deliberated concerning it, and in His secret counsel ordained how He would bring us thereto and preserve us therein. And since this counsel of God cannot fail nor be overthrown, we are thereby assured of our final salvation (Matt. 24: 24). (Cf., F. C., Th. D., Art. XI, 45. 46, *Triglot*, p. 1079).

We are also admonished: "Give diligence to make your calling and election sure" (2 Pet. 1: 10). No one should think that, because he is in faith today and thereby assured of his election, he may now discard the Gospel, lose faith, live in sin, and still regard himself as one of the elect who will unfailingly be saved. We find comfort in our election only *while* we are in the faith. Hence, to make our election sure *to ourselves,* we must give diligence that we remain steadfast in the faith. To this end we must make use of those means by which God assures us of His grace and thereby of our election.

7. **Relation of the election of grace to the work of grace.** —The work of the Holy Ghost, by which we are brought to Christ and to salvation, is the fulfillment and the execution of the election of grace. Hence, there is so intimate a connection between the two that an error in the one will result in an error in the other. Synergists teach that man contributes something toward his conversion; hence, they teach that men are elected in view of this "something" they would contribute. Calvinism teaches that many are foreordained to everlasting death; hence, they teach that the Holy Ghost does not intend to save all men. He who correctly understands and believes as is confessed in Luther's explanation of the Third Article of the Apostles' Creed, will have no difficulty in understanding and believing that, what the Holy Ghost does to bring us to Christ and through faith to heaven, God has purposed and resolved to do for us from eternity.

"This doctrine is the doctrine of the Third Article plus the idea of eternity; in other words, it is the eternal purpose and plan of God to do for the individual what, according to the Third Article, He actually does for him during his lifetime to bring him to heaven" (G. J. Fritschel in *The Lutheran Standard,* January, 1940).

8. **False teachings on election.**—Calvinism teaches: "By

the decree of God, for the manifestation of His glory, some men and angels are predestinated unto everlasting life, and others foreordained to everlasting death" (Westminster Confession); (cf., Schaff, 3608); (cf., *Triglot,* Introd., No. 225. 226). The Bible knows nothing of a predestination unto eternal death. On the contrary, it teaches that God will have all men to be saved (1 Tim. 2: 4), and that man alone is at fault, if he is lost (Matt. 23: 37; Hos. 13: 9).

Synergism, while upholding the universality of God's grace and of Christ's redemption, teaches that there must be something in man that influenced and determined God to elect just him and not another. (Cf., *Triglot,* Introd., No. 224). Even the expression that men are elected "in view of faith" makes sense only if there is an element of human merit in faith. But the Bible definitely excludes every merit or worthiness in man as a cause of his election (2 Tim. 1: 9; Rom. 11: 6).

Human reason cannot harmonize the two doctrines of the Bible, that God by grace for Christ's sake will have all men to be saved, and that God by grace for Christ's sake elected few to be saved; neither must men try to harmonize them. We can only restate what God has revealed to us in His Word, and we must not begin to guess what He has reserved in His hidden wisdom concerning this mystery. God has not revealed to us all He knows, all He did and intends to do for our salvation, nor His reasons for His acts. But God did reveal as much as He wants us to know and as much as we need to know regarding salvation through Christ. He does not satisfy our curiosity as to His secret counsels. Hence, we say with Paul: "O the depth of the riches both of the wisdom and knowledge of God! how unsearchable are His judgments, and His ways past finding out!" (Rom. 11: 33). (Read F. C., Art. XI.)

PART VIII. SALVATION THROUGH THE MEANS OF GRACE

XXXII. THE GOSPEL

1. **Necessity of the means of grace.**—The life and the death of Jesus are historic facts, witnessed by Jews and Gentiles of His day. But the meaning thereof no man could know if it were not revealed to us by God (1 Cor. 2: 9-12). If ever sinners are to profit by the merits of Christ's redemption, these merits must be offered and imparted to them. Hence, the necessity of means, by which the merits of Christ are revealed, offered, and imparted to us.—God determined the means by which salvation was procured for the world, namely, by the life and death of His Son. He also is the only one who can determine by which means this salvation is to be revealed and transmitted to us. It is exceedingly foolish for man to say how and by what means God should impart to us His grace. "God was in Christ, reconciling the world unto Himself, not imputing their trespasses unto them; and hath committed unto us the Word of reconciliation" (2 Cor. 5: 19).

The means of grace presuppose that God is gracious to all men for Christ's sake. A denial of universal justification is necessarily reflected in the doctrine of the means of grace. If God had not forgiven all sins, there could be no means by which forgiveness is offered. In that case the means of grace would become means by the use of which man earns grace, and they would be no longer means by which God offers grace.

2. **Which are the means of grace?**— (a) The Law is not a means of grace. "By the Law is the knowledge of sin" (Rom. 3: 20); it proclaims the curse of God (Gal. 3: 10). Prayer is not a means of grace (see p. 172). Self-imposed works and exercises are no means of grace; through them God does not convey grace and blessing to man; but man, erroneously however, often hopes thereby to earn favor with God.

(b) The means of grace are the Gospel and the Sacraments. The Sacraments are means only because of the Gospel promise connected therewith. Therefore we may say that there is

189

but one means by which the knowledge of grace and salvation, and grace and salvation itself, are imparted to us; it is the Gospel, the glad tidings of the grace of God in Christ Jesus. For this reason it is called "the Gospel of grace" (Acts 20: 24), "the Gospel of peace" (Rom. 10: 15), "the Word of reconciliation" (2 Cor. 5: 19), "the Gospel of our salvation" (Eph. 1: 13). This Gospel is made known to men by preaching and teaching (Mark 16: 15). In a more specific manner it is applied to men in the form of absolution (John 20: 23), and, connected with visible elements, in the Sacraments.

"Therefore we ought and must constantly maintain this point, that God does not wish to deal with us otherwise than through the spoken Word and the Sacraments. It is the devil himself whatsoever is extolled as Spirit without the Word and the Sacraments" (S. A., Part III, Art. VIII, 10, *Triglot*, p. 497).

3. **The functions of the Gospel.**— (Compare "The purpose of the Law," p. 59 ff.).— (a) The Gospel is not merely a biography of Christ, the story of His life and death as witnessed by men, but it *reveals to us the meaning and the achievements of His life and death.* It tells us of the love of God, who sent His Son into the world (John 3: 16; Rom. 5: 8). It tells us that Christ made full atonement for our sins (Hebr. 9: 12), and reconciled us to God; "when we were enemies, we were reconciled to God by the death of His Son" (Rom. 5: 10). It reveals to us that righteousness which we must have before God, if we would be saved (Rom. 1: 17). The Gospel does not reveal a possible grace of God, a possible reconciliation and forgiveness, contingent on certain conditions we are to fulfill; *redemption, reconciliation, forgiveness are revealed as accomplished facts,* which are not affected by what we may or may not do (Rom. 3: 3).

(b) Because the Gospel is God's own proclamation of universal grace and pardon, *it actually offers and conveys this grace to men.* The Gospel "talks" forgiveness, preaches forgiveness. "Through this Man" (Jesus, the Mediator) "is preached unto you the forgiveness of sins" (Acts 13: 38). In the Gospel God tells every sin-sick soul: "Be of good cheer; thy sins be forgiven thee" (Matt. 9: 2). The Gospel is, therefore, God's own absolution, His free and unconditional promise of grace and forgiveness. Whoever hedges this promise with all manner of conditions, virtually destroys the essence of the Gospel. —All means of grace offer the same grace and have the same purpose and power. Baptism and the Lord's Supper are but different ways or modes of conveying to man the grace of God and the merits of Christ. They offer no other, no greater, no better grace than the Gospel; nor do they offer it in portions and parts, for the grace of God and the merits of Christ are a unit, which in every instance is offered full and complete. Through the Gospel and the Sacraments "are granted not bodily, but eternal things, as eternal righteousness" (A. C., Art. XXVIII, 8, *Triglot*, p. 85).

(c) While such promise on the part of God requires faith on the part of man, such faith is not a condition on which the promise is based and on which it depends. Faith is only the means, the hand, by which the promise is accepted, and it is the only means by which it can be accepted. The free promise of grace precedes faith, and this grace is in no wise dependent on faith. Illustration: There must be food before we can eat it. However, as food will not benefit us unless we eat it, so the promise of grace will not benefit us personally unless we accept it by faith (Hebr. 4: 2).—Now, as it is the nature of a promise to work faith in him to whom it is made, so *the promise of God in the Gospel works in man that very faith by which he accepts the promise* and what the promise offers. "Faith cometh by hearing, and hearing by the Word of God" (Rom. 10: 17); (John 17: 20; 1 Thess. 2: 13). Therefore we are "born again" by the Word of God (1 Pet. 1: 23); we are begotten through the Gospel (1 Cor. 4: 15; James 1: 18).

However, this power of the Gospel to touch and turn the heart is not a natural power, such as inheres also in a promise spoken by men, but it is a supernatural and divine power. Since the Gospel is God's Word, and since the Holy Ghost is inseparably connected with it, there is inherent in the Gospel at all times and under all conditions, whether read, heard, or remembered, a supernatural and divine power and efficacy. Therefore the Word of God is never a lifeless instrument, but, as Christ says: "The words that I speak unto you, they are spirit, and they are life" (John 6: 63). "The Word of God is quick and powerful and sharper than any two-edged sword"

(Hebr. 4: 12). And Paul tells us that the Gospel "is the power of God unto salvation to every one that believeth" (Rom. 1: 16). Thus the Gospel is not a dead hand, which merely holds out to us the blessings of salvation for our acceptance, but it is the power of God, through which the Holy Ghost operates, bringing such influence to bear on the heart of man that it turns to Christ in faith and accepts the promised gifts. "Through the same Word and forgiveness the Holy Ghost bestows, increases, and strengthens faith" (Large Cat., Art. III, 62, *Triglot,* p. 695).

If God offered His grace and worked faith in the hearts of men independently of the means of grace, we could dispense entirely with the Gospel and the Sacraments, as the Quakers do. If, as Calvin maintains, the "external invitation" does not carry with it the "internal efficacy of grace," there is no purpose in reading the Bible or hearing the Gospel. (Cf., *Popular Symbolics,* p. 77. 215).

4. **The validity and the efficacy of the means of grace** do not depend on the personal or the official character of the minister. Their validity rests on their divine institution, and they have their efficacy in themselves.

The evil works of the scribes did not deprive the Word of God they preached of its authority (Matt. 23: 2. 3). The insincerity of the preachers characterized in Phil. 1: 16-19 did not affect the truth of their message. The personal character of the minister affects the truth, authority, and efficacy of the Word of God he preaches as little as does the grade of paper on which it is printed in our Bibles. The minister is only a steward, an ambassador, a messenger of God, and it is the message that counts, not the messenger. If he deals with us according to the Word of God, his personal impiety cannot invalidate the message he brings, nor render the divine power inherent in the Word and the Sacraments inefficacious. "Both the Sacraments and the Word are effectual by reason of the institution and commandment of Christ, notwithstanding they be administered by evil men" (A. C., Art. VIII, 2, *Triglot,* p. 47). (Cf., Apol., Art. VII, VIII, 28, *Triglot,* p. 237).

Neither does the official status of the minister, the fact that he is properly ordained (Apostolic Succession), contribute anything towards the validity and efficacy of the means of grace. A promise of God, when quoted by a layman, is as valid and certain as it is when pronounced by an ordained clergyman. The official character of the minister does not add virtue and power to any statement of the Word of God.

The Word and the Sacraments are valid because God Himself ordained them (Matt. 28: 19), and when administered in His name, that is, in the sense and meaning He Himself put into them, they are valid and efficacious (Hebr. 4: 12).

Luther says: "Our faith and Sacrament must not rest on the person, be he godly or wicked, ordained or unordained, called or sneaking in, the devil or his mother, but on Christ, His Word, His office, His command and ordinance" (St. Louis Edition, XIX, 1272). "Neither does the ministry avail on account of the authority of any person, but on account of the Word given by Christ (Nor does the person of the teacher add anything to this word and office)" (S. A., Power and Primacy of Pope, 26, *Triglot*, p. 511). (Cf., *Popular Symbolics*, p. 77).

5. **The Gospel is always efficacious**, always able to produce an effect, and to turn the hearts of men to God. It is powerful and quick to touch the heart (Hebr. 4: 12; Jer. 23: 29), and able to convert the soul and to comfort the distressed (Ps. 19: 7. 8; James 1: 21). Its promise is always sincere (Is. 1: 18; Jer. 3: 12; Rom. 10: 21). Even the unbelief of man, which rejects the promise, cannot invalidate it, as we learn from Rom. 3: 3. 4, where we read: "For what if some did not believe? shall their unbelief make the faith of God without effect? God forbid: yea, let God be true, but every man a liar."

6. **The Gospel is not always effective;** it does not in every case produce the intended effect. It does not always work faith, because the power of God, operating through the Gospel, can be resisted by men. "Ye do always resist the Holy Ghost; as your fathers did, so do ye" (Acts 7: 51). The fault lies not with God, nor with the Gospel, but with the perverse will of man, which, dominated by other considerations, will not yield to the persuasive influence of the Holy Ghost. Illustration: The seed we put into the ground has inherent power to germinate, grow, and bring fruit; but adverse weather conditions may prevent it from doing so. Thus the seed of the Gospel

has power to affect the heart and to work faith, but inhibitions such as love of sin, self-righteousness, etc., often prevent it from taking root. For whichever thought dominates the mind to the exclusion of others will also prevent other thoughts to make an impression on the heart. Thus inhibitory influences, emanating from the old Adam, often control the heart and thus frustrate the purpose of the Gospel. An inimical attitude of man cannot render the Word of God inefficacious (Rom. 3: 3. 4), but it may prevent the Word from being effective (Acts 7: 51). Such resistance to the power of God is possible when He deals with us through means; but it is impossible when He deals with us in His uncovered majesty, as when He will raise the dead on the Last Day.

XXXIII. THE LAW AND THE GOSPEL

1. **The Law and the Gospel.**—Both terms are used in the Bible in a wider and in a narrower sense. In the wider sense, either of the terms denotes the entire revelation of God. In the narrower and proper sense, the Law is the Law of the Commandments, and the Gospel is the glad tidings of God's grace. The Law and the Gospel have this in common: both are the Word of God; both pertain to all men; both must be taught side by side in the Church unto the end of time. Nevertheless, they are fundamentally different, and must be carefully distinguished; "rightly dividing the Word of truth" (2 Tim. 2: 15).

2. **Differences between the Law and the Gospel.**—(a) The Law, originally written in the heart of man, is still partly known to man by nature (Rom. 2: 14. 15).—The Gospel is absolutely unknown to natural man; there is not even a trace of it in the religions of heathen people. We learn of it only from God's own revelation (1 Cor. 2: 6-12).

(b) In the Law God tells us what we must do or may not do. It is "the Law of commandments contained in ordinances" (Eph. 2: 15). "Thou shalt" (Matt. 22: 37); "Thou shalt not" (Ex. 20: 3). It demands perfect obedience (Gal. 3: 10; Matt. 5: 48).—The Gospel reveals what God has done and is still doing for our salvation (John 3: 16; Luke 4: 18. 19). It contains no commands, but only promises of grace and forgiveness (Rom. 1: 16. 17; 3: 21; Matt. 9: 2). The command of the

Gospel calling for faith (1 John 3: 23), is not a legal command, but a gracious invitation, expressed in the most forcible way, to accept the proffered blessings.

(c) The Law promises eternal life on condition of a perfect obedience. "This do, and thou shalt live" (Luke 10: 28); (Lev. 18: 5; Gal. 3: 12). The promise of the Law must be earned by keeping all the Commandments. — The Gospel-promise is free, gratuitous, unconditional. "Being justified freely by His grace" (Rom. 3: 24); (Rom. 4: 16; 11: 6; Is. 1: 18; 43: 25). There are "no strings attached" to the Gospel-promise. Faith is not a condition of the promise in the sense that thereby we earn or become worthy of the promised gift, but only in the sense that thereby we accept what the promise offers.

(d) The Law convinces man of his sinfulness. "By the Law is the knowledge of sin" (Rom. 3: 20). Its transgressions provoke the wrath of God. Hence, it pronounces the curse of God on the evildoer; "cursed be he that confirmeth not all the words of this Law to do them" (Deut. 27: 26). Thus, the Law proves us to be ungodly, and condemns us.—The Gospel reveals to ungodly sinners the love and grace of God (John 3: 16; Acts 20: 24). It offers and imparts forgiveness of sins (Luke 24: 47), and the righteousness which Christ merited for man (Rom. 1: 17). Hence, it declares the ungodly just (Rom. 4: 5; 2 Cor. 5: 19).—In the Law God tells the sinner: Thou shalt die for thy sins and be damned. In the Gospel God tells the sinner: Thou art redeemed; thou shalt live and be saved.

(e) Because the Law reveals the wrath of God against all ungodliness and unrighteousness of man (Rom. 1: 18), it works fear of punishment, sorrow and regret, despair, and hatred of God in the heart of man. It demands love (Matt. 22: 37), but cannot inspire it; it kills love. "For sin, taking occasion by the commandment, deceived me, and by it slew me" (Rom. 7: 11); (2 Cor. 3: 6). It cannot make us Christians (Gal. 3: 2).—The Gospel comforts those who are depressed because of their sins (Is. 40: 1. 2); it works faith and trust in God (Rom. 10: 17), love of God and the neighbor (1 John 4: 19. 21), joy and hope (1 Pet. 1: 3. 6). Thus it regenerates us

(1 Pet. 1: 23), creating a new spiritual life and a willing obedience (John 6: 63; Ps. 119: 32).

3. **The use of the Law and the Gospel.**—While radically different as to content, purpose, and effect, both, the Law and the Gospel, must be used.

(a) By the Law man is brought to the knowledge of his sins, to regret, sorrow and despair. The Law "was added because of transgressions" (Gal. 3: 19). The Law shows transgressions to be what they truly are, namely, transgressions. It, therefore, demolishes all self-righteousness and trust in one's own merit, and makes one realize his helpless and hopeless condition. The Law must be preached to all men, but especially to *impenitent* sinners.

(b) The Gospel brings the message of grace, offers forgiveness of sins, works in the heart the acceptance of its offer, and thus converts man. (Cf., The functions of the Gospel, p. 190). The Gospel must be preached to sinners who are *troubled* in their minds because of their sins.

(c) But the Law must be used also after conversion. By faith we are perfectly righteous before God; the Law does not concern us at all as to our justification and salvation (Rom. 3: 28). But with respect to Christian living the regenerate need the Law as a curb, as a mirror, and as a guide.—As a curb: "For the old Adam, as an intractable, refractory ass, is still a part of them, which must be coerced to obedience of Christ, not only by the teaching, admonition, force, and threatening of the Law, but oftentimes by the club of punishments and troubles" (F. C., Th. D., Art. VI, 24, *Triglot,* p. 969).—As a mirror: "Therefore, as often as believers stumble, they are reproved by the Holy Spirit from the Law, and by the same Spirit are raised up and comforted again with the preaching of the Gospel" (F. C., Th. D., Art. VI, 14, *Triglot,* p. 967).—As a guide: "This doctrine is needful for believers, in order that they may not hit upon a holiness and devotion of their own, and under pretext of the Spirit of God set up a self-chosen worship, without God's Word and command" (F. C., Th. D., Art. VI, 14, *Triglot,* p. 967). Thus the Law is to be the guide which shows Christians the way they should go, and in which works they should exercise their faith. The Gospel is the power which makes them able and willing to follow this guide and do these good works (Rom. 12: 1. 2). Christians, "so far as they have been born anew according to the inner man, do what is pleasing to God, not from coercion of the Law, but by the renewing of the Holy Ghost, voluntarily and spontaneously from their hearts" (F. C., Th. D., Art. VI, 24, *Triglot*, p. 969).

(d) The reason why both, the Law and the Gospel, must be used in the life of the Christian, is that he has a double nature; he has the old Adam, who is under the Law, and he has the new man, who is under the Gospel. The difficulty in using both properly lies in the fact, that in actual life it is difficult to determine to what extent a given behavior of a Christian is the expression of his old Adam or of his new man. Yet the proper distinction between Law and Gospel is of utmost importance, as a confusion or commingling of the two will make it impossible for anyone to become a Christian, or to remain in the faith.

(Cf., F. C., Epit., Art. V, Of the Law and the Gospel, Art. VI, Of the Third Use of the Law, *Triglot*, p. 801-807; F. C., Th. D., Art. V, Of the Law and the Gospel, Art. VI, Of the Third Use of the Law, *Triglot*, p. 951-971.)

XXXIV. THE SACRAMENTS

1. **The term.** — The word "sacrament" is not a Biblical term. Originally it signified an oath or a solemn engagement, as the military oath of a Roman soldier. Because in the early Church adult Christians at their Baptism renounced all idols, and swore allegiance to Christ, which vow really was their "sacramentum," the term was by and by applied to Baptism itself, and later also to the Lord's Supper. In church parlance, Sacraments are visible means of spiritual blessings, religious rites instituted by Christ.

2. **Definition.**—Sacraments must be distinguished from sacrifices. In a sacrifice man deals with God, offering something to God; in a Sacrament God deals with man, offering and giving something to man. "A Sacrament is a ceremony or work in which God presents to us that which the promise annexed to the ceremony offers. A sacrifice, on the contrary, is a ceremony or work which we render God in order to afford Him honor" (Apol., Art. XXIV, 18, *Triglot*, p. 389). A Sacra-

ment, then, is a sacred act, ordained by God, wherein He, by certain external means, connected with His Word, offers, conveys, and seals unto men the grace which Christ merited.

As distinguished from the Gospel, the Sacraments are acts; water is applied in Baptism, eating of bread and drinking of wine take place in the Lord's Supper. As sacred acts they must be distinguished from ordinary acts of washing, eating, and drinking.—As it is God who deals with us through the Sacrament, it is He alone who can institute it; it does not belong to human authority. (Cf., Apol., Art. XIII, 3, *Triglot*, p. 309).. Likewise God alone designates the external means that are to be used: water in Baptism, bread and wine in the Lord's Supper. These external means are connected with the command and the promise of God, and that makes them Sacraments. "Accedit verbum ad elementum, et fit sacramentum."

Sacraments are not merely marks of profession, whereby men may know who are Christians; they do not merely symbolize spiritual gifts, which believers receive in some other way. The Sacraments are signs and tokens of grace; they are means through which God offers and assures His grace to man. (Cf., A. C., Art. XIII, *Triglot*, p. 49; Apol., Art. XII, 42, *Triglot*, p. 261).

3. **The validity of the Sacraments.**—The validity of a Sacrament, or the question: "When is it really that Sacrament which Christ instituted?", does not depend on the piety and faith of him who administers it (Matt. 23: 3. 4), nor on the opinion and faith of him who receives it (Rom. 3: 3. 4). Illustration: A jewel retains its nature and value irrespective of the personal opinion of those who handle it. On the other hand, if the very nature of a thing is changed, as when a polished pebble is substituted for a diamond, then, regardless of what the people may believe and label the stone, it is not a jewel.—The nature and essence of a Sacrament is determined by the Word of God, and it really is what it is intended to be, when it is administered according to the words of institution. It is not sufficient merely to use the prescribed elements and repeat the correct words of institution, for this may be done in sheer mockery, but the words must expressly be taken in the sense and meaning in which Christ would have us understand them, for it is not the sound of the words, but the mean-

ing of the words, that counts.—The divinely intended sense of the words of institution can be learned only from the Scriptures; but the sense in which churches understand and use these words must be learned from their public confessions. It is, therefore, the church, or denomination, which determines in what sense the Sacraments are to be administered in its midst. If this sense does not agree with the sense in which Christ instituted them and would have us understand them, then it is evident that such a church has not those Sacraments which Christ instituted. Illustration: If any man quotes my very words, but puts into them a meaning entirely different from the one in which I used them, then he is misquoting me, making me say what I did not say. So it is here. We must take the words of institution in that sense and meaning in which Christ used them.—Thus, if in Baptism one were to use the Trinitarian formula, but by public confession declare that there is no Triune God, and that, therefore, one does not baptize in the name of the Triune God, as is the case with Unitarian and other anti-Trinitarian bodies, then that baptism is not valid. Likewise, if the words of institution of the Lord's Supper are repeated, but if the official declaration of the church, celebrating this supper, gives an entirely different meaning to these words, as the Catholic and Reformed churches do, then these churches have a Catholic or a Reformed supper, but not the Supper which the Lord instituted. If, on the other hand, a church or congregation abides by the true meaning of the words of institution, and confessedly administers the Sacraments in this sense, then that church has the true Sacraments, and these Sacraments are valid, irrespective of the personal opinion of the administrant or of the recipient.—It should be noted that here we are speaking of the validity, nature or essence, of the Sacraments, and not of their benefit and blessings. As to essence, the Baptism of Catholics and Reformed is valid, but they err in what they teach about the benefit of Baptism. Whoever partakes of the Lord's Supper in the Lutheran Church certainly receives that Sacrament which the Lord instituted, but not every one receives also the blessings of this Sacrament. Hence we must distinguish, as also our Catechism does, between the nature of the Sacrament and the benefit of the Sacrament.

4. **The power of the Sacraments** is none other than that of the Gospel. The Sacraments assure to us the grace of God, offer to us the forgiveness of sins, and work or strengthen in us the faith by which we accept these heavenly gifts. The difference is this, that in the Sacraments God deals with us individually and personally, and that His promise is connected with external means, water in Baptism, and bread and wine in the Lord's Supper. The power, however, lies not in these external elements, but solely and exclusively in the Word of promise connected therewith. Therefore we confess with Luther in the Small Catechism: "It is not the water indeed that does them (such great things), but the Word of God which is in and with the water." "It is not the eating and drinking indeed that does them, but the words here written, 'Given and shed for you for the remission of sins.'" It is the promise of God that conveys these blessings, and in the Sacraments this promise of grace is by Christ's command definitely linked up with the visible elements.

5. **The benefit of the Sacraments.** — While the personal faith of the recipient does not affect the essence of the Sacrament, it does affect the benefit to the recipient. As it is the promise of God that connects the blessings of grace with the Sacrament, so it is faith, which trusts in this promise, that receives them. The promise itself is always valid and good, offering grace and forgiveness to all that partake of the Sacrament, but if "not mixed with faith in them that hear it," it does not profit (Hebr. 4: 2). Hence, the Sacraments do not benefit "ex opere operato," i.e., by the mere outward act or performance. (Cf., A. C., Art. XIII, *Triglot,* p. 49; Apol., Art. XIII, 18-23, *Triglot,* p. 313).

6. **Number of Sacraments.**—"No prudent man will strive greatly concerning the number or the term, if only those objects still be retained which have God's command and promise" (Apol., Art. XIII, 17, *Triglot,* p. 313). If the Romish Church wishes to speak of seven Sacraments, we do not object, but in that case our definition of a Sacrament differs widely from theirs. As we define and understand the term, there are but two Sacraments: Baptism and the Lord's Supper.

The five supernumerary Catholic "sacraments" lack one or more of the features which make Baptism and the Lord's

Supper Sacraments, namely, either the divine institution, or
the visible element, or the promise of the forgiveness of sins.
These three things are essential to a Sacrament, as we understand the term.

Confirmation is a praiseworthy church rite, but not a divine
institution; it also lacks the visible element.

Penance of the Catholic Church is not identical with Biblical repentance, which consists in sorrow over sin and faith in
the merits of Christ. (Cf., A. C., Art. XII, *Triglot*, p. 49). The
Catholic Church does not deny that "the satisfaction which
Christ made for sin released the sinner from guilt and from
eternal punishment due him for mortal sins, and such remission he receives by absolution of the priest. However, there
remain the temporal punishments due to sin, and these must
be suffered either here or in purgatory and are remitted only
by works of satisfaction, or penance. Its essential parts are
contrition, confession, and satisfaction" (*Popular Symbolics*,
p. 179). "An indulgence is the remission in whole or in part
of the temporal punishment due to sin after sacramental absolution," and "is made by transferring to the sinner's account
righteousness from the exhaustless treasury of superabundant
works laid up by Christ and the saints and entrusted to the
church's keeping" (*Popular Symbolics*, p. 181. 182). (Cf.,
S. A., Part III, Art. III, 10-12, *Triglot*, p. 481). This Romish
penance lacks every essential feature of a Sacrament, and is
a pure invention of man.

Order.—The office of the ministry, through which Christ
continues to perform His prophetic office, was, indeed, instituted by the Lord. But formal ordination to the ministry is
not commanded; it is an apostolic institution. Rome teaches
that "there is in the New Testament a visible and external
priesthood," whose proper and especial functions are the forgiving and retaining of sins and the sacrifice of the Mass. For
this reason the Catholic clergy are called priests. The universal priesthood of believers is denied. Ordination, performed
by the bishop, is said to imprint an indelible character on the
candidate for the priesthood.

Matrimony was instituted by God in the beginning. Christ
did not elevate it to a New Testament Sacrament, which, according to the Roman Church, can be validly administered

only by a Romish priest. Like civil government (Rom. 13), it belongs into the kingdom of power, and does not confer spiritual blessings. According to the Scriptures also non-Catholics are validly married without the benefit of the Romish clergy. (Cf., Apol., Art. XIII, 14. 15, *Triglot*, p. 311).

Extreme unction.—Using olive oil, blessed by the bishop, the priest with the oil makes the sign of the cross on eyes, ears, nostrils, hands, feet, and loins, saying: "Through this anointing and His precious mercy may the Lord forgive thee all thy sins of sight . . . ," and likewise of the other organs.— The anointing described in Mark 6: 13 and James 5: 14 was for the healing of the sick; it did not forgive sins and strengthen the soul. The forgiveness of sin is ascribed not to the anointing, but to the prayer of faith (James 5: 15). The object of this anointing was not to prepare for death and salvation, but to aid the sick in his return to health.

(For more information on the Seven Sacraments see *Popular Symbolics*, p. 175-196.)

XXXV. THE SACRAMENT OF BAPTISM

1. **The baptism of John** was a Baptism with water (John 1: 33), of repentance for the remission of sin (Mark 1: 4). It was administered in the name of the Triune God, who had commanded it (John 1: 33), and was an effective means of grace (John 3: 5). (Cf., Ylvisaker, *The Gospels*, p. 111).

During the public ministry of Christ His disciples likewise baptized (John 3: 22; 4: 2), which Baptism was essentially the same as John's. And it does not appear that those who were baptized by John or by the disciples of Jesus were later re-baptized, when Christ instituted His Baptism. However, after John had died, some of his disciples did not join themselves to Christ, to whom the Baptism of John pointed, but continued as a separate sect, and baptized "unto John's baptism" (Acts 19: 3). The baptism of these later disciples of John was not commanded by God, did not point to Christ as the Savior from sin, and was, therefore, not valid. Hence, those men who had been baptized with the now spurious baptism of John were baptized "in the name of the Lord Jesus" (Acts 19: 5).

2. **Baptism a divine and permanent institution.**—Baptism

was instituted by Christ to be administered in the Church unto the end of time. From Matt. 28: 18-20 we see that Christ
commanded Baptism, that it is to be administered by His disciples ("ye"), with whom He promised to be "unto the end
of the world." Baptism, therefore, is a permanent ordinance,
and those church bodies which have discarded Baptism, asserting that it was meant only for the primitive Church, nul-
lify a plain command of Jesus, and violate a basic institution
of the Christian Church.

While the right and duty to baptize was given to the whole
Church, and to each local congregation, Baptism is ordinarily
administered by the pastor, who is the public executive of the
congregation, which called him. (Cf., A. C., Art. XIV, *Triglot*,
p. 49). But in case of necessity also a Christian layman may
validly administer Baptism. (Cf., S. A., Of the Power, 67, *Triglot*, p. 523).

3. **The external element in Baptism is water.**—John baptized with water (John 1: 33); Philip baptized the eunuch
with water (Acts 8: 36); Peter baptized Cornelius with water
(Acts 10: 47); Paul speaks of Baptism as of "the washing of
water by the Word" (Eph. 5: 26); Christ says that we must
be born again of water and the Spirit (John 3: 5). We have
no right to substitute any other liquid. Without water it is
no Baptism.

4. **The mode of Baptism.**—While the application of water
is essential in Baptism (Matt. 28: 19; Acts 10: 47; Eph. 5: 26),
the mode of application, whether by immersion, pouring, or
sprinkling, is an adiaphoron. (Cf., Large Cat., Art. IV, 36. 45.
65. 78, *Triglot*, p. 741. 743. 749. 751). "Baptizein" and cognate
words mean any kind of cleansing by water.

Some churches teach that unless a person is completely immersed into water, he is not baptized. While they have little
to say about the spiritual benefit of Baptism and the significance of such immersion, they make much of the outward
form and mode of Baptism. The word "baptize" is derived
from the Greek "baptizein," which also means to dip in or
under water. Hence we admit that *we may baptize also by
immersion.*—Still, this is not the only meaning of the word as
used in the Bible. In Mark 7: 3 we find that the Pharisees
"washed (niptein) their hands" before they ate. This word

ʐas commonly used when only a part of the body was washed, while "louein" was used when washing or bathing the whole body. Yet this partial washing is in Mark 7: 4 and in Luke 11: 38 called "baptizing." Hence if only a part of the body is washed with water, it is a true baptism. The Pharisees may have immersed cups, pots, and brazen vessels, but hardly "tables," or rather, the "couches," on which they reclined when at table.—In Hebr. 9: 10 we read of "divers washings," baptisms, and from Num. 19 we learn that some ritual baptisms were indeed performed by immersion (v. 7), others by sprinkling (vv. 13. 18. 19). Yet also this sprinkling of water upon tents, vessels, and persons is called a baptism. Hence *we may baptize by sprinkling.*—In Matt. 3: 11 John tells the people that he was indeed baptizing with water, but that Christ would baptize them with the Holy Ghost and with fire. From the fulfillment of this prophecy (Acts 2: 16. 17) we learn that the disciples were not immersed into the Holy Ghost and into fire, but that the Holy Ghost was "poured out" on them, and that cloven tongues like as of fire sat upon each of them (v. 3). Still, this outpouring of the Spirit is called a baptism. Hence *we may baptize by the pouring on of water.* —In 1 Cor. 10: 2 we read that all the children of Israel were baptized unto Moses in the cloud and in the sea. Yet from Ex. 13: 21 and Ex. 14: 22 we do not get the impression that they were immersed into the cloud and into the sea. Hence immersion is by no means the only valid mode of Baptism. It is essential that water is applied, which may be done also by pouring or sprinkling. It does not depend upon the amount of water used, nor upon where and how it is applied. We do not immerse, because we do not wish to support the erroneous teaching of the immersionists, and so we let our liberty be judged by their conscience (1 Cor. 10: 29).

5. **The formula of Baptism** is definitely fixed: "In the name of the Father and of the Son and of the Holy Ghost" (Matt. 28: 19). We have neither reason nor authority to substitute another. Its use is essential; its non-use would render the so-called Baptism invalid. "Baptism is nothing else than the Word of God in the water, commanded by His institution, or, as Paul says, 'a washing in the Word'; as also Augustine says: 'Let the Word come to the element, and it becomes a

Sacrament'" (S. A., Part III, Art. V, 1, *Triglot*, p. 491). However, it does not depend upon the phonetic sound of the words, which is different in every language; it depends upon the sense. The Trinitarian formula must, therefore, admittedly and confessedly also be taken in the Trinitarian sense. Repeating the words, but denying their sense and meaning as referring to the Triune God, as the anti-Trinitarians do, invalidates Baptism. Such texts as Acts 2: 38; 8: 16; 10: 48; Rom. 6: 3; Gal. 3: 27, do not state that the apostles substituted a different formula; these texts merely describe Baptism as the Baptism instituted by Christ. And the Baptism which Christ instituted is the Baptism in the name of the Triune God.

To baptize in the name of the Father and of the Son and of the Holy Ghost does not mean to baptize at the command of the Triune God, for the command to do so lies in the words of Christ: "Go ye therefore and make disciples of all nations baptizing them." The words "in the name of the Father and of the Son and of the Holy Ghost" have a deeper meaning. As by Baptism men are made the disciples of Christ, these words indicate the blessings Baptism bestows. We are baptized "into" (Greek: eis) the name of the Triune God.—What do we mean by the name of God? We mean not merely those names by which we call upon Him, but we mean all He has revealed to us concerning Himself, and all that He means to us. (Cf., Second Commandment and First Petition). We have a brief summary of "the name of the Father and of the Son and of the Holy Ghost" in the three Articles of the Creed, and Luther's explanations.—What it means to baptize "unto some one" or "in the name of some one," we learn from 1 Cor. 10: 2 and 1 Cor. 1: 13. The children of Israel were baptized "unto (eis) Moses," and Paul denies that anyone was baptized "in (eis) the name of Paul." In both cases the meaning is not to have been baptized at the command of these men, but rather that by baptism they entered into a definite relationship, discipleship with them. So here, by being baptized in, unto, the name of the Father and the Son and the Holy Ghost we enter into an intimate and blessed relationship with the Triune God. We are, as it were, immersed into God, are initiated into His communion; we enter into covenant relation with Him and are made partakers of all the blessings of His grace. In Baptism God promises to be our Father, and adopts us as His children; in Baptism we put on Christ (Gal. 3: 26. 27), and receive the gift of the Holy Ghost (Acts 2: 38). Thus these words are a brief summary of all the blessings *into* and *unto* which we are baptized. To have been baptized into the name of the Triune God should mean more to us than merely to have been baptized at His command. We are baptized at the command of Christ in order that by such Baptism we may enter into communion with the Father and the Son and the Holy Ghost.

6. **Who is to be baptized?**—The Baptism which Christ instituted should not be administered to lifeless things, to animals, to dead persons. According to the Bible "all nations" are to be baptized, and this includes men, women, and children.

From Acts 2: 41; 8: 26-40; 10: 47. 48 we learn that adults were first instructed; hence we do likewise. These people are not converted or made disciples by Baptism; they are such by faith in Christ, which they confess before their Baptism (Acts 8: 37). In their case Baptism confirms upon them the grace of God, and strengthens them in their faith, even as the Lord's Supper does.

Little children, born within the Christian Church and brought to Baptism by those who have authority over them, are baptized without previous instruction, and are by such Baptism born into the Christian Church. Matt. 28: 19 does not say that we must first teach and then baptize, but that we should make all nations disciples of Christ by baptizing and by teaching them. Thus little children are made disciples of Christ through Baptism and are then taught to observe all that Christ has commanded.—As Christ blessed those little children which were brought to Him (Mark 10: 13-15), so we should not baptize children against the will and without the knowledge of those who have authority over them, but only when they are brought to us to be baptized. (Compare on this point the circumcision of the Old Testament, Gen. 17: 9-14.)

Infant Baptism.—Infants are to be baptized, because they certainly are included in "all nations." As little as they can be excluded from the term "nation," so little dare we exclude them from Baptism.—Also to infants Christ promises the kingdom of God (Luke 18: 15-17). To enter the kingdom of God, they must be born again of water and of the Spirit (John 3: 5. 6). Hence, infants should be baptized.—In the Old Testament little children were received into the covenant of God's grace through circumcision (Gen. 17: 9-14). In the New Testament Baptism is compared with circumcision (Col. 2: 11-13). As little children were then circumcised, so they should now be baptized.

The fact that children are not specifically mentioned in the Bible need not surprise us, for according to Jewish authorities it was a common practice to baptize proselytes and their children when they embraced the religion of Israel. As the Jews —men, women, and children—were baptized unto Moses in the cloud and in the sea (1 Cor. 10: 1. 2), so they held that any proselyte, whether he be man, woman, or child, must also be baptized. "So in all ages when an Ethnic is willing to enter into the covenant . . . he must be circumcised, and baptized, and bring a sacrifice, or, if it be a woman, be baptized and bring a sacrifice" (Maimonides, *Isuri Bia*, c. XIII and XIV). The Mishna of both the Babylonian and Jerusalem Talmud speaks of children being made proselytes. "They are wont to baptize such a proselyte in infancy upon the profession of the House of Judgment" (Gemara Babylon). (Cf., *The History of Infant Baptism*, by W. Wall).

We need not examine the authority on which such baptism was based; the point here is that it seems to have been an established custom among the Jews to baptize also the children of proselytes.—If Christ did not want His Baptism to be administered unto children, we should certainly expect a definite statement to that effect. *But there is no text in the Bible which bars children from Baptism.* When, therefore, Lydia and her household and the jailor and all his were baptized, it is probable that there were among them also children that were baptized (Acts 16: 33).

That the early church understood the command of Christ regarding Baptism to include children is evidenced by the testimony of such early fathers as Justin Martyr and Irenaeus. (Cf., A. C., Art. IX, *Triglot*, p. 47; Apol., Art. IX, 51, *Triglot*, p. 245; Large Cat., Of Infant Baptism, *Triglot*, p. 743).

The objection that little children cannot believe and that,

therefore, Baptism does not benefit them, is not valid, since Christ definitely tells us that children do believe (Matt. 18: 6), and we learn that the Holy Ghost works faith in them through this washing of regeneration (Tit. 3: 5). It is the Spirit of God who works faith in both, adults and children. It is not for us to question how little children can believe, but to accept what the Scriptures say. Conversion is a miracle of God whether it be in the case of a child or of an adult.

With regard to unbaptized children we have reason to assume that, as in the Old Testament the girls were received into the covenant without circumcision, so God has a way to save infants of Christian parents if they die before it is possible to baptize them. We do not dare to assume this with regard to the children of unbelievers; here we are in the realm of the unsearchable judgments of God.

7. **Baptism is a means of grace.**— (a) According to Matt. 28: 19 men are made disciples of Christ by Baptism, and in Mark 16: 16 we read: "He that believeth and is baptized shall be saved; but he that believeth not shall be damned." By faith we accept, and by unbelief we reject salvation; hence, Baptism must be the means through which this salvation is offered to man. Since the Pharisees rejected the counsel of God by not being baptized, there must have been in Baptism that counsel of God whereby they could have been saved (Luke 7: 30). Forgiveness of sin, gained by Christ, is offered and imparted through Baptism, for we are baptized "for the remission of sins" (Acts 2: 38). In Baptism sins are washed away (Acts 22: 16). In Baptism we "put on Christ" and are clothed with His merits (Gal. 3: 27), are sanctified and cleansed (Eph. 5: 26). Washing away the filth of sin, Baptism gives us a good conscience before God (1 Pet. 3: 21). Baptism, therefore, really offers and imparts to us the grace of God.

(b) Baptism regenerates us by working that faith which lays hold of the promised forgiveness. We are born again of water and of the Spirit; a new spiritual life is worked in us, which is faith (John 3: 5); in Baptism we are risen with Christ through faith of the operation of God (Col. 2: 12); we are converted and saved by the washing of regeneration and renewing of the Holy Ghost (Tit. 3: 5); in Baptism the Holy Ghost regenerates and renews us.—In the early Church the term regeneration was commonly used to designate Baptism. Justin Martyr (100-166 A.D.) says: "Then we bring them to some place where there is water, and they are regenerated by the same regeneration by which we were regenerated; for they are washed with water in the name of God the Father and Lord of all things, and of our Savior Jesus Christ, and of the Holy Spirit. For Christ says: 'Unless you are regenerated, you cannot enter into the kingdom of heaven.'"

Thus Baptism not only offers grace, but it also works the faith by which this offer is accepted. In the case of those who believe before they are baptized, Baptism strengthens their faith. Hence we confess in the Small Catechism: "Baptism works (or, imparts) forgiveness of sins, delivers from death and the devil, and gives eternal salvation to all who believe this, as the words and promises of God declare."

8. **The power of Baptism** to offer grace and to work faith lies not in the water. It is the Word of God, connected with the water, and the Holy Ghost, operating through this Word, that does these things. With the Word of God the water of Baptism is a "washing of regeneration and renewing of the Holy Ghost" (Tit. 3: 5). The Holy Ghost is the active agent, and the Word, which in Baptism is connected with the water, is His instrument. (Cf., Small Cat.: How can water do such great things?)

The water of the Jordan river did not in itself possess the power to cleanse Naaman from leprosy. Yet, since God had promised to heal him if he would wash in the Jordan seven times, the healing power was by this Word of God connected and joined with the water of this river. And Naaman could not have been healed, had he not used this water. But he did, and the Word of God in and with the water cleansed him from his leprosy (2 Kings 5: 6-14). In Baptism the Word of God cleanses us from the spiritual leprosy of sin.

"Catholicism limits the saving efficacy of Baptism, teaching that it forgives only original sin and the sins committed prior to Baptism, and holding out to the lapsed 'the second plank after shipwreck,' penance. It thus deprives the sinner of the abiding comfort which Baptism offers. Acts 2: 38 and parallel passages carry no such limitation" (*Popular Symbolics*, §118). The covenant and the promise of Baptism cover the entire life of a Christian, and at any time, even in old age, he may comfort himself with the assurance of God's grace, made to him in Baptism. (Cf., Large Cat., Part IV, 44. 60. 77. 80-82, *Triglot*, p. 751). "The Catholic doctrine that Baptism eradicates sin, the concupiscence remaining being no longer truly and properly sin, denies Rom. 7: 18-24; 8: 1; Gal. 5: 24, and fosters carnal security. Augustine: 'Sin is remitted in Baptism, not in such a manner that it no longer exists, but so that it is not imputed' " (*Popular Symbolics*, §118).

Reformed churches deny that Baptism conveys forgiveness of sins and works regeneration, and regard it merely as a token or symbol of the blessings wrought and conveyed otherwise by some alleged immediate operation of the Holy Ghost. This deprives men of the assurance of the forgiveness and the consequent strengthening of faith and spiritual life, which God would impart to them through Baptism, since they have no evidence at all that the Spirit has conveyed these blessings to them. Baptism is to them the performance of a duty, which God requires of all Christians. (Cf., *Popular Symbolics*, §118).

9. **Baptism is not to be repeated.**—Of the Lord's Supper Christ tells us that we should partake of it often. But there is no command, indication, or example in the Bible which tells us that we should be baptized more than once. Neither are those to be re-baptized, who have fallen away from the faith and then returned; Peter was not re-baptized. Baptism once validly performed remains valid; our Baptism abides forever. The covenant of God's peace shall not be removed (Is. 54: 10). "Even though some one should fall from Baptism and sin, nevertheless, we always have access thereto. . . . But we need not again be sprinkled with water" (Large Cat., Infant Baptism, 77, *Triglot*, p. 751).

A Baptism, performed in a church which according to the command of Christ baptizes in the name of the Triune God, must be recognized as valid, even though that church hold erroneous views with respect to the benefit and efficacy of Baptism. Thus the Baptism of the Catholic and of the Reformed churches is valid as to essence, which essence is as little invalidated by their false views of the benefit and the power of Baptism as the wrong idea a person may have of the benefit and power of a certain medicine will affect the essence of that medicine. The case is quite different when a person is baptized in an anti-Trinitarian denomination, where they do not baptize in the name of the Triune God; here the very nature of Baptism is changed; such a person must be baptized.

A doubtful Baptism affords no comfort. Persons who do not know whether they were baptized at all, or validly, and have no evidence of their Baptism, should be baptized. If the blessings of Baptism are to be sure to us, the fact of Baptism must be certain. Hence it is important to have witnesses to the Baptism and to issue Baptism certificates.

While in the rite of confirmation children and adults renew their baptismal vow, confirmation is not to be regarded as a repetition of Baptism, or as a complement thereof. We must guard against ascribing to confirmation a sacramental character; confirmation merely emphasizes the importance of Baptism.

10. **Necessity of Baptism.**—Baptism is necessary because the Lord instituted it, and commanded that all nations should be baptized (Matt. 28: 19). It is necessary because it is a means of grace (Mark 16: 16). But it is not absolutely necessary in this sense, that without it a person could not obtain grace, or, at least, not full grace. All means of grace offer the same plenary grace and work the same faith. While faith, being the only means by which we can accept the grace of God, is absolutely necessary for salvation, Baptism is not absolutely necessary, because it is not the only means through which this grace is offered to us. (Cf., S. A., Part III, Art. IV, *Triglot*, p. 491). He, who cannot be baptized, but believes the Gospel, will be saved. Presumably the malefactor (Luke 23: 43) was in this class. For this reason Christ did not say: "He that believeth not and is not baptized shall be damned," but He said: "He that believeth not shall be damned" (Mark 16: 16). It is unbelief that damns. Faith can exist with the lack of Baptism, or of the proper understanding of the necessity and the benefit of Baptism, but it cannot exist with the contempt of Baptism. He who rejects Baptism, rejects what Baptism offers (Luke 7: 30).

11. **The use we should make of our Baptism.**—Many forget their Baptism and thus deprive themselves of much comfort and strengthening. While Baptism is administered but

once, it is of use to us every day of our lives, and we should make it profitable to ourselves.—The daily remembrance of our Baptism strengthens us in the faith, that in Christ all our sins are forgiven, and that we are the children of God (Gal. 3: 26. 27).—It also admonishes us that "by daily contrition and repentance the old Adam in us should be drowned and die with all sins and evil lusts, and, again, a new man daily come forth and arise, who shall live before God in righteousness and purity forever." (Cf., Small Cat.). For "we are buried with Christ by Baptism into death, that like as He was raised up from the dead by the glory of the Father, even so we also should walk in newness of life" (Rom. 6: 4).—Our Baptism should also remind us of the communion and fellowship we have with all who are baptized; "for by one Spirit are we all baptized into one body" (1 Cor. 12: 13). Thus our Baptism should mean much to us in our daily lives.

XXXVI. THE SACRAMENT OF THE ALTAR

1. **Names.**—The Sacrament of the Altar is known by a number of names: the Lord's Table (1 Cor. 10: 21); the Lord's Supper (1 Cor. 11: 20); the Breaking of Bread (Acts 2: 42); the Holy Supper, as distinguished from the ordinary supper at home; the Eucharist, because of the giving of thanks ("eucharistesas") (Mark 14: 23); Holy Communion, because of the communion between bread and body, wine and blood (1 Cor. 10: 16), and also because of the union and communion of all communicants effected by partaking of the Sacrament (1 Cor. 10: 17). Our Confessions also use the term Mass, Missa, which term probably developed from the custom in the early Church to *dismiss* from the common service those, who were not yet entitled to partake of the Sacrament. As long as no heterodox ideas are connected with any of these names, we should not quarrel over them. However, we should not introduce needless innovations in our terminology, especially since some terms have become tainted with false connotations, as is the case with "Eucharist" and "Mass."

2. **A divine and permanent institution.**—Because human reason cannot comprehend what the Bible teaches concerning this Sacrament, it is well to remember at the very outset that it is the Son of God who instituted this Supper. His words

are plain and express what He meant; they must be taken as they read. Even though we are not able to comprehend how these things can be, we should bear in mind that He, who instituted the Sacrament, is able to do exceeding abundantly above all we can think (Eph. 3: 20).—Over against those, who hold that this Sacrament was intended only for the primitive Church, we maintain that it is a permanent institution to be observed in the Church unto the end of time. Christ told His disciples to do this in remembrance of Him (Luke 22: 19); and the believers continued steadfastly in the breaking of bread (Acts 2: 42), and to this day are admonished to do this often "till He come" (1 Cor. 11: 26).

3. **The visible elements.**—As to the visible elements to be used in this Supper we must be guided by what Christ used when He instituted it.—Christ took bread and gave it to His disciples; hence, we also use bread in the Lord's Supper. Because the Supper was instituted during the feast of the unleavened bread (Luke 22: 7), Christ used the bread that was at hand; but the disciples continued to celebrate this Supper also after the days of the unleavened bread were past, and they likewise took such bread as they had. It is, therefore, not essential that we use unleavened bread; but we are to use bread. We do use unleavened bread during our celebrations of the Lord's Supper, but we do not regard it wrong to use leavened bread. Wafers are used because they are convenient for distribution.—As to the contents of the cup we know that it was the "fruit of the vine" (Matt. 26: 29). From history we know that wine was used at the Passover, and that, therefore, Christ also used wine when He instituted the Lord's Supper; so did also the early Christians (1 Cor. 11: 21). To substitute grape juice would, to say the least, make the validity of the Sacrament uncertain.

4. **The heavenly elements.** — "They confess, according to the words of Irenaeus, that in this Sacrament there are two things, a heavenly and an earthly. Accordingly, they hold and teach that with the bread and wine the body and blood of Christ are truly and essentially present, offered, and received" (F. C., Th. D., Art. VII, 14, *Triglot*, p. 977). We confess with Luther in his Small Catechism: "It is the true body and blood of our Lord Jesus Christ, under the bread and the wine, for

us Christians to eat and to drink." Thus the body and the blood of Christ are the heavenly elements that are essentially present, and are offered, eaten and drunk in, with, and under the visible elements.

As to the elements in the Lord's Supper three divergent doctrines are taught in the visible Christian Church. These are discussed in the following paragraphs.

5. **Transubstantiation.**—The Catholic Church, both Greek and Roman, teaches that when Christ said: "This do in remembrance of Me," He gave unto His apostles the power to change bread and wine into His body and blood, and that even now, by virtue of the consecration by a properly ordained priest, bread and wine, while retaining their natural appearance and physical qualities, are changed, transubstantiated, into the substance of the Savior's body and blood. According to them, bread and wine are no longer present; nor are only the body and the blood of Christ present; but "Christ whole and entire," inclusive of His body, blood, soul, and His divinity, is present, distributed, eaten and drunk. Thus the priest performs a miracle comparable to the Incarnation of Christ. Transubstantiation became the official doctrine of the Romish Church at the Lateran Council of 1215, and was re-stated at the Council of Trent, 1545-1563. (Cf., *Popular Symbolics*, §239, p. 184; *Concordia Cyclopedia*, p. 417).

However, we read in 1 Cor. 11: 26-28: "As often as ye eat this bread and drink this cup, ye do show the Lord's death till He come. Wherefore, whosoever shall eat this bread and drink this cup of the Lord unworthily shall be guilty of the body and blood of the Lord. But let a man examine himself, and so let him eat of that bread, and drink of that cup." Eating and drinking takes place *after* the consecration; still the communicants, according to this text, eat bread and drink the cup (wine). Hence, bread and wine must still be present. Furthermore, if a transubstantiation had taken place, there could no longer be a communion between bread and body, wine and blood (1 Cor. 10: 16).—Illustration: Pointing to a barrel of flour, I may say: "This is flour"; yet, this does not mean that the barrel has been changed into flour, or that it represents flour, but that in this barrel we have flour.—"As regards transubstantiation, we care nothing about the sophistical subtlety by which they teach that bread and wine leave their own natural substance, and there remain only the appearance and color of bread, and not true bread. For it is in perfect agreement with Holy Scriptures that there is, and remains, bread, as Paul himself calls it, 1 Cor. 10: 16: The bread which we break. And in 1 Cor. 11: 28: Let him so eat of that bread" (S. A., Part III, Art. VI, 5, *Triglot,* p. 493).

6. **Representation.**— All Reformed bodies agree in this, that there is present in the Sacrament natural bread and wine, but "that the true essential body and blood of Christ is absent from the consecrated bread and wine in the Holy Supper as far as the highest heaven is from the earth" (F. C., Th. D., Art. VII, 2, *Triglot,* p. 973). Because of the rationalistic consideration that the condition of a body is such, that it must occupy one particular place and have its proper form and dimension, they hold that it is impossible for the body of Christ, which ascended into heaven, to be essentially present in the Sacrament. For this reason they take the words of institution in a figurative sense, stating that the bread and wine merely signify or represent the absent body and blood of Christ.

However, none of these words: "This is My body," may be taken in a figurative sense. "This" can refer to nothing else than to the bread which Christ gave to His disciples. (Cf., F. C., Th. D., Art. VII, 64, *Triglot,* p. 995). The word "is" can never be taken in a figurative sense to mean "represent" or "signify." "Is" always remains "is," and nothing else. When Christ says that He "is" the vine (John 15: 5), the figure of speech is not in the word "is," but in the word "vine." Christ really "is" to His Christians what the vine is to the branches; from Him they receive nourishment and strength. Also in the sentence: "This"—pointing to a picture—"is my father," the figure of speech is not in the word "is," but in the word "this"; the person here portrayed really "is" my father. Nor may the word "body" be taken in a figurative sense, because it is definitely stated which body is meant, namely, "which is given for you." When we read that the Church is Christ's body (Eph. 1: 22. 23), it is evident that the word "body" is taken figuratively, because the Church is not the body of Christ which was given for us. Besides, it is an established rule that a word must be taken in its native meaning, unless circumstances or context plainly indicate the figurative sense. But there is nothing in the words of institution that compels us to depart from the literal and native meaning. Nor has any one of the holy writers indicated that these words must be interpreted figuratively. On the contrary, speaking to the Corinthians, Paul says that the bread is the communion of the body of Christ (1 Cor. 10: 16), and that the unworthy communicant becomes guilty, not of the sign or symbol of the body of Christ, but of the body itself (1 Cor. 11: 27). This could not be if he had not in some way received it; and since the unworthy cannot receive it spiritually, because he has no faith, he must have received it orally when he ate the bread. Therefore the body and the blood of Christ must be really present, and are received by all that take the bread and the wine.

John 6: 53-56 does not treat of the Lord's Supper, because the Lord's Supper was not yet instituted. It teaches that by faith one must receive the merits of Christ, which He procured by giving His body and by shedding His blood, and that all those who so eat His flesh and drink His blood have eternal life. But not all who eat and drink the body and blood of Christ in the Sacrament shall have life (1 Cor. 11: 27-29). Besides, the expression "My flesh is meat" is by no means the same as "the bread is My body." Illustration: "God is a spirit" is not the same as "a spirit is God." For the sake of emphasis we may place the predicate noun at the beginning, but it can never become the subject, of which something is said. (Cf., F. C., Th. D., Art. VII, Of the Holy Supper, *Triglot*, pp. 971-1015).

7. **Bible doctrine.**—In the night in which He was betrayed Christ took bread, gave this bread to His disciples, and told them to eat it. Thus, the disciples indeed ate bread. However, as Jesus gave them the bread, He said: "This is My body, which is given for you." According to the words of the Lord, therefore, it was not only bread the disciples took and ate, but together with the bread they took and ate the body of Christ. For the presence of the body of Christ in, with, and under the bread there was absolutely no other proof and evidence than the words of the Master: "This is My body." The same is true of the wine, which is the blood of Christ.

The disciples did not doubt the words of Christ, nor did

they argue the question as to how it were possible for them to receive the body and blood of Christ, seeing that Christ was still visibly and physically present at the table. They took the words of Jesus in their simple and natural meaning, namely, that they ate bread and also the body of Christ, that they drank wine and also the blood of Christ. That such was the understanding of these words is evident from the words of Paul: "The cup of blessing which we bless, is it not the communion of the blood of Christ? The bread which we break, is it not the communion of the body of Christ?" (1 Cor. 10: 16). There could be no communion between the bread and the body, if the body of Christ were not essentially present. For we may not conceive of the communion in this manner, that the communicant by faith establishes a spiritual communion between the bread he eats and the body of Christ in heaven; this is true because the unworthy communicant, who has no faith wherewith to effect this spiritual communion, becomes guilty of the body and blood of Christ. "Whosoever shall eat this bread, and drink this cup of the Lord, unworthily, shall be guilty of the body and the blood of the Lord" (1 Cor. 11: 27). Eating the bread and drinking the wine, the unworthy communicant becomes guilty of the body and the blood of the Lord; hence, the body and the blood of the Lord must be present in, with, and under the bread and wine, which he eats and drinks.

The heavenly elements present, distributed, and received in the Sacrament are the true body and the true blood of our Lord Jesus Christ. We have no right to add to, or to detract from, this. The "Person of Christ" is indeed present at the Lord's Supper, as it is present everywhere; but it is not "Christ whole and entire," His body and soul, His humanity and divinity, that constitutes the heavenly element, as Rome declares, but only the body and blood of Christ. Nor may we substitute for body and blood spiritual benefits and powers, for these were not given and shed for us, neither can they be eaten and drunk with the mouth. Under the bread and the wine we receive nothing more and nothing less than the body Christ gave for us and the blood He shed for us.

The three different doctrines concerning the essence of the Lord's Supper may briefly be stated thus:

Catholic doctrine: No bread and wine, but "Christ whole and entire" is present;

Reformed doctrine: No body and blood, but only bread and wine are present;

Bible doctrine, which Lutherans accept: Both bread and body, both wine and blood are present.

8. **Which Church has the Lord's Supper?**—To make sure that we are celebrating that Sacrament which Christ instituted, it is not sufficient to eat bread and to drink wine, and to recite on such occasions the words of institution. A person may do all this in sheer mockery or play. There must be the purpose and sincere intention of celebrating the Lord's Supper (1 Cor. 11: 20-22). But the sincere intention does not make the Sacrament valid; it must confessedly also be administered in the sense and meaning, in which it was instituted. If, therefore, a church according to its public confession puts a different interpretation on the words of institution than the words warrant, and celebrates the Supper in that sense, as the Catholic and Reformed churches do, then these churches have a supper of their own invention, but not the Supper which Christ instituted. "If the institution of Christ is not observed as He appointed it, there is no Sacrament" (F. C., Th. D., Art. VII, 85, *Triglot*, p. 1001). Christ never instituted a supper in which bread and wine are changed into the body and blood of Christ, including His humanity and divinity; nor did Christ institute a supper in which bread and wine merely represent His body and blood. In the Supper, which He ordained, the communicants receive under the bread and wine the true body and blood of their Lord. And only those churches which celebrate Holy Communion in this sense have the *Lord's Supper*.

"For it does not depend upon the faith or the unbelief of men, but upon God's Word and ordinance, unless they first change God's Word and ordinance and interpret it otherwise, as the enemies of the Sacrament do at the present day, who, of course, have nothing but bread and wine; for they also do not have the words and appointed ordinance of God, but have perverted and changed them according to their own (false) notion" (F. C., Th. D., Art. VII, 32, *Triglot*, p. 983).

9. **The sacramental union.** — Four things are really and truly present in the Sacrament: bread and wine, and the body

and blood of Christ. In no other place and at no other time does such union obtain except in the Sacrament. It is not a natural, physical, local union, but a *supernatural* one, peculiar to the Sacrament, and is for this reason called a sacramental union. The Bible does not explain this union, nor can we understand its nature; but the fact is clearly taught in the Bible, and for this reason we believe it and confess it.—"It was the Word that spake it, He took the bread and break it, And what the Word doth make it, That I believe and take it."

This sacramental union obtains only during the sacramental action. "Nothing has the nature of a sacrament apart from the use instituted by Christ" (F. C., Th. D., Art. VII, 85, *Triglot*, p. 1001). Though the entire Communion liturgy be chanted or spoken, if no one actually ate and drank, there would be no Sacrament. The words of Christ: "This is My body," "This is My blood," did not refer to all the bread and wine on the table, over which He spoke the blessing, but only to that bread and that wine, that was actually eaten and drunk. Says Quenstedt (quoted by Pieper in *Christliche Dogmatik*, III, p. 434): "Christ does not say absolutely of the consecrated bread that it is His body, but of the bread that was broken and given to eat. First He says, 'Take and eat,' and then He says, 'This is My body.'" The sacramental union, therefore, is not effected by the pastor's consecration of the bread and the wine, but it obtains only in the bread and the wine we eat and drink, and while we eat and drink them. We have no Biblical ground to assume that the bread is the body of Christ before we eat it, and that it continues to be the body of Christ after we have eaten it. The sacramental union ceases with the sacramental action. Contrary to Romish opinion, bread and wine, though consecrated, are not the body and blood of Christ if they be not eaten and drunk, or if the bread falls on the floor, or the wine is spilled. Nor does the sacramental union continue beyond the eating and drinking; we do not chew, swallow, digest, and assimilate the body and blood of Christ, as we do the bread and the wine. "Hence, we hereby utterly condemn the Capernaitic eating of the body of Christ, as though His body were rent with the teeth, and digested like other food" (F. C., Epit., Art. VIII, 42, *Triglot*, p. 817). We do not "hold that the body and blood of Christ are included in the bread locally, or are otherwise permanently united therewith apart from the use of the Sacrament" (F. C., Th. D., Art. VII, 14, *Triglot*, p. 977).

The Lutheran Church does not teach "consubstantiation," which means that bread and body form one substance, or that the body is present, like the bread, in a *natural manner;* nor does it teach "impanation," which means that the body of Christ is locally inclosed in the bread. The purpose of the words "in, with, and under the bread" is not to explain the sacramental union, which cannot be explained, but to reject the papistical transubstantiation. (Cf., F. C., Th. D., Art. VII, 35. 38, *Triglot*, p. 983. 985). The body and blood of Christ are *really,* but *supernaturally,* present in the Sacrament, and all communicants receive them orally, with their mouths, together with the bread and the wine.

10. **Whereby is this sacramental union effected,** or by what power is the bread and wine made the carrier of the body and blood of Christ? "Not the word and work of any man produces the true presence of the body and blood of Christ in the Supper, whether it be the merit or recitation of the minister, or the eating and drinking, or the faith of the communicants; but all this should be ascribed alone to the power of Almighty God and the word, institution, and ordination of our Lord Jesus Christ. For the true and almighty words of Jesus Christ which He spake at the first institution were efficacious not only at the first Supper, but they endure, are valid, operate, and are still efficacious, so that in all places where the Supper is celebrated according to the institution of Christ, and His words are used, the body and the blood are truly present, distributed, and received, because of the power and efficacy of the words which Christ spake at the first Supper. For where His institution is observed and His words are spoken over the bread and cup (wine), and the consecrated bread and cup (wine) are distributed, Christ Himself, through the spoken words, is still efficacious by virtue of the first institution, through His word, which He wishes to be there repeated. . . . Just as the declaration, Gen. 1: 28: 'Be fruitful and multiply, and replenish the earth,' was spoken once only, but is ever efficacious in nature, so that it is fruitful and multiplies, so also this declaration (This is My body; this is My

blood) was spoken once, but even to this day and to His advent it is efficacious, and works so that in the Supper of the Church His true body and blood are present" (F. C., Th. D., Art. VII, 74-76, *Triglot*, p. 999).

11. **The validity of the Sacrament.**—Since it is the Word of Christ, which effects or makes the Sacrament, its validity is not affected by the faith or impiety of the minister or of the communicant. "For the Word, by which it became a Sacrament and was instituted, does not become false because of the person or his unbelief. For He does not say: If you believe or are worthy, you will receive My body and blood, but: Take, eat and drink, this is My body and blood; likewise: Do this. ... No matter whether you be worthy or unworthy, you have here His body and blood, by virtue of these words which are added to the bread and wine" (F. C., Th. D., Art. VII, 25, *Triglot*, p. 981). "There the body and blood of Christ are in truth eaten and drunk in the bread and wine, even though the priest (minister) who administers it, or those who receive it, should not believe or otherwise misuse it. For it does not depend upon the faith or the unbelief of men, but upon God's Word and ordinance, unless they first change God's Word and ordinance and interpret it otherwise, as the enemies of the Sacrament do at the present day, who, of course, have nothing but bread and wine; for they also have not the words and appointed ordinance of God, but have perverted and changed them according to their notion" (F. C., Th. D., Art. VII, 32, *Triglot*, p. 983).

12. **Consecration.**—The words Christ used when He gave thanks over the bread and the cup are not recorded, but they, no doubt, referred to what He was about to do. Also Paul speaks of "the cup of blessing which we bless" (1 Cor. 10: 16). Thus we likewise bless, consecrate the bread and wine. And as these elements are to be used in the Supper which Christ instituted, it is self-evident that we should use those words by which He instituted this Supper and commanded us to celebrate it. However, these words do not work like a magic formula, whereby the body and blood are instantly and automatically joined with the bread and wine, for Christ did not say that the bread which He blessed was His body, but the bread which He gave to His disciples, and which they ate.

(Cf., 9. The sacramental union). By such consecration we merely indicate that we are about to celebrate that Supper which Christ instituted with these words, and thereby we set aside this bread and wine for the sacred use that it should be the carrier of the body and blood of Christ. "However, this blessing, or recitation of the words of institution of Christ alone does not make a sacrament, if the entire action of the Supper, as it was instituted by Christ, is not observed (as when the consecrated bread is not distributed, received, and partaken of, but is enclosed, sacrificed, or carried about), but the command of Christ, This do (which embraces the entire action or administration in the Sacrament, that in an assembly of Christians bread and wine are taken, consecrated, distributed, received, eaten, drunk, and the Lord's death is shown forth at the same time) must be observed unseparated and inviolate, as Paul places before our eyes the entire action of the breaking of the bread, or distribution and reception, 1 Cor. 10: 16" (F. C., Th. D., Art. VII, 83. 84, *Triglot,* p. 1001).

13. **The sacramental action.**—The sacramental action *proper* is indicated by the words of Christ: "Take — eat — drink." This is what the disciples did at the first Supper, and what they were commanded to do in remembrance of Christ. The breaking of bread served only the purpose of distribution, and is, therefore, not an essential part of the sacramental action. If the command "This do" included the breaking of the bread, then the communicants would have to break the bread; this was not done by the communicants at the first Supper. It is also immaterial whether the elements are directly conveyed to the mouth of the communicants, or whether they are first placed into their hands to be conveyed to the mouth by them. The word "take" does not necessarily imply that they must take it with their hands. How the bread is distributed, and how it is taken are adiaphora. The essential part of the sacramental action is that we take and eat, take and drink.

Since the year 1415 (Council of Constance) the Catholic Church practices "communion under one form," giving to the laity only the consecrated wafer, which, they say, has been changed into the body of Christ and, therefore, contains blood. Only the officiating priest takes both, bread and wine. But Christ says: "Drink ye all of it" (Matt. 26: 27). And Mark

tells us: "And they all drank of it" (Mark 14: 23). From
1 Cor. 11: 26-30 we learn that the Corinthian Christians, and
not only the officiating minister, received the Sacrament under
both forms. "We condemn the sacrilege that to laymen one
form only of the Sacrament is given, and, contrary to the plain
words of Christ, the cup is withheld from them, and they are
deprived of the blood" (F. C., Epit., Art. VII, 24, *Triglot*, p.
815).

"Intinction," as observed in the Greek Catholic Church and
others, is the practice of dipping the consecrated bread into
the consecrated wine and giving it to the communicant in a
spoon, who thus receives both elements in one action; others
have the communicant dip the wafer into the wine. But Christ
says: "Take and eat" and "Take and drink."

14. **Sacramental eating and drinking.**—In the Small Catechism Luther speaks of a "bodily eating and drinking," because it is done *with the mouth,* which is a part of the body.
By virtue of the sacramental union "the true, essential body
and blood of Christ are also orally received and partaken of
in the Holy Supper by all who eat and drink the consecrated
bread and wine in the Supper" (F. C., Th. D., Art. VII, 63. 64,
Triglot, p. 995). The bread and wine we eat and drink with
our mouth in a *natural* way, as we eat and drink other food.
The body and blood of Christ we eat and drink also with our
mouth, but in a *supernatural,* indefinable, incomprehensible
way. The words of Christ: "Take, eat: this is My body"
(Mark 14: 22), and the term "communion" (1 Cor. 10: 16)
can mean nothing else than that the bread and the body of
Christ are received in one and the same action, and that a
real, albeit supernatural, eating of the Lord's body takes place.

From such sacramental eating we must distinguish spiritual
eating, which consists in this that *by faith* we appropriate to
ourselves the merits and blessings of Christ. (Cf., F. C., Th. D.,
Art. VII, 61-65, *Triglot*, p. 995). The unworthy communicant
receives sacramentally the body and blood of Christ under
the bread and wine (1 Cor. 11: 27), but he does not spiritually receive the blessings of the Sacrament. (Cf., F. C., Th. D.,
Art. VII, 60, *Triglot*, p. 993).

15. **"This do in remembrance of Me."**—The command of
Christ: "This do," refers only to what Christ had just told

His disciples to do, namely, "Take, eat; . . . drink ye all of it." And that is what the early Christians understood these words to mean, for Paul says: "As often as ye eat this bread and drink this cup, ye do show the Lord's death till He come" (1 Cor. 11: 26). (See above §13.)

The adoration of the consecrated host, a concomitant of Romish transubstantiation, is not only not commanded, but is a perversion of the Sacrament instituted by Christ. The bread is to be eaten, not to be adored. What the Catholics adore as Christ, as God, is plain bread, their pious opinion notwithstanding. "Accordingly, with heart and mouth we reject and condemn as false, erroneous, and misleading . . . when it is taught that the elements or visible species or forms of the consecrated bread and wine must be adored" (F. C., Th. D., Art. VII, 126, *Triglot*, p. 1015).

The papistical Mass. — (Cf., *Popular Symbolics*, p. 188). With the words "This do" etc., Christ did not give to His disciples the power to change the bread and the wine into His body and blood; Christ Himself did not do this at the first Supper. Nor were they, in celebrating the Holy Supper in remembrance of Him, to re-enact Christ's sacrifice in an unbloody manner "for the sins, penalties, and satisfactions of the living and the dead," as Romanists pretend to do. Christ says: "Eat . . . drink" (Matt. 26: 26. 27), not: "Sacrifice My body and blood." And Paul says (1 Cor. 11: 26): "Show the Lord's death," not: "Re-enact it." Furthermore, the words: "Given and shed for you," were addressed to the communicants present, not to the absent nor the dead. The Sacrament brings no blessings to those who do not partake of it. Masses for the dead are absolutely futile. (Cf., Luke 22: 19).

Mass celebrated as an expiatory sacrifice for the sins of those present or absent, for the living or the dead, is a most blasphemous practice of the Catholic Church. It is an invention of men; it belittles the sacrifice of Christ on the cross as being insufficient (Hebr. 10: 14. 18). Nor is there such a thing as an unbloody sacrifice for sin (Hebr. 9: 22). It denies justification by faith alone, because in the Mass justification is to be accomplished by the work of man, ex opere operato, by the mere outward performance of the act. It denies the necessity of personal faith (Hebr. 11: 6), and of the end of the period of grace at the time of death (Hebr. 9: 27). (Cf., *Popular Symbolics*, §138, for other papistical abominations, which derive their chief support from the Mass). (Cf., A. C., Art. XXIV, 24-33, *Triglot*, p. 67).

"This do" was addressed, not to the general public, but to the disciples of Christ. We also learn that the members of the Christian congregation continued steadfastly in the breaking of bread (Acts 2: 42). Hence, this Sacrament is not to be administered to all people indiscriminately, but "is for us Christians to eat and to drink," as Luther states in the Small Catechism. However, it is not optional with Christians, whether or not they will do so. "This do" is a command of Christ, whereby this Supper was instituted to be observed among Christians "until He come" (1 Cor. 11: 26). While Baptism is to be administered once only, the Lord's Supper is to be celebrated "often." "For Christ did not say, Omit this, or Despise this; but This do ye, as often as ye drink it, etc. Truly, He wants it done, and by no means neglected and despised. This do ye, is His command" (Introduction to Small Catechism).—While we may not force people by laws to go to the Sacrament, it is well to remember the words of Luther: "If a person does not seek nor desire the Lord's Supper some four times a year, it is to be feared that he despises the Sacrament and is not a Christian" (Introduction to Small Catechism). In these words Luther does not wish to emphasize the number of times to commune each year, but he warns against despising the Lord's Supper. Better advice cannot be given than that Christians commune whenever the Lord's Supper is being celebrated in the congrgation, where they hold communicant membership.

"In remembrance of Me." — "But Christ commands us, Luke 22: 19 'This do in remembrance of Me'; therefore the Mass was instituted that the faith of those who use the Sacrament should remember what benefits it receives through Christ, and cheer and comfort the anxious conscience. For to remember Christ is to remember His benefits, and to realize that they are truly offered to us. It is not enough only to remember the history, for this also the Jews and the ungodly can remember. Wherefore Mass is to be used to this end, that there the Sacrament may be administered to them that have need of consolation" (A. C., Art. XXIV, 34, *Triglot*, p. 67). By partaking of the Sacrament we do not remind God of what we are doing in order that He might forgive us our sins; but in the Sacrament God rather reminds us of what He has done and is doing that we might have forgiveness of sins. The Lord's Supper is, therefore, not a sacrifice by which we procure and merit forgiveness; but, being a remembrance of Christ's sacrifice, it is a Sacrament by which the benefits of His sacrifice are offered and conveyed to those who believingly remember His death.

16. **The Lord's Supper is a means of grace.**—Because of the words, "This is My body, This is My blood," we receive the true body and blood of Christ under the bread and the wine. From the words "Given and shed for you for the remission of sins," we learn that also spiritual blessings are offered in the Sacrament, "namely, that forgiveness of sins, life, and salvation are given us through these words," as we confess with Luther in the explanation of the Sixth Chief Part. Without these words, we should still have to eat and drink His body and blood under the bread and wine; but this would then be only an act of obedience. The words of promise, however, make this Sacrament an actual means of grace, assuring and sealing to us forgiveness of sins. Hence these words are of chief importance, since in them lies the power to convey spiritual blessings.

"This cup is the new testament in My blood" (Luke 22: 20). "This is My blood of the new testament" (Matt. 26: 28). The Old Testament, or covenant, was of the Law; it required a perfect obedience, imputed sin, and pronounced the curse on all transgressors; hence it was called "the ministration of condemnation" (2 Cor. 3: 9). Also this first testament, mediated by Moses, was dedicated with blood (Hebr. 9: 18-20).— But already Jeremiah spoke of a new covenant, which consists in this that God will forgive iniquity (Jer. 31: 31-34). This new covenant is referred to in Rom. 11: 27 and in Hebr. 8: 6-13. The Mediator of this new covenant is Christ, and by His blood was this new testament established (Hebr. 9: 12-28). When, therefore, Christ gives us the cup, which "is the new testament in His blood," He thereby confirms on us the new covenant of grace which consists in the forgiveness of sins.

17. The power to convey this grace and forgiveness lies not in the bread and wine, nor in the body and blood of Christ, otherwise also the unworthy would receive these blessings (1 Cor. 11: 27-29). The assurance of grace is given us through these words: "Given and shed for you for the remission of sins." The body and blood of Christ serve as a seal to make this promise more sure to us.

Forgiveness of sins is given us in the Sacrament not in the sense as though we did not have any before; for a believer has forgiveness as long as he is in the faith.—Nor do we receive a new supply of forgiveness every time we go to the Lord's Table; for forgiveness and grace are not offered in parts and portions; we either have forgiveness for all sins, or we have none; we either stand in the grace of God, or we do not.—Nor is there a difference in the gift itself, whether offered in Baptism, or in the Lord's Supper, or in the Gospel.—But there is a difference in the manner and mode of assuring and confirming this gift of grace to us. In the Holy Supper Christ deals with each communicant individually and personally, and seals to him His promise of grace and forgiveness.

18. The beneficial use of the Sacrament.—"The promise is useless unless it is received by faith. But the Sacraments are signs and seals of the promises. Therefore, in the use of the Sacraments faith ought to be added" (Apol., Art. XIII, 20, *Triglot,* p. 313); (A. C., Art. XXIV, 30, *Triglot,* p. 67). This faith is spiritual eating and drinking. (Cf., F. C., Th. D., Art. VII, 62, *Triglot,* p. 995). The worthy or believing communicant eats and drinks sacramentally the body and blood of Christ under the bread and wine; spiritually he eats and drinks, or receives, the blessings and benefits, namely, forgiveness of sins, life, and salvation. Belief in the real presence of the body and blood of Christ in the Sacrament is indeed necessary, but it does not put one into possession of the benefits of the Sacrament; for this, faith in the promise is necessary. The salutary use of the Sacrament requires faith. "The words 'for you' require all hearts to believe."

The Catholic dogma that the Sacraments profit without faith on the part of the recipient, ex opere operato, turns them into pagan rites and subverts the fundamental article of the Christian religion, that faith justifies and saves, as taught in Rom. 3: 28. (Cf., *Popular Symbolics*, §233).

We must guard against a frivolous and superstitious use of the Sacrament. We are not to partake of the Holy Supper to prove our innocence of a crime, of which we are accused; nor are we thereby to secure for ourselves help in some bodily ailment; nor are we to build up in ourselves the resurrection-body; nor are we to symbolize the marital union between groom and bride by giving to each one half of the broken wafer.

The chief purpose of the Sacrament is to assure and offer to each communicant the forgiveness of his sins. To earn this forgiveness, Christ gave His body and shed His blood on the cross. In order to assure and impart to each penitent sinner personally and individually the forgiveness of his sins, life, and eternal salvation, Christ instituted the Holy Supper, where He gives as a seal of His promise the very body and blood, wherewith He earned these heavenly treasures for us. And he that believes these words of promise, "has what they say and express, namely, the forgiveness of sins."—The effect of this is that it will strengthen our faith, which under the impact of our daily sins so easily weakens and fails. By strengthening our faith and comforting our hearts the Lord's Supper also increases our love toward God and toward our neighbor, so that we make greater efforts in leading a God-pleasing life. It also quickens our hope of eternal salvation. —We also confess our faith when we partake of the Lord's Supper. "For as often as ye eat this bread and drink this cup, ye do show the Lord's death till He come" (1 Cor. 11: 26). The very act of going to the Lord's Table is the confession of a Christian's faith; he confesses that he trusts for grace and salvation in the merits of Christ's death, and that he personally regards the doctrines of the church, where he communes, as the true teachings of the apostles (Acts 2: 42). At whose altar we worship, his religion we confess. Paul shows this in 1 Cor. 10: 18. He who partakes of an idol-feast, thereby confesses his worship of the idol. Speaking of Israel, Paul said that every Israelite, who did eat of the sacrifice in the Temple at Jerusalem, by that eating shared in everything for which the altar stood, and which that altar intended to communicate to him. So, if one goes to Holy Communion in the Lutheran Church, one thereby confesses the doctrine of the Lutheran Church; if one goes to another church, teaching otherwise, one confesses that religion. For this reason a person who is known to be an unbeliever, or who does not agree with us in the confession of our faith, should not be admitted to our altar. Neither may a Lutheran commune in any church which according to its public confession upholds false doctrines. Neither may he believe that it is possible to receive the Sacrament according to his private Lutheran conviction in a Catholic or in a Reformed church. In the first place, he does not receive the Sacrament of Christ in these churches (cf., §8. Which Church has the Lord's Supper?); in the second place, he by this act makes public confession of those doctrines, for which these churches stand.

19. Self-examination.—To partake of the Sacrament worthily, and to receive its blessings, one is to examine himself. "Let a man examine himself, and so let him eat of that bread and drink of that cup" (1 Cor 11: 28). Every communicant should examine himself:

(a) Whether he understands and believes the words of institution, for he must "discern," distinguish and recognize the Lord's body and blood in, with, and under the bread and wine. (Cf., 1 Cor. 11: 29). To discern the Lord's body means to perceive that body in the Sacrament as really present and received.

(b) Whether he knows himself to be a sinner before God, and is sincerely sorry for his sins. Neither the number nor the greatness of our sins make us unworthy; it depends on how we feel about our sins, whether we are penitent or not, that determines our worthiness or unworthiness. He, who does not know his sins, cannot repent, and sees no need of forgiveness, and, therefore, has no faith in the forgiveness through Christ. God wants us to realize our natural evil condition and our total insufficiency before Him.

(c) Whether he knows what Christ did for him, whether he truly desires forgiveness and applies the promise of Christ to himself, believing that all his sins are forgiven. No special degree of faith is required. The weak in faith, who lack the firm assurance of, and experience only a sincere longing for, the forgiveness of their sins, should by all means approach the Lord's Table for the strengthening of their faith.

(d) Whether he is willing to amend his life and bring forth fruit meet for repentance (Matt. 3: 8). For this we need the help of God, who through the Sacrament will so strengthen our faith, that we grow in holiness of life. A willingness and a desire to improve one's life before God go hand in hand with faith in God's promise of forgiveness.

Whoever partakes of the Lord's Supper unworthily, "shall be guilty of the body and blood of the Lord" (1 Cor. 11: 27). Man becomes guilty, not of a thing, but of an act, of a sin. Thus the unworthy communicant becomes guilty of a sin with respect to the body and blood of Christ, guilty of desecrating and profaning it. Hence he is liable to punishment (1 Cor. 11: 28. 29). The word "damnation" in this text, as in Rom. 13: 2, does not specifically refer to eternal damnation in hell, although it could lead to this. Final damnation may result from communing unworthily, especially when continued indefinitely. The word "judgment" in the sense of "a sentence of judgment" is the proper translation in place of the word "damnation"; such a "sentence of judgment" may be removed by repentance. (Cf., 1 Cor. 11: 30-32). (Cf., F. C., Th. D., 68, *Triglot*, p. 997). The sin of having in the past partaken of the Lord's Supper unworthily will be forgiven if we repent and believe that Christ has atoned also for this sin.

20. **Open and close Communion.**—The Lord's Supper was instituted for Christians. Christ gave the Supper not to the general public promiscuously, as He gave food for bodily sustenance when He fed the five thousand (John 6: 1-13). Christ gave the Lord's Supper to the disciples. In the Apostolic Church the Gospel was preached to all that would listen; but the Sacrament was given to baptized Christians only (Acts 2: 42; 1 Cor. 11: 20; 10: 17).—Some churches in our day practice "open Communion," permitting anyone to partake of their supper. "Close Communion," as practised in our church, is that we admit to the Lord's Table those only, of whom we feel reasonably certain that they are able and willing to examine themselves (1 Cor. 11: 28). From obedience to the Word of God and from charity to those concerned the Sacrament is denied to all who cannot or will not examine themselves. (Cf.,

§19 on "Self-examination").—Christians, who may otherwise be well able and willing to examine themselves, must not partake of Communion, unless they have been baptized. For on Pentecost the new converts were not told to commune, but to be baptized (Acts 2: 38). Baptism, "sacramentum initiationis," must precede Communion, "sacramentum confirmationis." Also in the Old Testament only they that were circumcised partook of the Passover (Ex. 12: 48). (Cf., §18, on "The beneficial use of the Sacrament").

While the Lord's Supper should indeed be celebrated with due reverence and solemnity, we must guard against making a liturgical show of it, and extolling it above the other means of grace.

21. **As to the necessity of the Lord's Supper,** the same is true what was said concerning Baptism. (Cf., §10, on "The necessity of Baptism").

22. **Reasons for frequent attendance at the Lord's Supper.**—In the early Christian Church it was not necessary to discuss this question, for the disciples well understood, and were mindful of, the words of their Master (Acts 2: 42). Such frequent Communion was of spiritual benefit to those Christians.—In the course of time things changed. In 1530 Luther complained of the infrequency of attendance at the Lord's Supper; he reproves not only the people, but blames in part also the pastors. (St. Louis Edit., Vol. X, 2171. 2173). In our present day it is well to emphasize the reasons for frequent Communion attendance, because the average attendance is very low.

What prevents us from receiving the Sacrament frequently? (a) *Worldly-mindedness.* For many people temporal things and material advantages are more important and hence also more desirable than spiritual and eternal blessings. We do not really always seek first the kingdom of God and His righteousness. The care for the physical well-being of our body, the desire for temporal advancement and success, our financial and business worries, our daily needs, so occupy our attention that we forget to watch for our souls. This accounts in a large measure for our neglect of the Lord's Supper. (b) *Lack of a live knowledge of our sin.* In the Sacrament Christ offers a sure cure to every sin-sick soul. Do we fully realize how very sick we are? How superficial and shallow is this knowledge! Our sense of sin is dulled by the lax views prevailing in the world. This lack of a true knowledge of our sins is no doubt a cause, but also a result, of our neglect of the Sacrament. (c) *Lack of understanding of the true purpose of the Sacrament.* The Sacrament is not a sacrifice we make, a service we give, or an act of adoration in which we take part. It is something different, something greater. In the Sacrament God bestows on us glorious gifts of heaven and powers of eternal life. Do we really understand and appreciate the blessings of the Sacrament? (d) *Fear of receiving the Sacrament unworthily.* This is another, and quite different, reason why some stay away from the Sacrament. Sins and repeated lapses cause people to feel unworthy, so that they are afraid to partake of the Sacrament; this type of unworthiness is really a deeply felt shame and sorrow over sin, and does not render us unworthy of the Sacrament.

What should move us to receive the Sacrament frequently? Let us bear in mind that the admonition for frequent attendance at the Lord's Supper is addressed to Christians only.

(a) *The command and invitation of Christ should move us to receive the Sacrament frequently.* It is not optional for us whether or not we partake of this Sacrament. For very definitely Jesus says: "This do." Christ wants it done and by no means neglected or despised. "This do ye" is His command. Even if there were no benefit connected with the Sacrament, still the very fact that our Lord asks us to partake of it often should prompt us to do so. A Christian does not wilfully and intentionally ignore and neglect the wish and will of his Lord.

(b) *The promised blessings should induce us to receive the Sacrament frequently.* Viewed outwardly, the Sacrament is a very simple and plain affair. It is not a sumptuous banquet where one may satisfy his bodily hunger and thirst; there are no material, tangible benefits connected with it. Holy Communion, however, is not an empty ceremony in which we participate for the exercise of our obedience, nor is it a service by which we earn favor with God. But it is a means of grace, through and by which God offers, assures, imparts, and seals to us the forgiveness of sins, life, and salvation. These gifts are so great that they surpass and outlast anything this world might offer to us. Ought we, then, not to go frequently to the Sacrament? While these spiritual blessings are offered to us in Baptism, and in the Gospel, we should go to the Sacrament of the Lord's Supper because the Savior deals with each communicant individually, and because the promise of forgiveness is sealed to us.

The first and chief benefit of the Sacrament is that it strengthens our faith in the forgiveness of sins. God's promise of grace never becomes uncertain in itself; but when our faith weakens, it becomes uncertain to us. Thus it is important that our faith in the forgiveness of sins be preserved and strengthened. And this is exactly the purpose for which the Sacrament was instituted. Let no one say that he has no need of such strengthening of faith! (Cf., 1 Cor. 10: 12).

The second benefit is that the Sacrament will restore peace to our conscience. Conscience troubles and bothers us as long as we are burdened with the guilt of sin. A guilty conscience makes life miserable; there is no peace of mind, no joy of heart, but restlessness and fear and despair (Ps. 38: 4). Because of our sins we all have at times compunctions and pangs of conscience, and it is dangerous to continue therein. Now, there is absolutely no other cure for a guilty conscience than faith in the forgiveness of our sins (Eph. 6: 16; 1 John 1: 7). In the Sacrament God strengthens our faith, purifies our conscience from sin and guilt, and restores peace and joy to our troubled hearts. (Cf., Rom. 5: 1).

The third benefit of the Sacrament is that it kindles in our hearts a fervent love of God, and helps us to lead a godly life. As soon as the sinner is assured of God's grace, his attitude changes. "We love Him, because He first loved us" (1 John 4: 19) expresses the attitude of the Christian towards God.

In the Sacrament God manifests His unchanging love toward us; in spite of our gross offenses and repeated lapses He again and again assures us of His pardoning grace. Because we so often forget the loving-kindness of our God, our faith grows weak, and our love waxes cold. He who would warm his cold heart must get close to the fire of God's love. In the Sacrament God opens His loving heart to us; therefore let us frequently partake of Holy Communion in order that our hearts may again and again be kindled and fired with the love of God. And such love makes us willing to lead a godly life; faith worketh by love (Gal. 5: 6).

The fourth benefit is furtherance of brotherly love. In life there are social differences also among Christians. But whenever we approach the Lord's Table, all these differences cease. No one may exalt himself above another; no one may think he is better than his neighbor. (Cf., Rom. 3: 23). The fact that we all are equally guilty before God and receive from Him the same grace certainly should induce us to forget our differences and bring us closer together. (Cf., 1 Cor. 10: 17). One reason why we do not show more forbearance, kindness, and charity toward one another is that we do not receive the Sacrament as frequently as we should. For if we did, we should oftener be reminded of the fact that, though we are many, we are nevertheless one bread and one body, as we are partakers of that one bread.

The fifth benefit is comfort in tribulation. "In this world ye shall have tribulation," says Christ (John 16: 33). (Cf., Matt. 16: 24). Each one has and feels his cross. God does not always remove the cross, but the assurance of His grace helps us to bear it. For what else matters as long as God is gracious to us and leads us to heaven? And of this grace we are assured in the Lord's Supper; so patience and strength to bear our cross is supplied in the Lord's Supper through the strengthening of our faith.

The sixth benefit is strengthening our hope of eternal life. Whatever strengthens us in the certainty of forgiveness of sins strengthens us also in the certainty of our eternal salvation. For by faith we are the children of God (Gal. 3: 26), and if children, then heirs of God and joint-heirs with Christ (Rom. 8: 17). In this hope we must not weaken; it supports us on our way through life. This hope affords strong comfort, especially in the hour of death. (Cf., Phil. 1: 23). This hope is closely connected with our faith in the forgiveness of sins, of which we are assured in the Lord's Supper. Hence we should frequently partake of the Lord's Supper.

(c) *The trouble which lies heavy upon us should move us to receive the Sacrament frequently.* Our possession of God's blessings will not go uncontested in this world. There are three enemies at work, that would undermine our faith and deprive us of all the blessings we hold. These enemies are our flesh, the world, and the devil. Christ instituted the Lord's Supper to strengthen us against the temptations from these enemies. Our drooping spirit is revived and our faith is strengthened to counteract the insidious poison coming from the flesh, and to resist the allurements and to overcome the seductions of the world and the devil.

Thus we see that we have many and strong reasons why we should partake of the Lord's Supper frequently.

PART IX. OF THE CHURCH

XXXVII. THE INVISIBLE CHURCH

1. What is the Church?—The word "church" is derived from the Greek "kyriakon (doma)," Lord's (house), kirk, Kirche, church. In the New Testament the word "ecclesia" is used, which means an assembly called out or called together. — All those whom the Holy Ghost through the Gospel has "called out of darkness into His marvelous light," constitute that "chosen generation, royal priesthood, holy nation, people for God's own possession" (1 Pet. 2: 9), which is called the Church. "And believers were the more added to the Lord, multitudes both men and women" (Acts 5: 14). In John 10: 14-16. 26-28 Jesus speaks of the believers as His flock, and this flock constitutes the Church. In John 11: 52 He tells us that the scattered children of God shall be gathered, and this gathering is the Church. Paul speaks of "the household of faith" (Gal. 6: 10), and calls the Church "His (Christ's) body" (Eph. 1: 23), for which Christ gave Himself that He might sanctify and cleanse it with the washing of water by the Word (Eph. 5: 25-27). All this shows that the many individual persons, who have by faith entered into close and intimate relation with Christ, constitute one body, and this body is the Church.

The kingdom of God.—This term is often used in the Bible with reference to the Church. However, this term does not designate the *persons,* which make up the Church, but rather indicates the *actual exercise of the kingly rule of God in the hearts of these persons.* That the kingdom of God is not identical with the Church, appears from the Second Petition of the Lord's Prayer: "Thy kingdom come," and from Luke 17: 21, where it states that "the kingdom of God is within you." If the kingdom of God is to "come to us," and is "within us," then we ourselves cannot be this kingdom. But of those who by faith have become members of the Church the Lord says: "I will dwell in them, and walk in them; and I will be their God, and they shall be My people" (2 Cor. 6: 16); (John

14: 23). Dwelling in the hearts of His believers, God is not idle, but active. He governs, rules, leads, and guides them, as Paul says: "For as many as are led by the Spirit of God, they are the sons of God" (Rom. 8: 14). The kingdom of God within men, therefore, is that activity of God in the hearts of Christians, by which He governs and rules them by His Spirit. "And this Church alone is called the body of Christ, which the Spirit renews, sanctifies, and governs by His Spirit" (Apol., Art. IV, 5, *Triglot*, p. 227).—Faith in Christ and the kingdom of God within us are not identical. While God indeed works faith in our hearts, He does not do the believing for us; man does the believing; faith is a spiritual act of man by which he trusts in the merits of Christ. The kingdom of God within us is an activity of God, by which He rules in the hearts of the believers. Yet these two are never separate; where the one is, the other is bound to be also (Gal. 3: 26; Rom. 8: 14).—Neither one of the two, or both together, are the Church, for the Church consists of *people;* the Church is the total number of those people, that have faith in their hearts and are led by the Spirit of God.

Unbelievers and hypocrites, though affiliated with, and active in, a congregation, do not belong to the Church, because the terms used in the Scriptures to describe the Church indicate that there exists an inner relation and spiritual communion between its members and God. It is called "the house of God" (1 Tim. 3: 15); "a spiritual house" (1 Pet. 2: 5); "an holy temple in the Lord" (Eph. 2: 21); a kingdom, in which we are citizens, and a household, in which we are children (Eph. 2: 19); the body of Christ, of which we are members (Eph. 1: 22. 23); "a chosen generation, a royal priesthood, an holy nation, a peculiar people" (1 Pet. 2: 9). To be in this intimate and personal relation to God requires faith in Christ; "for ye are all the children of God by faith in Christ Jesus" (Gal. 3: 26). While all true believers, no matter to which denomination they may belong, are members of this Church, no one, though he be priest, minister, or pope, is a member thereof, if he has no faith.

"Wherefore we hold, according to the Scriptures, that the Church, properly so-called, is the congregation of saints (of those here and there in the world), who truly believe the

Gospel of Christ, and have the Holy Ghost" (Apol., Art. VII, 28, *Triglot,* p. 237); (S. A., Part III, Art. XII, *Triglot,* p. 499; Large Cat., Art. III, 47-53, *Triglot,* p. 689. 691). Luther, in his explanation of the Third Article of the Apostles' Creed in his Small Catechism, describes the whole Christian Church on earth as those, whom the Holy Ghost calls, gathers, enlightens, sanctifies, and keeps with Jesus Christ in the one true faith. The moment a person believes in Christ, he thereby at once becomes a member of the Church; and he ceases to be a member of the Church the moment he loses his faith. Membership in the Church is contingent upon faith. "Because of unbelief they were broken off, and thou standest by faith" (Rom. 11: 20). We have no right to demand, before we regard any one a member of this Church, a certain amount of doctrinal knowledge, or a certain degree of faith; but there must be sincere sorrow over sin and trust for forgiveness in the merits of Christ. The thief on the cross likely had no great amount of doctrinal knowledge, and yet he knew what was necessary to know (Luke 23: 42). (Cf., Is. 42: 3; John 6: 37).

While all believers are most intimately joined by faith to Christ, their Savior, they are for this very reason also most intimately joined to one another by the bond of a common faith, a common hope, and a mutual love, and thus they constitute, no matter how far apart locally they may be from each other, a single body, a great communion, which we call the Church (Eph. 4: 3-6).

The Church is also presented as "the whole family (of God) in heaven and on earth" (Eph. 3: 15). This concept of the Church includes all the Christians who have died in the faith and gone to heaven, and all the Christians still living in this world. It is customary to distinguish between the Church militant on earth and the Church triumphant in heaven. The latter is so called, because, having been faithful unto death, these Christians have entered into their rest (Hebr. 4: 9), and received a crown of life (Rev. 2: 10); (2 Tim. 4: 8). The Church militant is so called, because here on earth Christians wage a spiritual war, or battle, against the devil (Eph. 6: 10. 11), the world (1 John 5: 4), and their flesh (Gal. 5: 17; 1 Cor. 9: 26. 27); and it is by a victorious death that they enter the Church triumphant (2 Tim. 4: 7. 8). Our present discussion is limited to the Church on earth.

2. **The attributes of the Church.**— (a) The Church is *invisible*. Because faith, by which men become members of the Church, is invisible to human eyes, therefore the Church itself is invisible to man. "The kingdom of God cometh not with observation" (with outward show); "neither shall they say, Lo, here! or, Lo, there! for, behold, the kingdom of God is within you" (Luke 17: 20. 21). As little as we can with absolute certainty say: "This man has true faith and the kingdom of God in his heart," so little can we say with absolute certainty: "These people constitute the Church." Elias did not know of the seven thousand men in Israel who had not bowed the knee to Baal (Rom. 11: 2-4; 1 Kings 19: 8-18).—But while the Church is invisible to man, it is definitely known to God, for God knows all its members. "The Lord knoweth them that are His" (2 Tim. 2: 19). The individual Christian knows himself to be a believer (2 Cor. 13: 5; 2 Tim. 1: 12); he thereby also knows himself to belong to the communion of saints, which is the Church of God.

(b) The Church is *one*. As the Church includes all men the world over, who truly believe in Christ, it is evident that there can be but one Church. Therefore Christ speaks of "one fold and one Shepherd" (John 10: 16); (John 11: 52). Paul describes the oneness and unity of the Church thus: "Endeavoring to keep the unity of the Spirit in the bond of peace. There is one body and one Spirit, even as ye are called in the one hope of your calling; one Lord, one faith, one baptism, one God and Father of all, who is above all, and through all, and in you all" (Eph. 4: 3-6). "There is neither Jew nor Greek, there is neither bond nor free, there is neither male nor female: for ye are all one in Christ" (Gal. 3: 28). Also the terms which describe the Church as the "house of God," "the temple of the Lord," "the household or family of God," "one body in Christ," show that the Church is one.

(c) The Church is *holy*. By the justifying power of faith all believers have complete forgiveness and the perfect righteousness of Christ; hence, they are saints before God. "Christ loved the Church and gave Himself for it, that He might sanctify and cleanse it with the washing of water by the Word, that He might present it to Himself a glorious Church, not having spot, or wrinkle, or any such thing; but that it should be holy and without blemish" (Eph. 5: 25-27). For this reason the Church is called "the communion of saints."

By the sanctifying power of faith all true believers earnestly endeavor to lead holy lives, thus achieving a true, though imperfect, righteousness of life. "Ye also, as lively stones, are built up a spiritual house, an holy priesthood, to offer up spiritual sacrifices, acceptable to God by Jesus Christ" (1 Pet. 2: 5); (Rom. 12: 1. 2). Because of their old Adam, the members of the Church still commit sins, gross sins at times, which are indeed damnable. But as Christians repent of their sins and trust in the merits of Christ, they have forgiveness with God and shall not be damned (John 5: 24).

(d) The Church is *catholic, universal,* because it is gathered together from every nation under the sun. It embraces all true Christians that ever lived, are now living, and will live to the end of days. Whoever is a true believer in Christ, no matter when and where he lives, or to which race or nationality he may belong, or of which church denomination he may be a member, belongs to this Church. In this sense the word "catholic" fitly describes the universal character of the invisible Church. This Church had its beginning with Adam and Eve, who trusted in the promised Seed of the woman; it includes all the believers of the Old Testament (Acts 10: 43; Rom. 4), and all the believers to the end of time (John 17: 20).

Because Rome usurped this term "catholic," and wrongly applied it to its particular denomination, which is by no means universal, Luther substituted the word "Christian" in the Third Article of the Apostles' Creed. Thereby we wish to distinguish this association, or communion of believers, from the adherents of other religions, such as the Jewish, the Mohammedan, the Buddhist, and other religious bodies, and thereby we also wish to confess that Christ and His redemption is the foundation of faith of all its members (1 Cor. 3: 11; Eph. 2: 19-22).

(e) The Church is *imperishable.* Individual church bodies, particular denominations, and local congregations may pass away, but the invisible Church will continue. "The gates of hell shall not prevail against it" (Matt. 16: 18); (Ps. 46: 5; 48: 8; Luke 1: 33). There existed in every period of time, even in the dark Middle Ages when Popes ruled supreme, and there will exist to the end of days a communion of true believers, kept by the power of God from falling a prey to fundamental errors (Matt. 24: 24; John 10: 27-29; Rom. 11: 2-5). As the Gospel and the Sacraments will remain, so there will always be some who are brought to faith in Christ and thus become members of the Church. "The Church will nevertheless remain until the end of the world" (Apol., Art. VII, VIII, 9, *Triglot,* p. 229). (Cf., F. C., Th. D., Art. XI, 50, *Triglot,* p. 1079).

(f) The invisible Church is the *only saving* Church. Since faith in the vicarious atonement of Christ is the only thing that saves (John 3: 16), and since the Church embraces all those who have this faith, it is apparent that membership in this Church saves. Whoever rejects the faith, by which one is a member of this Church, cannot find salvation in any other religion. It is not true that every one is saved in his own fashion, no matter what his faith may be. Christ says: "I am the way, the truth, and the life; no man cometh unto the Father, but by Me" (John 14: 6). However, no visible church body, or denomination, may claim that it is the only saving church, as the Romish Church does. Boniface VIII in "Unam Sanctam" (1302) stated: "For every human creature it is absolutely necessary for salvation to be subject to the Roman Pontiff." Pius IX in his Allocution of December 9, 1854, stated: "It is to be held as a matter of faith that no one can be saved outside the apostolic Roman Church." According to the Bible teaching "no salvation outside of the Church" applies to the invisible Church alone.

3. **The building and the preservation of the Church is exclusively the work of God.**—As it is the Holy Ghost, who by means of the Gospel works and preserves that faith by which men become and remain members of the Church, so it is He who "gathers the whole Christian Church on earth and keeps it with Jesus Christ in the one true faith."—And the exalted Savior, sitting at the right hand of God, is the Head of the Church, and, as the Sovereign Ruler over all things, He governs the affairs of the world for the special benefit of

His body, which is the Church (Eph. 1: 20-23), so that the gates of hell shall not prevail against it (Matt. 16: 18); (Ps. 46).

The means by which the Church is built and preserved are the same as those by which men come to, and remain in, the faith, namely, the means of grace; "which shall believe on Me through their word" (John 17: 20). The Church is not built and preserved by the Law, nor by human measures and methods, nor by political force or ecclesiastical organization, but solely by the means of the Gospel. We make men disciples of Christ by teaching them to observe what Christ commanded (Matt. 28: 19. 20). The role of man in building, spreading, and preserving the Church is merely instrumental (1 Cor. 3: 5-10), inasmuch as by men the Gospel of the kingdom is to be preached in all the world (Mark 16: 15). The people whom God employs to do this are the members of the Church. Men are brought into the Church to be saved through faith in Christ; but having themselves been won, they must and will endeavor to win others (John 1: 40-42). Hence, mission work is the chief business of the Church (Is. 40: 9). In our teaching and preaching we must always be conscious of this, that we are to bring men to faith in Christ, and thus build and preserve the invisible Church. And there is no other means to accomplish this than the Gospel.

4. **Where is the Church?**— (a) We are assured that this invisible Church exists on earth (Matt. 16: 18). It is faith alone that makes men members of this Church. Such faith is worked in the hearts of men by the Holy Ghost through the means of grace, which are the Gospel and the Sacraments (Rom. 10: 17). (Cf., A. C., Art. V, *Triglot*, p. 45). Wherever the Word of God is not known, whether this be the case with a whole nation or with an individual person, there can be no faith (Rom. 10: 14); and where there is no faith, there is no Church. Hence, wherever and only where the Gospel of Christ is in use may we expect to find the Church. "The kingdom of Christ exists only with the Word and the Sacraments" (Apol., Art. IX, 52, *Triglot*, p. 245). "The Christian Church consists not alone in fellowship of outward signs, but it consists especially in inward communion of eternal blessings in the heart, as of the Holy Ghost, of faith, of fear and love of

God; which fellowship, nevertheless, has outward marks so that it can be recognized, namely, the pure doctrine of the Gospel, and the administration of the Sacraments in accordance with the Gospel of Christ" (Apol., Art. VII, VIII, 5, *Triglot*, p. 227).

While it is true that there can be neither faith nor the Church without the means of grace, whereby faith is wrought and the Church is built, still, the administration and use of these means are neither of the essence of the Church nor a visible side thereof. Illustration: The dynamo in the powerhouse produces electricity; but who would include the dynamo in any attempted definition of the essence of electricity? Or, who would call the generator the visible side of electricity? Both, the essence of faith and the essence of the Church, remain invisible to us; and there is no visible side to an invisible thing. But "the pure doctrine of the Gospel and the administration of the Sacraments in accordance with the Gospel of Christ" are "outward marks," by which we may know that the Church must be there.

(b) There are true Christians, or members of the invisible Church, also in those denominations which, besides teaching false doctrines, still adhere to the fundamental truths of the Gospel. Any Gospel text, if it really be Gospel, is potentially the whole Gospel, and, therefore, is capable of producing faith in the hearts of them that receive it. It is possible that in ignorance men err in some doctrines, while in their hearts they trust in Christ for the forgiveness of their sins, and hope to be saved by His grace. The theology of the head does not always agree with the theology of the heart. But where the essentials of the Gospel, which alone works saving faith, are unknown or denied, there can be no members of the Christian Church. Where the Gospel is taught in its truth and purity, the marks of the Church stand out more distinctly.

(c) In Is. 55: 11 we read: "So shall My Word be that goeth forth out of My mouth: it shall not return unto Me void, but it shall accomplish that which I please, and it shall prosper in the thing whereto I sent it." According to this text the Word of God is never taught in vain. However, this does not mean that all who hear the Gospel will also be won for Christ and the Church. From the Parable of the Sower (Luke 8:

11-15) we learn that with many who hear, the Word has not this effect. (Cf., Acts 13: 46). Nor does it mean that in every place or mission station, where we preach the Word, it will win at least a few for Christ; in Luke 10: 10. 11 Christ tells His disciples that on their missionary journey they may possibly enter a city, where the people will not receive the message of the kingdom of God. Thus, the preaching of the Gospel will not in every instance produce positive results by winning souls for Christ. Nevertheless, the Gospel is never preached in vain. By it men are brought to faith (John 17: 20), and wherever, because of the hardness of heart in men, this primary purpose is not accomplished, the Gospel is preached as a witness against them (Is. 6: 9. 10; Mark 4: 11. 12; Matt. 24: 12). He who wilfully hardens his heart against the Gospel, may under the judgment of God finally be hardened by the Gospel (2 Cor. 2: 14-16). And the fact that the Gospel was preached to such a person will count against him in the Day of Judgment (Matt. 12: 41. 42).

XXXVIII. THE VISIBLE CHURCH

1. **Definition.**—The faith, by which men are members of the Church, is itself invisible (Luke 17: 20. 21); but it manifests itself in various ways. All true believers will confess their faith; "with the heart man believeth unto righteousness, and with the mouth confession is made unto salvation" (Rom. 10: 10); (Matt. 10: 32). They will also prove their faith by a godly life, letting their light shine before men, that they may see their good works and glorify their Father in heaven (Matt. 5: 16). They will nurse their spiritual life by making diligent use of the means of grace; "he that is of God heareth God's Word" (John 8: 47); (1 Cor. 11: 26). Thus by their confession of faith, by their godly life, by their attendance upon public worship the believers become recognizable to others; these things are the outward evidence of their invisible faith. "Faith makes men Christians; but confession alone marks them as Christians. . . . By our faith we are known to the Lord as His; by our confession we are known to each other as His children" (C. P. Krauth in *Conservative Reformation*, p. 166). The total number of those people whom we must re-

gard, on the basis of their confession in word and deed, as Christians, constitute the visible Church.

However, hypocrites can simulate these outward manifestations of faith; they have the "form of godliness" (2 Tim. 3: 5). And as it is impossible to distinguish these tares from the wheat (Matt. 13: 24-26), they are counted in with the Christians in the visible Church. "The Church in its wide sense embraces good and evil; likewise that the wicked are in the Church only in name, not in fact; but that the good are in the Church both in fact and in name" (Apol., Art. VII, VIII, 11, *Triglot,* p. 229); (Apol., Art. VII, VIII, 17-19, *Triglot,* p. 231. 233). The unbelievers united with the visible Church do not form an integral part of the Church, but are rather a foreign element. The privileges and duties conferred upon the believers are not vested in them, although externally they participate in them. Nevertheless, as far as outward appearance is concerned, they are members of the visible Church, or congregation.

Briefly stated: The invisible Church is the total number of those who HAVE true faith in their hearts; the visible Church is the total number of those who PROFESS the faith. The invisible Church is hidden in the visible Church.

2. **Church denominations.**—The visible Church is divided into many separate denominations, also called churches. There are three large branches of the visible Church: the Catholic Church, both Greek and Roman; the Reformed Church, comprising a large number of denominations; the Lutheran Church, which is also divided into a number of bodies.

These denominations differ one from the other in points of doctrine, each asserting that its teachings are true. It is absurd to assume that all these churches have the true and right teachings. There can be but ONE truth. A doctrine is either true or false; it cannot be both. Truth is intolerant; it can have no communion with error, just as little as light has communion with darkness (2 Cor. 6: 14). There can be but one true doctrine concerning the creation of the world, the Holy Trinity, the Person of Christ, the redemption, the conversion of man, etc., and whatever does not agree with this one doctrine, must of necessity be false.

3. **True and false churches.**—The question whether or not a church is the true church may not be determined on the basis of the personal faith and the sincerity of its members, but on the basis of its public doctrine, as laid down in its official Confessions. If these agree with the Scriptures, then that church is a true church. If these agree with the Scriptures, but the church, nevertheless, tolerates individuals of its communion to teach and to spread false doctrines, then the entire church body must be held responsible for the wrong teachings of the individual. God demands that we not only hold fast the faithful Word, but that we also exhort and convince the gainsayer (Tit. 1: 9). If a false teacher persistently refuses to listen to the truth of God, we must part company with him (Rom. 16: 17; Tit. 3: 10). Church discipline must be applied not only with regard to sins of life (Matt. 18: 15-17), but also with regard to teaching contrary to the Scriptures (1 Tim. 1: 3).

To be true, a doctrine need not agree with human reason, modern science, public opinion, etc., but it must in all parts and points agree with the Word of God. "Thy Word is truth" (John 17: 17). "If ye continue in My Word . . . ye shall know the truth" (John 8: 31. 32). In God's Church nothing but God's Word shall be taught. "Teaching them to observe all things whatsoever I have commanded you" (Matt. 28: 20). "If any man speak, let him speak as the oracles of God" (1 Pet. 4: 11); (Is. 8: 20). To teach any other doctrine is contrary to the will of God; "that they teach no other doctrine" (1 Tim. 1: 3); (Jer. 23: 31). God's children are even charged to withdraw from such as persistently teach otherwise than God's Word teaches (1 Tim. 6: 3-5; Rom. 16: 17).

A true church, then, is one which in all its doctrines adheres strictly to the Word of God; a false church is one which in one or more points departs from the teachings of the Word of God. In designating a church a false church, we do not pass judgment on the personal faith of its individual members, but only on its public doctrines as laid down in its Confessions.

It thus becomes the duty of every Christian to examine for himself whether the teachings of his church agree with the plain teachings of the Bible (Acts 17: 11; 1 John 4: 1). He may not take another's word for it. This is a matter of personal conviction and personal responsibility. We may not accept any doctrine on the authority of a professor or pastor, priest or pope, nor because a synod or a church council has so decreed, but only because it is plainly taught in the Word of God. "The Word of God shall establish articles of faith, and no one else, not even an angel" (S. A., Part II, Art. II, 15, *Triglot*, p. 467).

On examination we find that the doctrines of the Lutheran Church, as they are laid down in the Book of Concord of the year 1580, agree with the Word of God in every respect. Therefore those church bodies, no matter what their names may be, which actually teach, and adhere to, these doctrines, are to be regarded as the true, or orthodox, visible church; while those church bodies which, besides teaching some true doctrines, confessedly uphold and defend erroneous teachings, must be regarded as heterodox churches.

When we say that the Lutheran Church is the true, or orthodox, church, we do not mean to say that it is the only saving church, or that all its members are true Christians and will unfailingly be saved. Membership in the Lutheran Church is not identical with membership in the invisible Church. But we do mean to say that all its official teachings agree with the Word of God and are, therefore, positively true, and that all doctrines differing from them are heterodox and false.

When we say that other churches are false churches, we do by no means wish to insinuate that there are no Christians in those churches, or that it is impossible for any one to be saved in them. We are passing judgment, not on the personal faith of their members, branding them hypocrites and heathen, but only on those public doctrines, which do not agree with the Word of God.

4. **Unity of faith, unity of doctrine, and unionism.**— (a) Unity of faith exists among all the members of the invisible Church, as we confess with Luther in the explanation of the Third Article of the Apostles' Creed, that the Holy Ghost keeps the whole Christian Church on earth with Jesus Christ in the one true faith. No matter to which denomination a person may belong, or whether or not he is formally a member of any denomination, if he trusts for the forgiveness of his sins and for his eternal salvation solely in the merits of

Jesus Christ, then he is in unity of faith with all other Christians. He may possibly be ignorant of some other teachings of the Bible, or, misunderstanding certain texts, he may possibly err in certain doctrines; yet, if his ignorance and misunderstanding do not pertain to the central doctrine, namely, to justification by grace through faith in Christ, then he is still in the unity of faith, is a member of the invisible Church, and will be saved. The unity of faith is not limited by denominational boundaries, but includes all those, wherever they may be, who trust for grace and salvation in the God-man Jesus Christ. On the other hand, such unity of faith does not necessarily exist among all the members of the same denomination or congregation, for the tares among the wheat are certainly not in the unity of faith.

(b) Unity of doctrine consists in this that the members of a church, or a denomination, are united in all the doctrines they teach and confess. There is no unity of doctrine among the various denominations of the visible Church; they are divided because of differences in doctrine. Such division of the visible Church into divers denominations is a grievous offense both to the world and to the church, especially to weak Christians; it is also most displeasing to God. Responsibility must be placed not on those who strictly adhere to the Word of God and refuse fellowship to those who teach otherwise, but on those "which cause divisions and offenses contrary to the doctrine" we have learned from the apostles (Rom. 16: 17; Acts 20: 29. 30; 2 Tim. 2: 16-18; 4: 3. 4).

As the invisible Church is one in faith, so the visible Church should, according to the will of God, be one in the confession of faith and doctrine. "Now I beseech you, ·brethren, by the name of our Lord Jesus Christ, that ye all speak the same thing, and that there be no divisions" (schisms) "among you; but that ye be perfectly joined together in the same mind and in the same judgment" (1 Cor. 1: 10); (Eph. 4: 3-5; Acts 2: 42). For this reason Christians should not perpetuate this offensive division in matters of doctrine, but should labor towards a true unity in doctrine, which does not consist in an external merger or union, but in this that they unite in believing, teaching, and confessing the same truths of the Word. "And to the true unity of the Church it is enough to agree concerning the doctrine of the Gospel and the Sacraments" (A. C., Art. VII, 2, *Triglot,* p. 47); (Cf., F. C., Th. D., Art. XI, 95. 96, *Triglot,* p. 1095).

(c) Unionism is quite a different thing from unity of doctrine. "Unionism, which asks the various denominations to form a union, or at least to maintain church-fellowship among themselves, despite their disagreement in doctrine—that allegedly being a matter of indifference—is a gross violation of the divine command. Furthermore, it does not serve the cause of unity, but perpetuates division, since it demands toleration of the original cause of division, false doctrine. It sins, further, against charity; instead of warning the errorist and the erring Christians, it palliates error. It is immoral; it pretends a unity that does not exist and operates with dishonest, ambiguous formulas of union. Finally, it involves a denial of the truth, since he who consciously compromises with error, compromises and betrays the corresponding truth, Matt. 12: 30, and since it springs from indifference and fosters indifference, it tends to bring on the loss of the entire truth" (*Popular Symbolics,* p. 106).

Insistence on purity of doctrine is by no means narrow-minded bigotry on the part of the Church. A false doctrine can never produce a right faith, nor can false teaching direct us in the right way (Matt. 15: 9). Beside "trembling" at God's Word (Is. 66: 2), and not daring to depart from its teachings, we know that we can accomplish the purpose of this Word only if we most conscientiously continue in its teachings; for the effect our teaching has on the hearts and the lives of men is determined by the content of what we teach. False doctrines create a false faith in those who accept them, and only the right doctrine can create the right concept in the mind and the right faith in the heart. To make men disciples of Christ the Church must teach ALL that Christ has commanded, and nothing but what He has commanded (Matt. 28: 20).

For this reason no Christian congregation has the right to tolerate false doctrines in its own midst, or to connive at erroneous teachings in others. "Beware of false prophets, which come to you in sheep's clothing, but inwardly they are ravening wolves" (Matt. 7: 15); (Tit. 3: 10; Rev. 2: 15). To whichever church-body Christians may belong, they must insist that nothing but the unadulterated truth of God's Word is taught in their churches. "If ye continue in My Word, then are ye My disciples indeed" (John 8: 31). If the unadulterated truth of God's Word is not taught, it is the duty of these people to withdraw from such churches and organizations, because they uphold and defend false doctrines. "Now I beseech you, brethren, mark them which cause divisions and offenses contrary to the doctrine which ye have learned; and avoid them" (Rom. 16: 17). "Impious teachers are to be deserted (are not to be received and heard)" (Apol., Art. VII, VIII, 48, *Triglot*, p. 243).—While avoiding false teachers, we are to join a church in which the doctrines of the Gospel are taught in their truth and purity and the Sacraments are administered according to Christ's institution. For according to Acts 2: 42 we are to maintain church-fellowship with those who continue steadfastly in the apostles' doctrine, the early Church being to us an example. If from the very beginning the Christians had tried the spirits (prophets) (1 John 4: 1), whether their teachings were of God, and had withdrawn from false teachers, we should today not have the diversity of denominations that confuses the simple.

5. **The local church, or congregation.**—The Bible speaks of "churches" throughout Judaea, Galilee, and Samaria (Acts 9: 31), of the "church which is at Corinth" (1 Cor. 1: 2), and of the "church which was at Jerusalem" (Acts 8: 1). In these texts the word "church" does not refer to Christians here and there in the world, but to those in a certain place or locality, among whom existed a definite fellowship (Acts 2: 42; 4: 32).

A local congregation is a visible organization; it is the natural outgrowth of following God's command to assemble for the hearing of God's Word and the administration of the Sacraments. Hypocrites belonging thereto are members in name only, and not in fact; they do not form an integral part of the congregation. Only they that were "sanctified in Christ, called to be saints" constituted the local church at Corinth (1 Cor. 1: 2); "all that believed" were members of the church at Jerusalem. Hence, only the true believers in a given congregation really constitute that church to which the Office of the

Keys is given by Christ. (Cf., Apol., Art. VII, VIII, 3, *Triglot*, p. 227).

Since Christians should establish the ministry of the Word in their midst, exercise brotherly discipline, partake of the Lord's Supper in testimony of the communion of faith, every Christian will gladly become, and remain, a member of a local church.

The local congregation is recognized as the visible Church in the Scriptures (Matt. 18: 17. 20; Acts 9: 31; 1 Cor. 1: 2; Acts 8: 1). We read nothing about synods and similar organizations in that day. In our day synods and similar organizations are formed by a number of congregations for purposes other than the establishment of the public ministry; they exist by human right, and because their purposes, while related, are not the fundamental purposes of a local congregation, they do not possess the prerogatives and powers of the local church. They, nevertheless, serve as great blessings to local congregations and to individual Christians, because by united effort certain great things can be achieved for the kingdom of God.

XXXIX. THE GOVERNMENT OF THE CHURCH

1. **The form of government** in the Church is, on the one hand, a monarchy, and on the other hand, a democracy.—The Church is a monarchy, because Christ is the sole Head and absolute Ruler of the Church (Eph. 1: 22. 23; Col. 1: 18). In spiritual matters, doctrines of faith and rules of life, Christians are subject to no other authority than that of Christ. "One is your Master, even Christ, and all ye are brethren" (Matt. 23: 8); (Eph. 5: 24; Matt. 28: 20). His Word must be accepted without question and reservation. He has bought us; we are His own; therefore we must not again become the servants of men (1 Cor. 7: 23).—The Church is a democracy, because in the Church "all ye are brethren." Whatever may otherwise be the social, economic, political, or ecclesiastical status of the individual member of a congregation, in the Church there is no distinction and difference of rank, of authority, and of superiority. There is neither Jew nor Gentile, neither bond nor free, neither male nor female; for they are all one in Christ Jesus (Gal. 3: 28); none is greater than his neighbor (Luke 22: 24-26).

2. Christ rules and governs His Church by His Word.— "My sheep hear My voice, and I know them, and they follow Me" (John 10: 27). "Every one that is of the truth heareth My voice" (John 18: 37). Christ's Word is the sole authority in the Church, to which all, clergy and laity, must bow, from which nothing may be taken away, to which nothing may be added (Matt. 28: 20; 1 Tim. 6: 3; 1 Pet. 4: 11; John 8: 31; Deut. 4: 2). Where God has spoken, no man is permitted to think and to speak otherwise. "Peter cites the agreement of all the prophets. This is truly to cite the authority of the Church" (Apol., Art. IV, 83, *Triglot*, p. 145). "No man's law, no vow, can annul the commandment of God" (A. C., Art. XXIII, 8, *Triglot*, p. 61). "Any custom introduced against the commandment of God is not to be allowed" (A. C., Art. XXII, 9, *Triglot*, p. 61).

This Word, by which Christ rules and governs His Church, is found in the canonical books of the Old and the New Testaments, which are the Scripture given by inspiration of God. When Christ says: "I have yet many things to say unto you, but ye cannot bear them now. Howbeit when He, the Spirit of truth, is come, He will guide you into all truth" (John 16: 12. 13), (cf., John 14: 26), He did not mean to say that also after the close of the New Testament canon the Holy Ghost would continue to guide the Church into new truths, which had not yet been revealed (progressive revelation through the Church), or that there would be a development of doctrine beyond the plain statements of the Bible. (Cf., *Popular Symbolics*, pp. 151-157).—The conscience of Christians is bound by the Word of God, and not by the word of men. Neither the Pope nor the entire Church has authority to promulgate as doctrines of faith such matters as are not plainly revealed in the Bible (Matt. 15: 9; Jer. 23: 31). (E.g., Transubstantiation, the immaculate conception and the assumption into heaven of the Virgin Mary, the infallibility of the Pope, etc.)

3. In matters not determined by the Word of God the Church cannot speak with divine authority. — Regulations and ordinances of the Church covering adiaphora are observed by Christians solely for the sake of "tranquility and good order in the Church" (A. C., Art. XV, 1, *Triglot*, p. 49). "Let all things be done decently and in order" (1 Cor. 14: 40); (1 Cor.

14: 26. 33; Rom. 14: 19; Eph. 5: 21). Neither the congregation as a whole nor individuals in the congregation may legislate in these matters, and demand obedience on the theory that by divine right they possess authority to decide them. To place the commandments of the Church on the same level with the Word of God offends against the sovereignty of Christ and the sanctity of the conscience. (Read: Apol., Art. XV: Of Human Traditions in the Church, *Triglot,* p. 315 ff.)

4. **Under Christ the local congregation is a sovereign self-governing body.**—The local congregation is not subject to the jurisdiction of any other congregation, nor to any higher ecclesiastical body, such as a synod, a conference, a superchurch, a pope, and the like. Christ gives supreme and final judgment to the church, when He says: "Tell it unto the church" (Matt. 18: 17. 20). The word "church" in this text cannot mean the invisible Church, for we cannot tell for a certainty who its members are; it cannot mean the visible Church at large, for it would be a practical impossibility to report the case of an erring brother to all that profess to be Christians in the world; nor does it mean the "teaching church," the priests and bishops of the Romish Church, or of any other Church; but it can mean only the local congregation, of which the offending brother is a member, and to which he is known. Thus it was the local congregation at Corinth that, at the instruction of Paul, excommunicated the man who had married his stepmother (1 Cor. 5). (Cf., S. A., Of the Power, 24, *Triglot,* p. 511).

5. **All Christians are royal priests** (1 Pet. 2: 9), and therefore have no need of a priesthood from among men to mediate between them and God. They themselves have free access unto the Father (Eph. 2: 18), to present their petitions to Him, and to receive from Him the fulness of His blessings without the mediation of priest or saint. No hierarchy stands between Christ and His people. (Cf., Apol., Art. XIII, 7, *Triglot,* p. 311; Art. XIV, 58, *Triglot,* p. 405).

The Scriptures give to laymen, no less than to the official teachers of the Church, the right of judging doctrine and of sitting in the councils of the Church. To all Christians it is said: "Try the spirits, whether they are of God" (1 John 4: 1); (Matt. 7: 15; Acts 17: 11; 1 Cor. 10: 15). Not the apostles only, but the whole congregation acted in sending chosen men to Antioch (Acts 15: 22), and in receiving the report of Paul on his mission work (Acts 21: 22). The Catholic Church denies these rights to the laity. (Cf., S. A., Of the Power, 45. 49, *Triglot*, p. 517. 519; F. C., Th. D., Comp. Sum., 8, *Triglot*, p. 853.)

6. **Elders and pastors are not lords over God's heritage** (1 Pet. 5: 3). When the Bible speaks of them as having rule over us (Hebr. 13: 17), it very definitely limits their rule and power as being over us "in the Lord" (1 Thess. 5: 12). (Cf., Apol., Art. XXVIII, 20. 21, *Triglot*, p. 449). They have no authority of their own; beyond, and aside from, the Word of God they have no power. "In 1 Cor. 3: 6, Paul makes all ministers equal, and teaches that the Church is above the minister . . . For he says thus: 'All things are yours, whether Paul, or Apollos, or Cephas,' i.e., let neither the other ministers nor Peter assume for themselves lordship or superiority over the Church . . . let not the authority of any avail more than the Word of God" (S. A., Of the Power, 11, *Triglot*, p. 507). "The Church can never be better governed and preserved than if we all live under one head, Christ, and all bishops, equal in office (although they be unequal in gifts), be diligently joined in the unity of doctrine, faith, Sacraments, prayer, and works of love" (S. A., Part II, Art. IV, 9, *Triglot*, p. 473.) (Cf., Chapter XLIII, 10).

The Romish Church subjects its members to the government and rule of the hierarchy, in which the Pope, as the visible and infallible head of this Church, exercises the supreme authority. As vicegerent of Christ on earth he makes laws and decisions and promulgates doctrines, which, even though they be contrary to the Word of God, he demands all Catholics to accept for conscience' sake. Thereby he despoils the Christians of their priestly and royal estate, abrogates the sole authority of Christ in the Church, and reveals himself as the very Antichrist (2 Thess. 2: 4). As to the claim that the Pope rules the Church as the successor of Peter, the first ruler of the Church, it is to be noted that Peter was not given any precedence over the other apostles and the other Christians. The keys of the kingdom of heaven were not given to Peter alone (Matt. 16: 19), but to the Church (Matt. 18: 18). Peter never claimed primacy or lordship over the Church for himself (1 Pet. 5: 3); he calls himself just "an apostle," "also an elder" like the others (1 Pet. 1: 1; 5: 1). He does not assume equal authority with the Word of God, but calls it the "more sure word of prophecy" (2 Pet. 1: 19). The Church did not accord him primacy (Acts 8: 14; 15: 6; 2 Cor. 11: 5; 12: 11). When by his wrong conduct he supported false doctrine, he was publicly reprimanded by Paul (Gal. 2: 9-18). The story of the Pope's successorship is a myth, and has no Biblical nor historical foundation. As to papal infallibility (cf., *Concordia Cyclopedia,* under "Infallibility"), the Scriptures teach that there is but ONE who is infallible, namely, God (Ex. 3: 14; Matt. 24: 35; Rom. 3: 4). The prophets and apostles are the infallible teachers of the Church, because they spake under inspiration of God (Eph. 2: 20; 2 Pet. 1: 21; 1 Cor. 2: 13). (Cf., *Popular Symbolics,* §160). (Cf., Apol., Art. VII. VIII, 23. 24, *Triglot,* p. 235; S. A., Power and Primacy of the Pope, *Triglot,* p. 503).

XL. THE POWER OF THE CHURCH OR THE OFFICE OF THE KEYS

1. **The Office of the Keys is a spiritual power,** which must be clearly distinguished from the temporal power of the sword, given to the civil government (Matt. 22: 21; Rom. 13: 1-7). It is a spiritual power, because it pertains to the spirit, the soul, of man (Hebr. 13: 17); it imparts spiritual blessings, forgiveness of sins, life, and salvation; it uses spiritual means, the Word of God (Acts 6: 4); it has a spiritual aim, the eternal salvation of the soul (1 Pet. 1: 9).

2. **This power was given by Christ to His Church on earth.**—"As My Father sent Me, even so send I you . . . Receive ye the Holy Ghost: whose soever sins ye remit, they are remitted unto them; and whose soever sins ye retain, they are retained" (John 20: 21-23); these words were addressed to the disciples on Easter Sunday evening. "I will give unto thee the keys of the kingdom of heaven" (Matt. 16: 19); while these words were indeed addressed to Peter, they do not prove that the power of the keys was given to him alone. A comparison of this text with Matt. 18: 18 clearly shows, that the power to bind and to loose is given to the church or the local

congregation.—Nor was this power given exclusively to the apostles, and by them through ordination transmitted to their successors, the ordained clergy (Apostolic Succession). Christ says: "Tell it to the church," and the church is to absolve the penitent, or retain the sins of the impenitent (Matt. 18: 17. 18). In the case of the incestuous person at Corinth, action was taken by the congregation (1 Cor. 5; 2 Cor. 2: 6-10). Although hypocrites within the congregation externally participate in the exercise of this power, they do not share in the right of possessing it, since it properly belongs to those only who have received the Holy Ghost (John 20: 22. 23), and who by faith are the royal priesthood (1 Pet. 2: 9).

"He grants the keys principally and immediately to the Church, just as also for this reason the Church has principally the right of calling" (S. A., Of the Power, 24, *Triglot,* p. 511). "Here belong the statements of Christ which testify that the keys have been given to the Church, and not merely to certain persons" (S. A., Of the Power, 69, *Triglot,* p. 523). "This true Church of believers and saints it is to which Christ has given the keys of the kingdom of heaven and which is, therefore, the real and only possessor and bearer of the spiritual, divine, and heavenly blessings, rights, powers, offices, etc., which Christ has procured, and which are to be found in His Church" (Walther: *Kirche und Amt,* I, Thesis 4).

3. **The Office of the Keys is the power of the Word.**— Christ gave to His Church God's Word (John 17: 8. 14); by the Word men are to be sanctified and brought to faith (John 17: 20). Hence, Peter speaks of the "ministry of the Word" (Acts 6: 4).—The Church, therefore, has no right to exercise secular power (John 18: 36), nor may it employ the power of the state to compel men to accept the teachings of the Gospel, and to enforce Christian living (2 Cor. 10: 4), nor to imprison and burn heretics. The police power of the state is neither an integral part of, nor an appendage to, the spiritual power of the Church. Contrary to the claim of Rome that the Pope has both the sword of temporal power and the sword of the spirit, we hold that the state has the power of the sword, and the Church has the power of the Word. Not by force and fines, but by teaching and persuasion the Church wins men for

Christ and induces them to live under Him in His kingdom. (Cf., A. C., Art. XXVIII, *Triglot,* p. 83).

4. **Extent and limit of this power.**—As the power of the Church is exercised through the Word, its compass is definitely fixed by this Word. It reaches as far as the Word of God reaches, and not a whit further. The Church is to teach men to observe all Christ has commanded, and only what He has commanded (Matt. 28: 20). Whatever the Bible teaches, commands, and promises, the Church must teach, command, and promise. Beyond this the Church has no power and authority. (Cf., Apol., Art. XXVIII, 18. 21, *Triglot,* p. 449).

5. **The cardinal truth of the Word and the commission of the Church.**—The chief truth of the Gospel is that for Christ's sake God has forgiven all sins to all men. This truth the Church is to proclaim to the world (Mark 16: 15; Luke 24: 47), assuring complete forgiveness to penitent sinners, but withholding it from impenitent sinners as long as they do not repent (John 20: 23). Paul writes: "God was in Christ, reconciling the world unto Himself, not imputing their trespasses unto them; and hath committed unto us the word of reconciliation. Now then we are ambassadors for Christ, as though God did beseech you by us; we pray you in Christ's stead, be ye reconciled to God" (2 Cor. 5: 19. 20). Because the Church has received from God the Gospel, the Word of reconciliation, it is thereby divinely authorized to proclaim to all men this blessed fact that, as Christ has fully atoned for all sins, God has also forgiven all sins to all men. It is, therefore, the purpose of this Office and the mission of the Church to make known to the world the forgiveness of sins procured by Christ, to persuade men to accept it; "be ye reconciled to God" is the inviting message. The Church is to tell those who will not repent and believe in Christ that they shall die in their sins (John 8: 24).

The Church is to perform its mission by preaching and teaching the Gospel (Mark 16: 15), by administering the Sacraments (Matt. 28: 18-20; 1 Cor. 11: 25), by remitting and retaining sins (John 20: 22. 23; Matt. 18: 17. 18). (Cf., A. C., Art. XXVIII, 5-9, *Triglot,* p. 85). As God Himself offers grace and forgiveness to men in and by these means of grace, and as the Church is to administer these means of grace, it cannot do so without at the same time transmitting these promised blessings to man. It is impossible to preach the Gospel without preaching forgiveness of sins, and to administer the Sacraments without offering remission of sins.

The Office of the Keys, then, is that authority and commission which Christ gave to His believers on earth, that they should administer the means of grace, through which the Holy Ghost will impart to men the blessings of Christ's redemption. Christ procured forgiveness of sins and salvation for all men; through the means of grace the Holy Ghost imparts these blessings to men; and the Church, or the believers, are to administer these means.

XLI. THE POWER TO REMIT AND TO RETAIN SINS

1. Objection to, and misuse of, this power of the Church is due partly to misunderstanding the nature of this power, and partly to the denial of universal justification as taught in 2 Cor. 5: 19.

2. **The releasing key is the power to remit sins,** to absolve the sinner, to declare him free from guilt and punishment. This is not a power beside and above the ordinary preaching of the Gospel; absolution is merely a specialized form of Gospel preaching. "The power of the keys administers and presents the Gospel through absolution, which proclaims peace to me and is the true voice of the Gospel" (Apol., Art. XII, 39, *Triglot*, p. 261). The meaning is not that sins are then and there first forgiven by God in heaven, when the absolution is spoken, for Luther correctly says: "The sins are already forgiven, before we confess them." There is not a soul in all the world which God has not already absolved from all its sins because of the reconciliation through Christ (2 Cor. 5: 19). Absolution merely applies the message of grace and forgiveness to the individual in a more formal and direct way. Christ says: "Whose soever sins ye remit, they are remitted unto them" (John 20: 23). And speaking of the local Christian congregation He says: "Whatsoever ye shall loose on earth shall be loosed in heaven" (Matt. 18: 18). If these words mean anything at all, they certainly mean that the Christian congregation, and the minister acting in the name of the congregation, have the power and authority to remit sins, and that they may

do so not only by telling the sinner: "God has forgiven your sins," but also by using a more direct and personal formula: "In the name of God I" or "we forgive unto you all your sins."

In so doing the Church does not act in its own name, but in the name of God, as His spokesman. Neither the Church nor the minister of the congregation does the actual forgiving; only God can do that (Mark 2: 7); the Church and the minister merely transmit to the individual the forgiveness of God; their function in this matter is purely instrumental. Illustration: As the warden of a penitentiary merely transmits the governor's pardon to the convict, so the minister merely announces and applies God's forgiveness to the penitent sinner. If God had not first absolved all men for Christ's sake, and had not told us so in the Gospel (2 Cor. 5: 19), no man on earth could absolve a sinner. Therefore God does not forgive sins in heaven because of the absolution which is pronounced by men on earth; but the Church on earth absolves and forgives, because God in heaven has long since for Christ's sake absolved all men of their sins. The absolution of the Church is based on the absolution of God. For this reason it is valid and certain, in heaven also, as if Christ, our dear Lord, dealt with us Himself. Absolution, therefore, is not an empty word; but real forgiveness, God's forgiveness is announced, offered, and assured to us.

Like the promise of the Gospel, absolution is unconditional and always true; it simply states a fact and applies this fact to the individual. But whether one will be personally benefited thereby, depends upon his faith (Hebr. 4: 2). To receive the comfort of absolution one must believe it. "Wherefore the voice of the one absolving must be believed not otherwise than we would believe a voice from heaven" (Apol., Art. XII, 40, *Triglot*, p. 261).

3. **The binding key is the power to retain sins.**—Christ says: "Whosoever sins ye retain, they are retained" (John 20: 23). "Whatsoever ye shall bind on earth shall be bound in heaven" (Matt. 18: 18). To retain sins or to bind them on some one does not mean that these sins were not atoned for and are, therefore, not yet forgiven before God. For the Bible teaches that God does not impute the trespasses unto the world (2 Cor. 5: 19), and that He justifies the ungodly (Rom.

4: 5). In the court and in the heart of God also the sins of
the impenitent are really and truly forgiven; there is forgiveness for all men. But this forgiveness, offered freely in the
Gospel and in absolution, is meant to be accepted in faith
(Rom. 1: 17), and can be apprehended in no other way than
by faith (Rom. 3: 28). But the impenitent, lacking this faith,
makes the grace and promise of God, as far as it concerns
him, ineffectual (Hebr. 4: 2), and thus he excludes himself
from the general amnesty proclaimed by God. He is like the
man before whom the table is spread, but who will not eat.
To such a one the Church should declare that, while there is
indeed forgiveness of sins with God also for him, he shall not
and cannot *have* it as long as he does not repent. To retain
sins, therefore, simply means to declare a certain fact, which
fact would obtain even though the declaration were not made,
namely, that the impenitent cannot and shall not have forgiveness as long as he does not repent. And lest such a person
think he could still have forgiveness despite his impenitence,
the Church has authority and power to make such declaration
formally and officially.

4. **The Church may not use this power indiscriminately
or arbitrarily,** but must strictly follow the instructions of
Christ, remitting sins to penitent sinners, and retaining the
sins of the impenitent as long as they do not repent. Objectively, forgiveness of sins is ready for all men, but repentance,
or sorrow over sin, is a necessary prerequisite for its acceptance. For this reason forgiveness should be offered and assured only to those who repent. "Repent ye, therefore, and
be converted, that your sins may be blotted out" (Acts 3: 19).
"The sacrifices of God are a broken spirit; a broken and a
contrite heart, O God, Thou wilt not despise" (Ps. 51: 17).
Paul told the Gentiles that they should repent and turn to
God (Acts 26: 20). While the jailer is told: "Believe on the
Lord Jesus Christ, and thou shalt be saved" (Acts 16: 31),
Jesus tells the Jews: "If ye believe not that I am He, ye shall
die in your sins" (John 8: 24). When David repented, Nathan
absolved him (2 Sam. 12: 13). From these texts it is clear
that sins should be remitted to those who repent, but be retained to those who remain impenitent.

Whenever the Church thus deals with sinners, its actions

are valid also in heaven (Matt. 18: 18). But whenever the Church errs in its judgment, forgiving sins to an impenitent, and retaining sins to a penitent sinner, then such action is not valid. The penitent sinner will receive forgiveness in spite of what the Church has said, and the impenitent sinner will not have forgiveness, even though the Church has thrice absolved him.

XLII. CHURCH DISCIPLINE

1. **The power of the Church carries with it the duty of church discipline.**—No congregation may tolerate in its midst the public teaching of false doctrine (Matt. 7: 15; 1 John 4: 1; Tit. 1: 9-14; 3: 10), or a manifest and persistent ungodly life on the part of its members (Matt. 18: 15-17; 1 Cor. 5; Gal. 6: 1; James 5: 19. 20). As members of the body of Christ, we must be concerned about the spiritual well-being of each other; each is his brother's keeper. From love to the erring brother the congregation must seek to restore him (Gal. 6: 1); from love to those who might be led astray by his evil example it must rebuke him (1 Tim. 5: 20).—While it may not always be possible in a congregation to carry a case of church discipline to its final conclusion, still the duty to do so is manifestly included in the Office of the Keys (Matt. 18: 15-18; 1 Cor. 5: 13).

"Excommunication is also pronounced against the openly wicked and despisers of the Sacraments" (Apol., Art. X. XI, 61, *Triglot*, p. 249). "The true Christian excommunication consists in this that manifest and obstinate sinners are not admitted to the Sacrament and other communion of the Church until they amend their lives and avoid sin" (S. A., Art. IX, *Triglot*, p. 497).

2. **The procedure in a case of church discipline is prescribed in the Scriptures.**—No congregation or pastor may act rashly in this matter, but, wherever possible, should observe certain steps of admonition according to Matt. 18: 15-18.

(a) If a brother has sinned against you (Matt. 18: 15), or is otherwise overtaken in a fault (Gal. 6: 1), then do not speak about this to others; do not wait till he comes to you; but you go to him, admonish him in private, speak kindly to him in the spirit of meekness with a view of winning him back to Christ. This may be repeated until he repents. Then forgive and forget, and the matter ends.

(b) If you do not succeed, then "take with thee two or three more," preferably his friends or men in whom he has confidence, and do likewise. If he repents, forgive and forget, and the matter ends, and no one should talk about it to others.

(c) If these do not succeed in winning him, "tell it to the church." At this point the pastor of the congregation should be informed, who may then make another effort to win the erring brother. If he fails, he will present the case to the congregation. The brethren should then speak to him earnestly, but kindly; the purpose is not to judge and condemn him, as in a trial at court, but to win the brother from the error of his way; not to humiliate him, but to raise him from his fall. This also may be repeated until we have gained the brother, or until it is evident to all that he is impenitent.

If the offense is a matter of public knowledge, the case may be taken up by the congregation at once (1 Tim. 5: 20). It is wise, however, that also in this case some one speak to him privately first. If he repents, his confession must be made public, so that all who know of his sin, may also know of his repentance. Whoever is too proud to confess his fault is not truly repentant (Prov. 28: 13; Matt. 5: 23. 24).

(d) "If he neglect to hear the church" by stubbornly refusing to repent of the wrong he has done, the congregation must regard him "as a heathen man and a publican," and must put away from among themselves that wicked person. Such action on the part of the congregation must be unanimous. This is a matter that concerns all members, and must, therefore, be done with the consent of all. If there be some who are not convinced of the person's impenitence, or who believe that he can still be won, then they must deal with the erring brother until they have either won him or are themselves also convinced of his impenitence.—Such excommunication pertains only to the one who is manifestly impenitent, not to his entire family. We do not excommunicate a group of persons, but only individuals.—While excommunication deprives a person of the rights and privileges of the Church, it does not forbid him to attend the public services.

Excommunication validly and rightly performed in one congregation must be recognized in every other congregation. Manifest impenitence, which excludes a person from one congregation, will certainly exclude him also from every other Christian congregation in the world.

It sometimes happens that a person refuses to deal with his brethren, and by word or deed (by joining a church of another denomination) declares his withdrawal from the congregation; then this congregation cannot really excommunicate him, because he is no longer a member. While it is very sinful to act in such a manner, we have no right to declare such a person manifestly impenitent, for we have not had the opportunity to establish this fact. In such a case we can only say that he in a very sinful way severed his connection with the congregation; we judge and condemn his act, but we do not judge and condemn his heart.

3. **Meaning of excommunication.** — To excommunicate means to exclude from the communion of the Church. By faith one holds membership in the invisible Church, in the communion of saints. Impenitence instantly kills faith. Hence, by his impenitence a person automatically excludes himself from the invisible Church, even though he may continue to hold membership in the visible Church, because his impenitence may not be manifest. (Cf., Chap. XXXVIII, 1). Thus the man at Corinth (1 Cor. 5) was, because of his impenitence, no longer a member of the invisible Church, although the congregation still carried him as one of its members. However, when the impenitence of a person becomes manifest, then, after due admonition, it is the duty of the congregation to regard such a one "a heathen man and a publican" (Matt. 18: 17), and to "put away from among yourselves that wicked person" (1 Cor. 5: 13). The congregation excludes him from the visible Church, and thereby impresses upon him the fact that by his impenitence he has excluded himself from the invisible Church. By his impenitence he has actually forfeited the forgiveness of sins, and the Church has authority to declare this officially. This declaration on the part of the congregation is as valid and certain as if Christ had made it Himself. A person, therefore, is never excommunicated because of a particular sin he has committed, because he is a drunkard, a thief, a lodge member, etc., but solely because he is impenitent.

A penitent malefactor remains a member of the congregation, but an impenitent Caiaphas must be excluded. Impenitence of the heart excludes from the invisible Church; manifest impenitence excludes from the visible Church.

Denial of, or exclusion from, church-fellowship is not equivalent to excommunication. While we may not tolerate the teaching and spreading of false doctrine, it is possible that a person errs in sincerity of heart, without losing his faith in Christ (2 Thess. 3: 14. 15; 1 Cor. 3: 11-15). We are to have no fellowship with false teachers (Rom. 16: 17), yet we do not regard them as "heathen men and publicans."

4. **The purpose of excommunication** is not to destroy the soul, but rather to save it (1 Cor. 5: 1-5). Thereby the Church in a very emphatic manner would impress upon a person whither his impenitence leads him, namely, that as long as he remains impenitent, he cannot have forgiveness of sins, and shall not inherit the kingdom of God. It does not matter where such a person may go; even if in some other place he were to join a congregation, he carries his impenitence with him, which excludes him from the kingdom of God. Change of place and change of church will not help him; he needs a change of heart.

When excommunication has had its desired effect, and the person sincerely repents, he by such repentance and faith again becomes a member of the communion of saints, of the invisible Church. Then he will also confess his sin before the congregation, which is authorized by God to declare to him that his sin is forgiven, and which will gladly receive him again as a brother in Christ (2 Cor. 2: 6-10). "There is joy in the presence of the angels of God over one sinner that repenteth" (Luke 15: 10).—In case it is impossible for one, who was excommunicated, to make confession to the congregation, as it might be in the case of death, he shall still have forgiveness of his sins and be saved, if he truly repents and believes in Jesus Christ, his Savior (John 3: 16).

XLIII. THE OFFICE OF THE MINISTRY

1. **The royal priesthood of all Christians.** — By faith in Christ all Christians are royal priests before God; "ye are . . . a royal priesthood" (1 Pet. 2: 9). Because of this fact they

are the real owners and possessors of the Office of the Keys, and of all this Office implies. "All things are yours. . . ." (1 Cor. 3: 21-23); (Matt. 28: 19. 20; John 20: 22).—Christians should also exercise the privileges and powers of their priesthood. In their homes, among their brethren and neighbors, in their contacts with the world they should by word and deed "show forth the praises of Him who hath called them out of darkness into His marvelous light" (1 Pet. 2: 9). They should be witnesses to Christ, confess Him before men, teach His Word, reprove sin and error, admonish and comfort, pray and intercede for others; in cases of necessity they may also baptize and absolve. (Cf., S. A., Of the Power, 67, *Triglot*, p. 523). And whatever a layman does in these things is as valid and certain as if an ordained minister had done it; the official character of the minister does not add virtue and validity to the means of grace.

2. **Difference between the personal priesthood of all Christians and the public ministry.** — Whenever Christians perform the rights and duties of their royal priesthood, they act as private persons and not as public officials of the Church. As we distinguish between a private citizen and a public official, so must we distinguish between an individual Christian and the called minister of the congregation. What both do may in a given case be exactly the same thing; the one acts as an individual Christian on the basis of his royal priesthood, which may not be curtailed in any manner; the other acts on the basis of the call he received from his fellow-Christians. One acts, under God, in his own name; the other acts, under God, in the name of the congregation which has called him.

This very distinction limits the sphere of a Christian as a royal priest to such things as he can do as an individual Christian, and it excludes those things in which many Christians act jointly as a congregation. Thus the public preaching of the Gospel and the administration of the Sacraments, church discipline, and the excommunication of the impenitent sinner from a congregation no individual Christian may claim for himself on the basis of his royal priesthood. In these matters the entire congregation acts, and it acts through its called minister.

3. **The ministry a divine institution.** — The office of the ministry was not invented by men, but instituted by God. It is the will of God that His children not only personally or privately teach the Word of God, but that they do this also jointly as a congregation. Since Christians should not be separatists, each remaining aloof from the other, but should seek and maintain fellowship with one another (Acts 2: 42), forming local congregations, so they should also unite in doing the Lord's work, and to this end should establish the public ministry in their midst. Thus Paul and Barnabas "ordained them elders in every church" (Acts 14: 23). To Timothy Paul writes of elders that labor in the Word and doctrine (1 Tim. 5: 17). And in 2 Cor. 5: 19. 20 Paul calls himself and his coworkers "ambassadors for Christ," because God had committed unto them the "word of reconciliation." This was true not only of the apostles, but also of the elders or bishops that were elected by the congregations, for Paul tells the elders of the congregation at Ephesus that the Holy Ghost had made them bishops over all the flock (Acts 20: 28). In his letter to the Ephesians he writes that it is the exalted Savior who gives to the church men for the work of the ministry (Eph. 4: 11-13). He writes (1 Cor. 9: 14): "The Lord hath ordained that they which preach the Gospel should live of the Gospel." From all this it follows that the office of the ministry must indeed be an institution of God. Hence, "wherever the Church is, there is authority (command) to administer the Gospel. Therefore it is necessary for the Church (local congregation) to retain the authority to call, elect, and ordain ministers" (S. A., Of the Power, 67, *Triglot,* p. 523).

4. **The right to call its own minister is vested in the local congregation.**— No prince, pope, conference, synod, or consistory has the divine right to appoint and assign pastors to congregations. The Office of the Keys belongs to all believers in a given congregation, and this includes the right to elect, call, and ordain those who are to administer this Office within said congregation. Nor may any one within this congregation assume for himself the right to administer this Office in the name of all without the consent and call of all the other members. "Are all teachers?" Paul asks (1 Cor. 12: 29), and the implied answer is that they are not. "How shall they

preach, except they be sent?" (Rom. 10: 15). Hence we teach "that no one should teach publicly in the Church or administer the Sacraments unless he be regularly called" (A. C., Art. XIV, *Triglot,* p. 49).

The apostles were directly appointed by Christ (Gal. 1: 1), and had the supervision over the entire Church (2 Cor. 11: 28). But the bishops or elders were elected by their congregations (Acts 1: 23; 6: 2-6; 14: 23); ordained means elected by a show of hands, to choose, as in 2 Cor. 8: 19. Titus is charged to ordain, to have elected, elders in every city (Tit. 1: 5). "The Church has the command to appoint ministers" (Apol., Art. XIII, 11, *Triglot,* p. 311). "The Church has principally the right of calling" (S. A., Power, 24, *Triglot,* p. 511). "Bishops should be elected by their own churches" (S. A., Power, 13, *Triglot,* p. 507).

The call to the ministry is not universal in the sense that a person called by one congregation may by virtue of this call administer the means of grace also in any other congregation; his call limits him to the congregation over which he has been made overseer (Acts 20: 28). He should not meddle in the business of another pastor, nor take charge of a vacant congregation without being called to do so.

5. **Ministers are called by God through the congregation.** —The apostles were called by Christ directly, without human intermediaries (Matt. 4: 19; Luke 10: 1; Matt. 28: 19; Gal. 1: 1). But they instructed the congregations, which they had gathered, and which were the real possessors of the plenitude of spiritual and ecclesiastical powers, to elect and commission fit men for the work of the ministry in their midst (Acts 14: 23) and in the mission field (Acts 13: 1-3). In exercising this divine right the congregation acts as the executive of God's will. Hence, these elders, also called pastors or bishops, are mediately called by God Himself. For this reason Paul tells the elders of the congregation at Ephesus that the Holy Ghost had made them overseers over all the flock (Acts 20: 28). And in 1 Cor. 12: 28 and Eph. 4: 11. 12 he tells us that it is God, Christ, who gives apostles, prophets, pastors, and teachers to His Church. In 2 Cor. 5: 20 he calls himself and his co-workers "ambassadors for Christ," and in 1 Cor. 4: 1 "ministers of Christ." Whoever, then, is properly and regularly

called by a Christian congregation to the ministry of the Word should regard himself, and should by his congregation be regarded, as being called by God Himself. He is a minister of God not only because he does the work God has commanded, but also because God has called him into His service.

The two essential features of a divine call are (a) that the call be issued by the congregation, which has the divine authority to call, and (b) that it is a call to do those things which Christ has commanded His Church to do. A call issued by any individuals within or without the congregation may not be regarded as a divine call. A congregation may decide to call a man for the ministry in its midst, and leave the selection of the person to be called to a committee or board; but without the original call or consent of the congregation no one has the divine right simply to appoint a pastor for a flock. On the other hand, a congregation may call or engage a person for various activities and duties, yet if the person is not to labor in "the Word and doctrine" and to do those things which God has commanded His Church to do, it is not a "divine call" in the restricted sense, as applied to the ministry of the Word, even though the work may be very pleasing to God.

This does not mean that in every instance the call extended by a Christian congregation must be accepted by the one called. God here acts through human intermediaries, the congregation, and these may err in their judgment and in the selection of the man that is called. Generally speaking, the divinity of a call is determined by this question: "Where can the man that is called be of greater service to the kingdom of Christ?" In answer to this question both, the qualifications of the man and the opportunities for service, must be considered. But when a man has actually become the minister of a congregation, then the "Holy Ghost has made him overseer of the flock."

6. **Who may be called into the ministry?**—While the authority to choose, call, and ordain ministers was given by Christ to His Church (cf., S. A., Power, 67, *Triglot*, p. 523), a congregation is not at liberty to elect and call into this office any one whom it pleases, but only such as are fit and competent to perform its duties. (Cf., 1 Tim. 3: 2-7; Tit. 2: 7. 8). The

congregation, therefore, has the right to inquire into the personal and professional qualifications of candidates for this office, and it is advisable to consult competent men in this matter.

The office of the ministry may not be committed to women. "Let your women keep silence in the churches, for it is not permitted unto them to speak, but they are commanded to be under obedience. . . ." (1 Cor. 14: 34. 35); (1 Tim. 2: 11-14). Luther: "The Holy Ghost has barred women from the public ministry" (St. Louis Edition, XVI, 2280). The Scriptures in Gal. 3: 28 give women an equal share with men in salvation, but abrogate neither the social order, nor 1 Cor. 14: 34. This does not mean that women may not in some auxiliary capacity be employed in the work of the Church, for in Rom. 16: 1 Paul calls Phebe "a servant of the church which is at Cenchrea." Thus women teachers in our schools and deaconesses in our congregation are also servants of the church, doing some work that lies within the office of the ministry, and which they do under the supervision of the pastor. But the full office of the ministry may not be committed to them, nor should we expect the "weaker vessel" to assume the great responsibility of this office.

7. **Call and ordination.**— It is the call of the congregation and the acceptance of this call that makes a person the pastor and minister of said congregation (cf., A. C., Art. XIV, *Triglot*, p. 49); the ordination and the installation do not make him the pastor. Ordination is indeed mentioned in the Scriptures (1 Tim. 4: 14; 5: 22; 2 Tim. 1: 6), but it is not commanded. We observe it as an apostolic and ecclesiastical rite, not as an institution of God. It is the solemn attestation and public ratification of a fact that was effected by the acceptance of the call (cf., S. A., Power, 70, *Triglot*, p. 525). Because of the Word of God and prayer connected therewith, ordination certainly carries with it divine blessings. But it is not a sacrament, ordained by God; it impresses no "indelible character"; once a priest, always a priest, is not true; it bestows no special powers which the Church as such does not possess; the efficacy of the means of grace does not depend on it; nor is it absolutely necessary for the valid and effective administration of the office of the ministry.

8. **The clergy does not constitute an holy "order" or "priesthood"** endowed with superior sanctity and spiritual powers. Ministers are not mediators between man and God, as though the salvation of the laity depended on them. The power to save resides neither in the person nor in the office, but in the means of grace (Rom. 1: 16). They are indeed overseers over the flock (Acts 20: 28), but they were made such by God through the congregation. Hence, the Church is above the minister (cf., S. A., Power, 11, *Triglot*, p. 507). "Sacerdotalism" militates against the office of Christ as the only Mediator, against the doctrine of the efficacy of the means of grace, against the doctrine that the Office of the Keys is a church power, and not a priest or clergy power.

Christians should indeed esteem their pastors highly in love for their work's sake (1 Thess. 5: 12. 13); the difference between laymen and clergy is not one of order, but of office; out of office, the minister is a layman. (Cf., Luther, St. Louis Edition, Vol. X, 272).

9. **No grades in the ministry.** — The very nature of the ministerial office shows that by divine right no minister holds a higher rank and possesses greater power and authority than the other. The Romish hierarchial system, in which the priest is subject to his bishop, and the bishop to the archbishop, and he again to the Pope, is not instituted by God, but invented by men. The Bible uses the term "elder," presbyter, and "overseer," bishop, interchangeably (Acts 20: 17. 28; Tit. 1: 5-7). "By divine authority the grades of bishop and pastor are not diverse" (S. A., Power, 65, *Triglot*, p. 523). "All the bishops are equal in office (although they be not equal in gifts)" (S. A., Part II, Art. IV, 9, *Triglot*, p. 473). By divine authority there is no difference in the status of those who are ordained, or licensed, or called.

10. **The purpose of this office** is not that the minister as a priest reconcile the people with God—this Christ has done —but that he as a prophet and an ambassador of God proclaim to men the accomplished redemption and reconciliation, and that he beseech and persuade them to accept in faith what God offers them (2 Cor. 5: 19. 20).—For this reason it is not the aim of this office to present the teachings of the Bible in a purely academic way, as a professor may teach a system of

philosophy; the Gospel is to be preached and the Sacraments are to be administered for a very definite and practical purpose. We are to make men disciples of Christ and teach them to observe what Christ has commanded (Matt. 28: 19. 20); we are to perfect the saints and edify the Church of God (Eph. 4: 12); we are to save immortal souls (1 Tim. 4: 16). We may, therefore, define the office of the ministry thus: It is the public administration of the means of grace for the purpose of saving souls.

11. **The power of this office** does not extend above and beyond the Word. Texts of the Scriptures which enjoin obedience to pastors (Hebr. 13: 17; Luke 10: 16), do not confer unlimited authority in matters spiritual, but an authority under and within the Word of God. "Teaching them to observe all things whatsoever I have commanded you" (Matt. 28: 20). Whenever the called ministers teach otherwise than the Word of God teaches, we must neither obey nor follow them (Rom. 16: 17). (Cf., Apol., Art. XXVIII, 14, *Triglot*, p. 447; A. C., Art. XXVIII, 30-34, *Triglot*, p. 87).

On the other hand, when the called ministers deal with us by Christ's command, i.e., when they teach, admonish, and comfort us from the Word of God, then we must receive their instruction, admonition, and comfort as though God spake to us Himself. "He that heareth you, heareth Me; and he that despiseth you, despiseth Me; and he that despiseth Me, despiseth Him that sent Me" (Luke 10: 16). Whenever they truly teach the Word of God, they are God's ambassadors to us, and as such must be respected and obeyed (2 Cor. 5: 20).

12. **The necessity of this office** is based on its divine institution. For this reason every local congregation should establish the office of the ministry in its midst. However, this office is not *absolutely* necessary in the sense that without it no man could be saved, for it is not the office itself that confers spiritual blessings; it merely administers those means through which grace and forgiveness are offered and conveyed to men. And these means of grace are effective unto salvation also without the benefit of the clergy. (Cf., Chapter XXXII, The Gospel, 4.)

13. **"The ministry is the highest office in the Church"** (Apol., Art. XV, 42, *Triglot*, p. 327). Because the Word of

God rules supreme in the Church, it is evident that there can be no higher office than the ministry of the Word. This, however, does not mean that there may be only one minister in a congregation; (cf., Acts 13: 1; 20: 17. 28). In this case the work of the one office was probably divided among the several ministers as the different names seem to indicate (Eph. 4: 11). Even in the ministry of Christ we find that He preached, but did not baptize (John 4: 2); (cf., also 1 Cor. 1: 14-17). Thus a congregation has the right to call more than one pastor, and to divide the work among them.

Such division in the work of the ministry is not mandatory, but is rather a matter of expediency; it is determined either directly by the congregation, or indirectly through the pastor in charge, in order that the work of the ministry may be done more efficiently. What the duties and positions of the several persons within the framework of the ministry are to be, is determined by the congregation and is usually stipulated in the call.

This applies also to the feeding of the lambs of Christ. The work of teaching and training the young most certainly is an integral and important part of the work of the public ministry. Since the Christian education of children requires much time and attention, the congregation may call a special man or men for this particular work. Not the entire work of the ministry is transmitted unto them, but only that part of it for which they have been called. Yet, inasmuch as parish school teachers are called by the congregation for the express purpose of instructing children in the Word of God and of teaching them to observe all Christ has commanded, they are indeed laborers in the Word and doctrine, and hence theirs is a divine call. As children, and not men, are to be taught, women may also be engaged for this work.—However, there is no divine command that under all circumstances this work must be assigned to a special person. The feeding of the lambs is indeed commanded (John 21: 15), but it is not commanded that special men must be called for this work. Where the flock is small, it is quite possible that one man feed both the sheep and the lambs. Therefore, as a position separate and distinct from that of the pastor, the office of a parish school teacher is not a divine institution.—The teaching of secular subjects in our parish schools is not a part of the ministry of the Word. Yet our teachers take on also this work, in order that they may have opportunity to teach children the "One Thing Needful," the Gospel of Christ, and to eliminate from all secular instruction whatever might prove harmful to the souls of the children, and to exert a positive Christian influence for their training also in those periods when they teach reading, writing, and arithmetic.

XLIV. OF ANTICHRIST

1. **The term "antichrist"** is used in a general and in a specific sense. In the broader sense it applies to all false teachers, who within the Church teach doctrines contrary to the Word of Christ. This spirit of antichrist was in the world at the time of John (1 John 4: 1-3). But John differentiates between the many antichrists of his day and the one antichrist that was to come, and in whom the spirit of the many antichrists would culminate. "Ye have heard that antichrist shall come, even now there are many antichrists, whereby ye know that it is the last time" (1 John 2: 18). And Paul writes: "That day shall not come, except there come a falling away first, and that man of sin be revealed, the son of perdition" (2 Thess. 2: 3). Both apostles speak of the same individual, whose coming was to be a sign of the last time. Both teach that the spirit of antichrist (1 John 4: 3), or the mystery of iniquity, was at work even in their day (2 Thess. 2: 7), but would in the course of time become more pronounced and recognizable.

2. **The marks whereby antichrist can be recognized.**— (a) There will be "a falling away" (2 Thess. 2: 3), i.e., a falling away from the truth of the Gospel by teaching false doctrines. While every antichrist teaches false doctrines, this one would do so on so large a scale that he stands out above all others. Because of this falling away from the truth, there would also be a large falling away from the faith in Christ by those who follow the antichrist and accept his teachings. More than any other he would "speak perverse things, to draw away disciples" after him (Acts 20: 30).

(b) The antichrist "sitteth in the temple of God" (2 Thess. 2: 4). There are some outside of the Church that teach anti-

christian doctrines, causing many to lose their faith (1 Tim.
6: 20. 21). But these are not the antichrist of whom Paul
speaks; they are not in the Church, but outside of the Church.
Julian Apostate, Mohammed, and other well-known enemies
of Christ and His Church are not this antichrist; their opposition to Christ and His teaching was known and open. But this
antichrist is called "a mystery of iniquity"; he works in secret,
under cover of Christ's name, and his "coming is . . . with all
deceivableness of unrighteousness" (2 Thess. 2: 9. 10). Not
outside, but within the visible Church does this "mystery of
iniquity" develop, until it culminates in "that man of sin . . .
the son of perdition," who sits in the temple of God.

(c) "Who opposeth and exalted himself above all that is
called God, or that is worshiped; so that he as God sitteth in
the temple of God, showing himself that he is God" (2 Thess.
2: 4). "The phrase points out what the extreme of lawlessness is: opposition and self-exaltation *against* no less than
every God 'said' to be God, plus every reverenced object 'said'
to be reverenced" (Lenski on 2 Thess. 2: 4). Over all these
the antichrist exalts himself, claiming authority and lordship
over them, as the vicegerent of God on earth, to whom the
God-appointed estates are subordinate. And in the temple, or
Church, of God he usurps for himself the authority of God,
claiming to be the infallible teacher in matters of faith and
morals, who must be obeyed by all Christendom as though he
were God himself.

(d) The rise of antichrist to his full form and stature will
be gradual. The spirit of antichrist, or the mystery of iniquity,
was working already in the days of the apostles (1 John 4: 3;
2 Thess. 2: 7). Even among the very disciples of Christ there
was strife; they wanted to know who should be the greatest
in the kingdom of God (Luke 22: 24); Peter had to warn the
elders against being lords over God's heritage (1 Pet. 5: 1-3).
From the beginning there were ambitious men who strove for
eminence, dominion, and lordship in the Church. The people
likewise were ready to exalt one pastor over the other (1 Cor.
1: 12). However, there was something which for the time
being checked and repressed this tendency (2 Thess. 2: 5-7).
This was, on the one hand, the authority of the apostles still
living (Acts 20: 29. 30); on the other hand, there was the

mighty power of the pagan Roman Empire, which was not too friendly towards the Christians, and would certainly not tolerate such extravagant claims of superiority. During the first centuries the Church, and particularly its leaders, were persecuted; it was, therefore, not safe to be too prominent in the Church. This out of the way, there would be nothing to "withhold that he (antichrist) might be revealed in his time." Slyly, surreptitiously, but persistently, men would strive for power and authority in the Church, until one would succeed in exalting himself above all that is called God and is worshiped, so that he as God sitteth in the temple of God, showing that he is God.

(e) The driving force behind this ambitious striving for pre-eminence and primacy in the Church is Satan himself, who with "all power and signs and lying wonders, and with all deceivableness of unrighteousness" will support and further this antichristian movement (2 Thess. 2: 9. 10). Purported miracles and signs, the outward display of power, pomp, and grandeur, the apparent success of establishing and spreading its regime would blind the eyes and deceive those who do not hold fast to the truth of God's Word; looking up to him who had made himself head of the Church, they would forget Him who is the Head of the Church.

(f) This antichrist shall continue in the visible Church unto the end of time; "whom the Lord shall consume with the spirit of His mouth, and shall destroy with the brightness of His coming" (2 Thess. 2: 8).

3. **Who is this antichrist?**—The Bible does not expressly state who this antichrist is, but it describes him, so that Christians may recognize him and be warned. As we endeavor to determine who this antichrist may be, we must not take just one or two traits, but the entire composite picture as here portrayed, and find who fits into this picture. As we study the history of the Church, we find but one institution which bears all the marks here ascribed to the antichrist, and that is the Roman Papacy.

Because there still are believers in the Catholic Church (baptized children and those who in spite of false doctrines, officially taught, personally cling to Christ and His merits), this church must be included in the visible Church of Christ on earth, the "temple of God." But as far as the official teachings are concerned, there has been a gross falling away from the truth of the Gospel; the doctrine that sinners are saved solely by grace through faith in Christ is officially damned (cf., Canons 9, 11, 12, of the Council of Trent, as quoted in *Popular Symbolics,* p. 179). Because of the false doctrines taught, there has been also a falling away from the faith; many simple souls have actually been led astray and were lost. The Pope is not without, but within the visible Church, and has "exalted himself above all that is called God, or that is worshiped" (2 Thess. 2: 4). He claims to be Christ's vicar on earth, and to have supremacy over all temporal power, and he certainly exercises supreme authority within his denomination. (For proof from Catholic sources regarding the teaching of the primacy of the Pope cf., *Popular Symbolics,* §225. 226).

The rise of the Papacy was gradual. When Constantine the Great became sole emperor, about 300 A.D., the Christian religion was at first tolerated and protected; then it became the state religion and was supported by the power and revenues of the empire. Thus the ascendency of the Papacy was made possible. The chief obstacle in the way of ambitious men, the pagan and inimical Roman Empire, had been "taken out of the way." Bishops would exalt themselves above the presbyters; metropolitan bishops would exalt themselves above the other bishops; finally the rivalry narrowed down to the bishop at Rome and the bishop at Constantinople, which rivalry ended with the schism between the East and the West, 1054 A.D. In the West the primacy of the Pope and his temporal power were universally acknowledged about 1100 A.D. As to the "lying wonders," we call attention to the miracles alleged to have been wrought by saints and relics, and by which to this very day people are deceived.

Princes and church councils have fought against the power and the primacy of the Pope, but he has not only survived, but within his church his position has been more firmly established. As recently as 1870 the infallibility of the Pope was decreed by the Vatican Council at the insistence of Pius IX; "We, the sacred council approving, teach, and so define as a dogma divinely revealed, that the Roman Pontiff, when he speaks ex cathedra—that is to say, when in the discharge of the office of pastor and teacher of all Christians, by virtue of his supreme apostolic authority, he defines a doctrine regarding faith and morals to be held by the universal Church—is, through the divine assistance promised to the blessed Peter himself, possessed of the infallibility with which the divine Redeemer willed that His Church should be endowed for defining doctrine concerning faith and morals; and that, therefore, such definitions of the Roman Pontiff are of themselves, and not from the consent of the Church, unalterable. But if any one shall venture (which may God avert) to contradict our definition, let him be accursed." (Quoted from *Popular Symbolics*, p. 162). This decree gives divine authority to the Pope in matters of faith and morals, and proves "that he as God sitteth in the temple of God, showing himself that he is God" (2 Thess. 2: 4). When Pius XII was ordained on March 3, 1939, the following formula was used, as reported in the Chicago Tribune of March 12, 1939: "I bestow upon you the tiara adorned by three crowns; let it be known by you that you are the father of princes and kings, the director of the entire world, and the vicar of our Lord Jesus Christ, to whom only honor and glory in century and century is due. Amen." All this shows that the claims of papal supremacy both in the Church and in the world are upheld to this day.

There is nothing in the history of man that so fully answers the description of the antichrist given in the Bible as the Roman Papacy. Saying that the Pope is the antichrist, we are not thinking of one individual person, but of a succession of persons, each carrying on where his predecessor left off. It applies to the system of the Papacy as it developed in the course of time, and of which each individual Pope is the head. While we designate the Pope as the antichrist, we do not deny that it is possible for the individual Pope to be saved. If in the hour of death he simply trusts in the saving merits of Christ, he will be saved even as the malefactor on the cross was saved. "Even in considering the Pope as in his claims and assumptions an Antichrist, she (the Lutheran Church) does not exclude him as a person from the possibility of salvation" (Krauth in *The Conservative Reformation and Its Theology*, p. 194). (Cf., S. A., Of the Power and Primacy of the Pope, *Triglot*, pp. 503-521; S. A., Part II, Art. IV, Of the Papacy, *Triglot*, pp. 471-477; *Popular Symbolics*, § 223. 225. 226).

PART X. CIVIL ESTATES

XLV. CIVIL GOVERNMENT

1. In speaking of civil government we distinguish (a) the basic essence of all government, which is the power and authority to govern and rule a people in its external affairs; (b) the form of government, through which this power functions, and of which there is a great variety; (c) the personnel of the government, which administers this power. The personnel and the forms of government change, but the basic power and authority remain the same.

2. **Origin.**—The power and authority of all government originates with God. "For there is no power but of God: the powers that be are ordained of God . . ." (Rom. 13: 1. 2); (Prov. 8: 15; Dan. 2: 21; Jer. 27: 5. 6). It is the will of God that there should be government among men; anarchy is contrary to His will. This power is primarily vested not in a particular person, family, or class, but in the people.

3. **Form.**—The form of government is determined by men. Israel had a theocratic form of government until the days of Samuel; but when the people asked to have a king, God granted their request (1 Sam. 8). While the Bible speaks of the rights and duties of government, it nowhere champions any particular form. It may, therefore, be an absolute or a limited monarchy, an oligarchy or a democracy, or any other form the people choose to have. Nor does the Bible tell us in which manner the power of government shall be conferred, whether by heredity or by appointment or by election. Nor does the fact that control of government is obtained by force, by fraud, by usurpation, and that the men in office are wicked and godless, invalidate the power and authority of the government itself. The conscience of Christians is not bound to any special type of government, but Christians must regard as an ordinance of God every form that actually possesses and exercises the power and authority of government.

4. **Purpose.**—The fall of man into sin disrupted not only man's relation to God, but also his relation to his fellowmen,

as the story of Cain and Abel shows (Gen. 4). By means of civil government God purposes to make it possible for men to live together in outward peace and security. Governments, therefore, are to protect the lives, the property, the honor and reputation of the people, to safeguard them in the pursuit of their occupations and in the enjoyment of their liberties, and to preserve order and discipline in the commonwealth. For while rulers are "not a terror to good works, but to the evil," they are "ministers of God to thee for good" (Rom. 13: 3. 4), "that we may lead a quiet and peaceable life in all godliness and honesty" (1 Tim. 2: 2).

The government may also engage in such other activities as will promote and secure the general welfare of the people, such as the education of its citizens, the conservation of national resources, the amelioration of untoward conditions and suffering, combating social, economic, and physical dangers, improving living conditions in general.

5. **Right.**—To accomplish its purpose the government has the right to enact suitable laws, ordinances (1 Pet. 2: 13), which we call legislative power; to enforce these laws it has executive power; to judge men according to these laws (John 18: 31) it has judicial power; to punish transgressors by means of such penalties as it sees fit to impose (1 Pet. 2: 14) it has punitive power; to levy taxes for its maintenance and for such other purposes as it has a right to pursue (Matt. 22: 17-21; Rom. 13: 7) it has taxing power.

The government has the right to inflict capital punishment (Matt. 26: 52; Rom. 13: 4; Gen. 9: 6) and to wage just wars for the protection of its people. From Luke 3: 14 and Matt. 8: 5 we learn that military men are not required to abandon their calling on being converted to the Christian faith. "It is right for Christians to engage in just wars, to serve as soldiers" (A. C., Art. XVI, 2, *Triglot*, p. 51). "The Emperor may follow the example of David in making war to drive away the Turk from his country" (A. C., Art. XXI, 1, *Triglot*, p. 57). Courts have the right to demand oaths (Hebr. 6: 16); as Jesus suffered Himself to be put under oath (Matt. 26: 63), it is not sinful for Christians to take an oath when required to do so by the magistrates.

6. **Limit of power.**—The civil government controls in a measure the outward conduct of man inasmuch as it affects other men or the commonweal; it regards the individual in relation to society. But there are certain personal and private matters over which the government has no jurisdiction; chief of these is man's religion, or man's relation to God. Being a temporal power, civil government does not concern itself about the spiritual welfare of its citizens, and has no right to dictate to them whom they must worship and what they must believe. The care of souls is not committed to the civil government. Civil government deals with men not in the spiritual, but in the secular sphere and is therefore guided in its work not by Scripture, but by reason. "For civil government deals with other things than does the Gospel. The civil rulers defend not minds, but bodies and bodily things against manifest injuries, and restrain men with the sword and bodily punishments in order to preserve civil justice and peace" (A. C., Art. XXVIII, 11, *Triglot*, p. 85).

While the government may allow what God forbids, and forbid what God allows, it may not command what God forbids and forbid what God commands. If it does, we must obey God rather than men (Acts 5: 29).

7. **The basic principle.**—The fact that the powers are ordained of God does not mean that they must govern according to the Scriptures, making the Bible the fundamental lawbook of the land. Nero certainly did not rule according to the precepts of the Bible, yet the power he represented was ordained of God (Rom. 13: 1 ff.). The Bible is the sole authority in the Church or the kingdom of grace, but not in those institutions which, as civil government, belong into the kingdom of power. (Cf., Apol., Art. XVI, 55, *Triglot*, p. 331).

The basic principle in civil government is human reason, which codifies the natural knowledge of God's Law written in the hearts of men, and devises such additional ordinances as promise to achieve the purpose of government. It is by these laws that the government rules, and by the power of the sword it enforces them.

8. **Our duty to the government** is that we honor, obey, and support it (Rom. 13: 5-7; Tit. 3: 1), and take a sympathetic and active interest in its affairs (Jer. 29: 7). Christians, there-

fore, are law-abiding citizens not for wrath's, but for conscience' sake (Rom. 13: 5). Obedience to constituted authorities
and good citizenship are with them not matters of expedience,
but of conscience; they are a part of their religion. (Cf., A. C.,
Art. XVI, *Triglot,* p. 51; Apol., Art. XVI, *Triglot,* p. 329-333).

XLVI. SEPARATION OF STATE AND CHURCH

1. **Difference.**—The power of the State and of the Church
are both ordained of God; yet they differ from each other
radically in the fields in which they work, in the means and
methods they employ, and in the aims and objects they seek
to achieve.—The State exercises authority over all that live
within its political borders, irrespective of their religious convictions and church affiliations; the Church exercises control
only over those who voluntarily join its communion. — The
State rules by its own laws, and enforces obedience, if need
be, by means of penalties; it wields the sword. The Church
rules by the Word of God; it seeks to convince and persuade
men to accept its teachings and to observe its precepts; it has
the ministry of the Word.—The State preserves outward peace
in the community, and secures for all its citizens the enjoyment
of their civil and religious liberties; the Church offers spiritual blessings and brings the peace of God to troubled souls.—
The State is interested in the temporal affairs of its citizens;
the Church is interested in the spiritual and eternal salvation
of its members.—The power of the State is world-centered;
the power of the Church is heaven-centered.

2. **Separation.**—Because of this difference these two powers must be kept separate according to the axiomatic statement of Jesus: "Render unto Caesar the things that are
Caesar's, and unto God the things that are God's" (Matt. 22:
21).

While it is highly desirable that all public officials be true
believers and take an active part in all things Christ has commanded His Church to do, yet, their official position in the
State does not confer upon them additional authority in the
Church; as a member of a Christian congregation the Presi-
dent of the country holds no higher rank than any other
member of the congregation.—The Office of the Keys was not
given to the State, which, therefore, has no right and power

to perform any of the functions of the Office of the Keys. The State is not to teach religion, try heretics, absolve or excommunicate sinners; it has no authority to call and appoint ministers and teachers of the Gospel, to levy taxes to pay their salaries, to build and to maintain places of worship. If the State pleases to exempt church property from taxation, it does so not for religious reasons, but for reasons of State, because it recognizes the distinct and valuable service the Church renders in maintaining peace and discipline and inculcating obedience to constituted authorities. The State merely protects Christians and churches in the free exercise of their civil and religious liberties; but it must not try to do the business of the Church. (Cf., Luther: "How Far We Owe Obedience to Civil Government," Part II, St. Louis Edition, X, column 395 ff.).

Beyond such protection the Church should not expect and ask assistance from the State in her work of soul-saving. The Church should not call upon the police power of the State to compel people to attend church, to enforce Christian living (as though that could be done), to punish and burn heretics, to share in "the care of things divine" (Calvin, Inst. IV, Cap. XX, 9), to insert a confession of faith into the Constitution of our country, to govern according to the tenets of the Bible. All this would subject the civil government to the control of the Church and the clergy. "The power of the Church and the civil power must not be confounded . . . Let it (Church) not prescribe laws to civil rulers concerning the form of the commonwealth" (A. C., Art. XXVIII, 12. 13, *Triglot*, p. 85); (cf., Apol., Art. XVI, 54, *Triglot*, p. 329).

No church-state and no state-church. — It is "right for Christians to bear civil office" (A. C., Art. XVI, *Triglot*, p. 51). Still, they do not receive the authority of this office from the Church. For as little as the power of the Word was given to the State, is the power of the sword given to the Church, the claims of Popes notwithstanding. The Church as such has no right to rule land and people, to enact and enforce laws, and to do any of the things which properly belong to the domain of the civil government. Christ refused to act as judge and arbiter in a civil suit (Luke 12: 13. 14); His kingdom is not of this world (John 18: 36). There is no Scriptural reason for a church-state even as there is no Scriptural reason for a state-church; wherever a church-state or a state-church exist, they exist not by the will of God, but by the will of man. It is a mark of antichrist to claim supremacy over all civil authorities (2 Thess. 2: 4). (Cf., *Popular Symbolics*, §226).

Princes and presidents do not derive their authority from priests and preachers, but through the people from God (Rom. 13: 1). Therefore the Church has no right to depose or set up kings and governments, to establish, occupy, or transfer the kingdoms of this earth. (Cf., S. A., Power, 32-36, *Triglot*, p. 513). On the other hand, pastors do not derive their office and authority from the civil government, but through their congregations from God. Hence, the civil government has no right to organize Christian congregations, to appoint ministers, and to legislate in things spiritual. As little as the State may rule and govern the Church, so little may the Church rule and govern the State. The twain must remain separate.

Any usurpation of power either by the Church or by the State in the domain of the other results in misrule and tyranny in both, and is destructive of religious and civil liberty, as the history of the past amply proves. The strict separation of State and Church is conducive to the welfare of both. When the State faithfully and effectively tends to its business, it is a minister of God for the good of the Church; its members may then lead a quiet and peaceable life in all godliness and honesty (1 Tim. 2: 1-3), and worship God according to the dictates of their conscience. When the Church faithfully tends to its business, it will teach its members to honor and obey magistrates, to support the government with their prayers, taxes, and service, and will thus train them to be loyal and law-abiding citizens. Speaking of Christian schools and of their benefit to the State, Luther says: "That is a city's best and richest prosperity, weal, and power to have many fine, educated, sensible, and well-trained citizens." (Cf., St. Louis Edition, X, column 467).

XLVII. MATRIMONY

1. **Matrimony is a divine institution.** — God instituted matrimony when in the garden of Eden He made a wife for man, brought her to him, and blessed their union to be one

flesh (Gen. 1: 27. 28; 2: 18-24). According to the will of God, this institution was to increase the happiness of both, and was to continue among all men also after the fall (Matt. 19: 4-6). He still joins husband and wife together, and guards the sanctity of their union in the Sixth Commandment, recommends it in the interest of chastity (1 Cor. 7: 2-9), and tells us that marriage is honorable in all (Hebr. 13: 4). The Scriptures extol matrimony (Ps. 127; 128), and Christ honored it by His presence and His first miracle at the wedding in Cana (John 2: 1-11). (Cf., A. C., Art. XXIII, 19, *Triglot*, p. 63; Apol., Art. XXIII, 7. 14. 33, pp. 365. 367. 373).

2. **Matrimony is not a sacrament.**—Christians will certainly sanctify also their marriage with the Word of God and with prayer (1 Tim. 4: 5); but matrimony does not confer on them any particular spiritual blessings. Instituted before the fall of man, it could not offer forgiveness of sins, and there is not a text in the Bible which shows that this virtue has since been added. Matrimony is called "a mystery" (Eph. 5: 32), not because it confers the grace of perfecting the natural love and of sanctifying those who are joined in marriage, but because the right relation between husband and wife portrays the spiritual relation between Christ and His Church. Like civil government, matrimony belongs into the kingdom of power, and not in the kingdom of grace. (Apol., Art. XXIII, 9, *Triglot*, p. 369). It is, therefore, not essential to matrimony that marriage be solemnized by a minister or a priest. People whose marriage was solemnized by civil authorities are as properly and validly married before God and man as those whose union was blessed by a minister or priest of a church. (Cf., Apol., Art. XIII, 14, *Triglot*, p. 311).

3. **Celibacy versus matrimony.** — Celibacy is not commanded by God, and, therefore, can not be superior in sanctity and be more pleasing to God than matrimony, the claims of Rome regarding the priesthood notwithstanding. Expressions in 1 Cor. 7: 1. 8. 38. 40, which recommend it, must be understood in the light of the reason given for such recommendation in 1 Cor. 7: 26-29. Under certain conditions we may even in our day recommend to young people that it is better for them not to marry. Thus Paul says that for "the present distress," and to avoid "trouble in the flesh," it is bet-

ter not to marry.—But all men are not fit to lead a single life (Matt. 19: 11. 12), since not all have the gift of continency (1 Cor. 7: 7). Therefore under normal conditions it is better to marry than to remain unmarried (1 Cor. 7: 2-5; 1 Tim. 5: 14). The Word of God: "It is not good that man should be alone" (Gen. 2: 18), is true to this day; and more so now than it was in Paradise, for history shows that enforced celibacy has always resulted in the corruption of morals. Contrary to the Word of God, Rome forbids the marriage of priests as sinful. The Scriptures denounce the forbidding of marriage as "a doctrine of devils" (1 Tim. 4: 1-3), and say: "A bishop, then, must be blameless, the husband of one wife . . . having his children in subjection with all gravity" (1 Tim. 3: 2. 4). Paul was not married, but he claimed for himself the right to have a wife, just as Peter and other apostles had wives (1 Cor. 9: 5). Not a second marriage, but bigamy is forbidden in 1 Tim. 3: 2. (Cf., A. C., Art. XXIII, *Triglot,* p. 61 ff.; Apol., Art. XXIII, *Triglot,* p. 363 ff.)

4. **Polygamy.**—"Polygamy is prohibited by Scripture and all Christian churches. Monogamous marriage is the only form of marriage recognized by Jesus as instituted by God for all times (Matt. 19: 4-6). . . . While Scripture records instances of polygamous marriage in the Old Testament, it does not thereby sanction polygamy. It is forbidden in the Moral Law (Lev. 18: 18). The Civil Law of Moses did indeed permit it (Deut. 21: 15-17), as it permitted also divorces not sanctioned by the Moral Law, and for the same reason, 'because of the hardness of your hearts' (Matt. 19: 8). This toleration and regulation of polygamy and of divorce does not carry with it the sanction of the Moral Law. A thing may be legally right, but not morally" (*Popular Symbolics,* §171).

While a man may not marry two or more wives at the same time (Lev. 18: 18), he may marry another wife, and the wife may marry another husband, after the first spouse has died. The marriage union between husband and wife is dissolved by the death of either, and the other is free to remarry (Rom. 7: 2. 3; 1 Cor. 7: 39).

5. **Prohibited marriages.**—One may not marry any one whom he or she pleases. In the first families on earth there was intermarriage of brothers and sisters and close relatives,

for all nations of men are "of one blood" (Acts 17: 26). But now it is forbidden to marry those who are "the flesh of his flesh," "near of kin" to us, i.e., who are related to us by blood (consanguinity) or by marriage (affinity) in the first or second degree (Lev. 18: 6-18; 20: 11-21; Deut. 27: 20-23).—Betrothal, though essentially marriage, does not create a prohibited degree of affinity, since no sexual intercouse has ensued, by which a man and a woman become one flesh.—That these stipulations of prohibited marriages are a part of the Moral Law, is evident from the fact that God punished the heathen nations for these abominations (Lev. 18: 24. 25). While the Gentiles do these things, they have, nevertheless, the feeling that such things ought not to be (1 Cor. 5: 1).—The Pope, again setting himself above God, assumes for himself the right to "dispense in some of these degrees" and to add others, such as spiritual relationship between sponsors, which God has not forbidden. (Cf., S. A., Power, 78, *Triglot*, p. 527).

As we are to obey every ordinance of man for the Lord's sake (1 Pet. 2: 13), we may not marry those whom the State, in which we live, forbids us to marry. If the State allows marriages which God forbids, we must obey God; if the State forbids marriages which God allows, we must obey the civil law of the State.

According to Matt. 5: 32 and Matt. 19: 9 one may not marry a person that is unlawfully divorced. Because of the danger of being turned from the true faith, Christians are warned not to marry a heathen person or one of another faith (Deut. 7: 3. 4; 1 Cor. 7: 16).

6. **Definition of marriage.**—Marriage, as a civil status, is determined by the civil laws of the State, which are diverse in different countries. As a civil status before man, marriage begins with the wedding ceremony, in which a person authorized to do so pronounces a man and a woman, who are agreed to marry and have obtained their marriage license, husband and wife.—The nature and essence of matrimony as a divine institution can be learned from the Word of God alone. "Marriage thus considered and determined is the joint status of one marriageable man and one marriageable woman (Matt. 19: 4-6), superinduced and sustained by their mutual consent (Gen. 22: 58; 1 Cor. 7: 12. 13; Deut. 22: 23. 24; Matt. 1: 1-20),

to be and to remain to each other husband and wife in a lifelong union (Rom. 7: 2. 3; 1 Cor. 7: 39) for legitimate sexual
intercourse (1 Cor. 7: 2-5), the procreation of children (Gen.
1: 28), and cohabitation for mutual care and assistance" (Dr.
A. L. Graebner in *Theological Quarterly,* Vol. III, p. 406).
Marriage, therefore, is not an external companionship, which
might be dissolved at will, but it is that lifelong and intimate
union in which persons so united may mutually gratify the
divinely implanted love and desire of one sex for the other
(1 Cor. 7: 2-5), for the purpose of avoiding fornication and of
propagating the race (Gen. 1: 28). (Apol., Art. XXIII, 7-13,
Triglot, pp. 365. 367).—What is lawful and pure within wedlock, is a sin and a shame outside of wedlock (Hebr. 13: 4).

7. **Betrothal.**—The status of matrimony before God does
not begin with the public wedding ceremony, and is not effected by the official pronouncement that the two are now
husband and wife. It is not the minister, priest, or judge that
actually unites a man and a woman in marriage; but before
the public wedding the parties themselves unite and bind
themselves in wedlock by their free and mutual consent and
agreement to be husband and wife; it is by their own consent and agreement that God joins them together (Matt. 19:
6). Since the very essence of marriage lies in this mutual
consent, it follows that before God the status of matrimony
exists as soon as the parties agree to be husband and wife; in
other words, marriage begins with the betrothal, or engagement. "Consensus, non concubitus, facit matrimonium," i.e.,
consent, not cohabitation, makes matrimony. Before God betrothal is tantamount to marriage, as we learn from Deut. 22:
23. 24 and from Matt. 1: 18-20, where God Himself calls a
virgin that is espoused to a man his wife, and he is called her
husband. Therefore we maintain that matrimony is entered
into by "a rightful betrothal, or engagement."—But not every
so-called engagement is a rightful betrothal. Clandestine engagements, engagements made in fun, or when people are in-
toxicated, or made for a limited time only, or where for some
reason or other the consent of either party is wanting, or was
secured by duress or fraud, or where there is an error of
person, or where the consent is given conditionally, or where
there is merely a promise to marry at some future time—all

such engagements are not properly betrothals, and marriage does not exist under these conditions. "Betrothal is not a promise of future marriage, and a promise of future marriage is not properly a betrothal" (A. L. Graebner in *Theological Quarterly,* Vol. IV, p. 459). However, when competent parties by contemporaneous and free consent agree *de praesenti,* from now on, to be husband and wife, the status of marriage exists. A valid engagement, therefore, should be public, and consists in this, that the parties concerned freely and willingly agree that from now on they are to be and remain husband and wife, even though the wedding ceremony and their "coming together" is postponed for some time.—If the respective parents are living, their consent should be obtained. Bethuel, the father, and Rebekah, the daughter, consented to the marriage proposed by Abraham and Isaac through their servant (Gen. 24). As parents may not force on their children a marriage against their will, so children should not marry any one against the will of their parents. Both the Old and the New Testament establish the right of parents to give their children in marriage (Deut. 7: 3; Neh. 13: 25; 1 Cor. 7: 38). Even the State recognizes this fundamental right by requiring the consent of parents in the case of minors. In so important a step as matrimony children should seek the counsel and consent of their parents, whose blessing or curse are equally potent, as the father's blessing can build homes for his children, but the curse of the mother can tear them down. However, it is a misuse of parental authority to forbid absolutely marriage to their children, or to prevent marriage from selfish reasons.

8. **The mutual relation between husband and wife is clearly set forth in Scripture.**—There is no difference in their relation to God; in Christ there is neither male nor female (Gal. 3: 28); husband and wife are both heirs of eternal life (1 Pet. 3: 7).—In their relation to each other there is indeed a difference. The woman was created for the man (1 Cor. 11: 9), to be an helpmeet for him (Gen. 2: 18), and he was to rule over her (Gen. 3: 16). Therefore the husband is the head of the wife (Eph. 5: 23). But husbands should not be hard and bitter against their wives (Col. 3: 19), but dwell with them according to knowledge, giving honor unto them as unto the weaker vessels (1 Pet. 3: 7), and should love them

as Christ loved the Church, and they love their own bodies (Eph. 5: 25. 28. 29). The wife should reverence her own husband (Eph. 5: 33; 1 Pet. 3: 5. 6), and submit to him (Eph. 5: 22. 23). Such submission should not be one of fear and dread (1 Pet. 3: 6), but one of confidence and love. "Each should love and honor his spouse" (Luther in the *Explanation of the Sixth Commandment*).

9. **Matrimony is a lifelong union.**—While voluntarily contracted, matrimony may not be voluntarily dissolved. "What God hath joined together, let no man put asunder" (Matt. 19: 6). The fact that courts according to the civil law grant divorces does not prove that such separations are sanctioned by God. God dissolves the bond of wedlock by the death of either husband or wife (Rom. 7: 1. 2). Marriage is not continued in heaven (Matt. 22: 30), as the Mormons teach. Every dissolution of marriage brought about by man involves a sin on the part of him who is the cause of such separation.

10. **Divorce.**—The mutual consent to be husband and wife, which is the essence of matrimony, includes the promise that each will "forsake all others, and keep himself only to his spouse so long as they both shall live." Conjugal unfaithfulness is indeed a gross violation of this promise, but, in itself, does not sever the marital bond. However, it does give to the injured party the right, not the obligation, to dissolve the marriage union by obtaining a divorce. "Whosoever shall put away his wife, saving for the cause of fornication, causeth her to commit adultery" (Matt. 5: 32); if any other reason, excepting reasons on Scriptural grounds, is the cause of divorce, adultery is committed, both by the complainant, in severing the marriage-tie, and by the accused that permits the dissolution on frivolous un-Scriptural grounds. "Whosoever shall put away his wife, except it be for fornication, and shall marry another, committeth adultery: and whoso marrieth her which is put away doth commit adultery" (Matt. 19: 9); he that for any reason puts away, rejects, his wife, except that of marital unfaithfulness, in which case the marriage-tie has already been torn asunder, is an adulterer before God, and, in the same way, he that marries a divorcee, one that has left her husband without Scriptural grounds, is guilty of adultery. From these two passages it follows that, whenever either husband or wife

is guilty of fornication, the innocent party has God's permission to divorce the guilty one, though he is not required to do so.

In malicious desertion the case is different. Here the "unbelieving departs" (1 Cor. 7: 15), positively refusing to return and to live with his or her spouse, thus actually disrupting the marital bond. "A brother or sister is not under bondage in such cases" (1 Cor. 7: 15), i.e., he or she is free from the law which binds husband and wife together for life. (Cf., Rom. 7: 2. 3). The innocent party may obtain a divorce in court, and is free to marry another.

With respect to divorces for other reasons than those stated above, we must bear in mind the words of Christ (Matt. 5: 32; Matt. 19: 9).

11. **Marriage of divorced persons and adulterers.**—The innocent person in a divorce case is free to marry again (Matt. 19: 9). The guilty party may not marry as long as the innocent party remains unmarried and there is reason to believe that a reconciliation can be effected; for it is in the very nature of the case that a guilty husband, for instance, if he is penitent, ought to prefer to return to his original wife rather than marry another. However, after the innocent party has procured a divorce, not being willing again to live with the guilty party, or after the marriage or the death of the innocent party, the guilty party may again marry with the blessings of God, provided, of course, that such a person is truly penitent. (Cf., Fritz, *Pastoral Theology*, p. 173).

PART XI. OF THE LAST THINGS

XLVIII. TEMPORAL DEATH

1. **Definition.**—Temporal death is not a total destruction or an annihilation of man, but the privation of physical life caused by the separation of the soul from the body. "This night thy soul shall be required of thee" (Luke 12: 20). Christ died when He "yielded up the ghost" (Matt. 27: 50). "Then shall the dust return to the earth as it was; and the spirit shall return unto God, who gave it" (Eccl. 12: 7).

2. **Cause.**—As God did not create man to die, man is not subject to death according to the order of creation. Thus it is that men experience a natural horror of death. Death was a part of God's threat as a punishment of sin (Gen. 2: 17; 3: 19). Death entered into the world by sin (Rom. 5: 12). "The wages of sin is death" (Rom. 6: 23). "Sin, when it is finished, bringeth forth death" (James 1: 15).

God imposes the death penalty; men live and die by the will of God (Deut. 31: 14; 2 Kings 20: 1. 6). "Thou turnest man to destruction" (Ps. 90: 3). "The number of his months are with Thee" (Job 14: 5). God terminates the lives of men in various ways, by various means (sickness, old age, accident, war, etc., Luke 13: 1-5), and at different ages (children were killed in Bethlehem, Matt. 2: 16; Simeon died at a ripe old age, Luke 2: 25-29). But whatever may be the physical cause of death, all men die of their sins (Ps. 90: 7-9).

3. **A universal fact.**—No sane person denies the fact of death. It is a tragic situation. Man who has the will to live, and does all he can to avoid death, must finally die; no charm, no medicine, no science, no will power can stay the fatal blow. "It is appointed unto men once to die" (Hebr. 9: 27). Man, who was created to live, is now born to die; his way through life leads but to the grave. "To every thing there is a season, and a time to every purpose under the heaven: a time to be born, and a time to die" (Eccl. 3: 1. 2). While man knows that he must die, he does not know when he will die; "for man knoweth not his time" (Eccl. 9: 12). Death is as certain

and as universal as sin is. "So death passed upon all men, for that all have sinned" (Rom. 5: 12).

Christians in their lives bear the external consequences of sin, even as other men, and, therefore, they also suffer physical death (Gen. 25: 8). But there is a vast difference between the death of a Christian and the death of an unbeliever. For the Christian death has lost its sting (1 Cor. 15: 55-57), because he has forgiveness of all his sins. To him death is not a punishment, but a deliverance (2 Tim. 4: 18), a change for the better (Phil. 1: 23). Therefore by faith the Christian overcomes the natural fear of death (Hebr. 2: 14. 15), and departs in peace (Luke 2: 29).

Those living at the coming of Christ unto judgment will not die, and therefore need not be raised from the dead. "We shall not all sleep, but we shall all be changed" (1 Cor. 15: 51); (1 Thess. 4: 16. 17). There are a few exceptional cases where men did not die a temporal death: Enoch (Gen. 5: 24); Elijah (2 Kings 2: 11).

4. **Temporal death is not the end of man.**—While lacking positive evidence, natural man senses that temporal death does not destroy his conscious existence and personal identity. Hence almost every heathen religion speaks of a life beyond the grave.

Reliable information on this point we have in the Bible. We learn that temporal death is not the end of man. Speaking of the God of Abraham, of Isaac, and of Jacob, Jesus tells the Sadducees: "For He is not a God of the dead, but of the living: for all live unto Him" (Luke 20: 38). When Abraham, Isaac, and Jacob died (Gen. 25: 8; 35: 29; 49: 33), they did not simply pass out of existence, but they continue to live as persons, as Abraham, Isaac, and Jacob. Also the stories of the rich man and Lazarus (Luke 16: 19-31) and of the Final Judgment (Matt. 25: 31-46) show that temporal death is not the end of man. As men rise from their sleep, so shall they rise from death; for this reason death is sometimes called a sleep (Dan. 12: 2; John 11: 11. 14).

XLIX. THE STATE OF DEATH

1. **Continued existence.**—The material body decays and returns to the ground, dust to dust (Gen. 3: 19; Eccl. 3: 20).

In this state it continues until the resurrection on the Last Day (Job 19: 25-27; John 11: 24). A metamorphism naturally takes place with regard to all material things; we may say that a chemical composition and decomposition takes place constantly; this applies also to the material of our bodies. The disembodied soul, an immaterial, spiritual essence, does not dissolve and vanish into the air, nor is it absorbed into the essence of God, becoming a part of Him; but being a created spirit, endowed with immortality by God, it continues to exist as a distinct personal entity. To the malefactor Jesus said: "*Thou* shalt be with Me in paradise" (Luke 23: 43). The story of the rich man and Lazarus shows that personal identity is not destroyed (Luke 16: 22. 23). *Paul* desires to be with Christ (Phil. 1: 23). This separate existence of the soul continues until it is reunited with its body on the Last Day (1 Kings 17: 22; John 5: 28. 29; 11: 24).

2. **Where are the souls?** — In the moment of death the souls of the believers enter the joy of heaven. Jesus said to the malefactor: "Today shalt thou be with Me in paradise" (Luke 23: 43). Stephen said in the hour of death: "Lord Jesus, receive my spirit" (Acts 7: 59). Whoever dies in the Lord is blessed "from henceforth" (Rev. 14: 13). Paul desires "to be with Christ," and adds that this is "far better" for him than to continue in the flesh (Phil. 1: 23. 24). For this reason we pray that finally, when our last hour has come, God would grant us a blessed end, and graciously take us from this vale of tears to Himself in heaven.—The spirits of the unbelievers are "in prison" (1 Pet. 3: 19. 20). Judas went to "his place" (Acts 1: 25). The story of the rich man and Lazarus, though a parable, teaches definitely that the condition of the wicked after death is one of torment (Luke 16: 23).—The departed souls remain in heaven or in hell until the Day of Judgment, when they shall be reunited with their own bodies. The believers shall in their flesh see God (Job 19: 26), and the unbelievers shall in body and soul be consigned to eternal torment (Matt. 10: 28).

3. **The souls of the departed do not return to earth** to communicate with the living. (Cf., *Concordia Cyclopedia*, Spiritism, p. 724 f.) The dead are ignorant of us (Is. 63: 16), and will not be sent even on a mission of mercy to warn a

sinner (Luke 16: 27-29). Nor is there a transmigration of souls, as taught by some heathen (Brahmanism), who believe that at death the soul passes into another body (that of a human being, an animal, or a plant) for the purpose of purification, until it finally returns to God. According to the Bible the departed souls stay where they are, either in "paradise" or in "prison." (Cf., *Concordia Cyclopedia*, Transmigration of Souls, p. 767).

There is no purgatory, in which the full and final salvation of the soul is accomplished by its own suffering and by masses, prayers, and alms offered in its behalf by the living. The Catholic Church teaches: "The guilt is remitted to every penitent sinner, but there remains a debt of temporal punishment to be discharged in this world or in the next in purgatory, before the entrance to the kingdom of heaven is opened to him" (Canon and Decrees of the Council of Trent, Sess. VI, Canon XXX). This teaching cannot be established from 2 Macc. 12: 39-45, which, besides being an apocryphal book, does not speak of a purgatory at all. Nor can it be established by the authority of the Church, since the Word of God alone is the source of all doctrine. Also 1 Cor. 3: 15 and 1 Pet. 1: 7 do not prove that there is a purgatory after death; the fire here spoken of refers to the tribulations we endure in this life for the trial and purification of our faith. Incidentally, this doctrine of purgatory denies the sufficiency of the merits of Christ, and of the free and full remission of sins through faith in Christ. (Cf., *Popular Symbolics*, §250).

There are but two places, in either of which the departed soul enters. "Enter ye in at the strait gate: for wide is the gate, and broad is the way that leadeth to destruction, and many there be that go in thereat: because strait is the gate, and narrow is the way, which leadeth unto life, and few there be that find it" (Matt. 7: 13. 14).

4. **The eternal destiny of man is decided the moment he dies.**—He that believes shall be saved, and he that believes not shall be damned (Mark 16: 16). After death there is no opportunity for improving one's condition, no second probation, no further offer of grace and forgiveness. "When the wicked man dieth, his expectation shall perish: and the hope of unjust men perisheth" (Prov. 11: 7). "Now is the day of

salvation" (2 Cor. 6: 2). "It is appointed unto men once to die, but after this the judgment" (Hebr. 9: 27). The question whether a man will go to heaven or to hell will not be decided on the Day of Judgment, but when a man dies. "He that believeth on the Son hath everlasting life; and he that believeth not the Son shall not see life; but the wrath of God abideth on him" (John 3: 36). The Last Judgment is the grand finale of this present world, in which the sentence pronounced in death over the individual will be publicly confirmed and extended to the body, which till then has returned to the dust, from whence it came. He who continues in the faith unto the end has nothing to fear for his soul after death, nor for his body and soul on the Day of Judgment (Rev. 2: 10; 14: 13).

L. THE SECOND COMING OF CHRIST

1. **The fact of His coming.**—The fact of Christ's return is clearly taught in Scripture. "This same Jesus, which is taken up from you into heaven, shall so come in like manner as ye have seen Him go into heaven" (Acts 1: 11). Having come the first time "to bear the sins of many," He shall "appear the second time without sin unto salvation" (Hebr. 9: 28); (Matt. 24: 30; 1 Thess. 4: 16). The fact of Christ's return must be firmly maintained against the scoffers who say: "Where is the promise of His coming?" (2 Pet. 3: 2-4). Also we Christians must be reminded of it again and again, lest, because of the delay, we sleep (Mark 13: 36. 37), or allow ourselves to be engrossed with the things of this world (Luke 21: 34-36). We should live in constant expectation of the coming of our Lord. "What I say unto you I say unto all, Watch," says Jesus (Mark 13: 37).

2. **The manner of His coming.**—Christ now comes to us invisibly, spiritually, through His Word and Sacraments (John 14: 23); but when He comes at the end of time, His coming will be visible. "And then shall all the tribes of the earth mourn, and they shall see the Son of Man coming in the clouds of heaven with power and great glory" (Matt. 24: 30); (Acts 1: 11). Christ will not appear successively to one people after the other, but as the lightning flashes over the sky, so shall the coming of the Son of Man be (Luke 17: 24), and as a snare

it shall come on all them that dwell on the face of the whole earth (Luke 21: 35). It is not for us to ask how this is possible; Christ tells us that all the tribes on earth shall see Him.

Christ will come in power and great glory (Matt. 24: 30). He will not come in humility and lowliness, as in the days of His flesh, when it was possible for some not to recognize Him as the Son of God (1 Cor. 2: 8). Christ will appear in heavenly splendor and majesty, so that all men shall know at once who He is.

"And all His holy angels with Him" (Matt. 25: 31). The business of these angels is not merely to accompany the Lord and to announce His coming (1 Thess. 4: 16), but also to gather the resurrected dead and the living before the judgment seat of Christ (Matt. 24: 31), to separate the wicked from the just (Matt. 13: 49; 25: 32. 33), and to cast the damned into hell (Matt. 13: 42).

3. **The time of His coming.**—Christ will come at the end of the world (Matt. 24: 29. 30). It will be the "last day" (John 6: 40) of this present order of things, after which there will be a "new heaven and a new earth" (2 Pet. 3: 10-13). The day of Christ's return has even now been appointed (Acts 17: 31), but the date is not revealed. "Of that day and hour knoweth no man" (Mark 13: 32). As we know the certainty, but not the date of our death, so we know that Christ will certainly return, but we do not know when He will come. The reason for withholding this knowledge from us is that we should be ready at all times (Matt. 24: 42-51).

4. **Signs of Christ's coming.**—The day will come soon, because the signs which are to indicate its near approach (Matt. 24; Luke 21; 2 Thess. 2) have been fulfilled and are being fulfilled. Signs in nature: earthquake, floods, storms, eclipses of sun and moon. Signs in the life of men and nations: wars and rumors of war, pestilence, famine, unrighteousness in business and politics, perilous times (2 Tim. 3: 1-4). Signs in the visible Church: false teachers, hypocrisy, love waxing cold, falling away from the truth and from the faith, the appearance of antichrist. Some of the things mentioned as signs of Christ's coming had happened before, and may even now be explained from natural causes. This, however, does not mean that they are not to be regarded as signs; Christ made

them signs of His coming, and as we observe them, we are to be reminded that the end is at hand. Illustration: A bodily ailment may have a natural cause, and yet it is a precursor of death; in like manner these things are precursors of the final dissolution of this present world.

The beginning of the end, or things that lead unto and develop into the end were noticeable even in the days of the apostles. The destruction of Jerusalem was, as it were, the prelude to the Final Judgment, a sign, and, at the same time, the beginning of the end. In Matt. 24: 2-51 the destruction of Jerusalem and the end of the world are pictured side by side, and are interwoven with each other. For this reason Peter already in his day could say: "The end of all things is at hand" (1 Pet. 4: 7). Today these signs are more evident and pronounced. The next thing we may look for is the end itself.

The purpose of these signs is to prepare us. "So likewise ye, when ye shall see all these things, know that it is near, even at the door" (Matt. 24: 33); (Luke 21: 28). Nevertheless, the day will come suddenly, as a snare (Luke 21: 35), and unexpectedly, as a thief (2 Pet. 3: 10; 1 Thess. 5: 2-6). "Watch ye therefore and pray always that ye may be accounted worthy to escape all these things that shall come to pass, and to stand before the Son of Man" (Luke 21: 36).

LI. THE MILLENNIUM

1. Although there is no such thing as a Millennium, it is necessary to discuss it, because there are many who look forward to it. In the Augsburg Confession the Lutheran Church says: "They condemn also others, who are now spreading certain Jewish opinions, that before the resurrection of the dead the godly shall take possession of the kingdom of the world, the ungodly being everywhere suppressed" (Art. XVII, 5). In these words the Lutheran Church rejects Chiliasm, which teaches that prior to the coming of Christ to judgment, He will establish a Millennium on earth. Chiliasts, however, do not agree among themselves as to the general character and numerous details of this millennial kingdom. Generally speaking, they may be divided into Premillenarians and Postmillenarians. (Cf., *Concordia Cyclopedia,* Millennium, p. 471-474).

2. **Premillenarians** teach that Christ will come visibly to this earth before, or at the beginning of, the Millennium. At that time the saints will arise (first resurrection), and reign with Christ on earth one thousand years. During this time Satan will be bound, iniquity will be repressed, and righteousness and peace will prevail on earth. All Israel and many others will turn to the Lord. After the thousand years are over, Satan will be loosed for a little season and wage a bitter war against the camp of the saints. But soon the Lord will appear to judge the world. At this time the other dead will be raised (second resurrection), and Satan, his angels, and all the wicked will be cast into the lake of fire and brimstone. The earth will be renewed and become the home of the redeemed.

3. **Postmillenarians** hold that there will be indeed a Millennium, but that Christ will return visibly, not before, but after the Millennium. They believe that for a thousand years or for an indefinitely long period of time the Church will be in a flourishing and dominating position. Through Christian agencies the Gospel will gradually permeate the entire world, becoming more effective than at present in social, commercial, political, and international life. All Israel will be converted, and large numbers will join the Church. After this period of universal Gospel acceptance there will be a falling away from the faith, and the forces of evil will attempt to destroy the beloved city. But they shall not succeed, for suddenly the Lord will come to judge the quick and the dead.

4. **The Bible does not teach Chiliasm.** — The Old Testament texts quoted in support of the Millennium are misunderstood and misapplied. They speak neither of a visible earthly kingdom of Christ nor of an external growth and flourishing condition of the Church, but in figurative language describe the spiritual nature and condition of the New Testament Church. What we read in Is. 2: 2. 3 was and is continually being fulfilled when people come to Christ, as we learn from Hebr. 12: 22. The peace of which Isaiah speaks (Is. 2: 4; 9: 4. 5; 11: 6-9), came to the world when the Christ-child was born (Is. 9: 6; Luke 2: 14), and is still proclaimed in the Gospel of peace (Eph. 6: 15), and given to all that believe in Jesus (John 16: 33). The reference in Joel 3: 1 ff. was ful-

filled Acts 2: 16, and Amos 9: 11. 12 is being fulfilled by the
entry of the Gentiles into the Church (Acts 15: 13 ff.).

However, Rev. 20 is generally regarded to be the chief
proof for the Millennium. But also this chapter is full of figurative language, as the first verse plainly shows. There is
not the slightest indication that the martyrs and saints will
rule with Christ on *earth* one thousand years (v. 4), for their
souls reign with Christ, and these souls are in heaven. And
such reign in heaven is promised to the Christian (2 Tim. 2:
12; Rev. 22: 5). The "thousand years" stand for a long period
in contrast to "a little season" (v. 3). The binding of Satan
(v. 2) denotes the period of the New Testament dispensation.
By His death Christ virtually delivered all men from the
power of the devil (Hebr. 2: 14. 15). This deliverance is proclaimed in the Gospel (Acts 26: 18), and it becomes actual
for the individual the moment he believes (Col. 1: 13. 14).
The first resurrection is the spiritual resurrection, when a
person comes to faith (Eph. 2: 5. 6). Christ Himself distinguishes this resurrection (John 5: 25) from the bodily resurrection (John 5: 28. 29). The "little season" during which
Satan will be loosed (Rev. 20: 3. 7-9), refers to the perilous
times which immediately precede the coming of Christ to
judgment (2 Tim. 3: 1-5; Matt. 24). The battle of Satan, Gog
and Magog, against the beloved city (Rev. 20: 8. 9) is not a
physical battle with all the murderous implements of modern
warfare, but it is of a spiritual nature, and consists in this that
Satan will marshal all his forces without and within the visible
Church to attack and to corrupt the doctrines of the Gospel,
and thus destroy in the hearts of men that faith, by which
alone they are and remain citizens in Christ's kingdom of
grace and heirs of salvation. What we read in Rev. 20: 8 is
the same as what we read in Matt. 24: 5. 24.

It is true that "all Israel shall be saved" (Rom. 11: 26). But
the term "all Israel" is used in this verse in the same sense
as the term "fulness of the Gentiles" is used in the preceding
verse. As little as every Gentile will be saved, so little will
every one who is an Israelite according to the flesh be saved.
But the full number of the elect out of Israel will be saved,
even as the full number of the elect out of the Gentiles will
be saved. As all the Gentiles that will be saved constitute the

"fulness of the Gentiles," so all the Israelites that will be saved constitute the "all Israel" of God. While and as long as God gathers His elect from among the Gentiles, He will also gather His elect from among the Jews. In Rom. 9: 6-12 Paul plainly teaches that not all who are Israelites according to the flesh are also the Israel God recognizes as His Israel; but only they are Abraham's children, who are of the faith of Abraham (Gal. 3: 7). These alone constitute the "all Israel" that will be saved.

5. Premillenarians teach a threefold visible coming of Christ. The Bible knows only of two (Hebr. 9: 28). They teach a first and a second bodily resurrection; Christ tells us that He will raise the believers on the Last Day (John 6: 40), and that the good and evil will be raised simultaneously (John 5: 28. 29). They divert the hope and expectation of Christians toward an earthly kingdom during the Millennium; the Bible teaches us to look forward to the kingdom of heaven (Acts 14: 22; Matt. 5: 12; Phil. 3: 20. 21). Texts like Matt. 24; 2 Thess. 2; 2 Tim. 3: 1-5 disprove the teaching of Postmillenarians. Chiliasm in all its forms has no foundation in Scripture, and is fraught with grave dangers for Christians.

LII. THE RESURRECTION

1. **The possibility of a resurrection.**—While human reason cannot prove that there will be no resurrection, it cannot comprehend the possibility of a resurrection. Hence, some doubt it (1 Cor. 15: 12. 35), and others ridicule it (Acts 17: 32). Experience and observation do not support it, and we cannot understand how a body that has returned to the dust, or has been devoured by wild beasts could possibly be revived and regain its former shape. But all these doubts and objections as to the possibility of the resurrection of the body may be answered with the words of Christ: "Ye do err . . . not knowing the power of God" (Matt. 22: 29). He who believes that there is an omnipotent God will have no trouble in believing that He is able to quicken the dead.

2. **The fact of the resurrection** of the body must be established from Scripture. Since it is God who raises the dead, only He can tell us whether He will do so. The Bible is very definite on this point.

Faith in the forgiveness of sins implies faith in the resurrection. Death is the wages of sin (Rom. 6: 23). Christ delivered us from sin, hence, also from death (Hebr. 2: 14. 15). Therefore faith in Christ carries with it the hope of resurrection (John 11: 25. 26).

The resurrection of our Lord proves that there is such a thing as a resurrection of the body. "For if the dead rise not, then is not Christ raised" (1 Cor. 15: 16). "But now is Christ risen from the dead, and become the firstfruits of them that slept" (1 Cor. 15: 20). "Now if Christ be preached that He arose from the dead, how say some among you that there is no resurrection of the dead?" (1 Cor. 15: 12).

Christ proves from the Old Testament that there is a resurrection of the dead (Matt. 22: 31. 32). Job confesses his faith in the resurrection (Job 19: 25-27). In Dan. 12: 2 we read: "Many of them that sleep in the dust of the earth shall awake, some to everlasting life, and some to shame and everlasting contempt." In the New Testament we read: "The hour is coming in which *all* that are in the graves shall hear His voice, and shall come forth; they that have done good, unto the resurrection of life; and they that have done evil, unto the resurrection of damnation" (John 5: 28. 29); (John 6: 40; 1 Thess. 4: 16; 1 Cor. 15). On the basis of Scripture, therefore, every Christian confesses: "I believe the resurrection of the dead."

3. **The time.**—Contrary to Premillenarians, who hold that the resurrection of the saints will take place at the beginning of the Millennium and the resurrection of all others at the coming of Christ unto judgment, the Bible teaches one general resurrection of all dead at the end of time. Speaking of believers, Christ says that He will raise them up at the Last Day (John 6: 40). He also informs us that the good and the evil will be raised at the same time (John 5: 28. 29). From 1 Cor. 15: 23. 24 and from 1 Thess. 4: 16 we learn that this resurrection will take place when Christ comes to judge the quick and the dead.

4. **The efficient cause.**—The resurrection is not a natural development, as when a plant grows from a dying seed. Nor is it effected by a voluntary act of the soul, which by its own impulse returns to its body. The resurrection of the dead is

an act of God's omnipotence. It is God, who raiseth the dead
(2 Cor. 1: 9; Rom. 4: 17). "As the Father raiseth up the dead
and quickeneth them, even so the Son quickeneth whom He
will" (John 5: 21). The same Jesus, who raised the youth
of Nain (Luke 7: 14) and the daughter of Jairus (Matt. 9:
25) and Lazarus (John 11: 43), will at the Last Day call all
the dead from their graves (John 5: 28. 29).

5. **Who will be raised?**—Not only those who believed in
Christ and looked forward to their resurrection, but also those
who did not believe and did not want to arise will come out
of their graves. "There shall be a resurrection of the dead,
both of the just and unjust" (Acts 24: 15). Christ's call to
repent and to believe is rejected by many (Matt. 23: 37); but
His call to arise on the Day of Judgment will be obeyed by
all. "All that are in the graves shall hear His voice, and shall
come forth" (John 5: 28. 29); (Rev. 20: 12. 13).

Men living on earth, when Christ will call the dead from
their graves, will not experience a reuniting of soul and body,
since no death has preceded. The change, however, which
takes place in the bodies of those who are raised from death
will take place in theirs also, but in a different manner; it will
be by transformation. "We shall not all sleep, but we shall
all be changed, in a moment, in the twinkling of an eye, at·
the last trump" (1 Cor. 15: 51. 52).

6. **Identity of persons in body and soul.** — When Elijah
raised the widow's son, "the soul of the child came back to
him, and he revived" (1 Kings 17: 22). When Christ raised
Lazarus, the soul of Lazarus came back to the body of Lazarus. Thus it will be in the resurrection of the dead. The
same body which died and decayed will be restored from the
dust and scattered particles, and the same soul which departed
from the body in death will again make this body its dwelling place. Each body will have its former soul, and each soul
will dwell in its own body. The identity of person will, therefore, be fully preserved in the resurrection. Job says: "In my
flesh shall I see God . . . and mine eyes shall behold, and not
another" (Job 19: 26. 27). Moses and Elias on the mount of
transfiguration were the same persons as the Moses and Elias
we read of in the Old Testament (Matt. 17: 2-4). The resurrected Savior was the identical person that died on the cross

(Luke 24: 39). The identity of persons is also taught in the story of the rich man and Lazarus (Luke 16: 19-31).

7. **Condition of the body.**—While the resurrected body will be the same in substance, it will be endowed with new attributes and qualities, adapted to the nature and the circumstances then existing. Because it is henceforth inseparably united with the immortal soul, the body will likewise be immortal and incorruptible. Nor will it be subject to those physical laws and conditions by which it was controlled in this earthly life; for the former things have passed away. In this sense, we might say, the bodies are "spiritual."

Yet, there is a great difference. The wicked are not annihilated, but God destroys them, both body and soul, in hell (Matt. 10: 28), where their worm shall not die, neither shall their fire be quenched (Mark 9: 43. 44). Susceptible to torment and suffering (Luke 16: 24), they shall be objects of contempt (Dan. 12: 2) and an abhorring to all flesh (Is. 66: 24).

"The righteous shall shine forth as the sun in the kingdom of their Father" (Matt. 13: 43). The believers in Christ shall be "raised in glory" (1 Cor. 15: 43); their vile body shall be fashioned like unto the glorious body of Christ (Phil. 3: 21). They shall be raised "in power"; they will be strong and vigorous, free from the weaknesses, infirmities, defects, and the devastating consequences of sin. They will be raised as "spiritual bodies"; this does not mean that they will be spirits or angels, but they will be like or as the angels of God (Matt. 22: 30). For their sustenance they are not dependent on seedtime and harvest, food and drink; they will not be subject to pain and sorrow (Rev. 21: 4).

LIII. THE JUDGMENT

The idea of some future judgment and retribution is not peculiar to the Christian religion; in some form we find it also in many pagan religions. The reason for this is the natural knowledge of the Law and the conscience of man, which not only hold him responsible for what he has done, but also hold him worthy of death for his evil deeds (Rom. 2: 15; 1: 32). Reliable information concerning the judgment we can get only from the Word of God.

1. When and where will the judgment be?—On the Last Day Christ will appear in all His glory (Matt. 25: 31), will raise the dead (John 5: 28. 29), and will judge the world in righteousness (Acts 17: 31; 2 Tim. 4: 1). The place of judgment is not a definite spot or locality on earth, but it will be above the earth. For the Son of Man shall come in the clouds of heaven, and send forth His angels to gather the elect (Matt. 24: 30. 31) and all the nations before Him (Matt. 25: 31. 32). Then the quick and the resurrected dead shall be caught up in the clouds and meet the Lord in the air (1 Thess. 4: 16. 17).

2. The Judge. — Concerning Jesus Christ the Christian Church confesses in the Second Article of the Apostles' Creed that "He will come to judge the quick and the dead." This is exactly what the Bible teaches. "He" (Jesus) "was ordained of God to be the Judge of quick and dead" (Acts 10: 42). Jesus informs us that the Father had given Him authority to execute judgment also, because He is the Son of Man (John 5: 27). The same Jesus, then, who stood before Caiaphas and Pontius Pilate and was judged and condemned by both, will at the Last Day pass judgment on all people, on the quick and the dead, also on Caiaphas and Pontius Pilate.

3. Who will be judged?—Whether a person will or will not submit to this judgment is not a matter of personal choice. *All* men *must* appear before the judgment seat of Christ (2 Cor. 5: 10; Rom. 14: 10. 11). All nations (Matt. 25: 32), the world (Acts 17: 31), the quick and the dead (2 Tim. 4: 1) will be judged. No one will be overlooked; no one can escape. Also the fallen angels will receive their final sentence (2 Pet. 2: 4; Matt. 8: 29).

4. By what will men be judged? — (a) A human judge finds sentence according to the laws of the State. If Christ were to judge men according to the Law of the Commandments, no one would be saved. "If Thou, Lord, shouldest mark iniquities, O Lord, who shall stand?" (Ps. 130: 3). "Enter not into judgment with Thy servant, for in Thy sight shall no man living be justified" (Ps. 143: 2). Scripture texts like Matt. 12: 36; Rom. 14: 12; 2 Cor. 5: 10 are statements of the Law, and are to impress upon us that, if judged according to the Law, we should all be lost. He who understands his sins, will not appeal for judgment to the Law and the justice of God.

And Christ will not judge according to the Law, for that would render the work of His redemption and the work of the Holy Ghost purposeless.

(b) Christ says: "The word, which I have spoken, the same shall judge him in the last day" (John 12: 48). From the preceding verse we must infer that this Word is the Gospel, which men receive in faith or reject in unbelief. And Paul writes: "In the day when God shall judge the secrets of men by Jesus Christ according to my Gospel" (Rom. 2: 16). (Cf., Stoeckhardt, *Roemerbrief*, p. 90-101). But how can God judge men according to the promise of grace, which He Himself has made to them in the Gospel? He judges the individual according to his personal attitude toward this Gospel, whether he accepted it in faith or rejected it in unbelief. For this reason Christ says: "He that believeth . . . shall be saved, and he that believeth not shall be damned" (Mark 16: 16). In John 3: 18 we read: "He that believeth on Him is not condemned; but he that believeth not is condemned already, because he hath not believed in the name of the only begotten Son of God." (Cf., John 5: 24; 2 Thess. 1: 7-10). This appears also from the story of the judgment (Matt. 25: 32), at the beginning of which the nations are divided into sheep and goats, believers and unbelievers (John 10: 26. 27). The eternal destiny of a person depends upon this one thing alone, whether or not he had faith in the Gospel of Christ.

(c) For the believers the sentence of condemnation, which under the Law they had deserved by their sins, is suspended and changed into a sentence of pardon and justification, because by faith they have appropriated to themselves the saving merits of Christ. Their sins are not investigated and published; they are not even mentioned. The Judge does not look at the rags of their sins, but sees only the perfect garment of righteousness, which He offered them in the Gospel, and which they put on by faith. As long as a person knows himself to be in faith, he also knows where he will stand in the Final Judgment, for Christ says: "Verily, verily, I say unto you, he that heareth My word, and believeth on Him that sent Me, hath everlasting life, and shall not come into condemnation; but is passed from death unto life" (John 5: 24).—"Jesus' blood and righteousness my jewels are, my glorious dress, wherein before my God I stand, when I shall reach the heavenly land."

Good works, indeed, are mentioned (Matt. 25: 35-40), and the counsel of the heart will be made manifest (1 Cor. 4: 5); but these are not the reason for the sentence which is pronounced (Matt. 25: 34); they are rather the public evidence of that faith whereby they became the sheep of Christ. Good works are the visible fruit of an invisible faith (John 15: 5; Gal. 5: 6).

(d) With respect to those on the left of the Judge it should be noted, that also in their case the individual sins are not investigated and published; but the Judge calls attention to their lack of good works (Matt. 25: 41-45), which proves their lack of faith. Where there are no Christian works in the life of a person, there is no Christian faith in the heart (James 2: 20). Having no faith, these people lack the righteousness of Christ, which alone avails in the judgment of God. Also their sins were atoned for and were forgiven (2 Cor. 5: 19); but, rejecting the counsel of God against themselves, they brought upon themselves swift destruction (Luke 7: 30; 2 Pet. 2: 1). Hence, "he that believeth not shall be damned."—Unbelief is a sin, even as faith is a good work; but as faith does not save us because it is a good work, so unbelief does not damn because it is a sin. The saving power lies in the grace of God and in the merits of Christ, which the believer accepts and the unbeliever rejects. Unbelievers are lost because they wear not the protective garment of Christ's righteousness.

With the unbelievers the curse of the Law takes its course. Having rejected the grace of God in Christ Jesus, offered freely in the Gospel, the wrath of God, which they provoked by their sins, abides on them (Eph. 5: 5. 6). Because they did not believe in Christ for the remission of their sins, they must now die in their sins (John 8: 24).

5. **This judgment is not an investigation** to ascertain who is and who is not a believer; for as "Jesus knew from the beginning who they were that believed not" (John 6: 64), so He also knows those who believe. "The Lord knoweth them that are His" (2 Tim. 2: 19). Therefore at the very beginning of the judgment the sheep are separated from the goats. Also we know by the faith we now have where we shall stand

on the Last Day. The question of eternal life and eternal death is not decided in the Final Judgment; that is decided by a sinner's conversion to Christ and by his continuance in the faith unto the end (Luke 23: 43; Rev. 14: 13; John 3: 16). He who dies in the faith will stand on the right of the Judge and will be saved; he who dies in unbelief will stand on the left side and will be lost.

This judgment will pronounce sentence (Matt. 25: 34. 41). While this sentence is definitely fixed in each individual case when a man dies (Prov. 11: 7; Rev. 2: 10), and is carried out immediately as far as it concerns the soul (Luke 23: 43), it is formally and publicly pronounced and solemnly declared, and extended and applied also to the body, on the Day of Judgment.

6. **The sentence carries with it punishment and reward** for the things done in the body (2 Cor. 5: 10; Rom. 2: 6-11). Thus, when a person is damned because of his unbelief, he will also be punished for all the evil he has done in this life (Eph. 5: 5. 6); and when a believer is received into heaven, he will be rewarded for all the good he has done on earth (Matt. 5: 10-12). But while punishment is of merit, the reward is of grace. (Cf., Stoeckhardt, *Roemerbrief*, p. 79).

LIV. THE END OF THE WORLD

1. **The fact.**—The solemn truth concerning the end of the world is denied by scoffers, saying: "Where is the promise of His coming? . . . all things continue as they were from the beginning of the creation" (2 Pet. 3: 4). Various pagan religions show that the idea of an end of this present world is not foreign to the thinking man.—Reliable information regarding the end of the world we get from the Word of God. "Heaven and earth shall pass away" (Luke 21: 33). "The fashion of this world passeth away" (1 Cor. 7: 31). Christ speaks of the signs of His coming and of the end of the world (Matt. 24).

2. **The time.**—The day on which this world will be destroyed is "the day of the Lord" (2 Pet. 3: 10), which is identical with the day of His coming (2 Pet. 3: 4); (Matt. 24: 3). The sequence of events on that day will be as follows: The Lord will descend from heaven visibly; the dead will be raised

and the living will be changed; then all will be caught up to-gether in the clouds and meet the Lord in the air to be judged (1 Thess. 4: 15-17); at the same time the world will be de-stroyed.

3. **Means of destruction.**—"Whereby the world that then was, being overflowed with water, perished: but the heavens and the earth, which are now, by the same word are kept in store, reserved unto fire against the day of judgment and perdition of ungodly men" (2 Pet. 3: 6. 7); (2 Pet. 3: 10-12). The first world perished in water; this world will perish in fire. No man living knows the nature and the power of this fire.

4. **Annihilation or renovation.**— (a) Some hold that, as in the beginning the world was created out of nothing, it will on the Last Day be reduced to nothing; they hold that the entire fabric and substance of heaven and earth and of all created things, intelligent creatures alone excepted, will be annihi-lated, and that a new heaven and a new earth will be created. In support of this, they refer to such texts as: "Heaven and earth shall pass away" (Luke 21: 33); "They shall perish" (Hebr. 1: 11); "The end of the world" (Matt. 24: 3); "Be-hold, I create new heavens and a new earth, and the former shall not be remembered" (Is. 65: 17).

While we do not doubt the possibility of a total annihilation of the very substance of the world, and the creation of a new one, the texts quoted are not absolutely convincing. To "cre-ate" does not only mean to make something out of nothing; for God created man (Gen. 1: 27; 6: 7), and yet man was made out of the dust of the ground. The word "perish" does not prove annihilation of substance; for the first world per-ished in water (2 Pet. 3: 6), but its substance was not annihi-lated, though its "fashion," form, condition, etc., were, no doubt, radically changed. The terms "end of the world" and "pass away" do not necessarily imply that the substance of this world will vanish; they may refer only to the present form and order, the "fashion of this world" (1 Cor. 7: 31). We might question why fire should be necessary to annihilate the world, which subsists only by the word and will of God. We should also have to make a notable exception to this annihilation of substance, namely, the bodies of men, which certainly will not be annihilated.

(b) Others hold that the "fashion" of this present world will certainly be destroyed by fire, but its fundamental substance will not be destroyed; they hold that from the atoms composing this substance a new heaven and a new earth will be fashioned, even as from the dust of our bodies a new resurrection-body will arise. They do not believe in the annihilation of substance, but in the renovation of substance. According to their belief the basic substance, from which heaven and earth were made, remains, but the fashion, the shape, size, condition, etc., will be changed.

Proponents of this view point to the following texts: "The fashion of this world passeth away" (1 Cor. 7: 31); fashion is the scheme, form, order of the world as it appears at present. Again: "The foundations of the earth and the heavens . . . they shall perish; . . . and as a vesture shalt Thou fold them up, and they shall be changed" (Hebr. 1: 10-12). Again: "All these things shall be dissolved . . . and the elements shall melt with fervent heat" (2 Pet. 3: 11. 12). Again: ". . . Because the creature itself also shall be delivered from the bondage of corruption into the glorious liberty of the children of God . . ." (Rom. 8: 18-22). When man sinned, not he alone was cursed (Gen. 2: 17), but a curse was laid upon all nature (Gen. 3: 17; Rom. 8: 20. 22). From the corruption caused by this curse all nature will be delivered (Rom. 8: 21. 23). This is "the regeneration when the Son of Man shall sit on the throne of His glory" (Matt. 19: 28). (Cf., Stoeckhardt, *Roemerbrief*, pp. 371-380; Ylvisaker, *The Gospels*, p. 455).—They do not hold that every individual plant, bird, and beast will be revived—only every human being will be raised—but that the present universe, which God fashioned during the first six days, will be dissolved into its basic substance, which God created at the beginning from nothing, and that from this substance God will fashion a new heaven and a new earth, entirely different from the present one, large enough for all the saints, one wherein dwelleth righteousness. Thus the original purpose of God's creation will, after all, be consummated.

The difference between these two views may be briefly stated thus: the one holds that the entire universe will be reduced by fire to nothing, and a new heaven and a new earth will be created out of nothing; the second holds that the entire universe will be reduced by fire to its original substance, which God will then refashion into a new heaven and a new earth. That the world will be destroyed by fire is clearly taught in the Bible; but we may not charge a person with heresy who holds that this destruction will be either an annihilation or a renovation.

LV. ETERNAL DAMNATION

1. **The fact.**—Hell and damnation are not a fiction, but a stern and dreadful reality. In Matt. 18: 8. 9 the Savior speaks of the everlasting hell-fire. Paul speaks of "everlasting destruction from the presence of the Lord" (2 Thess. 1: 9). When, therefore, on the Last Day the sentence of condemnation: "Depart from Me, ye cursed, into everlasting fire, prepared for the devil and his angels," is passed, it will be carried out immediately, for it reads: "And these shall go into everlasting punishment" (Matt. 25: 41. 46).

2. **State of damnation.**—As to the nature of this punishment and of conditions in hell we must not allow our imaginations to run wild (e.g., Dante's Inferno), but must confine ourselves to what the Scriptures say.

The punishment of the wicked does not consist in annihilation. It has been said that the word "destroy" in Matt. 10: 28 ("destroy both soul and body in hell") means annihilate. But the same Greek word, here rendered "destroy," is used in 2 Pet. 3: 6, where it is rendered "perish." As the world was not annihilated by water, so body and soul will not be annihilated in hell. Other arguments advanced in support of annihilation are nothing but human speculations and sentiments, without foundation of Scripture.

The damned in hell are forever rejected and banished from the blissful presence of God. "Depart from Me, ye cursed, into everlasting fire" (Matt. 25: 41). They shall be cast into outer darkness, where there is weeping and gnashing of teeth (Matt. 8: 12); "weeping" indicates pain and despair, while "gnashing of teeth" indicates raging and helpless fury. The suffering of the lost is intensified by the fact that they are aware of the bliss of the saints in heaven (Luke 13: 28). Being utterly forsaken of God, they are tormented in body and soul (Matt. 10: 28; Luke 16: 23. 24).—It is idle to speculate on the nature of this fire and of these torments; let us rather give heed that we never experience them. For the torment of hell there is no relief; even a drop of water is denied the rich man in the parable (Luke 16: 25. 26); from hell there is no escape; to the sufferings of hell there is no end, for it is an everlasting punishment (Matt. 25: 48), an everlasting destruction (2 Thess. 1: 9) in an unquenchable fire, where their worm, accusing conscience, shall not die (Mark 9: 43-48). In hell there is no hope.

The thought of eternal damnation is so terrifying, that men have endeavored to mitigate its terrors by teaching a universal restitution, which is to mean that after a shorter or longer period of suffering in hell—which suffering is not to be retributive, but remedial—all the lost will finally be restored to the communion of God. But the "restitution of all things" (Acts 3: 21), does not refer to the lost in hell, but to the fulfillment of all those things God has spoken by the mouths of His prophets (Matt. 17: 13). "Christ . . . shall condemn the ungodly to be punished with the devil without end" (Apol., Art. XVII, *Triglot*, p. 335).

While in each case the torment in hell is terrible beyond conception, there will be varying degrees of punishment. The general rule laid down in Luke 12: 47. 48 applies also to the lost in hell. For according to Matt. 11: 16-24 they, who rejected the Gospel preached to them, will fare worse in judgment than those who never heard it; it will be "more tolerable" in the Day of Judgment for Tyre and Sidon and the land of Sodom than for Chorazin, Bethsaida, and Capernaum, more tolerable for a damned heathen than for a damned "Christian."

3. As for **the cause of damnation,** cf., Chap. LIII, 4 under *Judgment.*

4. **The place of hell** cannot be fixed geographically. It is not in the center of the earth, as Romanists believe, because the earth will be destroyed on the Last Day.

5. **The purpose of revealing this doctrine** is not to satisfy a morbid curiosity, but to warn us to flee from the wrath to come (Matt. 3: 7. 12), and to pray that we may be accounted

worthy to escape all these things and to stand before the Son of Man (Luke 21: 36).

LVI. ETERNAL SALVATION

1. **The fact.**—While even the heathen sense the immortality of the soul, and speak of a better life beyond (Elysium, Nirvana, Valhalla, Happy Hunting Grounds, etc.), they still have "no hope" (Eph. 2: 12), because what they hope for will never be realized. How it is possible for sinful man, though deserving of death, to have a "lively hope" of eternal salvation, we learn only from the Word of God, which tells us: "God so loved the world that He gave His only begotten Son, that whosoever believeth in Him should not perish, but have everlasting life" (John 3: 16). This text teaches not only the fact of an everlasting life, but also the way in which we may attain it. This eternal life is a gift of God (Rom. 6: 23), which Christ gives to His sheep (John 10: 28). Unto these, therefore, He will say on the Day of Judgment: "Come, ye blessed of My Father, inherit the kingdom prepared for you from the foundation of the world" (Matt. 25: 34); and these shall go into eternal life (Matt. 25: 46).

2. **The state of bliss.**—Following their own fancy, men are likely to imagine the most curious things concerning conditions in the life to come. Also here we must confine ourselves to what the Scriptures say.

To convey to us some faint idea of the surpassing splendor and glory and joy of heaven, the Bible indeed employs terms and illustrations taken from this earthly life. It speaks of a marriage (Matt. 25: 10; Rev. 19: 9), of a banquet, of sitting upon thrones (Luke 22: 30), of a house with many mansions (John 14: 2); it gives a detailed description of the heavenly Jerusalem, that city fair and high (Rev. 21: 10-27). All this must not be taken literally, but figuratively, and is intended to set forth the beauty of that heavenly place.

External conditions.—Conditions in the world to come will be very different from present day conditions. Certain institutions, essential and fundamental to this life on earth, will not obtain in heaven. There will be no matrimony (Matt. 22: 30), no separate families, nationalities, and races. There will be no civil government for the punishment of evildoers, no earthly vocations to alleviate suffering and to provide the necessities of life (Rev. 7: 14-17). There will be no Office of the Keys, no mission work. The wicked shall not live among the saints to vex and harass them, for the tares will be separated from the wheat (Matt. 13: 30); (Rev. 22: 15). We shall live in the company of just men made perfect.

A changed body.—We ourselves shall be the same persons we now are, but we shall be changed (1 Cor. 15: 52). We shall have spiritual bodies, not subject to the same needs and laws which now govern us. We shall have incorruptible bodies, free from all traces and consequences of sin. We shall have strong bodies, free from all frailties, weaknesses, defects, and deformities. We shall have immortal bodies, which shall never die. We shall have glorious bodies, clothed with beauty, perfection, honor, and glory; God "shall change our vile body, that it may be fashioned like unto His glorious body" (Phil. 3: 21); (1 Cor. 15: 42-44; Matt. 13: 43; Rom. 8: 18).

A purified soul.—As for the soul, the image of God will be fully restored. "Beloved, now are we the sons of God, and it doth not yet appear what we shall be; but we know that, when He shall appear, we shall be like Him; for we shall see Him as He is" (1 John 3: 2); (Ps. 17: 15). As the image of God consists in blissful knowledge of God and in righteousness and true holiness, we shall then "know even as we are known," shall fully know God, His will, and His ways; we shall understand what now is still dark to us. All our questions both with respect to certain mysteries of doctrine and to happenings in our personal lives will be fully answered (1 Cor. 13: 9-12). There will be no old Adam, no temptation to contend with, no sin, no sorrow, no grief (Rev. 21: 4). There will be perfect righteousness and holiness. There will be no jarring discords and differences among the saints, but the thoughts, desires, and actions of all will be in complete harmony with the will of God. There will be full satisfaction, perfect contentment (Ps. 17: 15), absolute security. Jesus said regarding the saints: "Neither shall any man pluck them out of My hand" (John 10: 28). There will be unspeakable joy and pleasure, which no man shall take from us (John 16: 22; 1 Pet. 1: 8). The cause and source of all this bliss is God, in whose presence we shall live (Ps. 16: 11), and whom we shall see as He is (1 John 3: 2).

Degrees of glory.—The joys and pleasures of heaven are so great that it is not possible adequately to describe them in words of human tongue (2 Cor. 12: 2-4), and, unless we were "changed," we could not grasp them even in heaven. While all saints in heaven enjoy perfect bliss, there will be degrees of glory. As there are degrees of punishment for the lost in hell, and as there are degrees and ranks among the good angels in heaven, so there will be degrees of glory for the saints in heaven. Greater glory is given as a reward, not of merit, but of grace, to those who in their lives on earth showed their faith in consecrated service to the Lord (Luke 19: 12-19; Dan. 12: 3), in many good works done to their neighbors (2 Cor. 9: 6; Gal. 6: 8. 9), and in suffering for the Lord's sake (Matt. 5: 11. 12).

3. **Where is heaven?**—The location of the new heaven and new earth cannot be fixed and determined. (Cf., Chap. LIV, *The End of the World,* 4.) We may say that heaven is wherever God reveals Himself to us in His uncovered glory, and where we see Him face to face. This present universe will be destroyed by fire, and we are looking for a new heaven and a new earth (2 Pet. 3: 13). Where this will be, need not concern us. Let us rather labor that we too may enter into the rest which remaineth to the people of God (Hebr. 4: 9. 10). Speaking of the place prepared for us, Christ tells us: "And the way ye know" (John 14: 4).

4. **The way.**—"Thomas saith unto Him, Lord, we know not whither Thou goest; and how can we know the way? Jesus saith unto him, I am the way, the truth, and the life: no man cometh unto the Father but by Me" (John 14: 5. 6). Christ is the way to heaven; only those and all those who cling to Him in true faith unto the end shall be saved (John 3: 16; Matt. 24: 13). By faith in Christ we are even now the children of God (Gal. 3: 26), and, therefore, also heirs of eternal life and glory (Rom. 8: 17. 18). For the end of our faith is the salvation of the soul (1 Pet. 1: 9). Faith in the Redeemer is the only way and it is the sure way that leads to heaven. "Be thou faithful unto death, and I will give thee a crown of life" (Rev. 2: 10). Paul had kept the faith, and therefore he was sure of the crown of righteousness (2 Tim. 4: 7. 8).

Also the Law points out the way to heaven. "This do and thou shalt live" (Luke 10: 28). This promise of life is absolutely true; it does not help any man, because no man can fulfill the condition: "This do." Whoever seeks salvation under the Law, will find himself cursed, because he has not continued in all things demanded by the Law (Gal. 3: 10).

5. **The purpose of this doctrine.**—While the doctrine of eternal salvation pertains to the future, it has an important and a practical bearing on our present life.

(a) As by faith in Christ alone men may attain to this glorious inheritance, they should repent of their sins and believe in Christ for the salvation of their souls. "Believe on the Lord Jesus Christ, and thou shalt be saved" (Acts 16: 31); (John 3: 16). We, who are in the faith, should be careful to remain therein unto the end. "Examine yourselves whether ye be in the faith; prove your own selves" (2 Cor. 13: 5). "He that shall endure unto the end, the same shall be saved" (Matt. 24: 13).

(b) We Christians are still in the world, but we are not to be of the world (John 17: 14-16). Therefore we should avoid worldliness; we are not to be conformed to the ideas and ways of the world, but are to be transformed by the renewing of our mind, proving what is the acceptable will of God (Rom. 12: 2). We are not to set our affection on things of this earth, but on things above (Col. 3: 2), for we have here no continuing city, but seek one to come (Hebr. 13: 14). The state in which we hold citizenship is in heaven, from whence we look for the Savior, the Lord Jesus Christ (Phil. 3: 20. 21).

(c) The expectation of heaven should incite every Christian to greater efforts in holiness of life (2 Pet. 3: 13. 14). And as Christ has graciously promised to reward our service, we should lay up for ourselves treasures in heaven (Matt. 6: 20), and be zealous in good works (Tit. 2: 11-14). In particular should we be interested and constantly active in bringing Christ to the nations by spreading His Gospel among the lost children of men, as the Lord has commanded us (Mark 16: 15). We shall not be able to win all men (Matt. 24: 14), but let us, nonetheless, bring them the invitation of the Lord (Luke 14: 15-24); some will come and be saved.

(d) It is true that we shall be hated of all men for Christ's sake (Matt. 10: 22). But what of it? We are God's own people, and should show forth the fame of Him who has called us out of darkness into His marvelous light (1 Pet. 2: 9). Even when men reject our testimony and persecute us, we should rejoice, for great is our reward in heaven (Matt. 5: 11. 12). And no matter what may happen to us in our personal lives, and how heavy the cross we bear, we should never be discouraged, for "blessed is the man that endureth temptation: for when he is tried, he shall receive the crown of life, which the Lord promised to them that love Him" (James 1: 12), and "we must through much tribulation enter into the kingdom of God" (Acts 14: 22).

(e) The work of those who labor in the Word and doctrine is not always duly appreciated in this life, not even by all who are benefited thereby. Yet, looking forward, we take courage, for we are gathering fruit unto eternal life (John 4: 36), and the Scriptures also say: "They that turn many to righteousness" shall shine "as the stars for ever and ever" (Dan. 12: 3).

(f) The prospect of eternal salvation fills our hearts with courage and joy and with a sustaining hope in life and death. We hope in Christ not only in this life (1 Cor. 15: 19), but, like Paul, we are looking forward to the day when the Judge will give us a crown of righteousness (2 Tim. 4: 8), and when death shall be swallowed up in victory (1 Cor. 15: 54-57).

Thus this present life is lived in the light of the life to come, and this gives meaning and direction to our sojourn on earth.

REFERENCE ABBREVIATIONS OF THE LUTHERAN CONFESSIONS

A. C.—The Augsburg Confession.
Apol.—Apology of the Augsburg Confession.
F. C., Epit.—The Formula of Concord. Epitome.
F. C., Th. D.—The Formula of Concord. Thorough Declaration.
Large Cat.—The Large Catechism of Dr. Martin Luther.
Small Cat.—The Small Catechism of Dr. Martin Luther.
S. A.—The Smalcald Articles.

Example of reference: Apol., Art. XIII, 7, *Triglot*, p. 311— the paragraph number 7 is to be found only in the Latin text, while the page number 311 refers to the English text.

BIBLIOGRAPHY

Christliche Dogmatik, by Dr. Franz Pieper.
Concordia Cyclopedia. Edited by L. Fuerbringer, Th. Engelder, P. E. Kretzmann.
Concordia Triglotta. The Symbolical Books of the Ev. Lutheran Church.
Outlines of Doctrinal Theology, by Dr. A. L. Graebner.
Pastoral Theology, by Dr. John H. C. Fritz.
Popular Symbolics. The Doctrines of the Churches of Christendom and of other Religious Bodies. Edited by Th. Engelder, W. Arndt, Th. Graebner, F. E. Mayer.
Roemerbrief, by Dr. G. Stoeckhardt.
(The above mentioned books published by Concordia Publishing House, St. Louis, Mo.)
Doctrinal Theology of the Ev. Lutheran Church, by Dr. Heinrich Schmid.
(Published in 1876 by the Lutheran Publication Society, Philadelphia, Pa.)

INDEX

Confirmation, 201. 211.

Congregation. Local, 250. 251; Christians should be members of a c., 251; under Christ a c. is a self-governing body, 253; is the possessor of the Office of the Keys, 255; has the right to call its pastors, 266; has the duty to exercise church-discipline, 261; pastors are not lords over the c., 254.

Conscience. Definition, 53; functions, 54; proves the existence of God, 20; is bound only by the Word of God, 252; a doubting c., 55. 74; an erring c., 55. 74; sins against c., 55. 74; c. not an infallible guide, 55; remedy for an evil c., 114. 233.

Consequences of the fall of man, 51. 52. 67; of sin, 65; external c. of sin remain also for Christians, 114.

Content. Chief c. of God's revelation to man, 109. 257.

Contrition. Worldly and godly sorrow, 136.

Conversion. Man capable of c., 123; takes place in the heart, 130; is not the work of man, 124-127; is work of the Holy Ghost, 127; Holy Ghost makes use of man's psychic equipment in c., 129; is effected through the means of grace, 128; consists in the bestowal of faith, 132-134; is instantaneous, 134; knowledge of our c., 135; reiterated c., 134; synonyms for c., 135; c. of Israel, 300.

Creation. Source of information, 34; time, six days, 35; orderly progression, 35; c. of man, 36. 47; ultimate end of c., 36; c. myths and evolution, 36.

Creator, the Triune God, 34.

Cross. Life under the c., 172; what may be regarded as a c., 172; each Christian has his own c., 173; purpose of the c., 174.

Curse of the Law, 58.

Damnation. The fact and state of d., 311; purpose of this doctrine, 312.

Death. Definition, 292; cause, 292; universal fact, 292; not the end of man's existence, 293; d. of Christ a voluntary act, 87. 99; Christ redeemed us from d., 115.

Decalogue, 56.

Denomination. Church d. are divided by difference in doctrine, 245; true and heterodox d., 246; true Christians also in heterodox d., 243; no particular d. is the only saving church, 241.

Depravity. Hereditary d., 68; is not of the essence of man, but a corruption of his nature, 69.

Destiny. Eternal d. of man is decided when man dies, 295.

Development. No d. of doctrine, 252.

Devil (cf. evil angels). Prime cause of sin, 64; no redemption, nor grace, for d., 46. 101; Christ redeemed us from the power of the d., 116.

Dichotomy and trichotomy, 49.

Difference. No d. in the spiritual condition of natural man, 180; no d. in the gracious will of God toward man, 180; a d. in the ultimate destiny of man, 181; d. between Old Testament priests and Christ, 110.

Difficulty. Why are some saved, and not all, 180; Synergistic and Calvinistic explanations, 181.

Division of the Bible, 14; d. of visible Church into divers denominations is displeasing to God, 248.

Divorce, 290.

Doctrine. Christian d. must be taken from the Bible and agree with Bible, 1-3; no development of d. beyond the Bible, 252; difference in d. divides the Church, 245. 246; purity of d. must be maintained, 246; Churches are to be judged on the basis of their public d., 246; a false d. cannot create a right faith, 249; false d. on election, 187. 188.

Efficacy. E. of the Bible, 11; e. of grace, 81; e. of the means of grace, 192; e. of means of grace can be hindered by the perverse will of man, 193; Gospel invitation is always efficacious, 132. 193, but is not always effective, 132. 193, but when it is effective, it works faith, 132; e. of prayer, 170.

Election of grace. General statement, 182; in detail, 183; resume, 184; knowledge of e., 185; comfort of this doctrine, 186; e. in relation to the work of grace, 187; false teachings regarding e., 187. 188.

Element. External e. in Baptism, 203; external e. in the Lord's Supper, 213; heavenly e. in the Lord's Supper, 213.

End of world. The fact, 308; the time, 308; the means of destruction, 309.

Essence of God, 22; e. of faith, 137; e. of Sacraments depends on correct administration, 198. 199; e. of Sacraments is not affected by wrong views regarding their benefit and power, 210.

Evil (cf., sin). Cause of e., 64; control of e., 42. 47; concurrence of God in e. works, 40.

Evolution, 20. 36. 52.

Exaltation of Christ. Definition, 99; stages of e., 100-105; descent into hell, 100; resurrection, 102; forty days, 105; ascension, 105; session at the right hand of God, 105; return to judgment, 296. 305.

Examination of the doctrines of the Church, 246; self-examination on going to Communion, 229.

Excommunication. Meaning, 263; procedure, 261; purpose, 264.

Existence of God proved from nature, 20; proved by conscience, 20; is universally acknowledged, 21.

Extreme unction, 202.

Faith. Essence of f., 137; a work of God, an act of man, 136; personal f., 140; object of f. is not the Law, 141; object of f. is the Gospel and Christ, 141. 142; promise of God and f. are correlatives, 141; why f. saves, 139. 151; f. apprehends the merits of Christ, 148; f. is not a condition of the promise, but a means of accepting it, 149. 191. 195; f. holds complete forgiveness, 150; justifying and sanctifying power of f., 144; f. always justifies, 148; f. always sanctifies, 157; fluctuations of f., 142; weak and strong f., 142; loss of f., 143; preservation of f., 176; not any kind of f. saves, 141. 142.

Fall of man and its consequences, 51. 52.

Father. The F. is true God, 30.

Forgiveness of sins is earned by Christ for all men, 113. 146; is revealed as an accomplished fact, 147. 190; is freely and unconditionally offered in the Gospel, 147. 148. 190. 226; is accepted and held by faith, 147.

Fulfillment of the Law, 57. 58.

Functions of the Law, 59. 194-197; f. of the Gospel, 190. 191. 194-197; f. of faith, 144.

God. Essence, 22; Unity in Trinity, 29-32; attributes, 23-28; G. is incomprehensible, 32; creation is a work of G., 34; preservation is a work of G., 37; government is a work of G., 42; redemption is a work of G., 78; sanctification is work of G., 128; judgment is a work of G., 305.

Goodness of God, 28.

Gospel, 189; differs from **Law,**

Propagation, 49. 288.
Purgatory, 295.
Purity of doctrine necessary to accomplish the purpose of God's Word, 249. 250.
Purpose of the Bible, 14; p. of the Law, 59-61; p. of redemption, 121; p. of the Gospel, 190-192; p. of the ministry, 270.

Ransom. Christ's life and death a r. for sin, 111.
Reason. Instrumental and judicial use of r., 2; r. is not the source and norm of doctrine, 3; r. cannot produce faith, 124. 125; r. is the basic principle in civil government, 281.
Reconciliation. R. by the active and passive obedience of Christ, 103. 111-113. 145. 146; God reconciled us to God, 94. 111; the Gospel reveals not a possible, but an accomplished r., 146. 190.
Redeemer. Names of R., 82.
Redemption, 111-118; by whom r. was accomplished, 111. 112; whereby r. was accomplished, 112. 113; for whom r. was accomplished, 113; what did r. accomplish, 113-116.
Religion. Sincerity of faith does not prove the truth of a man's r., 11. 141; true r. is based on the grace of God in Christ, 141. 142; the Christian r. is of divine origin, 15. 78.
Remembrance. "This do in remembrance of Me," 223. 225.
Renewal of heart, 155.
Repentance, 135. 136.
Reproof. Bible used for r., 18.
Rest. God rested, 37; r. of the saved in heaven, 315.
Restitution of all things, 312.
Resurrection. Theories and fact of Christ's r., 102; Christ's r. proves His Deity, the universal justification, and our own r., 103. 104; the possibility and fact of the r. of the body, 301; time and cause of the r. of the

body, 302; condition of the resurrected body, 103. 304.
Revelation is not identical with inspiration, 6; r. is not progressive, 252.
Righteousness. Personal r. of God, 26; r. demanded of man by the Law, 26; the r. of Christ offered to man in the Gospel, 26.

Sabbath, 57. 77.
Sacrament. Term and definition of s., 197; s. a means of grace, 198. 208. 226; the power of the s., 200. 209. 227; the benefit of the s., 200. 211. 227; the validity of the s., 198. 221; the number of s., 200.
Sacrament of Baptism. (Cf., Baptism).
Sacrament of the Altar. Names, 212; a divine institution, 212; visible and heavenly elements, 213; transubstantiation, 214; representation, 215; Bible doctrine, 216. 217; validity, 221; a means of grace, 226; s. of the Roman and Reformed churches, 199. 218; consecration, 221; "This do in remembrance of Me," 223-226; "Testament in My blood," 226; to be received under one or both forms, 222; intinction, 223; use of s., 227; self-examination before partaking of s., 229; open and close communion, 230; why we should commune frequently, 231.
Sacramental union, 218; whereby effected, 220; sacramental action proper, 222; sacramental eating and drinking, 223.
Sacrifice. Meaning of Old Testament s., 110; s. of Christ, 111. 112; s. as distinguished from sacraments, 197; the Lord's Supper not a s. for sin, 224. 225.
Salvation. S. is exclusively a work of divine grace, 178; eternal s. is a fact, 313; eternal s. is a